SHAPING THE EIGHTEENTH AMENDMENT

STUDIES IN LEGAL HISTORY

Published by the University

of North Carolina Press in

association with the American

Society for Legal History

Thomas A. Green and

Hendrik Hartog, editors

RICHARD F. HAMM

SHAPING THE

EIGHTEENTH AMENDMENT

TEMPERANCE REFORM,

LEGAL CULTURE, AND

THE POLITY, 1880–1920

THE UNIVERSITY OF NORTH CAROLINA PRESS *Chapel Hill & London*

The paper in this book meets the guidelines for permanence and durability of the Committee on Production Guidelines for Book Longevity of the Council on Library Resources.

Library of Congress Cataloging-in-Publication Data

Hamm, Richard F.

Shaping the Eighteenth Amendment : temperance reform, legal culture, and the polity, 1880–1920 / Richard F. Hamm

 p.   cm.—(Studies in legal history)

Includes bibliographical references and index.

ISBN 0-8078-2181-0 (cloth : alk. paper).—ISBN 0-8078-4493-4 (pbk. : alk. paper)

 1. Prohibition—United States—History. 2. Liquor laws—United States—History. 3. Temperance—United States—History. 4. United States—Constitutional law—Amendments—18th—History. I. Title. II. Series.

KF3919.H35   1995

344.73'0541—dc20

[347.304541]   94-17948

                                                                 CIP

99   98   97   96   95   5   4   3   2   1

DEDICATED TO HILDA D. HAMM

CONTENTS

ACKNOWLEDGEMENTS

This book was a long time in the making. It began many years ago as a conversation with Charles W. McCurdy. Early in 1980 he mentioned as a paper topic the effect of interstate commerce doctrines on the prohibition movement. Since then the work has grown. It has put down roots in various literatures, sprawled across far larger periods of time, blossomed with unexpected fruits, and required more tending and effort than this historical gardener would ever have imagined. Along the way I have accumulated many debts that must be acknowledged.

The greatest debts are those I owe to my family. Without their intellectual, moral, and financial support this work would never have begun, let alone been completed. At various times I lived with family members while researching or writing this work, and they all endured my stays with good cheer. Elaine Cascio sustained me more than I can ever say. She read various versions two or three times, proving that love has great patience. Her sharp editorial eye and common sense has made this a better book.

Also this work has benefited from a number of suggestions from various people coerced into reading it. At different times both Phil Merkel and Denise Thompson read the entire manuscript with pen in hand and removed hundreds of convoluted constructions. Richard Fiesta and Candice Bredbenner pointed me to literatures and interpretations that enriched the work. Christopher Lee, Jean Lee, and Robert Stanley made suggestions about issues that proved especially useful in rethinking the work at a particularly critical stage. Christine Paquette suggested a number of changes that improved both the introduction and conclusion. Reid Mitchell performed a feat that few will equal: he read the work twice, each time making comments that bettered the book. William Harbaugh's observations aided the development of this work in its earliest stages. Joseph Kett, Edward Ayers, and Calvin Woodard closely read the manuscript and suggested paths to follow in making it into a book. Stanley Katz, Robert Wesser, and Lewis Bateman expressed strong faith in the project, keeping me on track during the vagaries of the publishing process. The far-reaching, lengthy, and constructive criticisms of the anonymous readers for Studies in Legal History prompted a total recasting of the work. Similarly, the coeditor of the Studies in Legal History, Thomas Green (a self-confessed Tab-drinking semi-teetotaler), pushed the work out of its previous insular boundaries, always insisting on deepening the analysis and integrating the prohibitionists' history with that of other reformers. Pamela Upton and Alison Tartt, editors for the University of North Carolina Press, polished this work with their many corrections and comments.

Charles W. McCurdy's aid and assistance to this project must have seemed to him endless. Through the years he has given generously of his time. His insightful comments—sometimes in letters, more often in late-night phone calls—have made this a better book and me a better scholar. He has been a mentor without par.

Like any long endeavor, writing a book becomes a process that intertwines with one's life. And in life no joy is unalloyed. The very day I learned that the manuscript had received its final approval for publication was the first anniversary of my mother's death. In her memory this book is dedicated.

Richard F. Hamm
Ballston Spa, New York

REFORMERS AND THE POLITY

On June 6, 1900, in one of her first forays from Medicine Lodge, Carry Nation traveled to nearby Kiowa to attack saloons. This small Kansas town had at least three bars in operation despite the two-decade-old state ban on the manufacture and sale of intoxicating liquor. Singing her favorite hymn—"Who Hath Sorrow? Who Hath Woe?"—Nation wrecked the liquor-selling establishments. In one of the saloons she demolished, Nation saw what she later admitted was "a very strange thing." In the midst of her destruction, she saw a vision of "Mr. McKinley, the President, sitting in an old fashion arm chair." She threw several stones at this apparition, and "as the stone[s] would strike I saw them hit the chair and the chair fell to pieces, and I saw Mr. McKinley fall over." In her 1909 autobiography she reflected on the meaning of this incident: "Now I know that the smashing in Kansas was intended to strike the head of this nation the hardest blow, for every saloon I smashed in Kansas had a license from the head of this government." To Nation, the government was "more responsible than the dive-keeper" for the evils caused by the liquor trade. She further justified her actions on two other grounds. First, that her experience as a "Jail Evangelist" convinced her that the bars "manufactured many criminals" who "burdened" the county and country. And, second, that if the town officials would not enforce the law, someone else—like herself—would. Upon completing her work, she dared the authorities to arrest her; when they did not, she returned home.[1]

This incident illuminates many of the themes of this book. It shows what motivated drys like Carry Nation; her assertion that alcohol caused suffering and her hymn singing reflected the forces that drove most prohibitionists: religious faith mixed with a desire to improve human life. Moreover, Nation's actions in Kiowa revealed that she was well aware that the barkeepers in Kansas violated law. Thus, she did not see her action as an infraction of civil law; rather, she saw her work as a demand that officials enforce the state prohibition law. In general, drys like Nation took law very seriously; they believed that positive law—that is, man-made law in statutes and constitutions—should contribute both to the morality of the community as well as to its general welfare. Finally, this incident raised the issue of the federal nature of the American polity that confronted the temperance reformers. The "license" that Nation identified was the barkeepers' special tax receipt issued by the government for payment of the federal tax on retailers of liquor. The saloons that Nation broke up probably paid the federal tax despite the state's liquor prohibition. The Kansas ban on manufacturing likely meant that these speakeasies obtained their liquor through interstate commerce. Clearly, as Nation perceived, the federal system complicated temperance reformers' tasks. There was much more to Nation's hatchetry, and prohibition's interaction with the American polity, than first meets the eye.

This book is a study of the prohibitionists' struggles to implement their reform from the late nineteenth century to their great victory in engineering the Eighteenth Amendment. Because temperance and prohibition "were the reform issues that made the most insistent claim on the postwar American polity," because the drys typified one pattern of reform, and because—in one way or another—most reformers felt the effects of the structure of American government, this is a tale that raises implications for every reform of the period. All reformers, in attempting to use the government to obtain their ends, to one degree or another, confronted problems within the polity. Thus, the experience of the prohibitionists within the American polity from 1880 to 1920 can illuminate much about the nature of the interaction of reform and the structure of government.[2]

Scholarly views of this age of reform—and especially the progressive era that stretched from the 1890s to the First World War—have undergone much change. In the 1930s progressivism came to be seen as the precursor to New Deal liberalism. This conception delineated some aspects of progressivism, but it also excluded various reforms—like prohibition—from the progressive panoply because they did not fit the liberal consensus. Following the Second World War, a generation of scholars altered the understanding of the period by advancing various theories to explain the origins and nature of reform in the progressive period. Thus, prior to 1970, a number of schools of thought, identified by short monickers—the status hypothesis, the urban and rural conflict theory, the rise of reform Darwinism theory, the corporatist instigation of reform theory, the good citizenship theory, the social control theory, and the organizational synthesis—attempted to explain reform activity in the period. These interpretations illuminated once obscure parts of reform history and made the topic one of most lively within the historical discipline.

The discord between these interpretations eventually undercut the notion that there was a single progressive movement and that one theory could explain the reform experience in those years. Scholars began to question the usefulness of the term "progressive." In a famous essay Peter G. Filene announced the death of the term. But announcing the "obituary" of progressivism did not stifle scholarly examination of the era; indeed, it liberated it. In the 1970s and 1980s there was a flowering in the studies of the period. Instead of studying a unitary progressive movement, scholars have explored the many different reforms from the period. Much of this monographic work has shifted the focus—in the phrase of Daniel T. Rodgers—away from "the essence of progressivism . . . toward questions of context." This study of prohibition follows in this new path. While it suggests a tentative typology of reform activity, it also examines "the structures of politics, power, and ideas" that shaped one reform.[3]

In particular, this work focuses on how one social reform—prohibition—interacted with the polity. The typology of reforms developed here best fits social reforms with a tightly defined movement. Reform movements of the late nineteenth and early twentieth centuries can be divided by their goals and their structures. Some reforms—like the direct election of senators; the establishment of systems of recall, initiative, and referendum; and the extension of suffrage to women—aimed to make a change in the nature of the polity itself in the hopes of reforming the nation. Other reform movements used the government to redress social evils. But these reforms differed in their structure; some—like antitrust—were broad and amorphous amalgamations of disparate groups with no set programs; others were focused social groups with fixed agendas. It is these latter reforms, which were like the prohibition movement, that are the proper subject of this typology of reform.[4]

These social reforms differed in the ways in which they used the government. Four well-known examples exemplify this diversity in social reformers' use of government. First, pure-food and -drug crusaders established both state and federal agencies for regulating the production and distribution of these products. Second, purity reformers, who significantly failed to change many cities' or towns' attitudes toward prostitution won increasing activity in the states against prostitution as well as a federal act, based on the commerce power, banning the transport of women across state lines for immoral purposes. This act remained mostly unused, and the reformers utilized a new power, the war emergency power, to close red-light districts during the world war. Third, advocates against child labor, while gaining many state bans on the employment of minors, could not root out the practice in all states; their attempts to use the federal power to aid their earlier efforts, be it through the commerce power or the taxing power, were held to be unconstitutional in the courts. Their proposed constitutional amendment failed. Fourth, proponents of a separate justice system for juveniles managed to gain the establishment of such programs in many states, but the reformers never attempted to use the federal power to aid their efforts in the states.

These four examples (pure food, antiprostitution, anti–child labor, and juvenile justice), along with other reforms—conservation, antiobscenity, antitrust, eugenics, and divorce, will be used to show the context of reform and polity interaction for a fifth reform, prohibition. In brief, drys achieved the creation of some state bans on liquor. Moreover, they were instrumental in shaping—under the commerce and tax powers—federal laws regulating liquor transport and changing the administration of the federal tax system to aid the dry states. Finally, they created a national constitutional amendment banning liquor. The nature of the reformers' means and their experience within the polity explains this diversity of outcomes in social reformers' efforts.

By sorting reformers according to their preferred means, we take the first step in understanding why reform groups interacted differently with the polity as it existed in the late nineteenth century and progressive era. The social reformers of this period shared the greater goal of improving life in the nation. While the range of proposed reforms seems almost endless, the means reformers used to invoke the aid of the government in reaching their goals were quite limited. There were just three means available to them. First, they could abolish through law the activity they saw as evil. Second, they could regulate actions they perceived as dangerous. Third, they could reshape the character of individuals so deviant behavior could be prevented.[5]

At first glance, it is not apparent that social reform groups showed distinct preferences for a certain means. Experimentation with other methods obscured reformers' main means. Almost all reforms experimented with the different means of abolition, regulation, and reformation, but internal dynamics as well as circumstances drove reformers to prefer one method over others. Also obscuring the distinctions between reformers' methods were their similarities in outlook and style. Indeed, in 1900 Theodore Roosevelt identified two gospels common to all reformers: the gospel of morality and the gospel of efficiency. All American reformers combined moral outcries with social science analysis in their exposure of problems. All reformers mixed moralism with practicality in fashioning solutions to problems. It is how they mixed the gospels of morality and efficiency that helped fix reformers upon their preferred means. Thus, to borrow another of Roosevelt's constructions, the latitude of morality and the longitude of efficiency determined where they stood on means. To understand the campaigns and outcomes of reforms it is profitable to examine them in light of primary method: abolition, regulation, or reformation.[6]

Abolitionists were those who would root out as completely as possible the evils they saw in the society. On a scale of morality and efficiency, they emphasized morality. Significantly, abolitionists would build no new state apparatus to carry on their end. They hoped to agitate on an issue to raise an outcry loud enough to change the law. In all cases they assumed that the governments, as constituted, would abolish old immoral laws, pass new moral regulations, and enforce these new policies. They included temperance advocates, crusaders against prostitution, opponents of gambling, crusaders against phosphorous matches, and preservationists.

Regulationists were most concerned with stopping abuses of practices that were not in themselves necessarily harmful. On a sliding scale of morality and efficiency, they seemed to have a rough balance of the two. Having become convinced that the current polity could not do what they wanted, regulationists wished to build new structures in government to achieve their ends. They also presumed that reformers—and the larger public—would remain involved in the process of administering the new agencies. Thus, advocates of trade commissions to govern commercial practices, creators of public utility commissions, members of the pure-food and -drug movement, antitrust advocates, slum renewal advocates, conservationists, anti–child labor forces, advocates of working restrictions for women, insurance reformers, and some divorce reformers can all be considered regulationists.

Reformationists were those who wanted to create new institutions to directly mold the behavior of individuals. Efficiency dominated morality in these categories of reform. They wanted to directly reform human behavior at the individual level. Most reformationists required special institutions to carry on this reformulation of character. Many of them believed in asylums or other institutions, where individuals to be remade were removed from society and subjected to individualized attention. But also in this period many reformationists experimented with new means, carried outside of institutional walls, to try and remake people. Of all the reformers, the reformationists were most closely associated with the day-to-day operations of the reform within the polity. Within this category were the advocates of better prisons, of Magdalen homes, of juvenile courts, of outpatient psychiatric clinics, and of institutions for the epileptic and feebleminded.

To see how the reformers' predilections for certain methods affected their interaction with the American polity, it helps to think of the polity as a big machine, with entrances and exits at opposite ends. The machine was complex with many paths and tracks, and reformers got caught in its various cogs and moved along in one direction, or in another, or even stalled inside. The reformers entered this machine, carrying with them their preferred means, which automatically directed them to certain cogs of the machine. For instance, the cog of federalism only touched certain reforms. If reformers wanted to change individuals by building institutions like juvenile court systems, they were relatively unaffected by federalism. But regulation and abolition often raised issues of federalism, and reforms relying on these means were shaped by the limitations that the "machine" placed on their means. Thus, many of the reformers' legislative proposals dealing with the problems of federalism for reform—say the Wilson Act of 1890, the Food and Drug Act of 1906, and the Anti-Convict Labor Goods Act of 1929—looked similar. However, it was not merely the means of the reformers that shaped the outcome of reforms.

Alterations within the polity, and the actions of opponents of reforms, played their part in the shaping of the history of reforms. The polity machine changed its internal structure over time, sometimes facilitating reformers' goals, sometimes stymieing them. Beyond that, the quality of the reformers' opponents contributed to the shaping of end results. For example, as the antiprostitution advocates had no legitimate opponents, their one federal victory, the passage of the Mann Act, which met a virtually nonexistent problem and required no additional action, either by new laws or organized enforcement campaigns. On the other hand, the opponents of the anti–child labor movement were so effective in mobilizing the limits of the polity that those reformers' efforts to gain legislation, based on the commerce power and later the tax power, were long delayed and eventually struck down in the courts. The prohibition movement's experience with the machine of the polity fell between these extremes.

A number of scholars have shown that the nature of the polity plays a key role in shaping society. Following the lead of Theda Skocpol, they argue that "the state" is in part autonomous, that it is more than a tool used by interest groups or dominant classes to express their will. This study shares the perception of the autonomy and importance of "the state," although it avoids the term. "The state" seems an inappropriate label for a governmental system that rejected centralism. Whatever the name, how the government was constituted and how the polity worked were important to understanding what happened in American society. Morton Keller, Richard McCormick,

Stephen Skowronek, and others have delineated the changing nature of the American state—or polity—in the late nineteenth and early twentieth centuries.[7]

In particular, Skowronek has posited that the polity existing in the late nineteenth century was "a State of Courts and Parties." Similar to Keller's portrait of the preindustrial polity, his argument showed that there was no real national state as localism and limited government were key notions. Yet two entities linked together the various parts of the polity: the courts and the political parties. The parties—not recognized in any constitution—operated as objects of worship and attachment. As McCormick showed, they dominated political life, mobilizing voters and subsuming their ethnic, religious, and class divisions into vague political platforms. As neither party could establish hegemony, they used the assets of government as resources in their struggles to win elections; patronage became key to building party organization and maintaining turnout during elections. Thus the policies of the period tended toward what McCormick called "distributive policies." At the same time, the federal courts emerged as the arbitrators of the boundaries of government action. For example, Herbert Hovenkamp has shown how the ideas of the judges shaped state and national economic policy. In general, the judiciary forbade or permitted various actions by government. But this state of courts and parties could not effectively respond to the many problems spawned by the changing economy and society.[8]

To remedy problems reformers and interest groups pushed against the barriers of this polity and, in Skowronek's phrase, "patched together" a new structure of government. In the progressive period—the last decade of the nineteenth century and the first two decades of the twentieth century—the press of reform, the rise of interest groups, and the realignment of politics created a new polity. Keller called it "the industrial polity," and Skowronek named it "the administrative state." McCormick, who refused to label it, described its contours: the old distributive policies and methods of operation of the parties came under attack and were limited while the government gained regulatory and administrative powers. This new polity's reach was longer, and its methods were different from its predecessor's. It laid a layer of bureaucratic and administrative agencies over the state of courts and parties and could do more. Significantly, the new polity had the means to implement various reformers' programs. But, as Keller has noted, it was also hobbled by "preexisting values, interests, procedural and structural arrangements."[9]

These pictures of a state of courts and parties and a new administrative state give us a base from which to explore how the American polity responded to reformers' demands in the period stretching from the late nineteenth century to the second decade of the twentieth century. These models have three common themes. First, they point out that there was a change (short of a constitutional revolution) in the nature of the polity during the period, much of it coming during the first two decades of the twentieth century. Second, they raise the notion of constraints on action. Third, as Keller points out, "institutional and ideological persistence" characterized the early twentieth-century polity. While the system underwent various incremental changes during the era, the polity of 1920 was closer to the polity of 1890 than that of 1940. It is important to note that the great age of reform took place before the constitutional revolution of the late 1930s. Thus, despite these changes, the salient characteristic of the polity that existed in the period from 1880 to 1920 was its many formal and informal constraints on policymaking. The national political parties, operating informally, controlled the policymaking bodies and limited their actions. Conversely, the formal constraints, expressed often—but not exclusively—by the courts, were taken quite seriously at all levels of the government. Rules set out in constitutions and elaborated in constitutional doctrines restrained the powers of state and federal governments. These standards changed through legislative action, judicial decisions, executive behavior, and administrative proceedings. Thus, the reformers faced a polity with rules that often proscribed their actions but that had enough flexibility to allow them to achieve their ends.[10]

One of the most important constraints on reformers' actions in the late nineteenth and early twentieth centuries was the concept of federalism. The Constitution's formal division of authority between the states and the federal government ingrained federalism into the polity. Most constitutional experts accepted federalism as an important principle and saw it as a limit on activity by various parts of government. For example, after the Supreme Court (in the 1922 case *Bailey v. Drexel Furniture Co.*) held the prohibitory federal tax on goods produced by child labor to be unconstitutional, Andrew C. McLaughlin, Felix Frankfurter, and even Thomas Reed Powell defended the ruling on the grounds of federalism. McLaughlin argued that the decision was necessary if "federal as distinguished from centralized nationalism is to survive." Powell thought the ruling "essential" to safeguard "the federal system from being warped beyond recognition," while Frankfurter admitted that "We must pay a price for federalism." That legal thinkers of such diverse views espoused the importance of federalism underscores its centrality to the American polity of this period.[11]

Operations of various state and federal institutions further determined where governmental powers lay and how they would be exercised. Throughout this period, the polity recognized a limited number of justifications for federal action. Thus, those reformers who sought to use the federal government hung their proposals on certain constitutional hooks. The Constitution and practice defined five federal powers of use to reformers: the territorial power, the treaty power, the postal power, the taxing power, and the commerce power. Moreover, in the second half of the nineteenth century the federal system was beginning the transition from an essentially decentralized system, in which the loci of real and formal power lay in the states, to one in which real power was centralized in the national government. Thus, four of these powers—treaty, postal, taxing, and commerce—were stretched to their limits; the changing contours of federalism touched many reforms of the period 1880–1920, including prohibition.[12]

The prohibitionists embraced abolitionist methods. Indeed, antiliquor advocates became so identified with their preferred means that the name "prohibition"—in effect the equivalent of abolition—became synonymous with their movement. Drys only flirted with regulation and reformation. The reformationist agenda showed up in two different forms within the prohibitionist crusade: fraternal organizations devoted to maintaining their members' abstinence from liquor and temperance asylums dedicated to saving drinkers. Fraternal organizations, like the Independent Order of Good Templars, were essentially limited to religious conversion and moral suasion. Temperance asylums provided various medical cures for drinkers. While reformation of the individual through pledge signing and temperance remained an important component of the movement, the reshaping of individual drunkards in institutions moved outside the movement. The inebriate institutions established in the period 1880–1920 quickly became the private preserve of experts. There was little overlapping between the scientific experts of the institutions and the dry crusaders. Similarly, plans to better manage liquor in society existed mostly outside the prohibition movement. Regulation did not lead to abolition of liquor and indeed led the government into the liquor-selling business. So drys turned away from regulation to focus on the complete ban of the liquor evil. Yet the regulationist approach persisted, mostly clearly in the Anti-Saloon League's program of pragmatically striving for the enforcement of all liquor laws in the hopes that it would lead to prohibition. But, in the final analysis, only one means was their main weapon: abolition. It is this predilection that drys brought into the machine of the polity.[13]

By focusing on the temperance crusaders' interaction with the polity and the legal environment, this study stands in contrast to the bulk of the literature on the topic of prohibition. Much of what earlier scholars have discovered about the temperance movement's social origins, operations, and ideas shapes and informs this work. But gaps remain in prohibition scholarship. Paul Aaron and David Musto identify two subjects with which this work is directly concerned; they state that the "explicit, self-identified concerns around which people in the antiliquor movement mobilized" and the "particular regulatory techniques that were experimented with . . . to a large extent, have lain historically fallow." Thus, this book differs in two ways from previous works on prohibition. First, it takes the ideology of the drys, as a shaper of their actions, more seriously than many earlier works. Second, it pays more attention to the role of law in the prohibition movement.[14]

The ideology of the drys has not received all the attention it deserves. Jack Blocker, Ruth Bordin, Harry Levine, James Timberlake, and other scholars have explored some of the ideas of the movement. Yet many other writers have given the topic short shrift. Andrew Sinclair and Peter Odegard saw dry ideas as mere propaganda. Scholars following in the path of Joseph Gusfield have tended to ground the prohibition movement so firmly in social context that the ideas of the drys were reduced to merely evidence of cultural values. I do not deny the cultural context of dry ideas but instead examine the implications of ideology on the prohibition reform. Thus, my exploration of dry ideology is a focused one, aimed at showing how their ideas helped determine their legal means.[15]

This study also emphasizes law and its effects on the prohibition crusade more than earlier works. With few exceptions, the scholars who have written about the prohibition movement have devoted little attention to the subject of law. For the most part, what law has been covered by scholars has been the creation by drys of constitutional provisions and statutes. Case law, administrative law, enforcement efforts, and the interaction of legal institutions and ideas with the prohibition movement have received little attention. This deficiency in the study of the workings of prohibition law stems from the view of Gusfield and others that the prohibition laws were mere symbols. In this interpretation, the "symbolic import" of passage was "important to the reformer" in itself. Passage settled "the controversies between those who represent clashing cultures" by adopting one set of values and rejecting another. The structure and enforcement of symbolic laws were of less importance to reformers than passage. While not discounting the theory that prohibition laws and constitutional provisions symbolized cultural values, my account disagrees with the view that prohibitory enactments were not practical. I hope to prove that the drys created the laws to meet certain problems posed by the structure of government and to work within the polity of their day. Federalism pervaded the American polity in the period

1880–1920, and it is the interaction of federalism and the prohibition movement that is the focus of this study.[16]

Drys viewed the polity's federal limits through the lens of their legal culture. Legal culture, according to Lawrence M. Friedman, is: "the ideas, attitudes, values, and opinions about law held by people in a society." It is legal culture "which determines when and why and where people turn to law or government or turn away." Friedman paints his picture of legal culture with the broadest of brushstrokes: "Social change leads to changes in legal culture, which in turn produce legal change." Thus, grand transformations in society—like the industrial revolution or the rise of the welfare-regulatory state—placed indirect demands on the legal system to change and led to the creation of modern legal culture. While he paints broadly, Friedman admits that "there is no such thing as *the* legal culture. . . . In a country as large and diverse as the United States, there are all sorts of attitudes and opinions about law." Clearly drawing an analogy to the notion of high and popular cultures, he divides legal culture into two parts, general legal culture and high legal culture. High legal culture consists of the "formal, high-level writings and philosophies" about law—implicitly created by legal professionals. This higher culture reflects and influences popular ideas and opinions. General legal culture, Friedman argues, are the "attitudes and values held by people who exert explicit or implicit pressure on the legal system." Friedman thinks general legal culture does not reflect simply the "culture of the man and woman in the street" but also "rich and powerful people." In other words, general legal culture encompasses "the legal ideas and attitudes of those outside higher [legal] culture."[17]

Building upon and extending Friedman's analogy, this work asserts that there are legal subcultures within any legal culture. While there are larger general and high legal cultures, each can be divided into various complementary and conflicting subcultures. The full legal culture is thus created by the interplay of various legal subcultures. At the bottom of the legal subcultures are ideas; thus, a social group with an ideology—a consistently held set of beliefs drawn from whatever sources—can create its own legal subculture. Not every reform will have a legal subculture; for instance, very broadly based and amorphous reforms—such as antitrust or the movement for income taxation—apparently did not. Reforms with a subculture can borrow parts of the general legal culture and high culture in creating their own view of law. Drys had a variety of existing American legal cultures, which drew upon high and popular legal culture. Thus, the drys held specific ideas about law, and these views of law determined how they reacted to challenges of federalism.

In the 1880s and early 1890s, prohibitionists, led by the Prohibition party and the Woman's Christian Temperance Union (WCTU), saw law in Mosaic terms. Rooted in the idea of natural, God-given law, the Mosaic conception of law presented law as a list of ordinances that people were obliged to obey. Seeing law primarily as a code filled with moral meaning, drys thought human law should strive to reproduce God's commands. Law should promote morality and should not be used to legitimate evil. Therefore, laws that recognized the liquor traffic by regulating it were wicked as well as inadequate. Thus, total prohibition became the only legitimate legal response to liquor. Clearly this view of law complemented and flowed out of the drys' abolitionist means. Taking advantage of the diversity implicit under federalism, radical drys enacted prohibitory laws in some states. But these dry havens soon suffered from the eroding influences of the federal system.

In the 1880s and 1890s, federalism undermined state and local prohibition in two ways. First, the interstate commerce doctrines proclaimed by federal courts permitted liquor sellers based in wet states to introduce their products into dry territory legally. This flow of liquor made it impossible for prohibition areas to be truly dry. Second, the federal government's excise tax on liquor legitimated the industry and erected a barrier to the spread of the reform through fear of lost tax revenues. Initially, prohibitionists approached these problems with the Mosaic conception of law guiding their tactics. They urged the ban of liquor in interstate commerce and the abolition of the federal liquor tax. Though the polity did create a number of compromise solutions to the problems that federalism posed for prohibition states—offering limited federal aid to prohibition in the states—drys had no success in achieving their larger ends. Meanwhile, dry states suffered from loopholes and exceptions to federal policies designed to aid those states. Responding in part to the challenges of federalism, the prohibition movement changed its tactics.

A new organization, the Anti-Saloon League, arose in the 1890s and reoriented the movement's legal conception and response to federalism. While not abandoning the belief that law was in essence a moral command, the league adopted a pragmatic and functional approach to law. It rejected the notion that laws merely restricting the liquor traffic needed to be removed. Rather, it sought to enforce all liquor laws as a practical program of attacking the liquor evil. Thus, the league tried to use regulation as a means to abolition. This new legal culture allowed the league to build on previous compromises in the federal system to effectively curtail the sale of liquor in dry communities and spread prohibition to new jurisdictions. For drys, the federal system went from being a source of problems to a resource of promise. In using federalism for their own ends, they articulated a conception of concurrent state and federal action against liquor that reached its culmination in the creation of a prohibition amendment and its federal enforcement code.

Thus, the immediate origins of national prohibition lay in the prohibitionists' changing use of the federal system. And these very origins also limited the achievement of drys. The Eighteenth Amendment and Volstead Act mixed the two legal traditions of the dry movement. In prohibiting all beverage use of alcohol, they reflected the Mosaic concept of pure law, while their system of concurrent state and national enforcement embodied the pragmatic view of law. Strangely, both legal cultures also contributed to the failure of the prohibition. The total ban on alcohol, which earlier gave the movement such focus, prompted the drys' refusal to compromise on the sale of beer, which made them seem like intolerant fanatics. Similarly, concurrent power in the federal system, which had served the prohibition movement so well before the amendment, weakened nationwide prohibition. It diffused the power necessary for effective enforcement. Thus the drys' ambitious attempt to reform, through law, the drinking habits of the nation ended in failure. But both their successes and failures tell us much about the role of the polity in influencing reform.

While polity's structure did shape the reform history of prohibition, its constraining pathways did not determine what occurred. Reformers had options within the polity. For instance, that prohibitionists chose to remain with cooperative federal and state action in the progressive era instead of federalizing their reform was just that—a choice. If the drys had traveled the other path, then the history of their reform would have been different. Thus, the interplay of agency also directed the course of reforms. Moreover, the molding forces went both ways: the polity directed reformers to certain courses, and the pressure of reformers on the system recast the polity. Thus, while drys changed their legal culture to meet the demands of the polity, drys' actions (and those of other reformers) made part of the Treasury Department into a law enforcement agency. Finally, contingency modified the course of reforms within the polity. It is only by chance that the first crisis over interstate liquor occurred at one of the rare times when the Republican party controlled both houses of Congress and the presidency, enabling quick action in passing the Wilson Act of 1890. If the interstate commerce emergency had come at another time, when Democrats controlled one house of Congress or the presidency, the outcome might have been different. Certainly it is unlikely that the Democratic party would have come up with the same solution to the problem. As the Wilson Act was the foundation of dry legislative strategy for thirty years, different timing would have brought about dramatic consequences for the crusade's history with the polity. Thus, the structure may have been a molding force, but it was not the only force at work in the interaction of the polity and the prohibition reform, or any other reform.

Examination of a single reform to develop a larger point can lead to misunderstandings, as other historians have discovered. For example, in the preface to the reissued version of his classic *Conservation and the Gospel of Efficiency*, Samuel Hays remarked that earlier readers of his book had mistaken its "primary significance." It was not, as many assumed, about the "evolution of conservation" or the "idea of efficiency" in the progressive period. Rather he "hoped" that his discussion of conservation and efficiency "would turn" readers toward an understanding of "the history of the structure of power in modern America." He admitted that he left the main themes of the work implicit, which contributed to the readers missing his point. This work on the prohibition movement shares a similar purpose, but it tries to make the primary theme explicit. While it details the prohibitionists' interaction with the federal system from 1880 to 1920, its larger goal is to illuminate how the American polity shaped reform. The bulk of the book is an account of the prohibitionists' struggles to create a dry nation; yet it also speaks to the broader topic of how the polity influenced reforms. Throughout the text, to underscore the larger point of the book, the prohibition example is compared to the histories of other social reforms and interest groups within the polity, such as purity crusaders, antigambling advocates, pure-food reformers, opponents of child labor, and conservationists. Thus, this work is both a monograph and a conceptional model. My hope is that others will learn from what I say about the drys and test the model (which is more descriptive than theoretical) by detailed explorations of other reformers' legal cultures and experiences in the American polity.[18]

This work is divided into two parts. The first describes the interaction of the prohibitionists with the federal system when the Mosaic legal culture dominated the movement. The second explores how the new pragmatic legal culture helped drys conquer the federal system. In Part 1 the opening chapter profiles the prohibition movement in the 1880s and early 1890s, explores its Mosaic view of law, and examines the drys' enemy—the liquor industries. Chapter 2 shows how the liquor interests successfully invoked interstate commerce doctrines in federal courts and undermined the effectiveness of state prohibition; it also explains how the Congress, sidestepping the sweeping demands of drys, reshaped interstate commerce law to allow states a greater degree of control over liquor commerce. Chapter 3 examines the nature of the federal liquor excise tax, the radical prohibitionists' program for its abolition, the workings of the liquor tax in the federal system, and the drys' early efforts to use the tax as a means of tightening state liquor law enforcement.

To open Part 2, Chapter 4 discusses the transformations in the prohibition movement—including the new legal culture of practicality and pragmatism—that coincided with the rise of Anti-Saloon League. Chapter 5 returns to the tax issues and reveals how the new conception of law allowed the temperance advocates to turn the tax system into an enforcement tool of state liquor laws. Chapters 6 shows how the federal courts at the turn of the century made it easier to import liquor into dry areas and explores the new conceptions of federal power that emerged in the twentieth-century polity. Chapter 7 reveals how the Anti-Saloon League, alternately adopting purely national means and ideas of concurrent state and federal action, won legislation restricting interstate liquor commerce. Chapter 8 details the drive for creation of a dry nation and shows how both the Mosaic and pragmatic legal cultures combined in the Eighteenth Amendment. The conclusion explores the role of the polity in influencing three reform groups—advocates for juvenile justice, divorce reformers, and eugenicists—of the progressive period, examines the legacy of concurrent power for nationwide prohibition, and discusses the failure of national prohibition.

RADICALS AND THE POLITY

P A R T   O N E

THE RADICAL PROHIBITION MOVEMENT

AND THE LIQUOR INDUSTRY

C H A P T E R

The American polity in the last quarter of the nineteenth century saw both the rebirth of the prohibition movement and the emergence of the manufacture and sale of liquor as one of the nation's leading industries. Conflict between the two was inevitable. But the ideas of the prohibition movement, the qualities and actions of the drys' opponents, and the nature of the polity channeled that conflict into certain courses. A radical temperance ideology with its allied Mosaic legal culture predominated within the temperance crusade in the last two decades of the century. The drys' ideology and legal notions made it difficult for them to achieve much success in the American polity dominated by formal and informal rules administered by political parties and courts. Yet the popularity of temperance allowed drys to establish beachhead prohibition states. The liquor industry, after failing to block the adoption of prohibition in these states, challenged the policy in the federal courts. These legal confrontations set the parameters for the next three decades of liquor law struggles.

As old as the republic, temperance was a quintessential American reform. At the time of the Revolution, some leading figures, most notably Benjamin Rush, advised Americans to moderate their consumption of liquor. The early agitators focused on the relatively new distilled spirits, advocating that people drink the less powerful fermented and brewed beverages. Their appeals to the citizenry had little effect. By the early nineteenth century per capita consumption of alcohol ran at least two times the modern average. Use of liquor pervaded American life. Most of the population, from youth to old age, consumed it, often at every meal from breakfast through supper. It was common practice to drink at every social event and even at work.[1]

But the havoc that liquor worked in American life caused many to advocate temperance. Thus, in the early part of the nineteenth century, liquor lost its legitimate role in many parts of American society. The Second Great Awakening altered many middle-class Americans' view of alcoholic beverages. Going beyond the ideas of the earlier agitators, the new evangelicals saw liquor not as a necessary and benign part of life, but as an evil influence that threatened to weaken society by destroying individuals. They abstained from spirits themselves and sought to convince others to do so. In the 1840s the Washingtonians—a working-class temperance movement—emerged in the cities and spread across the nation. Members of this organization signed a temperance pledge not to drink any alcoholic liquors. In the next decade the pledge idea spread into the middle class, with the birth of other total-abstinence organizations. One of them, the Order of Good Templars, proclaimed their freedom from spirits by donning white ribbons and thus created the enduring symbol of the temperance movement. But moral suasion did not eliminate alcohol from American society, and this fact drove some temperance reformers to advocate legal means of controlling liquor.[2]

One legal means, state prohibition of liquor, became the goal of many antialcohol reformers. Between 1851 and 1855 thirteen states adopted prohibition. The drys even proposed writing prohibitory clauses into state constitutions to assure that the policy would prevail. But in many states, court rulings undermined the effective enforcement of these laws; in two states the highest courts declared the measures unconstitutional. Furthermore, the rise of the Republican party, which avoided prohibition while promoting temperance, and the Civil War's effect of diverting the energies of the "moral reform forces" stopped, and then reversed, prohibition progress. By the end of the war, only five states maintained their prohibition laws; a decade later only Maine, New Hampshire, and Vermont continued as dry states with admittedly lax enforcement. This early antiliquor agitation shared parallels with other reforms.[3]

The pattern of action shown by the temperance crusade in the early and middle nineteenth century corresponded roughly to the path followed by antigambling advocates. These reformers shared the drys' motivation, the goal of banning of a common social practice, and a similar decline during the sectional crisis. Before 1800 gambling was endemic in American society; indeed, colonial and early republic governments as well as private companies engaged in public works used lotteries extensively. In the early nineteenth century religious groups began to criticize lotteries, focusing on their abuses and urging people not to gamble. The Second Great Awakening added fuel to this antigambling movement and inspired it to urge the abolition of lotteries. Under this pressure, states began first to refuse licenses to new lotteries and then to ban them. By 1840 twelve states prohibited lotteries, and the movement put them on the defensive. But the war and Reconstruction slowed the campaign against lotteries, as they thrived in states where they were still legal and reappeared in some states where they had been outlawed as a means of raising revenue. The Louisiana State Lottery Company, created in 1868, became a powerhouse in that state's government and widely engaged in its trade in other states. Thus in the postwar period, reformers resumed their offensive against gambling.[4]

The experience of temperance and antigambling reforms points to the fundamental fact that in this era, when moral reformers wished to accomplish something, they turned first to the state governments. For instance, another reform, the pure food movement, began at the state level. Lawyer George Thorndike Angell led the late-nineteenth-century pure food movement. Angell, who shared the religious values of the prohibitionists, came to the cause through his work against animal cruelty. His goal was to create an abolitionist-style crusade to purify the nation's food; he began his work at the state level. This common pattern underscores the decentralized nature of the American polity before the war. After the war, these early crusades reverberated in a changed American society.[5]

The first temperance crusade made liquor drinking a public issue and changed Americans' drinking habits. Liquor lost its predominance as a drink for all occasions; when many had abandoned spirits, it became harder to include it in all activities. Thus, following the war, liquor consumption became centered in saloons. In 1873 about 100,000 of these establishments dotted the landscape. In 1890 cities with over 50,000 in population had a saloon for every 250 inhabitants. Besides their chief purpose of selling liquor, they served many important social functions on the frontiers and in the cities. But in doing so, they violated the most reasonable of restrictions, such as the prohibition on sales to minors, earning unsavory reputations. Nineteenth-century Americans sensitive to the liquor issue saw that drinking exacerbated certain illnesses, diverted income destined for subsistence, and led, in many cases, to violence and misery. They thought that banning liquor would alleviate, if not solve, these many social problems. These facts and arguments struck some Americans harder than others.[6]

In the late nineteenth century, religious affiliation and ethnicity predisposed many to see prohibition as a viable method of controlling the general disorder in society, and others to perceive it as foolish and dangerous governmental meddling in people's lives. In particular, pietists, members of evangelical sects, including Baptists, Methodists, and Presbyterians, whose religions rested on the bedrock of conversion and good behavior, saw prohibition as a needed corrective to the nation's moral laxity and resulting social problems. Liturgicals—Catholics, Episcopalians, and German Lutherans, espousing religions that emphasized belief over action—did not find prohibition an appealing method of remedying social ills. Since religion followed ethnic lines, old-stock Americans—of English and Scottish heritage—and some Scandinavian immigrants and their children more often supported prohibition than the Irish, German, Italian, and Polish immigrants, along with their descendants. The settling of immigrants in the cities added urban and rural dimensions to the division between wet and dry. Thus a cluster of factors—religious ideology, ethnic tradition, and place of residence—combined to create two different worldviews, which found alcohol use either acceptable or abhorrent.[7]

In the second half of the nineteenth century, despite the influx of immigrants and the collapse of state prohibition laws, temperance sentiment did not disappear. The temperance organizations, especially the Order of Good Templars and the newly founded National Temperance Society and Publication House (established in 1865), attempted to counteract the erosion of prohibitionist support. Their efforts centered on building favorable public opinion, chiefly through the publication of propaganda. Yet moral suasion did not forestall the repeal of state prohibition laws. So many drys determined to go beyond temperance tracts and speeches. From the rubble of the first, a second crusade emerged, becoming a national force in the 1880s. The revived temperance movement built a new structure on the antebellum reformers' foundation of moral suasion and legal remedies. New organizations, the National Prohibition party and the Woman's Christian Temperance Union, proposing programs more sweeping than the earlier reforms, dominated this second wave of temperance activity. Many drys blamed the earlier agitators' reversals on the political power of the liquor interests and entered politics to combat the influence of what they called the liquor traffic. In the wake of the organization of state prohibition parties in Michigan,

Illinois, and Ohio, an 1869 convention called and attended by prominent prohibitionists launched the National Prohibition party. Dry distrust of the major parties, which largely ignored temperance reform, led to their forming a party dedicated to prohibition. They did so on their own terms; radical drys defined a political party idealistically as "an agreement of some number of people upon" public issues.[8]

The formation of a new party underscores the difficulties the drys suffered in attempting to influence the polity to adopt their program. Other reformers of the period who shared similar origins, enunciated similar ideologies, and proposed abolishing other evils did not form political parties. They had no need to because the existing parties met their demands and they faced no organized opposition. For instance, the vice societies that sprang up in American cities in the 1870s—such as the New York Society for the Suppression of Vice and the Boston-based Watch and the Ward Society—remained societies and did not become political parties. Like the drys, members of these organizations, driven by religious and social values, sought to repress what they saw as a social evil. There was a close convergence between dry and vice-society ideas; for example, both movements believed, in the words of Anthony Comstock, that "private interests must be subservient to the general interests of the community" and that action was necessary "to prevent the moral diseases which lead to misery and crime." But the opponents of vice societies were "religious liberals and advocates of freedom of the press," which constituted a "small unheeded minority." Thus the existing parties acceded to the enactment and enforcement of stricter anti-obscenity laws; through reformers' agitation twenty-two states enacted general obscenity laws and another twenty-four banned birth control and abortion information. But the major parties rejected the prohibitionists, and given the constraints of the polity, they were forced to form their own party.[9]

The Prohibition party emerged as the leading temperance organization in the 1870s and 1880s. Looking to what they perceived as the antislavery success of the 1850s, they believed that their efforts could destroy the current party system and give birth to a new political era dominated by a party favorable to prohibition. It never succeeded in its grandiose plan to reshape the party system. Its members came primarily from the temperance wing of the Republican party. While it failed to become a true national organization, it gained strength in the northeastern and midwestern states, traditional bastions of Republicanism. The party grew sporadically from the 1870s into 1890s, responding to state Republican organizations' stands on prohibition. Where the Republicans retreated on the issue, the Prohibition party gained votes, reaching its electoral zenith in 1892, when it gleaned over a quarter of a million votes. Its chief accomplishment was proselytizing; through its plat-forms and candidates the Prohibition party brought the liquor issue into the public eye. The party also took the lead in the articulating and refining of prohibitionist ideas and programs. But the party was never able to defeat the liquor interests in the political arena or curtail the sale of liquor.[10]

After the war, the first temperance advocates to confront liquor sellers directly and demand a halt to alcohol sales were middle-class women of over four hundred midwestern villages, towns, and cities. In the winter of 1873–74 groups of women knelt in the snow before saloons and exhorted the proprietors and patrons to abandon "demon rum." The successes of these "women's crusades" in closing saloons and in capturing the nation's attention opened the eyes of many to the possibilities of direct action against the liquor interests. Overnight women organized temperance unions to channel female energy into the struggle. The next winter these local organizations federated into the National Woman's Christian Temperance Union.[11]

Paradoxically, building the WCTU organization diverted the women's energy from frontal assaults on liquor dealers. The women worked industri-ously, and in the 1880s the WCTU emerged as the nation's largest women's group. The WCTU's founders followed the pattern of trade unions in erect-ing an elaborate organizational structure. Each participating community had at least one union, formed under the authority of a state union. State organi-zations, while affiliated closely with the National WCTU, were in theory autonomous. In operation personality overcame these structural bonds.

The dynamic and charismatic Frances Willard, president of the National WCTU from 1879 to her death in 1898, dominated the formal organization and personally influenced the WCTU's rank and file as well as many other American women. Where Willard led they followed. Willard endorsed a "do everything" program that included women's suffrage, temperance edu-cation in schools, rights for laborers, and from 1884 to 1898 support of the Prohibition party. Since the lack of the franchise limited its political effec-tiveness, the WCTU's political program boiled down to lobbying legislators and circulating petitions. Thus, like the Prohibition party, the WCTU cen-tered its efforts on turning public opinion against the liquor traffic.[12]

The efforts of the Prohibition party and the WCTU in organizing and campaigning for prohibitionist candidates, along with their active programs of moral suasion, brought their message to the people. The extent of their activities was startling: John St. John, the 1884 Prohibitionist candidate for president, took to the lecture circuit in the late 1880s and by 1896 had delivered over 3,500 speeches. Frances Willard, Sallie Chapin, and other prominent white ribboners (members of the WCTU took the Templars' symbol as their own) kept a similar pace. During the late 1880s and early 1890s drys founded no fewer than three major weekly newspapers. By 1890 the party's papers (the *Voice* and the *Lever*) and the official WCTU newspaper (the *Union Signal*) had a combined subscribership of over 100,000. The success of these efforts in building public sentiment favorable to prohibition can be measured by the revival of agitation for state prohibition laws.[13]

In 1875 just three prohibition states (Maine, New Hampshire, and Vermont) remained from the first temperance wave. By 1890 a second surge doubled the number of dry states, with Kansas, North Dakota, and South Dakota joining the fold. Iowa and Rhode Island also adopted prohibition but quickly repudiated the policy. Moreover, between 1880 and 1890, prohibition became a serious issue before the legislatures of at least fourteen other states. In some states, legislatures referred the issue to the public through referenda, and 46 percent of those voting in all the referenda held in that decade favored prohibition. Yet the widespread popularity of the cause did not transfer to the major temperance organizations. Most American considered the members of the Prohibition party and the WCTU to be extremists, and many denounced them as fanatics; the drys' ideology contributed to this negative impression of the movement.[14]

A radical ideology dominated the national temperance organizations of the 1880s and 1890s. Radicals embraced an absolutist ideology and a crusading style. They followed the "radicalism of principle" and were "as constant in their devotion to the cause as the needle to the pole" because "the magnetism of right" directed them. For them, liquor, the embodiment of evil and sin, needed to be totally removed from society; they recognized no middle ground. Their views stemmed from the Christian heritage of come-outerism, combined with their perceptions that the liquor regulation programs of the 1870s and early 1880s had sorely failed to control demon rum. Support of total prohibition, rejection of all "halfway measures," hostility toward established party politics, and a conscious patterning of themselves on the abolitionists marked the philosophy and strategy of the radical prohibition movement.[15]

The ancillary reforms supported by the radical prohibitionists revealed the extent of their radicalism. While not socialists or economic radicals, they advocated a host of other reforms. These reforms centered on the common theme of protecting the family, the key institution of Christian civilization, from the forces of corruption. For drys, threats to family order came under the rubric of "immoral influence" and spurred them to opposition. Thus they favored legislation prohibiting gambling, tobacco, and pornography; promoted uniform divorce laws; and engaged in near-hysterical denunciations of the Mormon Church. Likewise, prohibitionist support of trust busting, the eight-hour day, profit sharing, and other far-ranging changes in the economic structure during the late 1880s and early 1890s also grew from fears that untrammeled capitalism endangered the foundations of Christian civilization. In sum, prohibition radicals were social crusaders who embraced absolutist positions. They regarded elimination of evil as the only acceptable solution.[16]

Radical prohibitionists saw liquor as a national sin, requiring a national solution. Drawing on Calvinist theology, the *Union Signal* summarized this view: "The evil is a national evil, the sin of perpetuating it is a national sin; God deals with nations as nations, and accepts no action of isolated members as expiation for the nation's sin." This view separated drys from the mainstream of American public opinion. Most Americans agreed with the *New York Times'* assessment of temperance: "The liquor question can hardly be called a national question." The prophet of national prohibition was Republican senator Henry W. Blair of New Hampshire, whom the *Times* characterized as a political prohibitionist save in name. Blair repeatedly called for a national prohibition amendment implemented through congressional legislation because he feared that piecemeal state prohibition would not be sufficient to curb the national liquor traffic. He argued that, under the current Constitution, wet states would contaminate dry utopias and that no state alone could limit interstate and foreign importation of liquor. In a stand similar to that of the Garrisonian abolitionists, he called the organic law of the nation corrupt: "The constitution . . . as it now is . . . is a law for the unrestricted manufacture, sale, importation, exportation and internal transportation of intoxicating liquors. It is the great legal fortress of intemperance in this country." Only by amendment, ceding part of the states' police powers to the national government, and subsequent legislation could national prohibition be achieved.[17]

In the 1880s Blair's conceptions and arguments for a strong national policy against drink became the cornerstone of the Prohibition party; from the party they spread throughout the movement to become the credo of the radicals. By the end of the 1870s, the WCTU, the Prohibition party, and most drys had abandoned "compromise measures" in dealing with the liquor traffic. They had replaced the "little schemes and halfway measures" with one solution: total national constitutional prohibition of the manufacture and sale of liquor. The radicals believed that, besides the practical benefits of removing prohibition from the "vagaries of every election," a constitutional amendment elevated their policy to the "highest attainable degree" of authority. It invoked the "dignity and power" of the nation. In their view their position was "comprehensive and complete."[18]

Temperance radicals renounced any measure but total prohibition. There could be "no compromise with wrong," and "separation from sin" was a necessity. They rejected regulation in all forms. For them there was "a law of gravitation in morals as well as nature," and any contact with sin led "steeply downward till the end is reached." Any other "palliative legislation" was "wrong in principle." The drys seriously wished to apply the scriptural passage "touch not the unclean thing" to state and federal regulation of liquor. They believed that governments should disassociate themselves from the liquor trade. Regulation merely created "a moneyed compromise on the part of the government," conferring legitimacy on the alcohol industry. To make their point, drys cited other instances in which the government had renounced its association with evil. For example, New York lawyer Herbert Shattuck, after denouncing the liquor traffic as the worst evil of the day, causing more "pauperism and immorality" than "all other evils together," asked, "What shall be done about it?" He followed this query with a series of rhetorical questions: "What was done about slavery, and the lottery, and polygamy? What is the attitude of government toward all public evils?" Then he supplied radical answers: regulation was no solution, as it would not remove the evils "inherent in the business or in the liquor itself." Only prohibition would be the moral solution for society. Following this reasoning, the radicals objected to the federal liquor tax (see Chapter 3) and the state policies of high license and local option.[19]

In the late 1880s and in the 1890s, the radical prohibitionists violently denounced the policy of high license. The high license program imposed exceptionally high license fees on wholesalers and retailers of liquor and also limited the number of such outlets. Ancillary provisions in most licensing legislation prohibited Sunday operations, sales to minors, and the employment of "immoral" persons. In the late 1870s and early 1880s, many prohibitionists supported the high license as a step in the proper direction. High license proponents contended that these restrictions assured a minimum of respectability in the liquor trade. The Republican party attempted to court the temperance vote by advocating high license, and in attempts to forestall prohibition the liquor manufacturers supported high license. As a result, the Republican party and the industry became identified with the policy. The rise of absolutist thinking and the dissatisfaction among temperance forces with the Republicans turned the movement against "seductive" high license.[20]

The radicals based some of their opposition to high license on the liquor industry's support of it, but more important was its failure to lead to total prohibition. Their opposition centered in their abolitionist principles. The

Prohibition party reduced its opposition to a banner in its 1888 convention: "No Evil can be Exterminated by Selling it the Right to Exist." Along the same lines, radicals responded to the claim "a license law is a partial prohibition" with the rejoinder "a partial prohibition means a partial permission." High license was "nothing else than a recognition of the liquor dealers' claim" to legitimacy. It was "the monopoly of abomination," and it made the "community itself a rumseller." Indeed, "licensing the liquor traffic" lowered the "moral tone of the community." An article in the *Cyclopaedia of Temperance and Prohibition* on the ethics of licensing determined that it was in essence unethical. Establishing the saloon as an honest business, the radicals argued, only increased its evils. One sin would lead to others. They believed prostitution so endemic to high license establishments that they reduced their belief to a phrase: "Low license says, give me your son; high license says, give me your daughter also." The dry assumption that prostitution and high license went together was probably deepened by the attempts of urban reformers in the early 1870s to institute systems of regulated prostitution. Such attempts only made abolitionist reformers more suspicious of instituting any progress through regulation. In sum, the nature of high license was permissive, not restrictive, and therefore unworthy of prohibitionist support.[21]

Similarly, the radical prohibitionists also attacked local option. A state local option law usually authorized the people of any township, county, city, or precinct to decide in a special election to allow liquor sales in their locality. In the 1870s and early 1880s drys supported this policy; their struggles and victories in local option campaigns—usually in this period framed in terms of granting or denying the local authority power to issue liquor licenses—helped define the movement. Ironically, what emerged was a radical movement, which, although it still used local option, found it tainted. Like high license, local option failed the critical criterion—absoluteness. According to the *Cyclopaedia of Temperance and Prohibition*, "Local option grew up as a kind of natural fungus upon the license system stock." It remained a "compromise measure" because it permitted the liquor traffic to flourish where localities voted wet. The survival of wet enclaves, especially in the cities, made the policy "too local" and "too optional" for the radicals. Their questioning of local option elections exposed the thinness of their commitment to majority rule. "No government ought to leave to the vicious, ignorant masses the option of deciding whether they shall have a traffic which makes them more ignorant and vicious," said the *Union Signal* in 1889. The radicals asserted that local option stripped the morality from law, substituting mere changeable majorities for God's "unchanging" and "all-pervading" law. Since compromise with sin was unthinkable, absolute prohibition, decreed by a higher law, was the only solution. The radicals, unlike drys still in the major political parties, contemplated "no other side—no alternative."[22]

The radical prohibitionists' hostility toward party politics distinguished them from more moderate temperance advocates. They found that traditional party loyalty, which they labeled worship before "the mightiest God in the United States . . . the party fetich," impeded temperance reform. The major parties were "hopelessly unwilling to adopt an adequate policy toward prohibition." Thus, many radicals joined or supported the Prohibition party. Its very nature guaranteed the party's radicalism, but the WCTU was not always so committed. From 1884 to 1898 the National WCTU endorsed temperance radicalism and the party, but this action provoked dissent and eventually split the organization. In an age of strong party loyalties, cutting the ties to major political parties symbolized the radical nature of the dry position.[23]

The radicals vented their spleen on both parties. Most prohibition radicals saw no hope of instituting temperance reform under the auspices of the Democratic party. Its record was bad in the eyes of the prohibitionists; in the 1870s Democratic victories prompted the repeal of prohibitory legislation in five states. The *Cyclopaedia of Temperance and Prohibition*, while admitting the existence of a few local exceptions in the south, characterized the national Democratic party as the "special champion and protector of the liquor interests." The party existed as "the avowed and persevering opponent of prohibitory legislation." The radicals did not find the Republicans to be more congenial. In 1881 a temperance speaker asserted that the only difference between the two was that "Republicans drink wine at the Fifth Avenue Hotel, and Democrats 'bug juice' at the distilleries, the latter ending up in the station house and the former going home in coaches."[24]

If anything, the radicals reserved their strongest venom for the Republicans. Typical of these attacks was a description of the 1892 Republican National Convention as "a period of the most stupendous debauchery known in all the extended history of drunkenness." No gathering, not even a "brewers' congress . . . has been more famous in its continued maudlin carousal than has characterized this national convention of the grand old party of temperance and reform." Republican Vice President Levi Morton's ownership of a restaurant with a liquor license earned him the prohibitionist epithet of "Rumseller Morton." Republican espousal of liquor regulation, not prohibition, angered the radicals. The Republicans' long association with reform and the Prohibition party's origins as a Republican splinter group deepened radical hostility. They guarded constantly against the allure of the old party. For example, the *Union Signal* asserted that the plank in the 1892 Republican platform expressing sympathy with temperance reform was meaningless "soundings of brass and tinkling cymbals."[25]

In general, the major political parties dismissed prohibitionists as dangerous fanatics who advocated unrealistic plans: "they are people whose sentiments and emotions are too much for their reason." The Democrats—committed to limited government and localism and opposed to moral experiments—remained ideologically opposed to prohibition, and their large foreign-born constituency reinforced this view. The Democratic *Richmond Times* concluded that the prohibitionists' "single-idea party" was doomed to fail because "the majority of the voters will not join" a party that wished to eliminate "the habit" most voters practiced. The Democratic party also liked to attack the Republican party for its courting of the drys, tarring it as a proponent of what it labeled "sumptuary legislation."

The prohibition revival presented the Republicans with a dilemma. In brief, rejecting prohibition would alienate many of their supporters, while promoting it would anger the equally important German-American wing of their party and might rouse the electorate against them. In the 1880s divisions between wet and dry Republicans rent the party in traditional Republican strongholds. Afraid to act, they presented the issue to the people. The 1886 Republican platforms in ten states endorsed referenda on the question. In states that were already dry the Republican party stood on platforms favoring law enforcement, not prohibition. The party refused to support prohibition openly. Fearing the Prohibition party might erode their own electoral base, they worked to undercut the drys. For instance, during the 1888 campaign, Republicans obtained the subscription list of the *Voice* and mailed propaganda to the subscribers. In essence, both parties—in different ways—tried to make political hay from the prohibition issue without giving in to the radical prohibitionists.[26]

Given the major parties' dominance of state and national legislatures, the radicals were unsuccessful in the legislative arena. For instance, neither the white ribboners nor the party played any role in the greatest victory for their cause in the 1880s, the adoption of constitutional prohibition by Kansas. Radicals exacerbated their difficulties by spending inordinate effort on lambasting the legislatures for public "carousals" or for allowing the sale of liquor in assembly buildings. They also mocked the actions taken by legislatures. "The Ohio Legislature has 'got its courage up to the sticking point'; and has actually prohibited the sale and use of—the toy pistol." Such attacks assured that radical dry programs would be poorly received by the professional politicians who controlled the legislatures. Thus while they bemoaned the political power of the liquor interests, the radicals undercut their ability to compete directly with the liquor lobby. Prohibitionist victories in the states came about primarily through the efforts of local drys who subverted Republican state parties to their own ends. The radical ideology of the national dry organizations proved more a hindrance than a help.[27]

That they did not fare well before the policymakers did not upset the drys. The radicals comforted themselves with their conception of themselves as latter-day abolitionists, guardians of the truth that would eventually sweep the nation. They argued that "in the fifties it was the oppressed negro" who "aroused public sentiment" and that in the 1880s and 1890s it would be the "innocent victims of the liquor traffic" who would spark another purifying crusade. The attraction to antislavery was natural, as many temperance reformers of the antebellum period were sympathetic to abolition if not abolitionists. Similarly, the radicals portrayed the liquor industry as analogous to the slave power. "The liquor traffic is like the slave traffic. . . . It will not submit to restriction and legal supervisions; it is arrogant, defiant and independent." Beyond reviving memories of past successes, this self-glorifying image emphasized the crusading nature of their movement.[28]

In their accounts the drys blurred pure abolition with the political antislavery of the 1850s. This enabled them to claim Phillips, Garrison, and Lincoln as progenitors of their own crusade. It also justified their using the sectional crisis and Northern victory in the Civil War in their propaganda. A phrase in the Prohibition party's 1872 platform, "the abolition of those foul enormities, polygamy and the social evil," recalled the language of the 1856 Republican platform, which condemned "those twin relics of barbarism— polygamy and slavery." Every judicial setback for temperance became another "Dred Scot decision." The prohibitionists honored the Republican party "for its past" but believed it had failed to foster further reforms and therefore needed replacement. Just as the destruction of the Whigs had advanced the cause of antislavery, the radical prohibitionists argued that the collapse of the Republicans would promote prohibition. Most of all, the past provided powerful images of hope. In decrying the striking down of the Iowa prohibition constitutional amendment by the state supreme court, the state WCTU declared, "We had our Bull Run Disaster before we had vanquished Richmond." This type of retelling of history comforted the drys, assuring them that prohibition "will follow as inevitably as abolition came."[29]

The prohibitionists attempted, by constant agitation, to bring about what they hoped was the inevitable. Beyond speeches, tracts, and newspapers they sought to spread the word by example. Radical drys devoted much time and energy to the creation of permanent temperance institutions—such as temperance hotels—and the founding of utopian prohibition communities.

Their purpose was to convince the public of the benefits of temperance and prohibition. In the late nineteenth century various drys founded a number of temperance towns—Greely in Colorado, Palo Alto in California, Harvey near Chicago, and Vineland in New Jersey. But three other ventures were associated directly with national radical organizations: the Women's Temple in Chicago, Prohibition Park on Staten Island, and the dry town of Harriman, Tennessee. In each case the leaders of the Prohibition party and the WCTU directly promoted these schemes. These enterprises were a visible manifestation of the radical prohibition spirit.[30]

In 1887 the Chicago and National WCTUs began planning the construction of a Chicago office building. Its name, the Women's Temple, revealed that this was more than another commercial structure. Drys conceived the Gothic-style, twelve-story building as a temperance response to the lavish structures erected by the liquor industry. Although its builders intended the Women's Temple to provide needed office space for the WCTU and anticipated its financial success, these were not its major purposes. To the officers, and especially to the rank and file, the Women's Temple became a tangible symbol of what women could accomplish outside the home. As one wrote, "My heart throbbed with delight that it was a woman's work that planned and completed such an undertaking." White ribboners showed their ardor for the undertaking by donating over one quarter of a million dollars to the Women's Temple. Beyond symbolizing woman in the public sphere, the WCTUs expected the Women's Temple to bring the message of prohibition and home protection into the financial capital of the Midwest. They missed few opportunities to proselytize. In 1890, at the laying of the cornerstone, 2,000 children bearing banners marched through the Loop chanting, "Saloons, Saloons, Saloons must go." The building's auditorium, Willard Hall, was the physical incarnation of the dry women's desire to spread the word.[31]

The leaders of the Prohibition party shared the proselytizing spirit of their sisters who planned the Women's Temple. On the Fourth of July 1888, they opened Prohibition Park on Staten Island. As conceived by the party's leaders, especially Issac K. Funk, the nature park and open air auditorium, "supplied by springs of pure water," were not another "money-making scheme" but rather "a grand enterprise to bless humanity by establishing an educational center to advance the cause of reform and prohibition." The promoters' vision quickly expanded as they decided to surround the park with a temperance town of summer homes. They sought to attract "New York business people" to what they advertised as a cross between Chautauqua and Ocean Grove. Like any real estate promoter, the radical prohibitionists lauded the park's ideal location, scenic beauty, superior transportation system, fine utilities, low taxes, and resale value. Initially their plans succeeded, and while they were trying to expand the park into a full-time prohibition community, they also decided to extend their real estate ventures.[32]

Soon after the founding of Prohibition Park, many of its founders decided to establish an industrial town that would serve as a prohibition utopia. They intended to educate through action, proving that the "practical result of prohibition" was prosperity. They chose to build their dream town in east Tennessee, an area with abundant natural resources located in a state with a unique law that prohibited the sale of liquor within four miles of a schoolhouse in unincorporated areas. This law would protect their venture in its infancy before it developed a government. In October 1889 they organized the East Tennessee Land Company. Within months they had purchased several thousand acres and laid out the town of Harriman. Once established, the key to guaranteeing prohibition in their town lay in the company's special restrictive title deeds. They required "every contract, deed or other conveyance to lease of real estate" to "contain a proviso" forbidding "the use of the property, or any building there on, for the purpose of making, storing, or selling intoxicating beverages." Advertised heavily in the prohibition press, this scheme enthralled drys. Prohibitionists and others flocked to the opening sale, and the company sold 573 lots for over $600,000. Subsequent sales and bond offers, while less spectacular, were also successful. These prohibition and industrial dreams flourished, and by July 1891 Harriman boasted several factories, fifty stores, three hundred dwellings, four churches, and two WCTUs. The creation of such experiments underscores the insular nature of the radical dry movement.[33]

In general, the radical prohibitionists' isolation from the major political parties, their aping of the crusading style of the abolitionists, and their obsession with absolute purity compelled them to lead the temperance movement down the path of pure agitation. Their ideology did not make them effective manipulators of the parts of the polity controlled by the major political parties. And their legal culture made them equally maladroit in handling the legal environment.

At the first National WCTU convention in 1874, a speaker noted, "We began with the fond hope of converting saloon keepers and reforming drunkards, but experience has taught the liquor traffic would never be stopped by that means alone." Similarly, in 1884, the prohibitionist Catholic archbishop John Ireland told a group of reformers that "the state only can save us" because it alone could control the sale of liquor through law. These speeches underscored how quickly the revived temperance movement adopted legal means. Although the radical prohibitionists never abandoned moral suasion, legal suasion became their standard. Some radicals saw little difference between the two, arguing that legal means were "really a phase of moral suasion," constructing an "artificial conscience" that reshaped public opinion and morals. Henry Blair argued vigorously for the connection between the two when he wrote, "Law is the inevitable result of moral suasion whenever moral suasion is effective." He saw them as "allies." So "just as the law against theft grows out of the universal sentiment of mankind that theft is wrong," prohibition laws "grow out of moral suasion" of society's "general conscience."[34]

Though law was integral to the revived temperance movement, it was a particular conception of law, the Mosaic ideal, that held sway in dry ranks. Radical drys tended to see law as essentially didactic. Law represented the distillation of social conscience, which reflected God-given principles and thus functioned as a means to deliver moral messages. This sort of legal suasion became the hallmark of the prohibition renaissance. Dry radical ideology shaped prohibitionist legal culture—their ideas about what law was and how it was to be used. The Mosaic conception stemmed directly from the religious values prominent in the prohibitionist crusade. As their legal culture echoed their theological ideas, the drys seldom systematically recorded their legal views. Nevertheless, their vast literature reveals this consistent conception of the law. Radical drys saw law as a list of commands that people were obliged to obey. These commands were rooted in the idea of natural law. They saw law primarily as the equivalent of God's commandments—a code filled with moral meaning. Moreover, human law should strive to emulate God's commands. Law should promote morality and should not be used to legitimate evil. Thus the radical drys tended to portray human law as a statement of moral truth. Their legal culture allowed drys to envision the use of law and the power of the government for a great social end. But it also hampered their application of legal means to the day-by-day operation of their reform.

One of the oldest traditions of Anglo-American law assumed that the chief goal of law was to enforce morality. This tradition was long established in America by the time the drys adopted it; significantly, it had been embraced by groups that the drys respected and emulated. For instance, when drys described human law as aspiring to progress toward God's unchanging moral rules, they echoed Puritan notions. The Puritans argued that human law ought "to comport with a higher divine law." Some abolitionists also enunciated a similar view of human law being rooted in natural law. For instance, the Liberty party, influenced by Lysander Spooner's ideas, believed "that law expressed Christian benevolence" and "that law and morality were one." Thus Alvan Stewart in 1837 argued that the due process clause of the Fifth Amendment sanctioned the immediate abolition of slavery, as God's law was the only source of human law and provided the only means of interpreting and applying human law. In Stewart's view, laws protecting the property rights of slaveholders were "carved out of the natural ones of the slave" and therefore "null and void in the court of conscience."[35]

Indeed, up until the middle of the nineteenth century, the melding of law and Christian morality was prevalent in the American legal community. In the wake of the great revivals of the antebellum era, American lawyers defended law from the charge that it was un-Christian and merely utilitarian, "with no voice from heaven or from the depths of the human soul." In reply to the charges of awakened Christians eager to remake the nation, the lawyers argued that law embodied the moral principles of Christianity. For instance, Samuel Chapin said that law went beyond "rules of procedures" to embrace the basic principle that civil society was "an ordinance of heaven." Thus law was as important as the church in meeting human needs: "It is not a combination simply for the protection of life and property; but it is an association for moral improvement." Many of the lawyers' defenses revolved around the notion that human laws and "the principles which underlie and regulate them" were "designed to be modelled after and built upon the principles of Divine Truth." As Washington Van Hamm wrote in the 1849 *Western Law Journal*, if the statute or common law violated divine principles, as embodied in the Ten Commandments, "then we will cheerfully admit that our laws should be so altered as to conform to this great code of Divine Law."[36]

But by the time drys embraced this tradition, its prevalence in legal circles had faded. The argument that the law came from the will of the sovereign people, the idea that a nation could shape law for its own purposes, and the concept of laissez-faire eroded the connection between law and morality. Before the Civil War the legal profession had lost its allegiance to this conception of the law. When the abolitionists asked the courts to equate law with natural law and morality, American jurists and lawyers refused. Rather, they retreated behind the shield of legal formalism, asserting that the law was what the constituted authority said it was, not God-given natural law. Following the war, the idea of the convergence of law and morality did not reestablish itself within the main legal tradition; instead, the legal community became dominated by ideas of individual rights. But the drys drew upon the older tradition to build their legal culture, thus putting themselves out of step with the predominant legal culture in the nation.[37]

Prohibitionists built on the existing idea of the affinity of law and morality according to their own blueprints; thus, the drys' religion deeply shaped their legal ideas. Prohibitionists tended to be native-born Americans of Northern European descent and pietistic Protestants. Since they were evangelical Christians for the most part, theological notions—some of them derived from liberalized Calvinism—tended to spill over into their political and legal ideas. In Calvinist theology individuals exist in a community that had contracted with God to follow his laws. Thus everyone had explicit duties to perform. All were under obligation to the community to use their wealth and talents for public good. In political affairs this influence was seen in the tendency for prohibitionists—like Frances Willard—to embrace a form of Christian Socialism. In legal affairs this strain emerged most clearly in the drys' decided predilection to equate law and morality.[38]

The prohibitionist Mosaic conception of law assumed that the purpose of government was to foster morality. Prohibitionists saw law as a means to extend morality, by which they meant their morality as they saw it: unchangeable God-given truths. People created law to embody God's just rules. Thus "good" law needed to promote morality. The prohibitionists did not worship government per se. Rather, they advocated governmental action to create a moral and just society. Drys sought to change the law to protect the rest of society from those whom they considered sinners, the sellers and consumers of liquor. Since no one had a right to make others suffer by offering them temptations to sin, the government needed to command the end to such temptations. Thus, the drys never questioned the government's authority to regulate private behavior.

Reformers with comparable backgrounds to that of the prohibitionists embraced similar legal subcultures. For instance, the Populists—another group of the 1890s who shared the same traditions and religious heritage as the drys—also advanced legal ideas much like the Mosaic notions in their plans to remake the nation. The notion that social values and legal means coincided and supported each other characterized reformers who favored abolitionist means. For example, the Boston Watch and Ward Society, in its campaigns against obscene literature from 1879 to the turn of the century, mixed moral suasion and legal suasion. Through a petition campaign of three hundred "leading citizens," it successfully pressured the railroad companies to remove "degrading" literature from their stations. The society followed this moral suasion effort with successful agitation for stricter state obscenity laws. After enactment it turned to bringing prosecutions under them. Punishment of a few booksellers was not the goal of these prosecutions. Rather, the society hoped through enforcement to deter all "others throughout New England reading the account in the daily papers" from engaging in the same activities. In short, the law established a moral conscience for society.[39]

Prohibitionists and other reformers who espoused the basic tenets of the Mosaic conception of law had little interest in individual rights. To them, the protection of society demanded action against sin if the sinners would not reform themselves. Thus the anti-obscenity reformers denied that anyone had any legitimate reason to read smutty work, Populists were willing to limit property rights to benefit the larger community, and drys rejected the notion that people had a right to drink liquor. Similar views existed in the pure food and antiprostitution movements. All these reformers sought to use the power of the state to achieve their goals, believing that the purpose of government was to advance a moral general welfare, even at the expense of individual liberties. Indeed, drys dismissed challenges to the control of individual behavior based on individual interest and rights. To them, the notion of individualism expressed in the term "personal liberty" was contrary to the general welfare of all. When people objected that prohibition destroyed the property rights of liquor makers and liquor sellers, drys retorted that property used in sinful businesses hurt the general good and thus were beyond the protections accorded to regular property. Drys envisioned a moral general welfare implemented through law. In their view, the polity had a duty to carry on such actions. In short, government, through law, was responsible for governing social behavior. And it should do so by creating pure laws that clearly delineated the proper path.[40]

These notions about morality and law filled prohibitionist speeches and writings, and a particularly clear statement of them occurred in an odd genre of temperance work: Lincoln biographies. The prohibitionist James B. Merwin claimed for years that Abraham Lincoln was a radical prohibitionist. His assertions were accepted in dry circles and widely repeated. Thus prohibitionists ascribed to Lincoln their fundamental values, including the purpose of law. According to drys, in the 1850s Lincoln was reported to have said that law existed "for the protection, conservation and extension of right things," not for the "protection of evil." Thus good legislation must reflect "this principle." A just society—one that concerned itself with extending "right conditions, right conduct, righteousness"—would "be secured and preserved, not by indifference, not by a toleration of evils, not by attempting to throw around any evil the shield of law, never by any attempt to license the evil." It could come only through prohibitory legislation, which set clear boundaries between good and evil. The "sentiment of right conduct for the protection" of society "must be taken up, embodied in legislation, and thus become a positive factor active in the State. This is the most important function in the legislation of the modern State." These statements succinctly summarize the radicals' conception of legislation.[41]

Another work completely delineated their working assumptions about law in general. Eli Ritter wrote the fullest statement of the radicals' view of law in his 1896 treatise *Moral Law and Civil Law: Parts of the Same Thing*. In this book he defined morality as good conduct within civil society; morality was both public necessity and public good. It was not a human construct subject to change but God-given and permanent. According to Ritter, "Morality like truth . . . has no varieties." Thus Ritter recognized no "absolute rights in conflict with public necessity," and he had little fear of government power. Both statute and common law should be "in harmony with morality." It was the goal of law to promote morality and suppress immorality. If law violated the standards of morality, it was destined to change. As an axiom, no act of immorality could be long "protected by legislation." The "legal principles are fixed," and as society's general intelligence and public necessity increased, law that recognized immorality would wither. To back up his point, he showed how legal institutions in both England and America ended slavery. Moreover, he claimed, the American states had recently and for similar reasons abolished lotteries and prizefights. Ritter then portrayed liquor licensing as another example of law that was "wrong in principle." He contended that if the "authority and protection given" by legislation "were withdrawn from the saloons," they would quickly be condemned as nuisances. Ritter's work incorporated several key Mosaic ideas about law: the belief that law was sanctioned by God, the idea that law should equate to moral rules, and the assumption that abolishing bad law would advance the cause.[42]

In general, guided by the purity of the Mosaic ideal, the radical drys were not interested in the intricacies of legal procedure. Rather, they were intent on the larger goal: establishing good law, which was pure and moral. Their Mosaic conception of law inclined them to see current legal rules concerning liquor as obstacles in their path. Thus, even when they used methods like high license and local option laws, the radical drys condemned them. In their eyes, legislatures had not written statutes that clearly laid out the moral rules and judges had not drafted doctrines to limit the liquor evil. Radical drys were uninterested in hammering out compromise measures that would meet the needs of competing interest groups; they wanted to use the law to root out what they saw as an evil and its fomenters, saloonkeepers and liquor manufacturers. So when they looked to law, either statute or common law, they looked to make clear statements. In general, the radical prohibitionist Mosaic legal culture limited their effective use of legal means. Moreover, their legal ideas conflicted with the lawyers' support for individual rights. And even without their ideas, the drys were somewhat alienated from the world of bench and bar of the late nineteenth century. But nevertheless the drys seemed obsessed with law.

As a result of this recourse to law, the radical drys evidenced great desire to learn it. They became so obsessed with law that they formed legal self-education groups. Typical of these efforts were the "Constitution parties" supported by the WCTU. In 1887 "Aunt Hilary" and her friends formed a typical student group in Sunrise, Illinois. They asserted that since crusaders needed better understanding of law, "We who can read must teach the law at home to our children." The group's meetings opened with the song "America," quickly followed by a reading from scriptures and the Lord's Prayer. A reading from the state constitution or statutes, followed by discussion, constituted the meat of the program. Others within the movement advised drys to take up law books. One writer argued that "legal reports are just now very profitable handbooks for temperance people." Mary E. Metzgar, head of the Illinois WCTU law enforcement division, extended this idea. She contended that every white ribboner ought to own three books: "the Bible, a copy of the state laws and a copy of the city laws."[43]

As shown by Metzgar's statement, when radical prohibitionists spoke of law, more often than not they meant statutory or constitutional provisions. For instance, the 1891 *Cyclopaedia of Temperance and Prohibition* contained an eighty-eight-page section tracing the history of each state's liquor legislation and a mere two-page article on common law. The relative clarity of positive law compared with common law helped to guide the drys toward this preference. A speech by J. Ellen Foster listed the Justinian Code, Magna Charta, Bills of Rights, Declaration of Independence, Constitution, state and city laws, and even "the petty regulations of our school districts" as the "crystallization" of the moral sentiment of society. These positive forms of law came closest to Mosaic law of clear prohibitions. Radical drys argued that all law was in essence a list of "Thou Shall Nots" embodying moral truths. This tendency to see law as moral truths put forth in clear codes paralleled one of the drys' favorite forms of literature—catechisms comprised of likely questions and definitive answers. With these notions in mind, they wanted to rewrite the nation's law to make it "righteous law," which "will be a terror to evil doers and a praise to them that do well." They sought to place prohibition of the liquor traffic on the highest available secular pedestal, the state constitutions. Following this inclination, in the 1880s, the people of Maine, Kansas, Rhode Island, North Dakota, and South Dakota appended prohibition amendments onto their states' fundamental law. And in every state where prohibition was an issue, drys tried to write prohibition into the state constitution. This virtual obsession with statutory and constitutional means of limiting the liquor traffic in part diverted drys from using the common law.[44]

The nature of dry legal culture, with its roots in a higher law, should have lent itself to the use of the courts, in the oracular tradition, to enunciate "higher law" against the liquor traffic. That most drys of the 1880s and early 1890s did not turn to the courts to invoke "higher law" was a result of both the Mosaic conception of clear and definitive law and their times. The model of abolitionist efforts to use higher law against positive law was one of failure. And higher law had been utilized against prohibition statutes by the courts, most notably in the 1856 *Wynehamer* ruling. Thus their answer to bad, liquor-sanctioning legislation was to repeal and replace such laws, not to seek judicial review of them. Judicial rulings, up to the 1887 U.S. Supreme Court's decision in *Mugler v. Kansas*, bolstered the prohibitionist predilection for statutory law. Their exclusion from the inner world of bench and bar hampered their appreciation of the possibilities of judge-made law for their reform.

Generally, when radical drys did examine judge-made law, they viewed it from a formalistic perspective. The radicals saw precedent as absolutely controlling. Thus the common law could be of little use because it legitimated liquor selling and reflected the "view entertained on the subject by a half-civilized people ages ago." It had no application to an "enlightened people" who had by statute or constitutional amendment prohibited slavery, polygamy, and lotteries as well as granted property rights to married women. According to some drys, the only way to change the law, to bring it into line with "every advance made by society in civilization," was to enact a statute. This focus on the formalistic nature of the common law no doubt arose from the drys' familiarity with the abolitionists' efforts to use the courts to end slavery. The U.S. courts had retreated into formalism in the face of abolitionists' efforts to utilize natural law doctrines against the institution, and positive law had been used instead.[45]

Also undermining the radical drys' respect for the common law were the recent actions by courts ruling prohibition unconstitutional in various jurisdictions. In the 1880s, decisions of state and federal judges gave radical prohibitionists reason to dismiss the common law as a means of reform. In

1883 the Iowa Supreme Court declared that mistakes made during the adoption of a prohibition amendment voided the provision. This ruling prompted the *Union Signal* to quote from prohibitionist attacks on the judiciary in the 1850s and to conclude: "The Evil One has available material ready to his hand on every side, and the judicial ermine ever and anon covers some of his most efficient agents." In 1885 Atlanta voted dry under the Georgia local option law, but within a week of the city's "glorious victory" the courts had "already rushed to the 'poor oppressed saloon keeper.'" Such rulings reinforced drys' belief that the "whiskey interest" dominated politics, including judicial selections and elections. The courts became another of many rum-soaked institutions, and their decisions were all too often a "Bull Run disaster," opening further loopholes for the liquor industry "to crawl through."[46]

No judge provoked more ire among the radical prohibitionists of the 1880s and 1890s than David Brewer. As a Kansas Supreme Court justice and as a federal circuit court judge, Brewer asserted that prohibition states had to compensate liquor manufacturers and sellers for the taking of their property. Prohibitionists believed his rulings were "calculated to crush" prohibition "utterly." After one of his rulings the *Voice* commented, "What's in a name? Read Judge Brewer's decision in favor of the Kansas brewer before you answer." Even after the U.S. Supreme Court declared, in *Mugler v. Kansas*, that dry states did not have to compensate the liquor interests, the radical drys refused to relent. Upon Brewer's elevation to the U.S. Supreme Court they denounced him as "man of very distasteful record" who favored "the liquor side of disputed questions." Party prohibitionists feared that his appointment was a Republican attempt to crush judicially prohibition in Kansas. Their fanciful ideas that the appointment of one justice would somehow bring about the reversal of the 7-1 *Mugler* decision underscored the radical prohibitionist misconceptions about appellate judging, misconceptions that hindered their application of legal means to their reform. Thus, judges and judge-made law had little role in their campaign to build a utopia.[47]

In part, some of the difficulty the radicals had in understanding the workings of the Supreme Court stemmed directly from their alienation from the culture of the appellate bar. A letter written to the *Union Signal* describing the festivities surrounding the centennial celebration of the U.S. Supreme Court revealed how far the prohibitionists stood outside the high legal culture. The writer condemned the "sumptuous feast" honoring the Court, held in New York City's Lenox Lyceum, because "everything was furnished" including, "four kinds of wine—champagne flowed more freely than water—brandy, whisky and the most costly cigars that money could procure!" By the time several hundred women entered the balcony boxes to listen to the after-dinner orations, "clouds of incense began to rise from multitudinous cigars," making the air "blue with smoke." The prohibitionists found the speeches lauding American institutions to be overwhelmed by the "thick fumes of tobacco smoke and popping of champagne corks." They believed that the members of the bar should "hang their heads in shame" over these proceedings. The radical drys' desire to civilize America by emancipating "the individual from appetite and passion" had little place in the traditions of American legal society.[48]

The general alienation from the world of judges and lawyers did not keep lawyers from the ranks of the radical prohibitionists. Many lawyers joined the movement, but legal training did not automatically make a person a member of the bar fraternity. Lawyers in the dry camp, for the most part, remained outside the usual orbit of lawyers for various reasons. Three of the most prominent temperance lawyers were women: J. Ellen Foster (called "Our Temperance Portia" by Mother Eliza Stewart), Ada M. Bittenbender, and Helen Mar Jackson Gougar. Their sex excluded them from the usual convivialities of the male-oriented bar. They all read law with their husbands, training that ran counter to the growing law school movement, and thus lost the opportunity to form valuable professional connections. More generally, lawyers who advocated reform separated themselves from their legal brethren. The pillars of the American bar were not noted for social radicalism. Indeed, many of them found the dry programs repugnant. The legal profession's intimate relations with party politics and the prohibitionists' abhorrence of the traditional parties only widened the gulf between the two groups. Thus it is not surprising that the prohibitionists lacked influence in legal circles.[49]

Moreover, the drys' ideas about law separated them from the larger legal community. As Morton Horwitz has shown, the dominant high legal culture (which he calls classical legal thought) established a separate realm for law, free from "the dangers of state interference." Legal thinkers of the late nineteenth century favored "a self-regulating, competitive market economy presided over by a neutral, impartial, and decentralized 'nightwatchman' state." Limited government and autonomous law, to them, explained "why Americans had uniquely been able to avoid falling victim to tyranny." At the same time, American lawyers loudly advocated individual rights and liberties. Drawing on Enlightenment and republican ideas, they saw rights as the individual's bulwark against governmental tyranny and as a shield from other individuals.[50]

In two ways this legal culture blocked the prohibitionists from integrating their ideas with the mainstream. First, the reliance on the small state stood as an obstacle to the prohibitionists who wished a more active government involved in promoting morality. The limited government notions so popular in legal circles would not give the polity the power needed to destroy the liquor evil; so drys refused to adopt it. Second, the ideology of rights became the first weapon liquor sellers picked up to defend themselves against drys, prompting drys to renounce it. Prohibitionists parodied the actions of liquor sellers who, when shut down by prohibition law, went "to see mein gounsel when I no got some right to mein own proberty." But the rights defense—based so strongly in the American experience—stung. So radical drys, in turn, dismissed "constitutional lawyers . . . loaded to the muzzle with legal lore, mounted on the Constitution" as mere mercenaries "selling their skills to the highest bidder." Drys, seeing lawyers as friends to their enemies, also rejected the lawyers' canonization of individual rights. Drawing on their religious inspiration, they asserted a different view of liberties.[51]

At the WCTU's annual convention in 1892 Frances Willard stated most fully the radical drys' rejection of individual rights. She postulated three evolutionary stages of rights. The first was that held most dear by American lawyers, that of "personal rights." She asserted that these rights of "life, liberty, and the pursuit of happiness" were "set up in the camp of the savage" and clearly deficient. She saw their replacement with a new era of social rights based on the realization that government, acting for the morality of all, must have the power to declare "thou shalt, and thou shalt not." When fully exercised, this stage represented the fulfillment of the Mosaic ideal of law, but Willard did not want to stop there. She saw the highest stage to be a true Christian polity in which "government by law is exchanged for that mightiest of all government—public sentiment. The moral tone of society declared by resistless common consent what the law" previously proscribed and punished. The golden rule was the only rule, and there was no need for rights. Thus their rejection of the dominant legal ideology, their alienation from the world of bench and bar, and their legal culture aimed at producing prohibitory legislation made the radical drys weak warriors in the legal arena.[52]

In the 1880s the drys' deficiencies in legal matters were readily apparent. A sympathetic lawyer commented that the prohibitionists "have been singularly neglectful of the conditions for maintaining their position in the courts, particularly in the courts of last resort." For instance, in this period, prohibitionists failed to file an amicus curiae brief in the important *Mugler* case. Similarly, the *Union Signal* took no notice of the Supreme Court's

March 1888 ruling in the important interstate commerce case of *Bowman Brothers v. Chicago and Northwestern Railroad*. Not until its annual convention in November 1888 did the WCTU discuss the opinion.

Yet the radical drys did not abandon the common law debated by lawyers and enunciated by courts. They occasionally consulted court decisions in search of moral truths. Reflecting the Mosaic conception of law, drys invariably cited the most general of phrases, often obiter, which they believed supported their programs. In 1888 the Anti-Nuisance League, a group of prohibitionists led by Eli F. Ritter, proposed to challenge the constitutionality of all state and local license systems before the U.S. Supreme Court. They based their action on Chief Justice Morrison Waite's phrase in the 1880 lottery case *Stone v. Mississippi*, "no legislature can bargain away public health or public morals." And they argued, before at least one state appellate court, that the liquor traffic was a "constant menace to public and private morals, health and safety" as well as a drain on the treasury and constituted a "public nuisance." The linking of prohibitionist values to the Court's general statement, removed from its context, and the discounting of the Supreme Court's (and all other courts') long recognition of the liquor trade and license systems revealed legal naïveté. But this idea, like the awareness of different judges, which could bring different outcomes, as evident in discussions of the *Mugler* case, showed that the drys could overcome their formalistic perception of the common law and could also use types of law other than their favored statutes and constitutions. Nevertheless, guided by their legal culture, the radicals drys intended to agitate until public opinion "advanced" on the liquor question, compelling the enactment of laws or constitutional provisions. Thus it was not the drys but their opponents who made prohibition an issue in federal court.[53]

Prohibitionists saw the liquor industry as a highly unified liquor power that was created by greed and that blighted American life and politics. The need to defend against the growing temperance movement sustained the unity of the liquor power. A temperance song, "They All Get There Together," expressed the key components of this view. "The brewers and distillers . . . would like to own the nation and also hold a mortgage on the balance of creation." And they had "a grip on politics that's mighty hard to break." But their vision was more colorful than accurate.[54]

Actually there were many separate liquor enterprises: brewers of beer, distillers of hard liquor, wine makers, and saloon keepers. Despite dry accounts, competition and hostility—not cooperation—dominated the relations between and within the liquor industries. Although all connected with producing and selling alcoholic drinks opposed prohibition, they seldom could unite to fight the temperance movement. The wine producers mostly limited their defensive efforts to California and did not affect the prohibition movement significantly. The distillers and brewers possessed the wherewithal to operate on the national level, while the retailers of liquor often became the foot soldiers in the battles against prohibition. For various reasons, the brewers, not the distillers, were the first to invoke the federal courts to protect their interests and the interests of all the liquor industries.[55]

The revival of the temperance movement coincided with a period of intense competition and frantic reorganization in the distilling trade. In the early nineteenth century the industry was characterized by small whisky distillers scattered across the nation who sold their product to a few large wholesalers. Beginning around 1850, increased competition, prompted by a growing market—created by increases in population and facilitated by improvements in transportation—and changes in federal tax policy, led to a decline in the number of producers. As the remaining distillers enlarged their output, the industry began to concentrate. Also at the same time, increased production and the rise of beer as a popular beverage sharpened competition. By 1891 a mere third of the distillers located in just four states (Illinois, Kentucky, Ohio, and Pennsylvania) accounted for nearly 85 percent of the industry's capacity. Fourteen plants in Peoria, Illinois, alone monopolized nearly 40 percent of the market, making that city the distilling capital of the world. In the late nineteenth century increasing competition in the once stable wholesaler network accompanied the concentration of producers. Thus a host of small middlemen fought for the distillers' output, and these businesses insulated distillers from the retailing aspects of the trade.[56]

The drys considered the distillers an organized threat, but nothing could be farther from reality. In the face of near ruinous competition the midwestern distillers formed pools, culminating in 1887 with the famous Whisky Trust. But the Peoria-based Whiskey Trust and successors organized after its collapse in 1895 never gained complete control of the industry. Its activities, including price manipulation and even an attempt to dynamite a competitor's plant, only sharpened the rivalries within the industry. Leading distillers, beset with such economic trials, failed to unite to fight the temperance movement. The drys misunderstood the near anarchic competitiveness in the distilling trade. Rather, they searched for hidden conspiracies. The *Cyclopaedia of Temperance and Prohibition* asserted that even though the "distillers have never revealed their organized national strength," it existed and controlled the country's politics. Yet the distilling industry's almost unique relations with the government made such an organized conspiracy superfluous.[57]

The federal government levied a heavy tax on hard liquor; from 1873 to 1917 the revenues raised by the internal revenue tax on distilled spirits averaged almost 23 percent of the nation's tax receipts. The government guaranteed these tax revenues by overseeing every step in the manufacture of distilled liquor. The cooperation between the government and distillers fostered by these day-to-day contacts, along with the heavy revenues provided by the liquor industry, led federal officials to perceive distilling as a benign and useful industry. Distillers worked to succor this relationship by presenting gifts to government officials. In 1886 the commissioner of internal revenue, Joseph S. Miller, and President Grover Cleveland received several bottles "of what is said to be pure old whisky" for Christmas. The gifts were mere symbols of the relationship between the industry and government; the liquor tax and its administration created a virtual partnership between the distillers and the government.[58]

The distillers' special relationship with the federal government, their isolation from retailing, and their geographic concentration shaped their responses to the emerging prohibition crusade. They did not act at the national level. In part, this inaction stemmed from the belief that the federal government would protect an industry that generated so much revenue. In addition, distillers' connections with the government stymied the formation of a trade organization; an active trade organization could have operated as a conduit for the distillers' opposition to prohibition during the 1880s and 1890s. But the National Wholesale Liquor Dealers Association was not formed until 1896. The industry's concentration in Illinois and Kentucky, with secondary centers in Ohio and Pennsylvania, shielded it from the effects of the prohibition movement. Prohibition in other states did not threaten to close its plants; indeed, the destruction of competing—especially brewing—plants in dry states perhaps offset the loss of markets in those states.[59]

Lacking a central organization to channel antidry sentiment and buffered by state boundaries from the direct effects of prohibition, the distillers centered their opposition to the temperance crusade on localities and states where prohibition was not in effect. It was never a coordinated counterattack. When prohibition agitation threatened individual distillers, they were likely to band together (and join with allies, like the brewers or saloon keepers) to fight the menace. Their weapons were suasion and a program of government regulation. They combated prohibition propaganda by printing their own literature. They sponsored politicians willing to defend the wet cause. Perhaps with the benefits of the federal tax in mind, the distillers promoted increased local taxation of the liquor trade. They also proposed to clean up saloons by restricting hours, sales to minors, and drunkards, as well as excluding the "immoral" from the establishments. Distillers sought to make the liquor trade more respectable and an essential part of the tax base of states and localities. Thus, their activities centered on preventing the adoption of prohibition laws, not on opposing the policy where established. That task fell to the brewers.[60]

The differences between the distilling industry and the brewing trade explain why the brewers used the federal courts to attack prohibition. Unlike the whisky business, brewing was spread across the nation. Virtually every town in America outside the south had at least one brewery. And unlike the distilled spirits industry, the brewers had a national trade organization, the United States Brewers' Association, formed in 1862. Competition within the brewing industry rivaled and perhaps surpassed the intense struggles of the hard liquor trade; but whereas sheer profit stimulated much of the competition in the liquor industry, improvements in technology opened a national market in beer that had not previously existed.[61]

The flood of German immigrants in the 1840s and 1850s laid the foundation of the late-nineteenth-century beer industry. The Germans brought with them a well-developed taste for light, effervescent lager beer and the technical skill necessary for its manufacture. The properties of lager shaped the early industry. Compared with most manufacturing, lager production required little capital; as a result, know-how and willingness launched many brewing careers. With an established market of consumers, the numbers of brewers rapidly multiplied; in 1880 over 2,266 brewers operated in the United States. The delicate nature of lager limited each brewer's market. Lager in kegs shipped poorly, and once the keg had been breached, it quickly turned stale. Thus, the breweries clustered in cities and towns. Its light, refreshing qualities and its low alcohol level made lager a popular beverage with many Americans across the nation. In 1880 only the states of Arkansas, Florida, Maine, North Carolina, and West Virginia lacked a brewery. By 1890 beer had replaced whisky as the leading alcoholic drink in the nation.[62]

Beginning in the 1870s and accelerating throughout the rest of the century, advances in brewing technology sharpened competition in the industry. Pasteurization, refrigeration, and improved bottling permitted a few brewers—all located in midwestern cities with limited markets—to penetrate markets located outside their cities and states. In the 1880s Anheuser-Busch, Best (Pabsts), Schlitz, Miller, Lemp, Blatz, and Morelein were called national brewers even though their systems of distribution did not cover the whole nation. Sharpened competition generated further efforts to secure a technological edge; the national brewers, especially Best and Anheuser-Busch, led the way in investing in new equipment. By 1890 a series of refinements made them the two largest breweries in the nation and in the world. Increasing competition led the nationals and many other brewers to focus on retailing. Brewers began to buy and operate saloons. This trend slowly grew through the late nineteenth century and sped up after the turn of the century.[63]

Sharp competition in the era did not sever the bonds that tied the brewers into a cohesive industry. The United States Brewers' Association, formed in 1862 when the newly imposed federal liquor tax threatened the industry, guaranteed some solidarity in the brewing ranks. The trade organization was remarkably long lived; it continued in operation until the implementation of national prohibition. Its founding before the era of intense national competition and its avoidance of the potentially divisive competition issue contributed to its longevity. Not all brewers belonged to the organization, but most, including all the nationals, did. In 1889 members of the United States Brewers' Association produced nearly 80 percent of the nation's beer. The association's fee structure, which had members pay in proportion to their production, gave the nationals control of the pursestrings.[64]

The predominance of German immigrants and their children within the industry and their common language and culture reinforced the members' shared values. The first meeting of the United States Brewers' Association was conducted in German, and occasionally its convention reports appeared in that language. An observer at a brewers' convention noted that the brewers enjoyed each other's company; "The Germans have the happy faculty of knowing just how and to what extent business and pleasure can successfully be combined, they always make such occasions enjoyable and profitable." While the social aspects of the organization proved a strong glue to bind the members, shared interests were the key to the association's viability. The business of the association included regulating the quality of beer, overseeing labeling of brands, lobbying with federal officials, setting labor policy, and protecting the industry from the prohibition movement.[65]

Like all liquor businesses, the brewers countered prohibition with propaganda and by backing antidry politicians, but in the 1880s their most important efforts centered on the federal courts. The brewers' interests in retailing and the geographical distribution of the industry brought producers face to face with state prohibition. In 1880 148 breweries operated in the two future prohibition states of Iowa and Kansas. These states were also important markets for the national brewers based in St. Louis and Milwaukee. Furthermore, the brewers possessed experience with the federal courts. The importance of technology in brewing had led them to use the courts to protect key patent rights. Their success in maintaining their patents made the courts look attractive as a forum to fight prohibition. If their court campaign was successful, prohibition would be ruled unconstitutional and the likelihood of the reform being enacted in the states reduced.[66]

Kansas's adoption of constitutional prohibition in 1880 and the prospect of Iowa following suit threatened the livelihood of many brewers located in those states. These brewers fought prohibition in many ways, including openly defying the laws, invoking the aid of local governments that favored liquor sales, and seeking to overturn prohibition in the courts. In Kansas, from 1882 to 1887, the state's highest court rendered opinions in sixty-four liquor cases. Significantly, the brewers turned to the federal as well as the state courts. But the cost of litigation was nearly prohibitive for small brewers: one brewery worth only $50,000 spent over $2,000 on suits. Lacking the resources to finance appeals to higher federal courts, both Iowa and Kansas brewers called upon the others (especially the United States Brewers' Association) to bankroll the litigation.[67]

At its twenty-first annual convention, held in Chicago in 1881, the United States Brewers' Association decided to challenge in the federal courts the "foolishness" of the state prohibition laws. The organization clearly feared the effect on the entire industry of this "active warfare on the part of prohibitionists." The potential for prohibition to disrupt the nationals' markets and the fraternal nature of the brewing network helped to settle the brewers' response. The gravity of the dry threat drove the association to seek a definitive ruling on state prohibition from the U.S. Supreme Court.[68]

The brewers hoped the Court would adopt, through the due process clause of the Fourteenth Amendment, the doctrine enunciated by the New York Court of Appeals in the 1856 case of *Wynehamer v. People*. During the prohibition wave of the 1850s the highest courts of New York and Indiana invalidated state prohibition laws, and the New York court did so in the strongest of terms. *Wynehamer* ruled unconstitutional the state's 1855 prohibition law on the grounds that it violated the state constitution's due process clause, because it took property without compensation. Liquor "innocently acquired" before the act's passage was property in the "most absolute and unqualified sense." The 1855 law banned the "right to sell" this property and thus "annihilated" it, thereby depriving property holders of their rights without due process of law. A similar ruling by the U.S. Supreme Court would erase the temperance movement's greatest triumphs and preclude the development of further prohibition measures.[69]

In the late nineteenth century, this doctrine of substantive due process became popular with legal thinkers and businessmen, and the brewers shared the enthusiasm for the doctrine as it fit with their view of rights. In general, the liquor industry believed in what it constantly called "personal liberty." By this term it meant that individuals should be largely free from government interference with basic human freedoms. In their view, individuals held the power to order their own personal lives, including choosing their religions, their spouses, and their drinks. In the United States the basic charters of government, the Declaration of Independence and the Constitution, guaranteed liberty in the private sphere. "Personal Liberty" was "that which no law framed by human mind can successfully abridge." This liberty against government was never absolute; the liquor industries recognized the need for government regulation as a means to support individual control. But the liquor industry did not concede that government's limited powers could be used to supplant individuals' right to choose. Government, they believed, lacked the power to legitimately ban personal liberties. No human law, said the wet propagandist Percy Andreae, could "suppress or govern a man's thoughts, or his beliefs, or his desires, or his appetites. It can only so regulate his exercise of them as to prevent him from thereby interfering with the rights, or endangering the safety of his neighbors." The brewers, grounded in their ideology of personal liberty, hoped that the Court would adopt the doctrine of substantive due process and protect their industry from destructive state regulation. Probably their reading of the legal treatises convinced them that the time had come for the Court to reverse its rulings in the *License Cases* and in *Boston Beer Company v. Massachusetts*; in these cases the Court had denied the claim that state prohibition disturbed vested property rights and found such laws to be a legitimate exercise of the police power. But, according to Morton Horwtiz, late-nineteenth-century legal treatises "sought not simply to report on the state of the law but to advance a highly abstract and integrated version" of what the law ought to be. Thus, the brewers sought a change in the law.[70]

The brewers' hopes were not totally unfounded, for as early as 1873 the Court had announced its willingness to adjudicate the Fourteenth Amendment's application to state prohibition. In *Bartemeyer v. Iowa* Justice Samuel Miller, writing for the Court, stated that although the issue was not properly before it, "two very grave questions" arose from the "passage of prohibition laws." The first was "whether such laws would deprive individuals of property without due process of law." The second was "whether if so, it would be so far a violation of the Fourteenth Amendment" requiring action from the Court. A concurring opinion written by Justice Joseph Bradley, and joined in by Justice Stephen Field, raised under the Fourteenth Amendment a potential relief for the brewers. It argued that a legislature "may prohibit the vending of articles deemed injurious to the safety of society" only when it did not "interfere with vested rights of property. When such rights stand in the way of public good they can be removed by awarding compensation to the owner." The United States Brewers' Association worked for six years to bring about a Supreme Court ruling on these issues.[71]

Not until 1883 did the United States Brewers' Association decide on counsel and a case to test state prohibition in the federal courts. On April 2 the Board of Trustees hired Senator George Vest of Missouri, an important pro-liquor politician and constitutional lawyer, to plead the association's case. They entrusted Vest with seeing Peter Mugler's case through the U.S. Supreme Court. Mugler, a Salina, Kansas, brewer, defied the state's 1880 prohibition amendment and challenged its constitutionality in the state courts. In January 1883 the Kansas Supreme Court held against him. No doubt the United States Brewers' Association selected his case because its evidence was restricted to a statement of facts that clearly raised the question whether the prohibition law interfered with vested property rights without due process of law. Yet the brewers were slow to bring Mugler's case before the Supreme Court. Wet politicians in Kansas and the Kansas brewers sought to use the prohibition issue to their advantage in the 1884 elections and feared any decision would reduce its electoral value. Thus a year after they hired Vest, and despite the report that the case was "progressing steadily," nothing had occurred.[72]

If the United States Brewers' Association was idle, other members of the liquor industry were not, and their actions, along with the reactions of prohibition states, forced changes in the association's plans. The liquor interests in the midwestern prohibition states, especially the brewers, combined to fight prohibition in the local courts. John Walruff of Lawrence, Kansas, the biggest brewer in the state, flamboyantly revealed that the brewers planned to "brew trouble for the courts as well as for the sports." He announced that he would continue to manufacture beer because he thought prohibition an unconstitutional deprivation of property without compensation. Following victories in local courts, Walruff would fly the American flag before his brewery. Walruff used other means beyond court tests to fight prohibition. In an 1882 letter he advised other brewers to cease selling beer while local courts were in session, to approach local officials to make "arrangements," to woo sheriffs to ensure appointment of jurors "who will hang the jury until dooms day," and to work against dry politicians in elections. Another firm, the small firm of Ziebold and Hagelien, based in Atchison, Kansas, succeeded in having part of the prohibition enforcement code of 1881 ruled void. In general, enforcement ills frustrated prohibitionists in both Kansas and Iowa. In response to the liquor counterattack and to assure better compliance with the law, the Kansas state legislature added a new provision to the prohibition law. It declared establishments that sold or manufactured liquor to be common nuisances and, if so adjudicated by a court, liable to abatement and confiscation. In the summer of 1886 Simon B. Bradford, the attorney general, tried to use this clause to dry up the state's cities. The firm of Ziebold and Hagelien, caught in the enforcement drive, challenged it in federal court. Reviewing these actions, one prohibitionist remarked that the enemies of prohibition "are determined to kill it by a court trial."[73]

The struggles between the Kansas brewers and the prohibitionists raised constitutional aspects about due process of law not covered in the original *Mugler* case. Walruff's contention represented a retreat from the *Wynehamer* rule, admitting the state's right to enact prohibition "for the public good," but it raised the idea that the prohibition laws could be legitimate only if compensation were paid for the taken property. Ziebold and Hagelien's argument against the 1885 law raised the strictly procedural due process question: did a chancery proceeding, abatement of nuisance—which was a trial that operated without a jury and deprived brewers of their property— constitute due process of law? The United States Brewers' Association, seeing the value of these points, moved to aid the litigants.[74]

The brewers' money at first appeared well spent, as *State v. Walruff*, decided in the Eighth Circuit Court of Appeals by Judge David Brewer, proved a resounding victory for the liquor trade. Brewer ruled that Kansas had the right to prohibit the manufacture of liquor only if it compensated owners for property damaged or taken "for the sake of the public." Since the state did not compensate Walruff for rendering his brewery virtually valueless, Judge Brewer ruled the prohibition law an unconstitutional deprivation of property without due process of law in violation of the Fourteenth Amendment. Soon after, a federal court in Iowa, in *Malin v. Pheiffer*, extended Judge Brewer's reasoning to liquor sellers. The *Walruff* rule delighted the brewers, as they believed compensation payments "will be so large that taxpayers will avoid prohibitory experiments." The United States Brewers' Association thought that it was "scarcely probable that this decision will be reversed."[75]

The setback in *Walruff* turned the prohibitionists' attention to constitutional law. They consulted law books, lawyers, and jurists who supplied them with material to refute the compensation argument. They compared the loss of liquor property to the taking of things without compensation brought about by the effect of state laws on other industries, such as gambling, obscene literature, and oleomargarine. They asserted that Brewer's ruling was an anomaly and subjected his reasoning to rigorous analysis. The key flaw they found in his opinion was that, in declaring that compensation was necessary for public taking, Brewer relied on principles deduced from eminent domain law. They argued that his decision "utterly confuses and blends two things which are essentially distinct: namely the police power and eminent domain." Since they were separate, principles of eminent domain did not extend to the taking of property under the police power. The prohibition press expressed the belief that, on appeal, the U.S. Supreme Court would reverse the compensation ruling and that the legal knife would cut "yet nearer to the cancerous growths of the age."[76]

While the drys increased their legal knowledge, the United States Brewers' Association acted. Knowing that " one of the most vital constitutional aspects of prohibition was concerned" and that a Supreme Court ruling would be virtually final, it moved to solicit postponement of argument on *Mugler*. The brewers hoped to bring up a new case that would incorporate the issues raised in *Walruff* and *Ziebold* cases and if possible "obtain a decision simultaneously with that in the Mugler case." But Senator Vest refused "to accede" to this plan, as he believed that *Mugler* would succeed. Although not willing to interfere "with the counsel's programme in the manner that might have injured the interests of our Association," the brewers refused to let all ride on Vest's argument, which he delivered in April 1887. The association hired "the best constitutional lawyer," Joseph H. Choate, as counsel for Ziebold's case, on the calendar for the Court's next term.[77]

Choate quickly got Attorney General Bradford of Kansas to agree to advance *Ziebold* to the current term and submit it on briefs alone. Once docketed, Choate orally argued this case, and Vest reargued *Mugler* on October 11, catching Bradford by surprise and outraging the prohibitionists. While the prohibition press castigated everyone, including Bradford and the members of the Supreme Court, the Prohibition party sent counsel to petition a reopening of arguments and the moving up of four other pending cases that they considered more favorable to their cause. When the Court rejected their pleas, many prohibitionists feared that it would rule against them. They worried that the Court was split 4-4 over the issues (there was a vacancy on the Court) and that the liquor interests had gained an unfair advantage by having their view presented by Choate's unopposed "masterly argument."[78]

Although their styles differed, Vest's and Choate's arguments taken together fully covered all the due process issues. Choate's presentation carried a heavy load of precedent and legal learning while Vest's tended toward emotional philosophizing. Together they advanced three arguments to show that Kansas prohibition laws violated the due process of law guaranteed by the Fourteenth Amendment. First, Vest asserted that beer manufacturing, but not sale, constituted a natural right that was beyond the state's interference. Thus the Kansas law prohibiting the manufacturing of liquor was "at war with the established axiomatic principles of free government" encapsulated in the words "due process of law." Second, Vest and Choate both argued that the Kansas law worked a taking of property for a public purpose without compensation. Citing eminent domain precedents, they argued that the lack of compensation deprived the individual of due process. Third, Choate alone challenged the 1885 enforcement law as a denial of the right to the due process of a jury trial in the taking of property.[79]

These arguments failed to persuade the U.S. Supreme Court. Justice John Harlan's opinion for the majority stated that the state police power encompassed the passage of absolute prohibition laws for the protection of the "peace and security of society." Stating that manufacture was not a right, Harlan refused to distinguish the manufacture from the sale of liquor. If the legislature thought its ban necessary to assure prohibition, the courts had no reason to interfere. Harlan denied compensation for takings under the police power, making it clear that breweries were not "unoffending property" taken under eminent domain, but objects subject to the state police power. That power could legitimately outlaw "a noxious use" of such property. Harlan also rejected the contention that equity proceedings denied due process, finding the jurisdiction applicable to the control of public nuisances. The nineteenth-century legal order's penchant for drawing, in Morton Horwitz's phrase, "clear, distinct, bright-line classifications" worked against the brewers. The Court placed them not in the class of private property protected from government action but in the class of potential nuisances that could be properly regulated. Thus the Court upheld the states' right to prohibit the manufacture and sale of alcohol. The brewers' long-sought "square decision" proved a disaster for them and a great victory for the prohibitionists.[80]

Prohibitionists hailed the Court's decision in *Mugler* as a "landmark in the history of prohibition." Its refutation of the due process arguments, so complete that it did not leave "a single loop to hang a doubt on," and the near unanimous agreement to the opinion particularly pleased prohibitionists. "How like clods on the coffin lid of the doomed traffic sound these sentences." The brewers took the defeat with dignity. They determined that "we must bow in respectful obedience" to the Court's decision even though it ran against what the brewers thought "natural justice." John Walruff spoke for the directly affected brewers when he complained that he had been "hounded worse than murders or horsethieves." Having lost to the "fanatics," he left Kansas. But other brewers also determined to continue their struggles against the temperance crusade.[81]

    Mugler secured for the prohibition movement a solid jurisdictional base. The Supreme Court, in construing the formal rules of the polity, granted the policy constitutional validity. Though the liquor interests would continue to raise the issue, the constitutionality of state prohibition would never be threatened seriously again. So *Mugler* guaranteed permanence for an achievable prohibitionist goal, state prohibition. And state prohibition fit in closely with the formal and informal rules of the existing polity that stressed government action in the states. Thus *Mugler* facilitated the state-by-state approach to drying the nation. It also reduced the liquor interests' legal alternatives and forced them to fight state prohibition at a different level. The legitimacy of state prohibition laws raised perplexing issues of federalism that the liquor industry could exploit in its struggle against the movement. Specifically, the federal government's power to tax and its power over interstate commerce impinged on state laws prohibiting liquor and challenged the drys' notions about law. In these clashes over the implementation of state prohibition in the federal system lay the genesis of the system of national prohibition.

CHAPTER

The U.S. Supreme Court's interpretation of the federal interstate commerce power shaped the course of the prohibition
movement. In the late nineteenth century, as various states took
a more active role in regulating the economy or promoting
reforms, interests opposed to these policies sought to use the federal nature of the polity to offset their losses in the states. Opponents of reform and regulation turned to the federal courts—
asking them to interpret the rules of the polity—to limit state
policies. Thus, the brewers, after failing to establish a Fourteenth Amendment right to make liquor, turned to the federal
commerce power to curtail the effects of state prohibition. Two
cases among the many they instigated reached the Supreme
Court, *Bowman v. Chicago and Northwestern Railroad* (1888) and
Leisy v. Hardin (1890). In these two cases, the Court attempted to
infuse old constitutional doctrines with new meaning. It sought
to define the limits of state action over liquor so as to insure
freedom of commerce within the nation and protect the federal
government's power to regulate commerce.

The outcome of the *Bowman* and *Leisy* cases also created a national crisis over liquor control and prompted Congress to act. While radical prohibitionist organizations called for federal legislation to undo the effects of these rulings, they played little role in shaping the legislation that Congress passed that year. The reformers were unequal to the task of influencing the political parties that controlled the polity. Congress, staffed with regular party politicians mostly unsympathetic to prohibition, responded instead to a political climate that demanded some action on the liquor importation issue. The Supreme Court's interstate commerce decisions created an "original package business" that threatened all liquor controls and created a crisis in alcohol policy. To advert the emergence of prohibition as a national issue, the Republican party wrote and passed a remedial act—the 1890 Wilson Act or Original Package Act. The Wilson Act did not build a federal agency to regulate liquor shipments; rather, it made it possible for states to control transported liquor. The prohibitionists, while they were more bystanders than creators, became the beneficiary of Congress's action.

No act was more important to the course of the temperance movement than the Wilson Act. In creating the Wilson Act, Congress followed the lead of the Court, which laid the first foundation stone for a system of concurrent state and federal jurisdiction over liquor. This pattern of a cooperative federal government was one that characterized much legislation achieved by reformers at the end of the "state of courts and parties." Prohibitionists persisted in following its conception of federal powers, even as the constitutional boundaries expanded in the progressive era. For the next thirty years drys would follow the course—with just two notable exceptions—laid down in the Original Package Act. From it a trail of failed bills and occasionally successful measures would lead ultimately to passage of the Eighteenth Amendment and the Volstead Act.[1]

The Constitution only outlined the nature of the federal commerce power in the two provisions that mention the subject. The first granted Congress power "to regulate Commerce with foreign Nations, and among the several States, and with the Indian Tribes." The second stipulated that "no State shall, without the consent of the Congress, lay any Imposts or Duties on Imports or Exports, except what may be absolutely necessary for executing its inspection Laws." The Constitution, especially the Tenth Amendment, which reserved to the states the powers not granted to the central government, implicitly recognized the legitimacy of state regulating and taxing powers that could affect commerce. The ambiguity in these clauses guaranteed friction between state and federal authority, and the Court stepped in to determine the boundary between the federal commerce power and the state police power.

The conflict between state power and federal authority to regulate interstate commerce first reached the U.S. Supreme Court in the 1824 case of *Gibbons v. Ogden*. New York granted a monopoly on steamboat operation to a company that licensed an agent—Ogden—to run routes from New York to New Jersey. To preserve his monopoly, Ogden won state court injunctions preventing a competitor—Gibbons—from landing his steamboats in New York. Gibbons, who had a federal license under the 1793 Coasting Act, claimed that the commerce clause and the federal law authorized his action and brought the case to the Supreme Court. For a unanimous Court, Chief Justice John Marshall broadly construed the grant of the federal commerce power and set limits on state action. He asserted that the commerce power extended to incidents of trade, such as navigation, and was "vested in Congress as absolutely as it would be in a single government." Furthermore, he argued that the power could not be stopped "at the external boundary line of each state." It must enter the interior to be effective but could not disturb commerce of a purely intrastate nature. Regulation of such commerce remained reserved to the states. Under the Constitution's supremacy clause, state laws that came "into collision with an act of Congress" enacted to carry out a legitimate enumerated power—like the regulation of commerce—were unconstitutional infringements on Congress's power. Since the New York law interfered with rights established under the commerce power by the 1793 Coasting Act, it was void.[2]

Three years later in *Brown v. Maryland* the Marshall Court elaborated its view of the relations between state action and the federal commerce power. Maryland levied a license tax on importers and wholesalers of foreign goods. Brown and other merchants were convicted of importing and selling one package of foreign dry goods without paying the tax. After losing their appeal in state court, they carried their case to the Supreme Court. Again the chief justice spoke for an unanimous Court. He wrote that the Maryland law violated the Constitution's provisions prohibiting states from levying duties on imports and granting foreign and interstate commerce regulation to Congress. But the chief justice did not intend to strip the states of their "sacred" and legitimate police powers, so he proposed to find the "point" where the "powers of the state commences."[3]

Marshall did not propose to build a "rule . . . universal in its application," for he thought the problem perplexing and the timing "premature." He proposed to point out the essential distinguishing point and, "as the cases arise," to mark it out more fully. His line dividing state and federal authority emerged from the facts of the *Brown* case, although he cloaked them in general language. Given the proposition that state power could not attach until international commerce ended, it was key to determine when such commerce stopped. Only when the thing became "incorporated and mixed up with the mass of property within the state" did it lose its "distinctive character as an import." While an item remained in its "original form or package in which it was imported," it was clearly still in federally protected commerce and beyond the power of the state. Similarly, since sale was "the object of importation" and an "essential ingredient" of commerce, state laws could not interfere before sale by the wholesaler. After sale by the wholesaler, the object was part of the state's general mass of property and so state law could regulate its sale by "retail, at auction, or as an itinerant peddler." Eventually this formula became known as the original package doctrine, and in obiter Marshall asserted that it extended "equally to importations from a sister state."[4]

The Court continued to refine its view of the proper spheres of state and federal action over commerce in the 1829 case *Wilson v. Black Bird Creek Marsh Company*. In a very brief opinion Chief Justice Marshall dismissed the claim that a Delaware law authorizing a dam across a navigable creek conflicted with the federal power to regulate interstate and foreign commerce. Since Congress had passed no act, the power to regulate commerce remained "in its dormant state," and state regulations affecting commerce were legitimate. If, however, Congress passed a law on a subject, "a state law coming into conflict with such act would be void." But this would not be the Court's last word on the topic of state action affecting foreign and interstate commerce.[5]

In a number of cases during the heyday of states' rights, the Court, under Chief Justice Roger Taney, redefined the relationship between the state powers and the federal commerce power. Two cases, the *License Cases* and *Cooley v. Port of Wardens of Port of Philadelphia*, were especially important to the later development of liquor law. The three cases comprising the 1847 *License Cases* arose from Massachusetts's, New Hampshire's, and Rhode Island's early experiments in temperance legislation. Rhode Island forbade liquor sales in quantities of less than ten gallons; New Hampshire required licenses for all liquor sellers; and Massachusetts combined the other two states' provisions requiring license fees to be paid by all retailers who sold at one time liquor in quantities less than twenty-eight gallons. The facts in the cases from Massachusetts and Rhode Island fell within the parameters of the original package test established in *Brown v. Maryland*. The liquors in question, imported from outside the nation, had clearly been broken from their original package because they were sold in containers of a different size than that required by federal customs law. Thus these cases did not require any extra elaboration of doctrine to sustain the state laws, although some justices did advance new justifications. But the other case, *Pierce v. New Hampshire*, involved "American gin purchased in Boston" and carried into and sold in New Hampshire in the same cask.[6]

The Supreme Court in the *License Cases* unanimously agreed that none of the state laws were inconsistent with the federal commerce clause or legislation under it. Yet the justices differed widely in their reasoning; six justices produced nine differing opinions. This "riot of diversity" made the ruling almost useless doctrinally. Virtually any view on the issues could be justified from the various opinions. Justice John Catron asserted that the states and nation shared a concurrent power over commerce. Generally national law overrode state action, but if the Congress had not spoken, the states were free to act as they saw fit. The chief justice's opinion followed Catron's reasoning, except that it did not see the state power as a commerce power but as part of its general reserved or police powers. Justice Levi Woodbury advanced the view that commerce by nature divided into local and national aspects. State regulations that did not conflict with "any uniform and general regulations" made by Congress and only affected local parts of commerce were legitimate. In effect, this ruling created a climate in which state prohibition could flourish, and soon after the decision the first wave of state prohibition laws swept the nation.[7]

In the 1851 case *Cooley v. Board of Wardens of the Port of Philadelphia*, the Court followed Justice Woodbury's path from the *License Cases* in setting new rules governing the division of authority over commerce. Justice Benjamin Curtis, for the Court, reasoned that commerce by nature divided into two categories: national and local. Commerce of a national nature required one uniform system of regulation provided exclusively by Congress. Local aspects of commerce, even of interstate and foreign commerce, remained the states' province. By this scheme state laws interfering with commerce requiring uniform, or national, regulation would be unconstitutional, but laws affecting commerce's local aspects would be legitimate. This rule established the necessity of a case-by-case review to draw the new line between local commerce and national commerce. In practice the *Cooley* decision granted legitimacy to the states' many activities in regulating commerce, including laws prohibiting the liquor trade.[8]

The postwar Court, less enamored of states' rights, advanced a new doctrine, the freedom of commerce. In the 1876 case *Welton v. Missouri*, the Court rejected the idea that when Congress let the commerce power be dormant, state regulation was permissible. Instead the Court interpreted the silence of Congress to mean that it intended commerce should remain free from interference. Thus state laws, like the Missouri law (at issue in *Welton*), which levied a special tax on peddlers who dealt in goods not made in the state, and a Michigan law that taxed liquor sellers who imported their liquor from outside the state and had no place of business in the state, were held to be barriers to commerce and unconstitutional infringements on the federal commerce power. The existence of the freedom of commerce doctrine raised the question whether state prohibition laws could be construed as a similar barrier to free commerce.[9]

The Supreme Court, while admitting it was an important issue, long refused to consider the interstate commerce implications of state prohibition. *Beer Company v. Massachusetts*, an 1877 case that challenged Massachusetts's 1869 prohibition law as a violation of the contracts clause by annulling the company's charter to brew beer, also raised the issue of the barrier to interstate commerce. In the majority opinion, Justice Joseph Bradley wrote, "Of course we do not mean to lay down any rule at variance with what this Court had decided with regard to" this question. He then cited a list of cases, including the *License Cases* and *Brown v. Maryland* and adding no further clarification. Ten years later, in *Mugler v. Kansas*, the Court faced assertions that state prohibition kept citizens from manufacturing beer for outside markets and thus interfered with the federal interstate commerce power. The Court decided that the issue was not properly before it, "and without expressing an opinion . . . we observe that it will be time enough to decide a case of that character when it shall come before us." Predictably, liquor men, state officials, and drys reacted differently to the muddled interstate commerce law.[10]

While the competitive world of liquor selling welcomed the confusion over the extent of the federal commerce power brought about by the emergence of the new doctrine, state officials differed in their reactions. Liquor dealers operated in the gray area, using the ambiguity of the law to protect their businesses. They invoked both the freedom of commerce and the original package doctrines as convenient shelters for lucrative liquor sales banned by state laws. Railroads gave liquor sellers their entry into dry areas. Liquor men shipped tremendous quantities of liquor into local option and prohibition jurisdictions. According to one estimate, the dry counties of Georgia received over 20,000 gallons in just six months. The railroad provided "speedy service for the thirsty." For instance, "most Iowa people lived where they could obtain whiskey in 24 hours by express from a neighboring state." State and local officials differed in which view of the commerce power they adopted. Some officials, like the mayor of prohibition Atlanta, accepted the contention that federal interstate commerce doctrines limited the effect of prohibitory laws. Many other officials did not share this view and, enforcing the rule of the *License Cases*, struggled against the flood of booze. But the efforts of lawmen with "educated" noses could not stem the tide of liquor flowing into dry areas concealed as "boots and shoes," "crockery," "glass—this side up," and the tongue-in-cheek "dry-goods." Still, their activities posed a threat to the liquor dealers. Arrests and seizure by officials who refused to countenance the original package or freedom of commerce rules reduced the liquor men's trade. As the vagaries of the law could also work against them, some liquor sellers sought a definitive ruling from the U.S. Supreme Court.[11]

Liquor dealers, including the Bowman Brothers brewery, hoped a decision based on the freedom of commerce doctrine would secure their right to ship liquor into dry areas. Their actions in invoking the federal commerce doctrine to protect their trade followed the same pattern of the earlier effort to use the doctrine of due process of law to invalidate state prohibition. At the root of each effort stood the liquor men's belief that they had a right to manufacture and sell liquor, free from government interference. Freedom of commerce was then in some ways just a judicial construct used to cover a framework of natural rights, and the enunciation of the freedom of commerce doctrine advanced their larger rights agenda. In another way, freedom of commerce was also an opening wedge to discredit prohibition. For if the demand for liquor was strong enough and if liquor dealers could meet it, prohibition would become a policy that failed to work, which perhaps might lead to its repudiation. Finally, the doctrine would keep their markets from shrinking through state action, permitting liquor men the chance to increase their profits. Thus, a Court victory upholding the new doctrines would have many benefits for the liquor industry.

Like the liquor men (and unlike most state officials, who clung to the *License Cases* rule as a shield against liquor dealers' claims to immunity), radical prohibitionists embraced the new doctrines. The drys accepted as foregone that "no state can effectively prevent interstate commerce" even if it "built a Chinese wall about herself." The modern doctrine of commerce fit well with the radicals' emphasis on national action against liquor. To overcome the problem of interstate liquor shipments, they called for two different types of remedial federal legislation. Thinking that nothing but root-and-branch prohibition would eradicate liquor commerce, most radical drys sought the enactment of a national prohibition amendment to the Constitution, buttressed by congressional acts banning liquor transportation and importation. Other drys, including J. Ellen Foster, one of the WCTU's leading lawyers, suggested a more realistic solution. Instead of complete federal prohibition, these prohibitionists called for limited congressional legislation excluding liquor importation and interstate shipment. No national prohibition organization called for state limitations on interstate commerce in liquor, but the state of Iowa enacted such a law. The Bowman brothers would challenge in the Supreme Court the constitutionality of that law.[12]

In the 1880s Iowa had great trouble in enforcing its prohibition laws. In its major cities, and especially in the towns along the Mississippi River, saloons flourished, often with contrivance of local officials. Since the state's prohibition on manufacture was effective, out-of-state distillers and brewers from Missouri, Illinois, and Indiana supplied Iowa's illegal sellers. To stem this tide of alcohol, the state legislature, in 1885 and 1886, enacted new restrictions on liquor transportation. The 1886 law removed a 1873 provision from the Iowa code that exempted liquor shipped in original packages from the state's restrictions. The 1886 law also prohibited carriers from shipping liquor within or into Iowa unless the consignees possessed a certificate showing that they were authorized (as druggists were) to sell liquor in Iowa. The law fined the carrier one hundred dollars and court costs per offense. By regulating interstate commerce, it was intended to improve enforcement of prohibition.[13]

As early as 1885 George A. Bowman and his brother Fred A. Bowman—brewers and wholesalers based in Marshalltown, Iowa—determined to challenge the state's prohibition laws as an infringement on the federal government's power over interstate commerce. They hoped that the courts would legitimate their liquor selling carried on in defiance of the law and also damage the law's effectiveness so much as to create a decline of confidence in prohibition and thus bring about its repeal. The Bowman brothers were not members of the United States Brewers' Association and proceeded without assistance from that organization. In fact, the association refused a request to pay the brothers' legal fees at the conclusion of the litigation, even though many members benefited from the Bowmans' action.[14]

Instead of confronting the state, the brothers sued the Chicago and Northwestern Railroad, which had refused to ship beer to their Iowa plant. Their first attempt failed when the U.S. Supreme Court decided that "the actual value of matter in dispute" was insufficient to justify federal court diversity jurisdiction. Undeterred, the Bowmans bought a larger shipment of beer to meet the jurisdictional requirement and again asked the railroad to ship the beer into Iowa. It declined on the grounds that the Bowman brothers lacked the certificate required by the 1886 law. The resulting case, *Bowman v. Chicago and Northwestern Rail Road*, reached the U.S. Supreme Court in 1888. Louis J. Blum, the attorney for the Bowman brothers, argued that the Iowa act interfered with a right vested exclusively with Congress and that Congress's inaction was a declaration that it intended that commerce remain free of restrictions. Counsel for the railroad and the State of Iowa contended that the law was a legitimate police regulation that protected the health and morals of the state's citizens. They also averred that it was an exercise of the state's power to inspect commerce and that the law did not discriminate against out-of-state products.[15]

Justice Stanley Matthews wrote the majority opinion, which at times sounded like a temperance tract. It characterized the Iowa prohibition laws as part of a "general design of protecting the health and morals of its people, and the peace and good order of the State, against the physical and moral evils resulting from the unrestricted manufacture and sale . . . of intoxicating liquors." Yet only the rhetoric pleased prohibitionists, as the Court ruled the Iowa liquor transportation law unconstitutional. The opinion dismissed the state's inspection defense and supported the claim that Congress intended commerce to be free and unrestricted. It declared that the Iowa law's effect carried beyond the state's borders. It "materially affects . . . the conduct of such carriers . . . in every other state" and conflicted with other states' laws, bringing about "commercial anarchy and confusion." Thus, the Court struck down the law because of its extraterritoriality and because it erected a barrier to commerce that Congress wished unrestrained.[16]

At the same time, the Court in *Bowman* addressed, but did not rule on, two issues of fundamental importance: the original package doctrine and Congress's power to act. First, on the question of sales in the original package, the majority seemingly accepted the rule of *Brown v. Maryland*. The *Bowman* opinion stated that commerce included "by necessary implication the right of the importer to sell in unbroken packages at the place where the transit terminates." Second, as Matthew's opinion tortuously wove its way through the issues, it constantly raised Congress's role in setting the boundaries of commerce. The opinion implied that Congress could somehow act, either by banning liquor commerce or by legitimating the states' efforts to regulate interstate liquor shipments.[17]

On the practical level the *Bowman* decision weakened the chances of the prohibition states of enforcing their liquor laws. Blum, the Bowmans' attorney, said that the effect of the ruling was "to render nugatory the prohibitory law." The *Voice* agreed, saying that the decision "opens the door for successful violations on a large scale." The attorney general of Iowa concurred and concluded that *Bowman* made it nearly impossible for the states to prevent directly the importation of liquor. Iowa officials proposed to stop the influx of liquor by creating state sanitary inspectors. These agents would examine all imported drinks to assure that they met "purity" standards—which excluded alcohol as an ingredient. This plan to circumvent the decision, based on the Constitution's provision allowing state inspections of commerce, provoked the United States Brewers' Association to denounce it as a "Siberian method" for enforcing "compulsory sobriety." Brewers, preoccupied with the disastrous *Mugler* decision, found little comfort in *Bowman* in general. They believed that it would not affect many brewers but admitted that the Bowman brothers' court victory "appears to have displeased the prohibitionists very much."[18]

The radical prohibition organizations reacted to *Bowman* by intensifying their focus on national action. Soon after the ruling, the *Voice* declared, "The Supreme Court makes prohibition a national question." In August 1888 Clinton B. Fisk, in accepting the Prohibition party's nomination for president, reiterated the nationalization theme; he argued that prohibition "can never be made of local and state limitations again." The party followed his lead and clamored for a federal prohibition law. The WCTU agreed; its 1888 convention adopted a resolution stating that it was "evident that all ultimately effective action for suppression of the liquor traffic must come through national legislation." The Kansas WCTU memorialized members of Congress to pass a law prohibiting transportation of liquor into states unless it was consigned to licensed sellers. Since the Court had rendered state limitations impotent, the drys contended that "national prohibition is the most direct road to state prohibition."[19]

U.S. Senators Henry Blair, William Frye, James Wilson, and John Ingalls attempted to fulfill the prohibitionists' desire for action. Of the four, James Wilson's proposal went the farthest. Even before the *Bowman* ruling, Wilson (a Republican from prohibition Iowa) had attempted to please his temperance constituents by introducing a bill allowing state laws to operate on liquor imported from outside the nation. After the ruling, Wilson added interstate commerce liquor importations to his bill. He contended that the revised bill would curtail "judicial interference with the effective exercise by states of the police powers." Wilson's colleagues seemed uninterested in the issue. He had trouble getting the bill to the Senate floor; and at the instigation of Senator George Vest, the Senate quickly moved on to other business following Wilson's first and only speech on the bill. Despite this failure,

Wilson kept the bill alive in the Senate Judiciary Committee. He was soon able to resurrect it when changes in legal and political environments guaranteed full debate on the measure.[20]

Meanwhile, the liquor industry saw opportunity in the *Bowman* ruling. For many in the trade it became a powerful wedge for them to use to force their wares into dry states. Liquor in transit could not be legally seized nor could it be stopped at the state's borders. Thus, the ruling increased the responsibilities of local jurisdictions in enforcing prohibition, including the sale of imported liquors. Liquor sellers reasoned from the language of the opinion that the Court would uphold liquor sales of unbroken shipping packages in dry territory. This was a grassroots notion, not one conjured up by the United States Brewers' Association or any other group. Only after the fact did the association assume the cost of the resulting litigation, and it did so over the objections of its Board of Trustees. Small-town liquor dealers were convinced that the law, for once, was on their side. One circular asserted that they "had a right to sell liquor in Kansas." Courts in prohibition states gave credence to these claims. One Iowa judge concluded that original package sales were constitutional provided the product came directly from the distiller or brewer with federal revenue stamps attached. Another Iowa judge found a liquor seller guilty of illegal sales because he had broken the shipping crate in dispensing his wares, a conviction that legitimated original package sales.[21]

To the consternation of drys, both liquor sellers and manufacturers took advantage of the rule. Often saloon keepers would continue in business just by moving most of their business across state lines into wet states, preserving only retail outlets in the dry states. For instance, J. F. Daugherty and Company publicized in a circular the company's move from dry Iowa to wet Illinois. It published its new phone number for the Illinois plant and Iowa office, promising that after the move "we will be better able to accommodate our friends and especially our Iowa customers." Other original package sellers came from the opposite end of the liquor business. The potential profits derived from tapping the thirsty market of the dry states pushed some manufacturing firms into retailing. Gus Leisy and Company, the largest brewery in Peoria, went into the original package trade. As a family-owned and -operated business that had been established in Keokuk, Iowa, the company had a good reputation there. So in its own brick brewery—closed by the prohibition law—the company opened a retail agency in the city. It depended on the original package doctrine as an umbrella for its liquor sales—selling full kegs or cases of beer with government revenue stamps attached and avoiding sales to minors and drunkards. It soon had problems with Iowa officials, problems that would end in the courts.[22]

Keokuk was an unlikely site for legal confrontations between prohibitionists and interstate liquor seller and shippers, as it was one of the wettest towns in Iowa. It was located in far southeastern Iowa, bordering on wet Illinois and Missouri, and it possessed an immigrant community totaling one-fifth of its population. The town had opposed Iowa's experience with prohibition in the 1850s and continued it opposition after the war. In 1882 it voted 62 percent against prohibition and after its implementation defied the law. In 1885 the town licensed liquor sellers, and by the next year forty saloons openly operated there. The *Voice* characterized the liquor men of Keokuk as "particularly arrogant." But an ambitious Republican reform mayor, John N. Irwin, who had studied law with Supreme Court justices Samuel F. Miller (of Keokuk) and Stanley Matthews, ended the license system and instigated a campaign of state liquor law enforcement. Irwin's efforts ran counter to the desires of many of the city's officials, including the city sheriff, A. J. Hardin. In June 1888 the mayor's enforcement campaign netted John Leisy, vice president and agent of the Leisy Company, along with 122 one-quarter barrels of beer, 171 one-eighth barrels of beer, and 11 sealed cases of beer, with a total value of $540. The malt liquor was all manufactured by the Leisy Company and shipped to Keokuk by rail and offered for sale in its original package. While the company continued its business and lost another 689 kegs of beer to a Christmas Eve raid, antiprohibitionist Sheriff Hardin found himself named in a suit that in 1890 reached the Supreme court.[23]

In the Leisy Company's pursuit of a definitive judicial ruling, principle replaced practicality. The case began in the local county court when the Leisy Company sought through an action of replevin to recover its seized beer. The trial court agreed with the company's contention "that they had the right to sell beer in the original package by virtue of interstate transportation." It ordered the beer returned and the payment of one dollar in damages. On appeal to the Iowa Supreme Court this judgment was reversed, so the Leisy Company sought a writ of error to the U.S. Supreme Court. By the time the Court heard the argument, the reform regime had been voted out of Keokuk and the town was again open to saloon keepers. The Leisy Company could ship in all the beer it wished. The beer originally seized was long spoiled, and attorneys' fees would probably outweigh any recovered damages. Only a desire to get a definitive ruling kept the company in court.[24]

Before the Court the counsel for the Leisy Company argued that the power to regulate interstate commerce rested exclusively with Congress, that interstate commerce extended within state borders, and that the Iowa law prohibiting the sale of liquor interfered with Congress's power over commerce by preventing sale of imported liquors. Thus, the law should be ruled unconstitutional. The State of Iowa contended that the prohibitory laws were universally regarded as legitimate regulations under the states' police power, that the silence of Congress affirmed the right of the state to enact such laws, and furthermore that the power to tax, regulate, and control took hold when the imported goods were delivered to the consignee. Thus, the sale of beer should not be protected by the federal interstate commerce power.[25]

On April 28, 1890, the Court delivered its ruling in *Leisy v. Hardin*. The majority opinion, written by Chief Justice Melville Fuller, reflected the chief justice's and the Court's determination to assert national authority over commerce and limit state restrictions on interstate commerce while preserving the prewar doctrinal language. The opinion divided into three major parts. First, it set up a model of the constitutional arrangements concerning the commerce power. It argued that the national power could limit the states' police power only in three instances: when the Constitution delegated the power to the federal government and denied it to the states; when the power was exclusively lodged in the national government; and when from the "nature and subjects of power it must be necessarily exercised by the national government." The Court ruled that under all three categories the regulation of foreign and interstate commerce—and alcoholic beverages were long recognized as legitimate objects of commerce—lay with the federal government.[26]

Next the opinion dealt with the issue of the silence of Congress in exercising the commerce power. Fuller declared that when a "particular power of the general government is one which must necessarily be exercised by it, and Congress remains silent," then "the only legitimate conclusion is that the general government intended that power should not be affirmatively exercised." Therefore, states could not be "permitted" to act in a manner "incompatible" with Congress's presumed intention. In short, the states could not regulate the transportation of alcohol even if the national government refused to act. The opinion determined that the federal courts were the proper agencies in the "absence of congressional legislation . . . to determine whether state action does or does not amount" to an unconstitutional exercise of the powers granted to Congress.[27]

Finally, elevating the rough test of *Brown v. Maryland* into a binding rule, the majority of the Court ruled that the federal commerce power extended until the commercial object had been mingled by the act of sale into the commerce within a state. Fuller concluded, speaking to the facts of the case, that the Leisy Company "had the right to import this beer" and "had the right to sell it." Only by sale did the beer become "mingled in the common mass of property" of the state. Thus "in the absence of congressional permission to do so, the state had no power to interfere by seizure or any other action." In the companion case *Ling v. Michigan*, the Court made it clear that "other action" included taxation. It struck down as interference with interstate commerce a Michigan law that levied a three-hundred-dollar tax on beer sellers in every township in which they operated but that excepted state brewers from the assessment because they paid a seventy-five-dollar manufacturers' tax. In a sweeping dictum the chief justice concluded that these rules applied to all legitimate commodities of trade, "natural or manufactured" including sugar, wine, hops, and tobacco. The Court borrowed from the *Brown* case its only limitation imposed on those engaged in importing liquor into the states. The Court stipulated that to be under federal protection, the imported article needed to be offered for sale and sold in its original package. Justice Horace Gray wrote a long dissent for Justices Harlan and Brewer that strongly condemned the majority's erosion of the state's police power. But few, including the Leisy Company, bothered to examine the dissenters' views. It had won its victory of principle.[28]

The *Leisy* ruling upset the leaders of the United States Brewers' Association but stimulated other liquor men into action. August Thomann, director of the association's publication program, when interviewed by a correspondent for the *Voice*, accused the drys of lobbying the Supreme Court for the decision. He asserted that "it's a blessing to you in disguise." Brewer Thomas M. Dukebarb of Baltimore agreed by saying the rule was "bad for brewing as it will lead Congress to take action that will make matters worse." A year later, at the 1891 convention, the Board of Trustees rebuked the Leisy Company for opening a Pandora's box by pressing the suit and the members for voting to assume the cost of the litigation. Other liquor men disproved the assertions of Neal Dow—the aged author of the first prohibition law—and the attorneys general of Kansas, Iowa, and Maine that the decision would have little effect on the enforcement of prohibition. Within a month of the ruling, "original package houses" and "supreme court saloons" had sprung up in every prohibition state. For brewers and distillers it became a profitable trip "over the border with a carload" into prohibition territory. The producers assumed the cost of test cases, and the liquor sellers went about discovering in the courts the limits, if any, of their new federal rights. Once shipping privileges were assured, large shipments, like "fifty-six barrels and a number of sixteen gallon kegs of beer," flowed into the dry states. In the quest for even greater profits some barkeepers risked the creation of their own "original packages" by bottling the bulk shipments into small, easily retailed bottles carrying forged U.S. revenue stamps. The *Leisy* ruling flooded the dry states with liquor.[29]

Leisy v. Hardin delivered "a serious blow to the maintenance of that extreme policy to which prohibitionists as such are wedded." It angered many prohibitionists, becoming the "favorite text" at dry gatherings. Prohibitionist protests over the ruling prompted at least one member of the Court to justify the decision. Justice Miller, by virtue of his residence in prohibition Iowa, probably received more complaints than other justices. J. P. Titer, a Methodist clergyman, wondered in a letter how Miller could give such aid to the violators of state law and common decency. Miller's response was published in the press. Miller wrote, "Many people like you . . . have the idea that the Supreme Court is oath-bound in its decisions" to follow "abstract moral rights." Actually the Court was "sworn to decide according to the Constitution of the United States as you are bound by your conscience to a faith in the Bible." Miller defended the original package doctrine, asserting that it commanded respect because it "fell from the lips of the greatest constitutional lawyer that this government ever had" and because it had not been altered in sixty years.[30]

But few prohibitionists and politicians cared how venerable the original package doctrine was; they wanted it erased because it precipitated a crisis in liquor control across the nation. And those unhappy with the results of the decision had only to look at the decision itself to find the means to overturn it. Several times the majority opinion employed the words "without congressional permission" when speaking of the states' regulation of commerce. The term by inference meant that Congress could give such permission to the states.

Overnight the *Leisy* ruling created a new liquor business: the original package house. As this trade grew, panic over the control of liquor began to sweep the country. The prohibition states' original package business, which in May was "budding to bloom," had in June and July spread like a pernicious weed. The business swamped the federal courts in dry states; the district court for Kansas was "almost exclusively given to habeas corpus proceedings" of jailed liquor merchants. The district court judges refused to recognize the states' power over interstate liquor before its sale in original packages and routinely released jailed original package merchants. The implementation of the *Leisy* rule opened the dry states to the liquor dealers. In

Kansas City, Kansas, during the summer of 1890 it was impossible to get cool water but "everywhere may be found iced beer." Soon every major town in the prohibition states had its own package house.[31]

Small containers, fierce competition, and the proprietors' ready familiarity with the law characterized the original package trade. The brewers and hard-liquor merchants fought over customers and quickly found that the smaller the package, the better the sales. To cut expensive glass costs, they used reusable bottles, experimenting with deposits. The brewers in the Kansas market created a package of three bottles of beer and "christened it 'the Trinity.'" In turn, the whiskey sellers reduced their bottles to two-ounce and four-ounce sizes. Shippers exercised care to keep within the letter of the Court's ruling, sending these "diminutive original packages" into the state unboxed, surrounded only by loose straw. Such shipments steeply multiplied shipping costs; on one order of fifty dollars of liquor the shipping bill ran to sixty-eight dollars.[32]

Initially, the package houses discouraged drinking on the premises, but eventually it became common practice, and the original package house became known as a "supreme court saloon." In such an establishment "the thirsty soul . . . on the payment of quarter of a dollar" received a bottle "corked and containing about sixteen fingers of straight stuff" or a quart of beer. After pulling the cork "he can absorb all the contents to his own cheeks or can invite his friends to share his imbibitions." The emphasis on the buyer uncorking the liquor was of course intended to preserve the originality of the package. In effect, the "supreme court saloon" sold original packages by the drink. The proprietors, often agents of brewing concerns or liquor wholesalers, possessed a working knowledge of interstate commerce law. Some permanently retained attorneys while others talked "as familiarly and shrewdly about the late decision as a lawyer." Such knowledge was essential to business as the prohibitionists and officials launched campaigns of harassment in response to the liquor invasion.[33]

In the dry states prohibitionists refused to stand idle while "the liquorites" set up shop. Church bells were rung to call the citizens together to fight this new menace. In Iowa, and especially Kansas, public meetings, town resolutions, and ad hoc committees of community leaders confronted the returning "Missouri ruffians" intending to open "these left handed saloons." The action taken in Ottawa, Kansas, was typical. The citizens, mostly steadfast drys, held a town meeting and raised $25,000 to fight the liquor sellers. They threatened "any man audacious enough to . . . open an original package store" with destruction of his spirits and "a brand new suit of tar and feathers." When threats failed, prohibitionists tried action. In Lawrence, Kansas, white ribboners revived the tactics of the 1873 women's crusade against a package merchant. The picketing by women and children reduced his clientele to those the women considered beyond moral appeal, "the bummers and darkies." WCTU members revealed their predilection for using suasion and building public opinion when they pronounced this crusade a success because it "made people *think*." When remonstrances failed, some individuals turned to violence. Mrs. James A. Smith in Girard, Kansas, broke the bottles of an original package store and assaulted the agent, striking him with a buggy whip.[34]

Officials in prohibition states also responded to public pressure and challenged the original package industry. Local judges ignored the *Leisy* ruling and gave the "business a black eye" by jailing liquor agents. While some argued that "it would be folly for a country judge in a one-horse town to put a chip on his shoulder and invite the United States Supreme Court to knock it off," others applauded such action and called for "the arrest of every man who is found dealing in the liquor traffic." State and local officials, especially in Kansas, followed such a course, going to the extremes of rearresting original package agents released by federal habeas corpus. Feeling the pressure, the liquor sellers turned to the federal district courts, which enjoined local officials from continuing their prosecutions of original package merchants. One group of liquor dealers even filed suit, seeking $10,000 in damages on the basis that state officials conspired against their business. This course of events prompted the *Union Signal* to answer the question "Has a state any rights the nation is bound to respect?" with a resounding "No."[35]

The original package house did not remain limited to the prohibition states. At first there was uncertainty as to whether wet states would be affected by the *Leisy* decision. While drys and prohibition state officials thought it did, the *New York Times* argued that it worked "no interference at all with the reasonable policy of regulation." At first events supported the *Times*, as liquor sellers concentrated on the markets with the greatest potential profits, the prohibition states. By mid-summer the license states had caught the eye of original package merchants. If the original package ruling shielded them from high state taxes and from state operating restrictions, they would gain a competitive edge over the traditional saloon. For liquor producers it was also an excellent chance to improve their retailing by cutting out the troublesome middleman, the saloon keeper.[36]

In Pennsylvania Charles Silverman, an agent for the Cincinnati Brewing Company of Hamilton, Ohio, tested the extent of the original package umbrella. Silverman met accusations that he violated Pennsylvania's laws prohibiting the selling of liquor without a license and selling intoxicants to minors and persons of "known intemperate habits" with the contention that he was "fully protected in selling original packages shipped from Ohio into Pennsylvania." In instructing the jury, the trial judge agreed with Silverman on the issue of licensing, but disagreed over the protection for sale to minors and inebriates. He ruled that the state's police power to protect its citizens was not constrained by the interstate commerce power of the federal government. The jury convicted Silverman on a charge of supplying liquor to drunkards, but nevertheless he was "overjoyed." Other out-of-state liquor men were jubilant; since Silverman won on the license issue, it made "the high license paid by local liquor dealers . . . practically money thrown away." The Cincinnati Brewing Company also planned an appeal on the grounds that a police regulation limiting to whom one could sell did not differ fundamentally from a law prohibiting all sales. Since the Supreme Court had restricted one, it would probably restrict the other. The *Washington Post* called the Silverman case "a blow to high license." Indeed, it did open the door for original package merchants to enter states and open shop without paying license fees, thus gaining a significant advantage over other liquor retailers.[37]

The air of crisis deepened when newspaper editorials began constructing scenarios of national disaster from the few violent episodes associated with the original package saloon. The Democratic *Washington Post* and *Atlanta Constitution* both escalated a number of small incidents in Iowa and Kansas into an "original package war." In a July editorial the *Post* argued that if the Court "despoiled" the people of their rights, their only recourse was to "become a law unto themselves." If Congress failed to protect the states' reserved powers, the state affected "must maintain its own sovereignty, Court and Congress to the contrary notwithstanding." The paper warned, "Either the Supreme Court must reverse its own judgment or Congress must nullify the Court's decision, or the battle of states' rights will have to be fought over again." The press warned against a "popular uprising" and danger to "public peace" created by the original package business, and pressured Congress to act.[38]

The Fifty-first Congress was, by nineteenth-century standards, an activist body, and this must have given some hope to the drys seeking legislation. It was this Congress—under Republican direction—that passed the McKinley Tariff, the Sherman Silver Purchase Act, and the Sherman Anti-Trust Act. Moreover, showing its willingness to tackle controversial issues, this Congress also extensively debated the Federal Elections Bill, which would have subjected elections to greater central government oversight. It also considered but did not pass the Blair Education Bill, which would have provided federal aid to public schools. Yet, in the eyes of prohibitionists, this Congress, like previous ones, had a dismal record on the issue of temperance. With one exception (banning liquor sales in the Capitol building), every temperance measure since 1875—including bills and resolutions calling for stricter liquor laws for the District of Columbia, national prohibition, bans on liquor sales at public exhibitions constructed with government money, and the creation of a federal commission to investigate the liquor trade—had died. Most were "never allowed to mature" but rather were ruthlessly "extinguished in committee." Louis Schade, lobbyist for the United States Brewers' Association and editor of the pro-liquor newspaper the *Washington Sentinel*, often claimed credit for engineering the smothering of these measures. Congress's hostile reception to even the most innocuous temperance proposal increased the burden of those calling for remedial legislation.[39]

A series of incidents from November 1889 to May 1890 exemplified the Fifty-first Congress's collective views toward liquor control. In the fall of 1889 Congress passed a resolution barring liquor sales in the restaurant located in the Capitol building. Its authors intended that it should satisfy temperance advocates who had long sought such action. The *New York Times* castigated Congress, charging that the resolution was "adopted for the purposes of pure buncombe" and to raise the lawmakers to an undeserved "plane of high morality." Evidence of the members' moral failings appeared in the restaurant's subsequent policy of serving hard liquor in tea cups and beer in coffee mugs. Other members, who desired to drink away from the "curious eyes" of the public, turned committee rooms "into safe and convenient places in which to keep and drink liquor." The so-called "House groggery" prevailed until mid-May 1890. With the debates on the Wilson Bill beginning, the "House bar room" became so embarrassing that House Speaker Thomas Reed ordered the trade halted. But the *Voice* reported that the restaurants were soon selling liquor in defiance of Reed's order, in violation of their contract, and without a valid liquor license. This incident underscored the apathy or hostility that characterized many members' views of temperance.[40]

Nevertheless, drys turned to Congress. Within a week of the ruling, prohibitionists proposed a common solution to the problems created by the ruling: congressional action. There was precedent for such joint action between the federal and state governments against moral menaces and dangerous substances. For instance, in the 1870s Congress and state legislatures had created new laws to prohibit obscenity: the 1873 federal Comstock Law and the states' "little Comstock laws." And these laws had been sustained in both the state and federal courts. Attempts to regulate food also revealed the federal possibilities and limits. In the 1870s pure food reformers, who had won state legislation, began calling for federal action. The House Committee on Manufactures proposed a law that would supplement proposed state laws regulating food and drugs. The federal law would make knowingly transporting adulterated foods in interstate commerce a federal crime. Two years later the food industry proposed a purely federal solution, the establishment of a national Board of Health, which would set standards for purity and would control all foods and drugs in interstate commerce. But the House Committee on Commerce balked at having the federal government control "domestic"—within the state—adulteration; it saw such action as an unconstitutional invasion of the state police power. Thus, Congress, like the Court, believed a cooperative federal law to be constitutional. Moreover, the majority opinion in *Leisy* hinted at such a possibility. In three places Chief Justice Fuller used the phrase "without congressional permission" in referring to the states' regulation of interstate commerce. This phrase logically implied that the Court believed that Congress could grant the states permission to impose their police powers on articles in interstate commerce. Drys thought a simple declaratory law by the Congress could restore prohibition to the prohibition states.[41]

The Prohibition party, the WCTU, and local temperance societies at first sought this type of congressional action. The Georgia State Temperance Alliance Convention, the Kansas State Temperance Union Convention, and the Maine State Prohibitory Convention all adopted resolutions condemning the Supreme Court's decision. They also called for a congressional act "to protect and make effective any and all prohibition legislation." According to the *Voice*, the decision offered "an opportunity for Congress to act." Its practical effect was to make prohibition a "national issue." The *Union Signal* promoted an identical view, and in a long editorial claimed to see "the hand of God in the Iowa saloon decision." The paper compared the *Leisy* ruling to the *Dred Scot* decision; just as that ruling had contributed to the growth of the Republican party, this ruling would "bring about a union of all the friends of temperance law and order" in a national party dedicated to the suppression of the saloon. If the minority opinion supporting the state's police power over commerce had prevailed, it would have retarded the temperance movement. Divine Providence guided the justices' pens; their ruling would elevate prohibition to the national level "where the drink traffic would be practically suppressed by congressional legislation."[42]

When it came to temperance legislation, the United States Brewers' Association did not intend to leave Congress to its own devices. The brewers were convinced that the prohibitionists, who had suffered defeats in amendment campaigns in Pennsylvania and Nebraska, intended "to accomplish through national channels that which the people of the states by their votes have refused to endorse." Thus, they scheduled their 1890 annual convention in Washington, D.C., to forestall the establishment of a congressional committee to investigate the liquor traffic as well as passage of injurious legislation (such as increases in tax duties and an interstate commerce act). The convention showcased the organization's economic power and political influence. Attendance of the commissioner of internal revenue, a commissioner of the District of Columbia, and at least six congressmen underscored the political purposes of the brewers' convention. Democratic Representatives (all from New York) Ashbel Fitch, Amos Cummings, James Covert, Roswell Flower, and Charles Turner, as well as Asher Caruth of Kentucky, came to the final banquet to hear their colleague, Republican Benjamin Butterworth of Ohio, toast America, where "every man should be accorded the privilege of drinking his own beer and kissing his own wife."[43]

Against this array of congressional indifference and brewer clout, the radical prohibitionists deployed limited resources. In their quest for remedial legislation the prohibitionists' assets included a small number of dry legislators willing to work for the cause, one WCTU lobbyist, and a sound grassroots organization. These modest forces could have been instrumental in shaping and pushing through the Wilson Act had the prohibitionists fully mobilized them. But the radical prohibitionist initiative was half-hearted. They had other plans that diverted their energy, and what measures they took were largely ineffective.

The WCTU's Office of National Legislation constituted the radical prohibition movement's only direct connection to Washington. The Prohibition party's refusal to work with regular parties precluded it from trying to influence Congress, so the burden fell to the white ribboners. From 1887 through 1890 Ada M. Bittenbender and her husband Henry (her part-time assistant) staffed the WCTU office. Describing them, the *Union Signal* wrote: "She works for nothing, and he pays her board." Bittenbender, a lawyer trained by her husband and only the third woman admitted to the bar of the U.S. Supreme Court, lobbied Congress (with no success) for prohibition in the territories, for prohibition in the District of Columbia, and for national prohibition. In mid-1890 the failure of temperance measures in Congress and the allure of the law prompted her to leave the WCTU. She returned to Nebraska and joined the Prohibition party, becoming that party's candidate for state judicial office in 1891.[44]

Bittenbender's planned departure crippled the prohibition organizations' chances to influence the shape of the legislation. It was a particularly hard blow in that she recognized more clearly than many prohibitionists how to work for the passage of an original package act. In a May 15 article for the *Union Signal* she outlined a plan of political pressure. She implored "every reader" to write her congressmen and "secure the writing of similar letters by . . . influential people of the same political faith . . . of the congressmen addressed." Organizations favoring temperance should petition Congress. The religious and temperance press should call repeatedly for passage of an original package bill. In all endeavors, prohibitionists should focus on the measure before Congress, identifying it by name. But Bittenbender had lost interest in her Washington job, so she did not press prohibitionists into following her plan. It presaged later dry campaigns to pass legislation, but it remained unfulfilled in 1890.[45]

Perhaps the weakest element of the Bittenbender plan, petition drives, became the dry organizations' staple in behalf of remedial legislation. The *Voice* declared that "Congress ought to be flooded at once with petitions." But the radical prohibitionists quickly lost sight of the attainable. The *Union Signal* suggested "a house to house canvass of the voters of the United States" in which all those disposed would sign pledges promoting elimination of the liquor evil "by the best attainable means." This proposed canvass ignored Bittenbender's stricture to focus on a clear goal. Obviously, the results of such an ambiguous poll would have swayed the minds of few congressmen. In general, petitions were ineffective tools of political pressure. They were easily ignored by politicians, as they were addressed to the entire Congress. Yet the radicals did not choose petitions for their short-term ends. Their predilection for building public opinion guided them to choose a propaganda weapon over more private forms of political suasion.[46]

Although the Prohibition party and the WCTU favored the Wilson Bill, neither worked assiduously for its passage. Their official papers reflected their lukewarm support for the measure. Editorials and coverage on the bill appeared only sporadically. While finding the bill in general a good thing and covering its debates in some detail, the temperance papers did not attempt to mobilize their readers behind the measure. Cogent criticism and analysis of the *Leisy* ruling pointing out the feasibility of congressional action appeared in these papers only after the Wilson Act passed. Drys portrayed Congress's deliberations as delaying tactics. The *Union Signal* dismissed the constitutional debates over the measure as an "astonishing" display of "Latin." Prominent drys, like the Prohibition party's 1884 presidential candidate, John St. John, predicted defeat by a Congress determined to "appease the wrath of the liquor power." Even after it passed, the *Union Signal* rated the Wilson Act as less important than the antilottery act, and the temperance papers did not celebrate its passage. The prohibition press's treatment of the Wilson Bill revealed that it was not a radical prohibitionist measure.[47]

In the wake of the original package decision, the major prohibition organizations placed promotion of their own agenda before working for passage of the Wilson Bill. They saw opportunity in the *Leisy* ruling: "it presages a new crystallization of political elements around a new center," the prohibition issue. Either one of the "existing political parties" must embrace "the great opportunity, and speedily advance to the actual abolition" of the liquor evil, or a new organization would arise and "execute the Will of God" against the saloon. Halfway measures were unacceptable; at the very least, radical prohibitionists wanted Congress to pass "a law declaring that intoxicating liquors . . . shall no longer be an article of interstate commerce." Some saw the *Leisy* ruling as "a part and parcel of that infernal internal revenue system" and wanted to mobilize the backlash against the ruling to abolish the federal liquor tax. Their hope was that public opinion would be so aroused that "'on to Washington' for national prohibition, will be the cry." Their appetite grew the more they considered the situation. The *Union Signal* called for "a COMPLETE code of regulations" of national prohibition enacted under the general welfare clause of the Constitution. The radical, abolitionist mind-set kept them from fully promoting the Wilson Bill; thus, the only prohibitionists who had any part in the shaping of the measure were the few prohibitionists in Congress.[48]

Senators Henry W. Blair (Republican from New Hampshire), William P. Frye (Republican from Maine), Alfred H. Colquitt (Democrat from Georgia), and John H. Regan (Democrat from Texas), along with Representative Isaac S. Struble (Republican of Iowa), constituted the prohibitionist contingent of the 1890 Congress. Of the group, only Blair was a tireless proponent of absolute prohibition. Like the radicals, he argued that state and local action would never be enough to control liquor. "Samson," he wrote, "was not more completely hampered by withes than is this giant reform by the geographical lines of states"; the "natural arena" of temperance supporters was the "national domain." The other legislators, while equally committed to temperance, advocated less dogmatic solutions to the liquor problem. Unlike most prohibitionists, all worked for the passage of the Wilson Bill; indeed, Frye and Struble had introduced similar measures. They frequently spoke in favor of the bill and defended it from congressional critics. If any prohibitionists can be credited with the shaping and passage of the Wilson Act, it was these men. But prohibitionists did not play such a key role.[49]

The Republican party, not prohibitionists, was chiefly responsible for the Wilson Act. The author of the bill, James Wilson, was a regular Republican and no temperance fanatic. The Republican party proposed legislation because it feared that the *Leisy* ruling would create "a political storm, the extent and outcome of which cannot be determined." The consensus among politicians was that the ruling worked "a great revolution in the temperance question," making it a national issue. Only quick action by Congress designed to stop the national government from becoming "party to violations of wholesome state laws" could advert this political transformation. Republicans dreaded the emergence of prohibition as a national question, thinking that it would work to the Democratic party's benefit. Indeed, in the next congressional elections Democrats would, in once solid Republican states like Iowa, ride the prohibition issue to victory. Thus, in "self-defense" the Republican party rode "to the rescue" of state prohibition.[50]

Republican dominance of the Senate elevated James Wilson of Iowa to the chairmanship of the powerful Judiciary Committee. Wilson's position permitted him to revive a bill he had introduced the previous year, which the Judiciary Committee had killed with an unfavorable report. With the apparent sanction of the majority of the Supreme Court, Wilson convinced members of his committee that the bill was constitutional. While other representatives and senators struggled to draft bills, Wilson had his placed on the Senate's docket in mid-May, a mere two weeks after the *Leisy* ruling.

When Wilson's proposal reached the Senate floor, it read as follows:

No state shall be held limited or restrained in its power to prohibit, regulate, control or tax the sale, keeping for sale, or transportation, as an article of commerce or otherwise, to be delivered within its own limits, of any fermented, distilled or other intoxicating liquids or liquors by reasons of the fact that the same have been imported into such state from beyond its limits, where there shall or shall not have been paid thereon any tax, duty, impost, or excise to the United States.

Wilson introduced it as an innocuous and straightforward remedial measure. He stressed that he drafted the bill "in response to the suggestion made by the Supreme Court in its opinion in the recent liquor case." He designed the bill to extend congressional permission for the states to control foreign and interstate liquor shipments, "to grant to the states what may be called a local option, to allow them to do as they please in regard to the liquor question. They can have prohibition, high license, local option, or free liquor." His remarks carefully distanced the bill from the extreme policy of prohibition, tying it to all forms of state liquor control. He stressed that the Supreme Court probably would approve of the measure.[51]

Missouri's Senator George Vest, a member of the Judiciary Committee who had dissented from the favorable report, interrupted Wilson's opening speech by questioning his interpretation of the *Leisy* case. Vest, a constitutional lawyer, had formulated his arguments against state regulation of the liquor industry when he argued for the brewers in *Mugler v. Kansas*. Vest articulated the theme that would form the touchstone for all Senate opponents of the Wilson Bill. Vest contended that he was defending a fundamental constitutional principle. To him, the bill threatened to alter the American constitutional order, since he saw it as the opening wedge for "a successive series of such bills." Soon demands would be made on Congress to except tobacco or oleomargarine from interstate commerce protection. He argued that the Wilson Bill threatened to tear the commerce clause from the Constitution.[52]

A corollary to the opponents' main theme was that the Wilson Bill unconstitutionally delegated congressional powers to the states. Senator Richard Coke, a Democrat from Texas, pointed out that the Constitution conferred upon Congress the power to regulate commerce; Congress could not "abdicate the power, as it is proposed to be done in the pending bill," and delegate it to the states. "It is a familiar principle of law . . . that delegated power can not be delegated." Such a delegation of the interstate commerce power would undermine the foundation of the Union. Designing states, through the manipulation of Congress, would eventually erode the foundation of national unity and order.[53]

Little in Vest's or Coke's backgrounds marked them as advocates of nationalism, and their emphasis on the bill's threat to national power was probably a deliberate strategy to woo Republican support. Vest had served in the Confederate military and Congress during the Civil War and had always considered himself a states' rights man. Even the Democratic *Washington Post* admitted that "he had never been selected nor will he be, to go into northern states to increase the Democratic vote there." Vest's interests, not his ideology, motivated his assault on the Wilson Bill. Missouri's powerful brewing businesses supported Vest's political machine. Amendments that Vest and his supporters offered to the Wilson Bill—when it was clear that the measure would pass the Senate—revealed that their stand originated in their opposition to prohibition, not in the constitutional principles. One proposed to except beer from the bill. Another offered to change the bill's title to "A bill to overrule the decision of the Supreme Court . . . and thereby relieve the state of Iowa from the consequences of their own misguided legislation." Coke, a native of Virginia, studied law with St. George Tucker, a noted strict constructionist and states' rights thinker. Coke had moved to Texas where he fought against the Union, and after the war he helped defeat Radical Republican rule. A firm opponent of the extension of federal power, he spoke against the Blair Education Bill and the Federal Elections Bill of 1890. The transformation of Vest, Coke, and other senators captured the eye of the *Union Signal*. The paper commented on how southern Democrats had suddenly become "old time Federalists." The opponents of the Wilson Bill probably embraced the "foreign" nationalistic ideology for the tactical reason of weakening Republican support for the measure.[54]

This strategy failed miserably. The opponents' tactic of focusing on the bill's danger to national authority actually aided its supporters. It removed prohibition, always a troublesome political issue, from the Senate debates on the Wilson Bill. Vest, in his introduction to a speech on the measure, explained that he would not discuss prohibition because "it would be entirely foreign to the debate now before the Senate." Filtering out prohibition from the deliberations carried a political benefit for the senators. They did not have to go on record as being for or against the policy. They did not have to fear the consequences of their remarks on wet or dry constituents. The proponents turned the attack into a states' rights justification for the bill.[55]

James George, a Mississippi Democrat and a states' rights advocate, was the first senator to articulate the states' rights potential of the original package bill. George's support was dramatic: as a member of the Judiciary Committee, he had voted against Wilson's first proposal the year before. Indeed, George's first position on the Wilson Bill, that Congress controlled commerce only while it was in the process of transportation, was consistent with his stand on the initial Sherman antitrust measure. But he voted with the majority in 1890 and championed the Wilson Bill in the Senate. He justified his switch on the grounds that the *Leisy* ruling destroyed the previously secure police power of the states over liquor. Aware that his states' rights stand conflicted with the underlying premise of the bill, supremacy of the federal commerce power, George argued that he felt "constrained to support the bill since only through such legislation can the states, under the decision of the Supreme Court, exercise their rightful and necessary jurisdiction" over liquor. He concluded that the bill would reduce the power of the federal government, something he considered a laudable goal.[56]

Supporters of the Wilson Bill rallied to the constitutional standard raised by Senator George. For the most part, northern Republicans, not known for their adherence to state sovereignty, backed the bill. The proponents' advocacy of states' rights was as alien to them as their opponents' espousal of nationalism. Former nationalists like James Wilson and George Edmunds experienced a "sudden conversion" and became "champions and defenders of states' rights." The opponents' constitutional tactics left the door open for the supporters to back the Wilson Bill with states' rights pronouncements, thus avoiding the prohibition issue. Restoration of the states' power was a shrewdly chosen theme to stress, as many perceived the *Leisy* ruling as a "juggernaut" of "centralization." States' rights rhetoric may have even gleaned some southern support for the bill.[57]

The Wilson Act passed the Senate by a vote of thirty-four to ten, with forty members not voting. The ten senators who voted against the act revealed themselves in the debates and in their votes as opponents of prohibition. Senators Vest and Francis Cockrell of Missouri, David Turpie and David Voorhees of Indiana, and William Bate and Isham Harris of Tennessee came from states where liquor manufacture was a key industry. These senators were not motivated by constitutional ideology. For instance, Vest was willing to use the commerce power in other areas; in the same year he supported the use of federal power to control trusts, and he even proposed an amendment for an explicit ban on railroad pooling. Four others, Coke of Texas, James Jones of Arkansas, Zebulon Vance of North Carolina, and Rufus Bloodgut of New Jersey, expressed their ideological opposition to the policy of prohibition.[58]

On the other hand, the proponents of the Wilson Act were not prohibitionists. Of the four prohibitionists in the Senate, only Blair and Colquitt cast their votes for the measure; both Regan and Frye missed the vote. Of the five southerners voting for the bill, four of the southern Democrats may have been swayed by its states' rights gloss. The states' rights ideology might have also led many of the seventeen southern Democrats who did not vote to withhold their votes. The final vote on the original package bill revealed it as a Republican measure. Significantly, no Republican opposed it, and 63 percent of the party members voted for it. Republicans from all sections—from states with prohibition policies, local option policies, and high license systems—supported the measure in roughly equal numbers.[59]

Republicans came warily to the rescue of state prohibition, and did so on their own terms. They did not seriously consider the far-reaching proposals of the radical prohibitionists, like banning liquor in interstate commerce, and they feared the effects of prohibition on the national level. Their proposed legislation kept the prohibition issue confined to the states, where they had worked out a strategy of controlling the issue by submitting the question to plebiscites. The Wilson Act, by removing the immediate problems of the prohibition states, turned attention away from national solutions. The constitutional focus of the Senate's debates not only avoided the prohibition issue, it obscured the Republicans' strategy. Other factors would keep the Republican plan hidden when the Wilson Bill moved into the House of Representatives.[60]

The course of the original package bill in the House differed from that in the Senate. The House Judiciary Committee broadened the bill beyond liquor to include all items of commerce. Members of the House also turned the states' rights arguments against the bill. And the lower chamber's deliberations took on a sense of urgency inspired by the spread of the original package industry. But one factor carried over from the Senate: the bill remained a Republican measure. The House Judiciary Committee produced a substitute bill; it recast the original package bill in general terms "that whenever any article of commerce is imported into any state from any other state, territory, or foreign nation, and held there or offered for sale, the same shall be subject to the laws of such state." This proposal would have reshaped the American federal system by increasing state police power over the new forms of interstate business that were transforming the economy. The tremendous ramifications implicit in the substitute sparked much discussion both in and out of Congress.[61]

The bill caught the eye of vacationing U.S. Supreme Court Justice David Brewer. He broke with judicial tradition by discussing impending congressional legislation with a reporter. Brewer stated the revolutionary aspects of the House's substitute in the simplest of terms. He said that it "prevents Armour from shipping into Kansas his diseased meats, it will drive out Louisiana sugar, and it will prevent the shipment of Texas cattle through Kansas if diseased." Although he thought the measure "far-reaching" and predicted a long and lively debate over its terms, he hoped the House substitute would become law. The *New York Times* believed that the substitute "covered the grounds in a much more satisfactory way than the Senate bill." The paper preferred this measure because it made no distinction between commodities and reinstituted what "most competent jurists" considered to be "the true doctrine of the Constitution."[62]

Brewer's and the *Times*'s assessment of the House substitute points to a broadly held conception of the polity, a view that radical prohibitionists did not share. From the debates and legislation from this period, it is apparent that many Americans shared an attitude concerning how the polity should respond to the challenge of big business and other problems. Seeking to preserve federalism as a governing principle, legal thinkers and politicians postulated a polity of shared powers between the federal and state governments. Thus, the Wilson Bill prompted constitutional discussions about the federal commerce power and state police power that duplicated the ideas advanced in legal periodicals, the courts, and Congress on the trust issue. The bill in all its forms reflected, complementary to state efforts, federal legislation based on the postal power that banned lottery materials, obscene works, and fraudulent inducements from the mails. Yet the prohibitionists seemed blind to this dimension of the substitute. They found the new version appealing only because it would control another moral evil: lottery tickets. Their focus on moral issues illuminates the gap between their ideas about law and the prevailing view within the society. Drys also did not see the tactical advantage of the substitute bill.[63]

The nature of the substitute steered the House debates away from prohibition. As in the Senate, the deliberations centered on constitutional issues, and many members defended the bill as a states' rights measure. But some southern representatives rejected this contention. For instance, David Culberson, a Texas Democrat, asserted that until the *Leisy* ruling it was established law that the states had jurisdiction over liquor, and it remained a desirable goal that states should retain this power. Furthermore, he argued, the Wilson Bill in either form was not the proper way to restore that authority. The bill offered no concessions to states' rights. "Instead of Congress being the grantee of powers from the states it assumes to become a grantor of power. The old rule is reversed, the creature becomes the creator." In this new role Congress could limit as well as expand state power. He declared the bill would reduce "the great state" he represented to "a mendicant at the footstool of federal power."[64]

The southern press echoed this new states' rights view of the bill. For example, in May of 1890 the *Atlanta Constitution* had decried the *Leisy* ruling and advocated the passage of a congressional act to restore power to the states. But in July, after the southern Congressmen had turned the states' rights argument against the bill, the paper opposed enactment of the Wilson Bill "in the interest of home rule." If it became law, it would be "another forward stride of centralization." The debates over the proposed Federal Election Law of 1890 (the so-called Force Bill) increased southerners' sensitivity to creeping nationalism and fueled their opposition to the Wilson Bill.[65]

Culberson and other ideological opponents of the original and substitute bills proposed alternatives intended to restore the states' power over liquor.

They suggested that Congress do nothing and hope that the Supreme Court would "correct" its view of the commerce clause. On a more active note, they argued that Congress should frame a constitutional amendment redefining the interstate commerce power. The supporters of the bill attacked these proposals and "those excellent gentlemen who always find a 'constitutional' objection in the way of right action." Proponents dismissed the alternatives as too time consuming, arguing that immediate action was required to advert a national crisis over liquor regulation.[66]

Indeed, Congress could not avoid hearing about the spread of the original package industry. Members of the House often read during debates newspaper articles that predicted disaster. These accounts reinforced the warnings of individuals. Attorney General Kellog of Kansas wrote his state's congressional delegation urging swift passage of the Wilson Bill. Friends of members kept Congress informed of the situation. "You can have no idea what a 'hell on earth' " the *Leisy* ruling "created here in Iowa. We have now four joints and they are starting in all the little towns in the country." Such pleas prompted Representative Byron Cutcheon, among others, to call for speedy action: "other questions of public policy can be put aside for a time," including plans for a silver purchase act and for an antitrust act, "without great detriment to the community, but this remedial measure . . . cannot be delayed with safety."[67]

In the House the crisis over liquor policy created by the *Leisy* ruling induced many members to speak openly about prohibition. This frankness changed few minds or votes. Congressmen tended to state their positions, defend them, and cast their votes accordingly. For example, Democrats John Chipman and William Oates maintained that they opposed all sumptuary laws and for that reason voted against the bill. Representative Struble defended prohibition and supported the measure. It was somewhat ironic that prohibition should even be mentioned in the House debates, as the substitute measure written by the Judiciary Committee applied to all items of commerce.[68]

Fear that the substitute would retard the passage of remedial legislation on the liquor issue was the most prevalent reaction to the committee's action. Many argued that "its sweeping effects" would keep the measure from quickly passing either house. Some speculated that it was introduced deliberately to slow the progress of the original bill. Justice Brewer thought that "a number of congressmen representing high license districts" were "filibustering for political purposes," supporting the measure in hopes that the Senate would refuse to concur. While perhaps accurate for some representatives, this theory does not satisfactorily explain the origins of the substitute. Trusts, big business, and state power were important issues in the 1890 Congress. The substitute's authors intended it to help the states regulate multistate concerns. It also met the fear that the Court's reasoning in *Leisy* would be extended to other items, like oleomargarine, wild game, and even obscene literature. The support for the substitute in the House demonstrated the importance of these issues.[69]

Analysis of the voting patterns on the substitute and the final version of the Wilson Act (limited only to liquor) revealed the reasons for the substitute's passage in the House and the forces at work behind it. These voting patterns can be explained by the interplay of party politics, constitutional ideology, and interest-group influence. A number of Democrats supported the broad substitute but not the limited final version. Some southern Democrats, despite the arguments of Representative Culberson and others, saw the substitute as too good an opportunity to pass up. Even though its sustaining theory undercut states' rights, its effect would increase the authority and power of the states at the expense of the national government. southern support eroded when the bill was confined to liquor. In general, the turning of the states' rights argument against the bill in the House increased southern opposition to the measure. In the House 41.5 percent of the southern members voted against the bill, compared with 17.8 percent in the Senate. Thus, ideology played a part in the shaping of the bill, but was not instrumental in its passage.[70]

The northern Democrats who voted for the substitute had no such ideological base. Economic interest drove them. Most came from states where dairying was an important industry. The strong dairy lobby, concerned about competitive oleomargarine, pressed for restrictive anti-oleo laws in many of these states. The House substitute would permit these laws to operate against interstate oleo shipments. When the bill was narrowed, the northern Democrats lost their reason for supporting it. Northern and southern Democrats who had supported the substitute differed in the way they cast their votes for the restricted final version of the bill: 85.7 percent of the northern Democratic supporters of the substitute voted against the final version, while only 42.1 percent of southerners followed this pattern. In other words, the northerners jumped from support to opposition, while the southerners shifted from support to not voting, and from not voting on the substitute to opposition on the final version. Perhaps many southerners' respect for states' rights kept them from opposing the final bill, while northern Democrats, driven by interest-group politics, opposed it when it did not suit their needs. The Republican party represented the core of the support for the Wilson Bill in all its forms: 66.4 percent of the party members in the House supported the final version, comprising 96.6 percent of its total yea votes; and 68.7 percent supported the substitute. Only twelve Republicans, less than 6.8 percent of the party membership, voted against the bill, and all were "living and breathing" within "the shadow of a brewery." The Republican party never wavered in its adherence to the measure, and the actions of Speaker Thomas Reed symbolized the party's commitment to the bill.[71]

One Republican observer with a German name complained that "no one was more assiduous or earnest in his efforts to push this thing through than your Speaker Reed." Thomas Reed was no prohibitionist; indeed, the *Voice* thought that Reed lacked "aggressive views on temperance." Yet Reed pushed for the bill in all forms, although he preferred the limited version. At one point during the vote on the Judiciary Committee proposal, "Speaker Reed was taking no chances, but turned the gavel over to a substitute and took his stand where he could give the particular managers suggestions with more ease and promptness." Reed used his powers as Speaker to further the bill. He appointed the conferees for the joint conference committee when the Senate refused to accept the House's version, packing it with members willing to accept the Senate's version of the bill. His final action in behalf of the bill was to set an early voting date on the conference committee's report.[72]

Among the three House members in the conference committee, James Reed and Albert Thompson seemed more interested in passing any form of the bill than in preserving the scope of the House substitute. Only William Oates was firmly wedded to the House version. Before August 1890, these three men met with Senators Wilson, George, and Edmunds, all strong advocates of the Senate's version. The inflexibility of the senators and the perception that the nation needed remedial legislation motivated the representatives to accept the Senate version of the bill. The conferees also adopted the Senate's language, which better expressed Wilson's purposes. The final form of the bill read as follows:

> . . . that all . . . intoxicating liquors . . . transported into any state or territory . . . for use, consumption, sale or storage therein, shall upon arrival . . . be subject to the operation and effect of the laws of such state or territory enacted in the exercise of its police powers, to the same extent and in the same manner as though such . . . liquors had been produced in such state . . . and shall not be exempt from by reason of being introduced there in original packages or otherwise.

They justified this decision when they returned to the House on the grounds that the Senate version would meet the emergency of the times.

They also added that it was all the Supreme Court had called for in the *Leisy* ruling. Enough members of the House agreed with this reasoning to insure passage of the Senate version. On August 8, 1890, less than four months after the *Leisy* ruling, President Benjamin Harrison signed the Wilson Act into law. With its passage the *Washington Post* concluded, "So endeth the original package business."[73]

As they were not the authors of the Wilson Act, prohibitionists expressed little joy over its passage. The prohibition newspapers limited their rejoicing to detailing the effect of the act. The adoption began what the *Voice* characterized as "the great exodus." Original package proprietors, on the advice of their attorneys, hurried to unload their stock. One advertised, "Get your beer to-day, for to-morrow you can't, the Wilson Bill has passed." Most were "rather more anxious to leave" than fight in the courts. "John Brown," a Topeka brewers' agent, arranged to ship his beer back to Missouri. Many liquor sellers thought that to remain open "would just be a bill of expense." But most liquor dealers, like the agent of Anheuser-Busch, admitted their willingness to resume the trade if the results of a test case of the Wilson Act proved satisfactory.[74]

Eager law enforcement officials and a few daring liquor sellers soon generated a host of cases. For instance, Iowa saloonist "Stormy" Jordon, who called his bar "The Road to Hell," remained in business by having his attorney "raise federal questions." In the lower federal courts and in the highest courts of Iowa and Kansas the cases centered on whether the parts of state prohibition laws affected by the *Leisy* ruling needed to be reenacted in the wake of the Wilson Act. For liquor sellers, the advantage of such a contention was obvious. It would keep original package stores open and unmolested until such laws passed. And with prohibition unpopular in three of the five dry states (Iowa, North Dakota, and South Dakota), chances of reenactment were slim. At first the courts that heard these cases decided that the Wilson Act's operation was not retroactive; but by late October courts were ruling that the prohibition laws were in full force and effect. The latter rulings prevented original package sales while a test case worked its way up to the U.S. Supreme Court.[75]

In Re Rahrer, the test case that eventually reached the Court, began the day after the Wilson Act passed. On August 9, 1890, Charles A. Rahrer, the Topeka agent of Maynard, Hopkins and Company, wholesale shippers of liquors based in Kansas City, Missouri, was arrested for selling one pint of original package whiskey. Rahrer quickly sought writ of habeas corpus in the federal courts. A syndicate of Chicago brewers and liquor dealers, and not the United States Brewers' Association, assumed the costs of the litigation and hired counsel to argue Raher's case before the Court. In their arguments on May 17, 1891, they added a general assault on the Wilson Act to earlier attacks against the state laws. Rahrer's counsel argued that since *Bowman* and *Leisy* had ruled unconstitutional parts of the prohibition codes and since unconstitutional acts were not law, no state law on the subject existed. Therefore, Rahrer was arrested under a state law "enacted by the national" Congress. Such action clearly exceeded Congress's authority and was unconstitutional. Counsel also contended that the act unconstitutionally delegated the national power to regulate interstate commerce to the states.[76]

These words carried little weight with the Court, which unanimously upheld the constitutionality of the Wilson Act. Chief Justice Fuller, who wrote the opinion in *In Re Rahrer*, replied to counsel's first argument by asserting that *Leisy v. Hardin* did not hold the state laws in question "absolutely void . . . as if they had never been enacted" but merely limited their operation "to property strictly within the jurisdiction of the state." When Congress, through the Wilson Act, "removed an impediment to the enforcement of state laws" on interstate liquor shipments "created by the absence of specific utterance" on the topic, the state laws attached. The chief justice forcefully rejected the unconstitutional delegation argument. He argued that the Congress had not "attempted to delegate" the commerce power to the states "or to adopt state laws." Rather, it took "its own course" in making "its own regulation," whose "uniformity is not affected by variation in state law." Further, Fuller asserted that the Court saw "no reason" why it was not within Congress's "competency" to designate that certain commodities in interstate commerce could "be governed by a rule which divests them of that character at an earlier period of time than would otherwise be the case." The Court thus ended the liquor sellers' remaining hope that the federal judiciary would allow interstate commerce in alcoholic beverages to flourish without state interference.[77]

The decision in *Rahrer* underscored how Congress and the Court thought the polity operated in the late nineteenth century. Indeed, it represented a pattern whereby the Court approved of Congress's use of its enumerated powers to aid the states in enforcing various laws. This framework of joint state and federal action could be instituted under the federal commerce, tax, treaty, or postal power. For instance, in the 1890s, the postal power was extended to prohibit from the mails lottery materials and fraudulent and obscene matter. These postal regulations functioned as adjuncts to state laws on gambling, obscenity, and fraud. The federal laws kept violators of state bans from using the federal system as a shield for their activities, and the

Wilson Act, once it was tested in the courts, functioned in the same way. Indeed, the *Rahrer* ruling forced liquor sellers to abandon their legal toeholds in the dry states. Some returned to the practice of operating outside the law, depending on the weakness of a locality's commitment to prohibition. For instance, Keokuk, Iowa, remained wet. Other liquor dealers specialized in personal-use, cash-on-delivery liquor shipments into dry areas, never entering the dry jurisdiction.[78]

The liquor dealers' enemy, the prohibition organizations, responded predictably to the *Rahrer* ruling. The *Union Signal* (which also mistakenly called the case *Raker*) printed a letter applauding the decision, saying that the day it was delivered "was a red-letter day for the prohibition states." The *Voice* wrote that the ruling was "received with great glee by all the prohibitionists of Kansas." Both papers commended the revival of enforcement efforts in Iowa, Kansas, and Maine. After the passage of the Wilson Act, radical prohibitionists warned against the abandonment of national goals. Ada M. Bittenbender argued that the law did not "do away with the necessity for national constitutional prohibition." The *Union Signal* editorialized, "It would be unfortunate in the extreme if prejudice in favor of the exclusive jurisdiction of the states over the traffic . . . should take root in the temperance mind." The prohibitionist press stressed that the movement needed to focus on the new reality, that the national government could cooperate with the states in fighting demon rum. Drys could not ignore the states, for they would do the bulk of the work in destroying the liquor octopus, and they could not forget the general government because piecemeal reform was doomed to failure. Thus the conception of the concurrent operations against liquor emerged from the Supreme Court's opinions and Congress's legislation.[79]

Following the disastrous defeat in *Mugler*, the federal nature of the American polity allowed the liquor industry to challenge state prohibition on different grounds. The Supreme Court's application of freedom of commerce and original package doctrines to the policy limited the effect of state prohibition laws. At first glance this resort to the "state of courts," which invoked formal rules against prohibition, seems to have been a great victory for the liquor forces. But the Court's references to congressional permission raised the potential for Congress to act. Moreover, the interstate commerce issues raised in *Bowman* and in *Leisy* briefly fulfilled the radicals' dream of transforming prohibition into a national issue. But what the Court gave to the drys the Republican party took away. Its quick action—derived from Republican control of the Congress and presidency—forestalled the development of prohibition into a national issue. Building on the ideas contained in the Court's decision in *Leisy*, the Wilson Act returned the prohibition issue to the states. By upholding the act in *Rahrer* the Supreme Court guaranteed that temperance would remain a state matter. But a new configuration emerged from these events: the national government had acted to support the liquor policies of the states. This new actuality was far different from the reality that existed in another area of state and federal relations, tax policy. In this area the federal policies stood squarely against the goals of the temperance crusaders and dry states.

THE FEDERAL LIQUOR TAX AND THE

RADICAL PROHIBITIONISTS

CHAPTER 3

The federal internal revenue system was the notable exception to the limited nature of the federal government that characterized the late-nineteenth-century polity. Part of the federal revenue system, the liquor excise taxes, required the government to take an active role in economic and daily life. It also fostered a benign view of the liquor industries within the federal government. Thus, the first budding of the modern bureaucratic polity stood in the way of prohibition. From 1880 to about 1900, most prohibitionists denounced the federal liquor tax as a hindrance to temperance progress. This view of the tax reflected the dominance of the abolitionist mind-set in the movement and a conscious rejection of regulation as a means to promote temperance. Radical drys viewed the tax not as a restriction on the liquor business but as a recognition of its legitimacy. To knock away this prop from underneath the evil liquor establishment, they demanded that the federal government abolish the tax. In this period the government ignored the prohibitionist agitation and kept the tax as a key part of government finance.

The existence of the federal tax also presented prohibitionists with an opportunity. Beginning in the 1880s, some drys proposed using the federal tax system as a tool to enforce state liquor laws. Overcoming their predilection for pure solutions, they shaped state laws to make use of the federal tax records and officials. But the federal Office of Internal Revenue obstructed the efforts of drys to use the liquor tax as an enforcement mechanism in prohibition territory. At first, this impediment was piecemeal since the government lacked an official policy toward use of federal tax materials in state prosecutions. Later, in the late 1880s, the Internal Revenue Office formulated a policy that was unsympathetic toward prohibitionist plans. By 1900, this policy had hardened into fixed rules tested in the federal courts.

The fiscal necessities of waging the Civil War compelled Congress to enact a host of internal revenue measures, among them a tax on alcoholic beverages. Political economists and government officials believed the liquor tax an excellent way to raise emergency revenue. It was a method tried and true. Alexander Hamilton had made taxes on distilled spirits a key part of his plan to retire the national debt, and even the Jeffersonians embraced a liquor tax during the War of 1812. But the tax fell out of favor and was repealed in 1818. Thus, in 1862 Congress, inexperienced in the logistics of excise taxation, made mistakes in creating the new system. It passed a high tax but endowed its administrators with woefully inadequate machinery to collect it.[1]

Tax avoidance and corruption kept the tax from raising the predicted revenue, and although the government struggled to refine the system, it initially had little success. Despite these troubles, officials persisted in their belief that the liquor tax had the potential for raising a large revenue; thus, it survived the general repeal of internal revenue taxes following the war. To combat continuing fraud and corruption, the commissioner of internal revenue and the Congress tinkered with the tax machinery, varying rates, closing loopholes, and enacting stiff penalties for myriad violations. The final spasm of reform following the Whisky Ring disclosures finally put the tax on a sound footing. By 1876, a mature tax system had been established, one that stood virtually unchanged until the implementation of federal prohibition.[2]

The structure of federal taxation of liquor contributed to the prohibitionists' denunciations of the policy. Two issues were of particular interest to the radical temperance crusaders. The first, the mechanics of collecting the liquor tax, created an intimate and cooperative relationship between federal officials and liquor producers and sellers. The second, the tremendous amount of revenue generated by the tax, legitimated the liquor trade.

Effective taxation of liquor, especially distilled spirits, required the federal government to oversee its manufacture. At first, the government taxed distilled spirits at an exceptionally high rate, and thus producers who avoided paying these burdensome taxes benefited. To assure accurate and full collection of its tax, the federal government supervised almost every aspect of distilling. Federal officials directed the construction and operation of all distilleries. They measured and recorded the amounts of raw materials brought into the plants and the amount of fuel consumed. At several points in the manufacturing process, officials gauged the amount of pure, taxable alcohol in the product. Since the distillers were not liable for the tax until the liquor was sold, provision was made for the storage of the product. Federal law required distillers to build a "government-bonded warehouse," to store all their spirits in the warehouse, and to pay a bond guaranteeing the payment of the tax. Government officials directly supervised the warehouse, measuring, sealing, and stamping every container as it entered. The liquor was released only on payment of the tax. Statutes limited the period that the spirits could remain "in bond," but the commissioner of internal revenue set allowances for leakage and loss. No detail was overlooked. Owners of distilleries could enter their plants only with the permission of the tax officials, who controlled all distillery keys.

The federal government did not interfere to the same extent in the brewing industry. The malt liquor tax rate was low compared with that on distilled liquors. The incentive to achieve extraordinary profits by defrauding the government did not exist in the brewing trade. Thus the government's direct supervision was relatively insignificant. The government merely required that every barrel of beer carry a U.S. tax stamp over its spigot hole. It also made an effort to prevent the counterfeiting and reuse of the stamps. In part, action by the brewers in shaping the liquor tax system curtailed the government's role. A group of brewers toured Europe to gather information on how other governments taxed liquor. These representatives and many other brewers conferred repeatedly with the drafters of the legislation, and many of their suggestions were accepted. Indeed, the United States Brewers' Association and other liquor makers, aware of the benefits of this relationship, worked to nurture it.[3]

The federal government's intervention into liquor manufacturing promoted a cooperative relationship between government officials and producers of intoxicating beverages. Despite their supposedly adversary status, the regulators and producers often became friends. Indeed, the frauds perpetuated by combinations of distillers and government agents reveal that cooperation, not conflict, characterized their relationships. Even after reforms reduced the incidence of fraud, the intertwining of the two groups in the production of spirits, their daily contacts, and their mutual dependence blurred the distinctions between the government's purposes and the liquor producers' interests.

This identification with the liquor industry pervaded the whole revenue bureaucracy. At its lowest levels the internal revenue system provided jobs to a large number of storekeepers, gaugers, inspectors, and collectors of revenue. Like the manufacturers and sellers of spirits, these federal officials perceived prohibition as a threat to their jobs. They publicly attacked prohibitionist ideas, emphasizing that prohibition did not work in the few areas where it had been adopted. Their access to federal statistics on the sale of liquor in dry areas added credence to their attacks. At the highest level the blending continued. At least two revenue commissioners, Green B. Raum and John W. Yerkes, became liquor lobbyists. One of the early administrators, Louis Schade, became the most prominent liquor spokesman of the nineteenth century as editor of the *Washington Sentinel* and chief attorney for the United States Brewers' Association. The change from regulator to industry spokesman was an easy one, as most officials developed a positive attitude toward the liquor industry and its products. As one secretary of the treasury expressed it, liquors were "things which are in very small measure necessary to health and happiness of mankind." No liquor propagandist could have said it better, and most federal officials concurred.[4]

The officials' pro-liquor attitudes, while shaped by their interest and direct contacts with the industry, also emerged from their backgrounds. In the era of party government, federal tax positions were an important source of political patronage. The high turnover in the offices reflected the professional politicians' desires to reward the faithful and to punish the errant. They seldom wasted positions on reformers, who were notoriously unreliable as political workers. For the most part, party hacks with no future or vision filled the offices. Temperance reformers rarely served in the Internal Revenue Office. I have found only two known drys, William Armstrong (solicitor, 1868–85) and Myron H. Clark (collector, 1862–68), who worked in the tax bureaucracy, and they gained their positions early on in the tax's history. Thus it is not surprising that almost all federal officials became convinced that the taxation of liquor benefited the nation; and the revenues that flowed into the federal treasury from the liquor tax only reinforced this view.[5]

The liquor tax was a very important source of revenue for the federal government, and revenue helped to shape the government's perceptions of the liquor industry. From 1873 to 1890, the alcohol tax, excluding the stamp tax on occupations, generated between 20 percent and 30 percent of the nation's total tax revenues. From 1891 to 1916 the tax never fell below 30 percent of the federal government's tax receipts. In the years 1894 and 1898 over 41 percent of the federal government tax income derived solely from the tax on spirits. Just as important as the magnitude of the liquor industry's contributions to the federal treasury was the government's tendency to raise liquor tax rates to meet extraordinary fiscal demands. For example, the government increased the liquor tax to defray the loss of revenue during the depression of the 1890s and to replace diminishing tariff revenues caused by the outbreak of World War I. This inclination lasted until the adoption of national prohibition. In fact, on January 16, 1919—the day the thirty-sixth state ratified the Eighteenth Amendment—House and Senate conferees were again considering raising liquor excise tax rates.[6]

More than anything else, revenue defined how the federal government viewed the liquor industry. As President Taft put it, "I know something about the manufacture of whiskey, because I was Collector of Internal Revenue, and we collected millions and millions of dollars' revenue on whiskey." At the annual convention of the United States Brewers' Association in 1890, the internal revenue commissioner, James W. Mason, said that he "was glad to be with the brewers," for he "regarded them as substantial businessmen, engaged in a legitimate business." He urged that "closer relations should be established between the brewers and the government." In 1892 Mason made an official tour of the nation's distillers, "with whom he was on friendly terms," to discuss problems of taxation.[7]

In turn, the liquor industry put their special tax status to good and different uses. Many representatives of the liquor industry asserted that the federal revenue system legitimated the manufacture and sale of liquor. Even the letterheads of liquor firms reflected this view. For instance, the letterhead of Clarke Brothers Company showed the operation of their "independent" (of the trust) Peoria distillery. Prominent in the picture is the American flag, flying over the label "U.S. Government bonded warehouse." Other liquor manufacturers argued that the tax made the industry patriotic. The United States Brewers' Association sang the glories of the federal tax, detailing how their sacrifices benefited the nation and in turn legitimated their trade. Liquor advertisements and circulars reflected this conception of the federal tax. The Seeba Company of Jacksonville, Florida, a liquor mail order house, ran a newspaper ad that claimed, "This whisky is bottled in bond under the supervision of the United States government. Uncle Sam guarantees it is a truly fine, straight whisky." Another circular summed up this view in a phrase, "Uncle Sam is our partner."[8]

Liquor makers also used the tax system against their competition and proposed using it against their enemies. For instance, Gallus Thomann wrote a book-length treatise under the auspices of the United States Brewers' Association in which he argued that the thrust of the federal liquor taxes was to promote temperance. By temperance, Thomann specifically meant the consumption of beer and wine as opposed to hard spirits. The most far-reaching attempt of the liquor industry to take advantage of the liquor tax came in 1884. In that year the pro-liquor Indiana representative John Jay Kleiner introduced a bill that forbade the states from prohibiting the manufacture and sale of commodities subject to federal internal revenue taxes. Such a law would have nipped the state prohibition movement in the bud. Louis Schade, the Brewers' Association agent in Washington, found the idea attractive. While the bill quickly died, it revealed the potential of the liquor tax for the industry.[9]

To the dismay of temperance reformers, the general government's tax system stood squarely against their goal of a nation free of alcohol. The liquor tax presented them a serious obstacle because it created an air of legitimacy about the trade. Obviously, temperance advocates did not share federal officials' beneficent view of the liquor industry. They were more likely to agree with J. Ellen Foster when she wrote, "the traffic in alcoholic beverages breeds disunion, overthrows justice, creates domestic strife, weakens the common defense, and fastens the chain of an ignoble slavery upon ourselves and our posterity." Yet these basic tenets of the prohibitionist faith did not necessarily shape their views toward the federal tax. Hostility to liquor did not automatically translate into opposition to the liquor tax. Indeed, in the 1860s and 1870s, many in the temperance movement supported the tax as a regulatory measure. The emergence of radical temperance organizations—the Prohibition party and the WCTU—changed drys' attitudes toward the tax.[10]

In the 1880s the radical temperance ideology rejected regulation as a suitable solution to the liquor problem. The rise of the abolitionist solution of complete prohibition made the liquor tax a hindrance to the stated goal of the movement. Radical temperance crusaders argued that the tax ran counter to public policy and moral law. Reflecting the pure stand of the radical temperance organizations, prohibitionists saw the tax not as a restriction but as a license. It sanctioned and strengthened the liquor industry and created a virtual partnership between the government and the liquor sellers. Corruption naturally followed in its wake. The federal action was as sinful, criminal, and evil as the liquor traffic itself.

This negative view of the federal tax also grew from experiences with local licensing and taxation. For example, tax revenues from liquor in Atlanta—one of the first major cities to experiment with local option prohibition—fell from $12,525 in 1886 (18.6 percent of total revenues) to $775 in 1887. At the same time, overall city revenues fell $12,169. Few communities could sustain such losses. Indeed, in 1888 Atlanta rejected prohibition and determined to make the liquor license tax a significant part of its fiscal system. In 1888 that tax generated 48.6 percent of the city's revenues. A wet appeal to voters in Portsmouth, Ohio, argued that "Portsmouth needs revenue . . . for . . . new water works, new schools, why vote to deprive the city of part of her present income? Vote wet." Martin Behrman, mayor of New Orleans, saw that "an increase in the saloon license taxes was the best way to get" money for the city's schools. From examples like this radical drys drew a lesson. As the *Nation* explained, prohibitionists "found in their municipal and state campaigns that the revenues derived from the saloon stand in the way of their agitation" and "some of them" moved to the position "that the national liquor taxes" had a similar effect. Prohibitionists denounced what they saw as government sponsorship of the liquor traffic. It outraged them to see kegs of bogus "near beer" shipped into prohibition states "made respectable with governmental stamps." The federal tax, they argued, "has made the infernal business appear as one of the pillars of the country, when it is nothing more than a caterpillar living upon the fruits of others' industry."[11]

The moral abhorrence that the prohibitionists felt toward the selling and consumption of liquor deepened their resentment of the federal government's sanction of the liquor trade. They labeled the liquor tax "our revenue from vice" and "legalized immorality." Since the saloon blighted the lives of young men, prohibitionists condemned the federal tax as "paying taxes with boys." As drys saw it, the federal government licensed sin, and they feared where this might lead. On hearing a rumor that the government proposed to tax slot machines, the *Union Signal* editorialized, "Should this wicked scheme actually prevail, the accelerated evil principle would still further be fortified by the general taxing (licensing) of houses of prostitution." In the heyday of prohibition radicalism, drys opposed licensing of any evil; they believed that vice and crimes were not the proper subjects for taxation. They compressed this view to an aphorism, "We do not tax a crime. We prohibit and punish it."[12]

Prohibitionists denounced the partnership of the government with the liquor industry. In 1896 the *Union Signal* lamented, "We feel just as much ashamed to have Uncle Sam in the liquor business as we would if he were a really truly uncle." They argued that this partnership corrupted the government, making it as responsible for the evils of liquor as the industry. A cartoon published on the front page of the *Voice* summed up the prohibitionist attitude. It depicted the marriage of a spry Uncle Sam to an overdressed, pig-faced harlot with "liquor traffic" written across her gown. As the preacher pronounces the benedictions Uncle Sam hands his bride a "license" that symbolizes their partnership. The prohibitionists buttressed their charge that Uncle Sam belonged to "the firm of Gambrinus, Bacchus, and Co." by detailing in long articles the mechanics of federal supervision of distilleries. Some drys argued that, because the government tax raised more revenue than what the distillers earned in profits, the "United States government is the senior partner in the concern."[13]

In the eyes of many temperance reformers, the federal liquor tax did more than legitimate the trade. It created the "scaffolding" that the industry used to build itself into the "liquor power." In short, the tax made the industry a potent political force, a "national institution." This view, pioneered by the Prohibition party and the white ribboners in the 1880s and 1890s, persisted through the era of national prohibition. The liquor power was "thoroughly organized, resourceful, cunning, vigilant, politically powerful, wealthy and carefully entrenched" in the structure of American life. The "rum power" was perceived as "an organized and aggressive factor in national politics, . . . a creation of the revenue legislation of the Civil War." The tax promoted the "compact and intelligent organization" of the liquor industry and forced it to establish "intimate relations with federal officials and influential politicians."[14]

According to Clinton B. Fisk, the Prohibition party's presidential candidate in 1888, the liquor tax "put whiskey producers and dealers besides the chairs of administration at Washington, enthroned them in congressional halls, and made of great statesmen suppliant servants." John G. Woolley, looking back at the development of temperance in the United States, asserted that the "federal special tax . . . endowed a federal Fagin's university of graft and spoils where assessors, collectors, gaugers and storekeepers [are] trained to steal and lie and pack conventions and stuff ballot boxes." Thus public service lost all "conscience and fairness" and important public problems remained unsolved. Many prohibitionists agreed with Henry George when he used this analogy to detail the evils flowing from the tax: "If the federal government" were to tax "the manufacture of corsets, as it does" alcohol, soon a "corset ring" would emerge "with [a] large pecuniary interest in the retention of the tax, in the rulings of the department, and in the appointment of internal revenue officials." Many drys believed that by its nature the liquor tax led to the corruption of federal officials and augmented the liquor industry's power.[15]

Prohibitionists held the federal tax responsible for the economic might of the liquor industry, and this "plethoric purse" translated directly into political influence. Especially during the 1880s and 1890s, drys infused their accounts of the liquor business with the terms and imagery of the antitrust movement. They denounced saloon keepers as dupes of the "whiskey trust" or of other "villainous combines." They used the octopus, that all-purpose symbol of monopoly, to represent the liquor power. In one 1892 cartoon, the "octopus saloon" was depicted with one tendril crushing a helpless American woman, another overseeing murder and mayhem, and using yet another to hold Uncle Sam's leg, while its agent—an evil ogre dressed in a checked suit—bought government protection with a packet marked "revenue." Similarly, Fisk referred to the "rum power" as a "huge devil fish, whose body is in Washington, and whose slimy tentacles reach clear across the land." The federal tax, then, was the key to the relationship of the government and the liquor industry. According to drys, "In its dealing with the liquor traffic the government set the pattern for and instituted the first of those gigantic trusts, crystallized monopolies, which now prey remorselessly upon the lives and substance of the people." The nurturing nature of the tax created a "gigantic monopoly" in the liquor trade that became the "mastering spirits in our politics."[16]

The radical prohibitionists argued that the liquor power first exercised its strength by compelling the federal government to preserve its liquor tax. Prohibitionists pointed out that historically excises were emergency measures usually relinquished "when the means necessary to defray the expenditures of the government could be obtained from customs receipts." They wondered why the liquor tax did not follow this pattern and why it survived the repeal of the other wartime direct and income taxes. They concluded that the "liquor power" conspired to preserve the tax, so as to use it as a shield against attack. In fact, nearly every wet defense of liquor raised the issue of revenue that would be lost if prohibition were adopted. For instance, the *National Liberty Herald* pointed out that national prohibition would cause "bankruptcy" of local, state, and national governments.[17]

In the prohibitionist view, the shortsightedness of modern politicians contributed to the retention of the liquor tax, which drys thought flatly contradicted the dictates of sound public policy. They believed that the economic costs of the liquor traffic more than offset the tax revenues; "for every dollar the government receives from the liquor traffic, the people must pay ten dollars in support of its consequent evils." Drys, who stoutly believed that intoxicating liquor impoverished people, stimulated crime, and endangered the good order of society, saw the government's participation in the degradation of the nation as monstrous. They were fond of comparing the attitude of the civilized, "professedly Christian" American government to that of the Chinese emperor and the queen of Madagascar, who resisted the opium trade. The emperor's reputed statement—"It is a shame for a government to derive revenue from that which debases and debauches its people"—summarized the radical prohibitionist attitude toward the public policy ramifications of the federal liquor tax.[18]

In the 1880s and 1890s most drys, guided by the radical temperance ideology and caught up in emotional attacks on trusts, condemned the excise tax. Essentially their position was that the tax strengthened the liquor industry, sanctioned its activities, and dirtied the nation's honor. As its revenues blunted the "conscience" of the public, it hurt the nation. In sum, the tax was "vicious and demoralizing" and stood "in the way of reform." This prohibitionist mentality similarly dictated their solution to the problem: repeal of the tax.[19]

In 1882 the national conventions of the WCTU and the Prohibition party called for repeal of the federal liquor tax as a way of erasing the evils sanctioned by that tax. Reflecting their absolutist ideology and their Mosaic ideal of law, they believed that repeal would dissolve the partnership between the government and the liquor industry. Ending the law's recognition of the trade, drys thought, would strip liquor of all pretense to legitimacy. Further, severing the fiscal tie, "the spinal column of the traffic," would diminish the industry's grip on the nation's economy and politics. Beyond these benefits, prohibitionists contended that the national government's example would be contagious. If Congress abolished its excise tax, the states would follow suit, repealing their tax and license laws. They reasoned that "the removal of all excise laws from the statute books would make prohibition a near certainty."[20]

Calls for abolition of the federal excise tax did not make repeal a reality. First, the repeal sentiment aroused dissenting views within the temperance crusade. Second, outside the movement the move for change met with a serious obstacle: what would replace the liquor tax's revenues if it were abolished? These factors undercut the repealers' arguments, but the key problem was that in the 1880s and 1890s the prohibitionists lacked political influence in Washington. Indeed, in the second decade of the twentieth century, after the temperance movement had gained muscle and urged national prohibition, the loss-of-revenue argument carried little weight.[21]

Even at its peak, the agitation for repeal of the federal tax had opponents within the temperance movement itself. These drys did not drink from the same cup as the radical prohibitionists. They looked back to the policies of the 1870s and offered a view of the tax that conflicted with that of the abolitionists. They argued that the tax was regulatory in effect. Typical of their arguments, though much longer and better researched than most, was a pamphlet written by William H. Armstrong and published by the National Temperance Society in 1889. Armstrong, a committed dry, had been assistant solicitor for the Office of Internal Revenue from 1868 to 1885. He hoped to see a liquor-free nation, but until that day, he announced, "I am for obstructing the business with as heavy burdens, and onerous restrictions, as it is possible to enforce against it." He argued that the federal liquor tax worked as such a restriction, resting "*ponderously upon* that business, crushing it into smaller compass than it would otherwise occupy, and depriving it of much of its vitality." To release the liquor industry from the prison of federal taxation, he argued, would be folly.[22]

Protaxers believed that its chief benefit lay in increasing the price of liquor, which lowered consumption. One prohibitionist, in an 1888 letter to the *Union Signal*, forecast the results of repeal of the liquor tax. Abolition "would reduce the price of whisky to twenty cents a gallon" and would debauch the people. "We would have drunken men, drunken women, drunken children." Since the extermination of liquor was not soon forthcoming, "we ought to make it high-priced, to keep it out of as many homes as possible." Temperance supporters of the federal tax feared that repeal would usher in an era of "free whiskey" and drown the nation in booze.[23]

Prohibitionists who opposed the repeal of the tax also raised the issue of lost revenue. They argued that abolition was impractical because politicians and policymakers would not surrender the money generated by the liquor tax. They read the era's politicians correctly. Leading Republicans and Democrats took stands against repeal or reduction of the tax. In the 1880s two presidential standard-bearers of the major parties—James G. Blaine and Grover Cleveland—opposed repeal of the internal revenue tax on liquor. Among politicians, only strong protectionists supported repeal of the liquor tax, but only as a way to guarantee the survival of their favored policy, a high tariff. Reformers were confronted with the sobering fact that repealing the liquor tax significantly reduced federal revenues. Naturally, they resented this argument and denounced it in the strongest of terms: "Ever since thirty pieces of silver bought the betrayal of the world's Redeemer the clink of silver coins has stilled all holy voices, all piteous appeal." But verbal bombast did not change fiscal reality.[24]

Up to 1890, the issue of how to replace the lost revenues seemed inconsequential as the high tariff and other taxes created a federal surplus. Prohibitionists argued that given the surplus, time was ripe for abolition of the liquor tax; the surplus would buffer the nation against fiscal disaster. In 1884 the *Voice* calculated that federal excise taxes could be done away with, leaving ten million dollars in federal coffers. Government officials scorned such proposals, and even the less drastic step of reducing the tax was dismissed by officials. Daniel Manning, President Cleveland's first secretary of the treasury, thought that reducing the tax would increase consumption. Therefore, "any probable reduction of the tax on whiskey would be more likely to increase the revenue than diminish it." But the activities of tariff reformers and the "billion-dollar" Congress of 1890 ended all hopes of a quick and painless repeal, and prohibitionists were forced to offer alternatives to the liquor tax.[25]

Drys argued that the federal government should replace "the dirty dollars it obtains from the liquor traffic" by enacting new taxes. To counter the loss-of-revenue argument, prohibitionists advocated direct taxes, inheritance taxes, and particularly graduated income taxes. They chose these methods of taxation because they reflected the drys' worldview that sacrifices must be made for the public good. Radical prohibitionists argued that replacing the liquor tax with a more direct tax would benefit everyone by diminishing the liquor industry, a result that would offset any additional tax burdens imposed on individuals.[26]

The impassioned denunciations of the federal liquor tax, the earnest discussion of the benefits of its repeal, and recommendations of alternatives produced little action. In 1906 the *Union Signal* noted that several temperance-backed proposals to alter the liquor tax were pending in Congress, but admitted that not one bill "asks for the entire removal of the revenue tax." The paper accurately characterized the whole period of radical prohibition. Until 1900 drys—under the leadership of the Prohibition party and the WCTU—lacked the political might to convince anyone to introduce a bill that would repeal the tax or even to call for its abolition on the floor of Congress. The radicals' proposals were merely "paper bullets of the partisan prohibition press"; they had no substance and little impact.[27]

In the 1880s and 1890s the radicals' conception of the liquor tax, which predominated within the temperance movement, acted as a hindrance to temperance progress. Most prohibitionists shared the visionary ideal of abolishing the federal excise tax on liquors. This view pitted the movement against the existing polity, dominated by the political parties that found the revenues from the liquor industry a convenient source of government funds. The abolitionist view also made the emerging bureaucratic state—epitomized by the revenue officers who oversaw and regulated the liquor industry—an enemy of their movement. Thus, not surprisingly, drys' plans to repeal the tax never left the realm of theory. While the radicals honed their arguments, other prohibitionists working in the states began to realize the possible value of the federal tax records to their cause.

The internal revenue taxes of the Civil War produced an innovation in federal taxation—the federal license tax on occupations. During the war the government levied a license fee on over thirty common trades, including liquor manufacturing, liquor wholesaling, and liquor retailing. In general the license taxes were short lived. In 1871 Congress repealed all except those imposed on the liquor and tobacco trades. The creation of the license system raised questions about the relationship between federal and state authority, and the perpetuation of the liquor license had important ramifications for the temperance movement.[28]

The key issue in the prohibition context was whether Congress could license a trade in a state where the state's law prohibited the practice of that trade. Congress attempted to meet this problem by inserting an explicit disclaimer into the tax act. The disclaimer provided that the payment of internal revenue tax did not "exempt any person" from state laws against "carrying on any trade" or "authorize the commencement or continuance of such trade." Despite this provision, dealers in the states that strictly regulated liquor selling and prohibited lotteries claimed immunity from state laws because they possessed "federal licenses." In Massachusetts the situation quickly became absurd. It presented a "singular spectacle" of "several people being arrested and put in jail by the state, in the morning" for selling intoxicants "*under* a federal license," but in the afternoon "an equal number of other persons were arrested and sent to the same jail, on behalf of the United States," for selling liquor without one.

In 1866 a group of cases arising from such circumstances reached the U.S. Supreme Court. But before judgment could be rendered, Congress sought to remove ambiguity by changing throughout the statute the term "license," which implied permission, to "special tax," which did not. In the *License Tax Cases*, the Supreme Court concurred with Congress's view of the tax, concluding that "these licenses give no authority, they are mere receipts for taxes." The Court also ruled that the states' prohibition of a trade did not justify nonpayment of the federal special tax. In essence the *License Tax Cases* ruling made permanent the status quo. While it settled the issues of federalism, it perpetuated the absurdity of a "federal license" that conferred nothing.[29]

Since Congress, the Supreme Court, and various state courts had declared that payment of the special federal tax on liquor selling did not authorize the violation of state prohibition laws, most Americans should have had some idea that the special tax receipt was not a license. After 1891 liquor dealers had no excuse for confusing the two. In that year, the certificate given to liquor dealers when they paid their tax had the substance of the federal government's 1866 law—which disclaimed any licensing effects—printed across it in red ink. Yet, as one Alabama prohibitionist claimed, "the idea remained abroad" that the federal tax conferred a license.[30]

Prohibitionists like the leader of the Maine WCTU, Lillian Stevens, often referred to their encounters with illegal sellers who claimed federal sanction for their operations. She reported a conversation with "a young man" who had "opened what seemed to me a drinking place. I talked with him about it and he replied 'I have my license' showing me the receipt for his United States tax." This young man went to jail to learn the distinction between a special tax receipt and a license. Many prohibitionists shared his misconception about the nuances of the law. The prohibition press strove to set them straight. The papers were fond of quoting the language of the federal statute, which stated that the tax did not afford any protection from state laws, and citing court decisions reaffirming this view. Indeed, temperance papers covered the topic so fully that the *Voice* announced that it was "growing weary" of explaining the subject.[31]

The radical prohibitionist ideology contributed to this confusion about the implications of the liquor tax. Drys loosely referred to the tax receipt as a license. In their desire to repeal the tax, some Prohibition party members asserted that the special stamp was, in fact, a license. They argued that the congressional substitution of "special tax" for "license" was merely cosmetic. "Its name alone is changed," wrote one. Others (most notably Finley C. Hendrickson) argued that the federal tax receipt was a license because it acted exactly like a state license. With such mixed signals, it is no wonder that some temperance advocates remained confused about the issue.[32]

This confusion helped to convince many drys that the federal government actively aided their opponents. They believed that by "licensing" illegal sellers in the states, the federal government cemented its partnership with the liquor interests. Federal policies added weight to this contention. For prohibitionists three practices proved especially galling: the auctioning of seized liquor; the compromise system used in tax evasion cases; and, most important, restrictions imposed on the use of federal tax lists. Taken together, these actions strengthened the drys' belief that national government aided their enemy. Speaking of these policies, one dry proclaimed, "The rum power with the federal government as its head and front trample[s] upon the rights and expressed wishes of the people."[33]

Without intending to, the national government exacerbated its poor relations with the temperance movement by auctioning liquor seized for nonpayment of taxes and by imposing light penalties on liquor dealers who failed to pay their special tax. In each instance, the government acted with just one end in mind, raising revenue. It pursued these policies nationwide with no complaints, except from prohibition states. In temperance territory these practices were tantamount to slaps in the face.

The Internal Revenue Office and the Customs Service routinely auctioned off materials seized to meet a taxpayer's delinquent bill. The government auctions were a good way of disposing of the seized material and generating revenue. Much to the dismay of prohibitionists, the government made no allowance for the local liquor laws in holding these auctions. The *Voice* pointed out an instance in which a quantity of liquor was sold in dry territory "in broad daylight, in a public place" after "its sale had been openly advertised for several days before in the Post Office." Despite local prohibition laws, "the great federal government was selling that rum" and without a license required of common vendors. Regardless of the prohibitionists' furor, such auctions continued unabated throughout the period.[34]

Government treatment of violators of the tax laws also angered drys. Federal statutes provided strict penalties, including jail sentences, for failure to pay liquor taxes. In practice, however, the Internal Revenue Office determined that, for purposes of raising revenues, jailing potential taxpayers made little sense. Officials routinely compromised in nonpayment cases, usually simply doubling the special tax or levying some other fine. The office processed so many of these cases that it vested individual collectors with the power to make such compromises. In dry territory the effect of this practice was that illegal sellers caught by the government had only to pay their tax due plus a penalty to resume their trade. Prohibitionists were convinced that this practice was merely the government's way of "protecting the liquor criminals." They also believed that another policy, restriction of access to the tax lists, extended further protection to the junior partner in the "government liquor business."[35]

The ruling in the *License Tax Cases*, when combined with an 1872 law, created an unexpected windfall for prohibitionists. As the government limited its taxes to excises on liquor and tobacco, it also cut back on the number of internal revenue officials. With fewer officials Congress determined that making the tax lists accessible to the public would reduce opportunities for graft and corruption. Thus, from 1872 forward, federal law required each internal revenue collector to "place and keep conspicuously in his office, for public inspection, an alphabetical list of the names of all persons who shall have paid special taxes within his district" and to "state thereon the time, place, and business for such special taxes have been paid." As a double check, the government also required, under threat of penalty, that the taxpayer "keep conspicuously in his establishment or place of business all stamps denoting the payment of the said special tax." In effect, this provision compelled all violators of state prohibition laws, under the duress of federal prosecution, to advertise their violation of state bans.[36]

Temperance advocates involved in enforcing local liquor laws tried to turn these documents to their own use. Since by common law rules of evidence such materials were admissible in court, prohibitionists and state officials used them to prosecute illegal liquor sellers. As most drys had no legal training—and possessed a predilection for statutory law—they moved to codify these common law rules. By making them into legislation drys sought to make the regulatory possibilities of the federal liquor tax records known to all. So, in the late 1880s, states began to pass laws embodying the common law rule.[37]

Within a three-month period in 1887, the legislatures of Maine and Massachusetts codified the common law rule that possession of the U.S. revenue stamp constituted prima facie evidence of liquor law violations. These laws were designed to ease the burden of proof in liquor prosecutions and were predicated on the idea that "it is evident that no one would pay the twenty-five dollar fee to the federal government unless he were really violating the state liquor law." The Massachusetts statute made the posting of the U.S. tax receipt as a liquor retailer or wholesaler (malt liquor excepted) prima facie evidence that the holder was engaged in illegal liquor selling. The Maine legislature cast its net wider, declaring that "the payment of the United States special tax, as a liquor seller . . . shall be held to be prima facie evidence that the person or persons paying said tax . . . are common sellers of intoxicating liquors." By not specifying that the posted tax receipt constituted evidence, the Maine legislature opened the door for state officials to use federal collectors' tax rolls as evidence. This dimension of the law caused "a stir" and was admitted by prohibitionists to be "a very radical clause." The timing of the creation Maine and Massachusetts statutes seeking to use the federal tax power to supplement state prohibition reflected developments in the polity prompted by the pure food movement.[38]

If temperance and prohibition were "the reform issues that made the most insistent claim on the postwar American polity," attempts to regulate and prohibit adulteration of foods and medicines were a close second. Indeed, between 1879 and 1906 almost 200 bills to protect the nation's consumers were introduced in Congress. In particular, one food—oleomargarine—prompted a full range of responses from the polity, including, in 1886, a federal regulatory tax. While the controversy over oleo to a great degree was a clash over economic interests, the parallels between its history and the history of liquor, in both the states and the federal system, make it a particularly instructive example of how reformers and interest groups, first frustrated by the nature of the polity, could creatively use its existing structure to their ends.[39]

The new foods like oleomargarine, the fruits of nineteenth-century science and industry, generated much governmental action. Oleo was manufactured by churning rendered animal oils (and after World War I vegetable oils) with skim milk to produce a white paste similar to butter in taste, appearance, and food value. In the United States, besides stand-alone manufacturers of the product, the large Chicago meat-packing companies like Armour and Swift made oleo production a valuable sideline to their business. Its relative cheapness made it a good substitute for butter. Indeed, oleo's low cost tempted many businesses to engage in fraud by adding color and passing the product off as butter. Thus, the new product threatened the dairy industry, directly and indirectly; and because of abuse in the food industry it also threatened the public. The oleomargarine industry, reflecting the larger food distribution network, had its share of unscrupulous vendors willing to sell adulterated and unwholesome products. In the bad food scares that periodically swept the nation, oleo gained an evil reputation.

In the late 1870s and early 1880s, when the manufacturing and marketing of food became more impersonal and mysterious, people began to become worried over the purity of their food and oleomargarine soon became a health concern. Moralistic denunciations of bogus butter, exposé stories on the alleged unhealthy materials that went into it, and accounts of adulteration of the product all appeared in the press. In states with a strong dairy industry these concerns were expressed in law. A number of states, and even Congress for the District of Columbia, required that the product be labeled as oleomargarine. In the 1880s, under pressure from dairy interests and reform groups, states moved beyond regulation to prohibit the product. By 1890 seven states had banned its manufacture and sale. At the same time the reformers and the dairy industry sought federal action to control oleo.

Early in 1886 a convention of dairy farmers and businesses proposed that Congress enact legislation to regulate or suppress oleo. Congressmen from dairy states listening to their constituents decided on a tax of ten cents per pound on oleo—which in effect was a regulatory tax. Its supporters claimed that the oleo industry had grown so strong that state legislatures could not control it and that it threatened one of the largest industries in the nation, dairying. Moreover, they pointed out that the exporting of oleo falsely labeled as butter threatened overseas markets. They justified the heavy tax rate by asserting that the liquor tax functioned in the same way. The opponents of the bill alleged that it was unconstitutional. Led by southern Democrats John Reagan, Zebulon Vance, and Richard Coke (all of whom used similar arguments in opposing the Wilson Bill four years later), they asserted that the tax trespassed on the states' police powers. But their arguments only induced Congress to reduce the tax rate from ten to two cents a pound when it passed the bill.

The oleo tax was the first post-Reconstruction federal regulatory tax and like many pioneer measures did not function perfectly. The 1886 law set up a tax system along the lines of the system used to tax liquor, imposing license fees on makers, wholesalers, and retailers. All involved in the trade were to file annual reports and fix tax stamps on oleo packages, showing that they paid the federal tax of two cents for domestic oleo and fifteen cents for oleo to be sent overseas. But the act's low tax rate meant that it did not destroy the oleo industry; rather, it led to the concentration of the industry around packing companies. As a potentially profitable sideline the packers continued to seek means to avoid discriminatory regulation and prohibition. Moreover, the tax conferred legitimacy on oleomargarine—it was now sanctioned by the federal government as a commodity in international and interstate commerce. Thus neither the pro-oleo nor anti-oleo forces remained satisfied, and they continued to seek more favorable action for their causes from the polity.

The legislative history of oleo was only part of the tale, as in "the state of courts" the manufacturers and retailers of oleo tested the bans through litigation. At first their efforts failed. In state courts the record was mixed. Many state courts upheld the bans, while others struck them down. For instance, Missouri's courts found that state's "Bogus Butter Act" a legitimate use of the police power, but New York's highest appellate court ruled the state's ban an unconstitutional deprivation of liberty. Then the oleo industry turned to the federal courts for relief; in *Powell v. Pennsylvania*, an 1886 case before the U.S. Supreme Court, the oleo industry asserted that the ban on oleo amounted to a taking of property without compensation and denied the liberty to engage in a trade contrary to the due process clause of the Fourteenth Amendment. As in the liquor case of *Mugler v. Kansas*, the Court rejected the claim and found the oleo ban a legitimate use of the police power.[40]

As most states did not ban the product, as the federal tax did not drive it from the market, and as the Court had said that oleo was a proper subject for state police action, the anti-oleo forces lobbied for new regulations to burden oleomargarine. Two types of regulations became the prime means of restricting the product. The first type prohibited oleo from being colored in imitation of butter. The second type required oleo to be colored pink to be sold in the jurisdiction. In the face of state action, just as the liquor industry persisted in raising federal questions after the defeat in *Mugler*, so the oleo industry returned to the courts in the 1890s. And in the 1890s it brought the state oleo laws before the Court on new federal questions.

For the oleo industry the result was mixed. When oleo manufacturers challenged a Massachusetts law that prohibited the sale of colored margarine as violating the national revenue law, they lost. The Court ruled that the ban on coloring was a reasonable statute designed to prevent fraud. But four years later the oleo industry won on an original package challenge to state oleo bans. States were prohibited from banning oleomargarine imported from other states while still in its original package. And the oleo makers succeeded in getting the Court to apply the original package doctrine to state laws that required oleo to be colored pink. But the victories for the industry in the courts were short lived. Following in the footsteps of the prohibitionists in interstate commerce doctrine and taking their own pioneering steps in tax law, anti-oleo forces returned to the Congress. There they won passage of a law styled after the Wilson Act for oleomargarine and a new federal tax law that dropped the rate on uncolored margarine to half a cent per pound but levied a tax of ten cents per pound on yellowed-colored oleo.[41]

Thus colored margarine—which might pass for butter—was driven from the market by the combination of federal and state law. But because of its cheapness, the uncolored product—sold with a packet of coloring to be mixed by consumers who could not endure its natural color—flourished. The oleo tax never raised significant revenue, as it was always designed as regulation and thus aroused little resistance among federal revenue officials. But this was not the case with the liquor tax. It had long been a key part of government finance; moreover, federal tax officials had good relations with the liquor industries. Not surprisingly, when faced with prohibition states that wished to use the tax system to prosecute illegal sellers, the Internal Revenue Office acted to preserve the tax-gathering functions of the liquor tax.

The officials of the Internal Revenue Office created and then maintained a consistent policy toward the states' desire to use internal revenue records as evidence in prosecuting illegal liquor dealers. Working within the confines of legislation, the officials determined that, while not actively hindering the states' actions, they would render no aid. After the policy was set, collectors and their subordinates would not impede anyone from reading the list of special taxpayers required by law to be posted and available for public inspection, but they would not testify or produce internal revenue records in the courts. In the late 1880s, after a period of some confusion, this view emerged as official policy. By 1900 it was hardened into a concrete rule tested by the federal courts.

From the inception of the liquor tax until the middle of the 1880s, the role of the federal tax records in state liquor law violations remained unclear. At this time, as the foundations for later policies were being laid, some federal officials acted contrary to the future policies of the government. The most glaring exception to the later rules was the willingness of collectors to testify in state courts. In Vermont around 1870 collector A. J. Crane and his deputy, E. A. Jewett, took the witness stand against liquor dealers accused of violating the state's prohibition laws. To corroborate their testimony both men produced their assessment rolls. Since the prohibition movement was moribund during this period, such instances were probably rare. The basis of the Internal Revenue Office policy regarding access to its tax rolls emerged not in conflicts between federal officials and state prohibition but in other areas.[42]

In the late 1870s Internal Revenue Office officials started refusing to allow their records to be entered as evidence in court. The issue first arose in a 1876 libel case, *Gardner v. Anderson*. The secretary of the treasury removed Thomas Gardner from his clerkship in the Internal Revenue Office on the recommendation of tax appraiser Ephraim Anderson. In federal district court Gardner contended that malice motivated Anderson, and he subpoenaed his correspondence with the secretary of the treasury. The secretary refused to appear or produce the documents, arguing that the letters "were official in their nature, confidential and protected from disclosure." The district court accepted the secretary's explanation and ruled against Gardner, who appealed to the U.S. Circuit Court for Maryland. The circuit court also agreed with the secretary's conclusion and extended his reasoning. It asserted that "communications in writing passing between officers of the government, in the course of official duty, relating to the business of their offices" were "on the grounds of public policy" considered "privileged from disclosure." Courts could not compel their production.[43]

A year later the issue of confidentiality of the internal revenue records was again before the federal courts. This time the Internal Revenue Office referred the question to the highest legal officer in the Hayes administration. In two separate cases Attorney General Charles Devens advised the Internal Revenue Office not to release its records to courts. The first instance arose when a group of lawyers sued for their attorney fees in an Illinois state court.

Their client had been convicted of internal revenue law violations, and they had the court subpoena the correspondence between the revenue official and the U.S. attorney. What they hoped to learn by production of these records remains unclear. What is important is the position that Attorney General Devens assumed in advising the Internal Revenue Office not to comply with the subpoena. Devens wrote that the correspondence was by nature "privileged," and its disclosure would "frustrate the ends sought to be accomplished by the federal government," proving "detrimental to public interest."[44]

The next year, Devens advised the Internal Revenue Office to refuse to obey a subpoena of a U.S. Circuit Court, which sought the internal revenue records in an attempt to prove that a collector "framed" defendants in a case of underpayment of federal taxes. Again Devens stressed that the records were privileged, as "they are in nature of confidential communications, intended by a sub-officer to enable a superior to perform the duty required of him by law." The idea that government records were confidential and that disclosure would violate public policy gained in stature by being espoused by the attorney general. When the semiofficial paper *Internal Revenue Record* published the attorney general's letters, these doctrines became readily available to tax officials. They would be applied to the novel situation where state officials requested federal records for state liquor law prosecutions.[45]

The revival of the prohibition movement in the 1880s provoked negative reactions from the internal revenue officers. It is impossible to determine whether their actions represented an Internal Revenue Office policy or simply the personal attitudes of the officials. Since evidence exists for both views, this was perhaps one of the times when officials' sentiments coincided with the government's plans. In 1886 and 1887 the federal government, in the person of the collectors and their subordinates, obstructed prohibition efforts in the states. Perhaps the most controversial action taken by the officials was the practice of hindering the examination of the list of special taxpayers that collectors were required to post.

In 1886 the collector for many of the dry counties of Georgia, Thomas C. Crenshaw, expressed his views about prohibition and the role the federal collectors should play in aiding the prohibition states. To the question "You have the record here: is it open to inspection?" Crenshaw replied, "The law says it shall be, but I have been advised to resist any attempt that may be made to secure the records to the purpose of prosecutions under the state laws." Crenshaw promised to "use every effort to defeat" the use of his records as "evidence against retailers." He thought it "manifestly wrong for the United States to license a man to retail liquor and then furnish the evidence on which he is convicted under state law"; he concluded, "I am a tax collector, not the guardian of the prohibition laws. I am not here to suppress liquor making or liquor selling." Crenshaw's words were reprinted without commentary in the *Internal Revenue Record*.[46]

Prohibitionists decried such "obstreperousness on the part of the revenue collectors" and believed that Crenshaw's remarks reflected official policy. To support this contention, the *Union Signal* altered his statement, changing "I have been advised" to "I have been advised by those higher in authority than I." For temperance advocates, Crenshaw's motivation, as well as other collectors' obstructions to making public their lists, stemmed from their desire to protect the government's lucrative tax revenues and their own jobs. Prohibition would limit the tax base and thus "would be like killing the goose that laid the golden egg." Whether the prohibitionists were correct in their view or not, the practice of limiting access to the posted list of special taxpayers quickly diminished.[47]

By mid-1887 the commissioner of internal revenue, Joseph S. Miller, set government policy concerning the posted tax lists. Commissioner Miller's ruling complied with the expressed wish of Congress that the tax lists be open for public inspection. He made clear his position in a letter to B. F. Wright, an Iowa prohibitionist, who complained to President Cleveland about the abuses in the Iowa collectors' offices. These practices included an abbreviation scheme that made the public lists incomprehensible as well as restrictions placed upon the users of the posted lists. On May 23 the commissioner replied for the president, and his letter was subsequently published by the *Voice*. He wrote that the Internal Revenue Office prescribed a form for the keeping of the records. By agency guidelines, the public list was to include "an alphabetical list of the *Names* of all persons who shall have paid special taxes . . . and the time, place, and business for which such special taxes have been paid." Miller reiterated that the list was to be "kept conspicuously in the collector's office, for public inspection." He then assured Wright that "if the collectors are not observing the law in good faith, a proper remedy will be applied." Fulfilling the letter of the law was as far as Commissioner Miller intended to go to placate the prohibitionists. In matters that Congress had not contemplated, such as testimony of collectors in courts and production of their records as evidence, he took a stand less pleasing to prohibitionists.[48]

In the late 1880s federal tax officials and authorities in the prohibition states clashed over the federal tax records; in every jurisdiction in which they were asked to be witnesses in prosecutions for state liquor law violations, revenue collectors refused either to testify or to produce their records for the courts. The states of Iowa, Kansas, and Maine jailed collectors for contempt because of their refusal to produce their records. From later action it is clear that the Internal Revenue Office under Commissioner Miller was forging a policy of limited cooperation with the prohibition states. The collectors jailed by the states sought habeas corpus in federal courts, perhaps indicating that these officials were eager to have a judicial determination of their emerging policy.[49]

The prohibitionists, while incensed by the actions of the collectors, misread the Internal Revenue Office's intentions. They did not perceive that the government wished to settle its relations with the prohibition states. Prohibitionists believed that the Cleveland administration, faced with Maine's jailing of revenue officials, sought to avoid the issue. They portrayed the combining of the revenue districts of prohibition Maine and Vermont with wet New Hampshire as "subterfuges" of a government "determined to shield its partners, the liquor sellers." To make this contention the crusaders wrenched the New England redistricting out of its context. It came during a general reorganization of all collection districts and reflected the decreased revenues produced by the two prohibition states. Nevertheless, the new district had one collector, Calvin Page, and he was no friend to temperance. Until directly ordered by Commissioner Miller, he denied prohibitionists use of the public tax lists. Page's residence in New Hampshire and the merging of districts transferred the records and the person of the collector beyond the reach of prohibition state law. Despite the reorganization, Maine used its new prima facie law to try to compel Page to testify and to produce his records.[50]

Prohibitionists were aware that prima facie laws raised the possibility of potential conflict between state and national officials. The *Voice* "doubted whether the state authorities can compel" federal revenue officers "to produce the needed evidence." Soon after the passage of the Maine law, Page was besieged with subpoenas, but he ignored the processes. As 1888 opened, the courts of Vermont and New Hampshire added their requests to his growing pile. In July 1888 Page referred the matter of the state court subpoenas to the commissioner's office.[51]

Commissioner Miller, in a letter to Page published in the *Internal Revenue Record*, publicly announced the Internal Revenue Office's policy and justifications. His letter summed up the agency's position for at least the next twenty years. He wrote that while his office had "no desire to throw any unnecessary obstacle in the way of enforcement of state laws, even though such enforcement should tend to diminish the internal revenue," it did "not concede the legal right of a state court to compel the production" of federal records. The legality of efforts made by several states "to compel their production" remained an open question. Until it was settled, the Internal Revenue Office ordered that the alphabetical list of taxpayers was "not to be removed from the collector's office." It was to be "kept conspicuously posted there for public inspection." He "respectfully insisted" that neither the tax return itself nor "information derived from it should be admitted on trial."

Miller rationalized this decision by arguing that a "special tax payer is required, under severe pains and penalties to make his return" and that this information was "extorted from him." Furthermore, it was "largely in the nature of a privileged communication which he is required to make to the revenue officer, *for revenue purposes and for these alone.*" He based this ruling on the case of *Gardner v. Anderson*. Admitting that the situation was not quite analogous, he nevertheless asserted that disclosure of communications "relating to public business" was contrary to "public policy and not to be permitted."[52]

In this letter Miller revealed mixed motives for the government's course. On one level he argued it was preserving national sovereignty from encroachments by the states, but he also admitted that the government was merely protecting its taxpayers. He put the public posting law to good use, arguing that, because the lists were public, there was no need for the collectors to bring them into court. Furthermore, since the lists were required to be kept in the collector's office, there was a statutory reason why it could not be removed to the court. His most creative moments came when he extended the doctrine of privileged communications to liquor dealers' tax returns. He glossed over the vast difference between protecting officials in the exercise of their duty and shielding liquor dealers suspected of violating state laws. His application of the language of "public policy" and "privileged communications" to the issue of collectors' testimony in state prohibition cases would become enshrined in later internal revenue circulars.

With the policy outlined and justified, Miller then turned to implementing it. He directed Page and his deputies to "respond to the subpoenas" but to "respectfully decline to produce" federal records. "If the Court should insist," he ordered them to consult the U.S. attorney and to remove the question to federal court, as the Internal Revenue Office "desires a careful consideration and authoritative decision of it." The procedures he detailed for Page to follow would become one of the hallmarks of the tax officials' responses in future confrontations with state courts. However, the "authoritative decision" on these issues would not be forthcoming quickly; it would not be announced until the first year of the twentieth century.[53]

From 1889 to 1897 the federal courts heard at least three habeas corpus petitions from U.S. deputy collectors of revenue. Each had been found in contempt of state court for refusing to testify or produce their records after being subpoenaed. Although Joseph Miller was no longer commissioner, his ideas shaped the course of each case, as the internal revenue officials justified their actions by invoking Miller's letter to Page.

The 1895 decision, *In Re Huttman*, the first case to reach the federal courts, produced a strong affirmation of the Internal Revenue Office's stand. Judge John A. Williams of the district court for Kansas argued that the case turned on the conflict between state police power and federal taxing power. The taxing power was essential to the government, for "if the general government has the power to do anything, it has the power to pass laws in relation to the raising of revenue. . . . This authority is supreme." Congress, under its taxing power, had granted authority to the secretary of the treasury and the commissioner of revenue to make regulations governing the collection of taxes. The court found Miller's guidelines to be such a regulation; since such regulations had the force of an act of Congress, the states had no right to hinder the officials. The judge declared that malice toward the prohibition policy of Kansas did not motivate his ruling when he wrote that the United States had no "desire to interfere with or prevent the enforcement of any criminal law." It acted only to protect the supremacy of national law.[54]

Within a year, another federal court had ruled against the Internal Revenue Office's standing policy, but this setback would be short lived. In *In Re Hirsch*, decided by the circuit court for Connecticut, the opinion of Judge Nathaniel Shipman refuted the arguments made by Commissioner Miller in his letter to Calvin Page. Judge Shipman brusquely dismissed Hirsch's contention that he was operating under the department's rules: "No regulation upon the subject . . . is contained in the printed book of general regulations which has been issued for the guidance of internal revenue officers." Judge Shipman ruled that Miller's letter was not a regulation but merely "instructions based on the Commissioner's legal opinion." The judge further argued that the supposed rule "would not seem to be in harmony with the principle of internal revenue legislation" that the payment of federal taxes afforded no immunity from state laws. He next attacked the idea that tax returns were privileged communications: "that they are papers of the United States does not make them superior to the ordinary means proved by law for the production of private and public papers for the use in courts." Finally, Shipman assailed the idea that disclosure of the tax information worked an unfairness on the liquor dealers. He noted, "There can be no implied obligation upon the government, because it has received a special tax from an offender against the laws of the state, to shield him from the consequences of his act." While this opinion tore a sizable hole in the fabric of the Internal Revenue Office's policy, it was easily patched.[55]

Two years later another court decision repaired the Internal Revenue Office's handiwork. *In Re Weeks*, decided by Judge Hoyt H. Wheeler for the district court for Vermont, took up where *Huttman* left off. The judge distinguished *Hirsch* by noting that Miller's letter applied to the collection district where *Weeks* arose. Judge Wheeler made it clear that the policy determined by Commissioner Miller was legitimate and "in accordance" with federal law and policy. He compared the revenue officers' determination not to reveal to state officials what they learned about liquor sellers through their official duties to the activities of the federal court system. He argued, "This is somewhat as if a federal district attorney or grand juror should be imprisoned to compel disclosure of proceedings before the grand jury which might be very material in a trial elsewhere." Just as such state interference would not be tolerated in the courts, it could not be tolerated in the tax system either. State officials had "no right to federal instruments of purely federal character for proof." In short, the tax records were privileged.[56]

Despite the doubt cast on the legitimacy of their policy by the *Hirsch* ruling, internal revenue officials continued to apply it. On April 1, 1898, Commissioner Nathan B. Scott denied requests for copies of records to be used as evidence against liquor dealers accused of violating Maryland's local option laws. Scott justified this ruling by arguing that the records were kept for tax purposes only and that any other use would be "contrary to public policy." He buttressed his assertions by concluding that this position was a "long-settled" rule, "fully sustained by decisions of United States courts," and cited *Huttman* and *Weeks* to support his claim. That he ignored the *Hirsch* ruling is telling. Scott was not ignorant of the case; at that very moment, his office was preparing a formal regulation to overcome Judge Shipman's decision.[57]

Two weeks later the Treasury Department and the Internal Revenue Office drafted explicit regulations on the subject. Promulgated on April 15, 1898, the new regulations relied heavily on the early work of Commissioner Miller. In some places the drafters incorporated his exact language into the regulations. They prohibited collectors from giving out any special tax records to local officials, private citizens, or to state magistrates in answer to subpoenas. If served with a subpoena, these individuals were required to appear in court and "respectfully decline to produce the records called for, on the grounds of being prohibited therefrom by the regulations of this department." The refusal was justified on the now familiar grounds of "public policy," and "records were to be used for taxation purposes only." If copies of the records were sought by parties to a suit, the matter, along with a copy of the request, should be sent to the treasury secretary's office, which would determine whether the circumstance merited their release.[58]

At the same time that federal officials wrote Miller's views on testifying into the official regulations, they also preserved his doctrine that officials should not interfere with the public inspection of the alphabetical lists of special tax payers. In two letters sent to collectors, published in *Treasury Decisions* and therefore carrying the weight of administrative law, the commissioner made it clear that collectors should not abridge the rights of individuals who wished to inspect the list. They should not prevent the copying of names and addresses from it, and no permission was required to use the list. But they should not let one individual monopolize the list to the interference with the rights of the rest of the public or official use of it. Thus, the officials perpetuated Miller's views on the role of the federal internal revenue system in relation to the states. It would be another two years before the Internal Revenue Office received its long-sought, conclusive judicial determination on its policy.[59]

Ironically, it was the distilling state of Kentucky that brought about U.S. Supreme Court review of Internal Revenue Office policies toward the use of tax records. Kentucky levied a tax on its distillers; in a case of underpayment of the state tax, the state auditor had the court subpoena the collector and the federal tax lists. The collector, citing the Treasury Department's new rule, refused to produce the records or to testify about knowledge he derived from them. The state court held him in contempt of court. The U.S. district court judge, former internal revenue commissioner Walter Evans, granted his habeas corpus petition, and Kentucky appealed the decision to the Supreme Court.[60]

In the resulting case, *Boske v. Comingore,* Justice Harlan delivered the opinion of a unanimous Court. He wrote that the Treasury Department could rightfully refuse access to its records. Congress had given the secretary of the treasury and the commissioner of internal revenue the power to make regulations, provided that they were consistent with the law for the maintenance or records. The Treasury Department rule of 1898 did not violate any statute and therefore was legitimate. Justice Harlan went so far as to give several justifications for such a rule, among them protection of taxpayers: "The interests of persons compelled under the revenue laws, to furnish information as their private business affairs would often be seriously affected if the records were not guarded by such a rule." Thus, by the decision of the Supreme Court, in a matter only vaguely related to the enforcement of prohibition laws, the Internal Revenue Office's policy of rendering little aid to the prohibition states became judicially unassailable.[61]

Boske v. Comingore fixed the ideas first developed by Commissioner Miller as permanent policy in the Internal Revenue Office. After the ruling the next two commissioners saw fit to reiterate the 1898 rule in circulars. Beyond stating the rule, the commissioner's office applied it; it routinely turned down requests for records, whether they were to be used in prosecutions arising from state tax or prohibition laws. The mixed motives of protecting the national government's authority and shielding the special taxpayers continued to surface, clearly guiding the government's actions. In a letter sent to Congressman Charles H. Weisee, a member of the commissioner's staff explained just what materials would be released by the office: "Information disclosing the business of individual brewers is not given out, but where the aggregate figures for a city or a state are desired no objections to furnishing the same is made." Thus the special taxpayer's privacy was protected by the government against business competitors and to a limited degree against state officials intent on discovering violators of liquor laws.[62]

To many drys, the very existence of the federal liquor tax and its unsympathetic operation by internal revenue officers in the federal system seemed to indicate that the government intentionally acted to impede prohibition. While that might have been the intentions of individual bureaucrats, it was not the government's purpose. The federal government created and maintained the liquor tax to raise revenue. The Internal Revenue Office wrote its policies—the ban on testifying, the compromise system for tax evasion, and the tax auctions—with this goal in mind. But whatever the larger purposes, federal tax policy put the central government on a collision course with the drys. Radical drys demanded its repeal; prohibition states (emulating the dairy states, which had turned the tax power to their own advantage through the oleo tax) tried to use the tax system to help enforce their policies. The federal government rejected repeal and resisted the use of its tax system in the states. Thus, from the 1880s to the second decade of the twentieth century, prohibitionists remained irritated with the federal government; they called for the government to change its ways. But changes in federal tax policies came only after changes in the prohibition movement.

PRAGMATISTS AND THE POLITY

P A R T   T W O

THE TRANSFORMATION OF

PROHIBITIONIST MEANS

CHAPTER

For drys the 1880s and early 1890s marked an era of accomplishment and progress. Four states—Kansas (1880), Iowa (1884), North Dakota (1889), and South Dakota (1889)—joined Maine, Vermont, and New Hampshire in the dry fold, bringing the total number of prohibition states to seven. The 1890 Wilson Act promised to protect these dry havens from the corruptions of their wet neighbors. The growth of the Prohibition party, which in the 1888 election received 150,957 votes, made it a political force. The WCTU grew into the largest women's organization in the nation. At the same time the radical drys launched three utopian ventures, the Women's Temple office building in Chicago, Prohibition Park on Staten Island, and the prohibition-industrial community experiment in Harriman, Tennessee. Thus, the final decade of the nineteenth century opened auspiciously for the temperance reformers.[1]

But the 1890s, which began so promisingly for drys, quickly turned into a decade of disaster. Temperance progress, as measured by the adoption of state prohibition laws, halted abruptly. Even worse, the prohibition states proved anything but dry utopias as enforcement of liquor bans ranged from sporadic to nonexistent. The depression, the rise of Populism, the realignment in the nation's politics, and the emergence of alternative methods for taming the liquor industry further damaged the radical prohibition movement. The national prohibition organizations collapsed into squabbling camps in their efforts to meet the challenges of the decade and to restore appeal to the movement. As they failed, a new organization, the Anti-Saloon League, arose to fill the leadership vacuum.

The emergence of the Anti-Saloon League was part of a larger trend sweeping American society in the progressive era. As dry propagandist Louis Albert Banks expressed it in *Ammunition for Final Drive on Booze*, "This is the age of combination. The personal age has disappeared." Scholars have called this pattern "the organizational impulse." Samuel Hays first explored the drive to organize in economic groups, and Robert Wiebe extended this analysis to reformers. Norman Clark, Jack Blocker, and K. Austin Kerr have delineated how the league fit into the pattern by replacing the democratic structure and partisan politics of the WCTU and Prohibition party with a bureaucratic structure and pragmatic politics. What other scholars have not noted is that the Anti-Saloon League also reoriented dry legal conceptions. Its political methods would give it power, and its legal ideas would transform the movement; together, interacting with the legal environment, they led to the Eighteenth Amendment.[2]

The 1889 adoption of prohibition in the Dakotas ended the second prohibition wave. No other state went dry for the next eighteen years. In the same year voters in Massachusetts, Connecticut, and Washington rejected prohibition by large majorities. Two years later Nebraska refused to go dry. Even more ominous to prohibitionists, in 1889 Rhode Island rescinded its prohibition law, and in 1894 Iowa circumvented its prohibitory policy by taxing, through the Mulct Law, the illegal sellers of liquor. In effect, the Mulct Law operated as local option. Where dry sentiments prevailed no saloons opened, but in wet-leaning areas saloons opened and the government collected taxes from them. In the early 1890s rollback movements emerged in South Dakota and New Hampshire, and the pressure to repudiate dry policy grew in the course of the decade. With some justification the United States Brewers' Association thought prohibition on the decline throughout the decade. By 1903 the ranks of dry states had been reduced to Maine, Kansas, and North Dakota. Another problem went along with defections from the arid list—the poor enforcement of prohibitory laws.[3]

Even prohibitionists admitted that prohibition laws, more often than not, went unenforced. In Iowa the *Union Signal* conceded that the law was "trampled." In March 1891 a Kansas legislative investigating committee reported that the prohibitory laws went unenforced in every city of the state and that many municipalities actually taxed the illegal saloons. Two years later the Prohibition party paper the *Lever* found that in Kansas "the loft in the livery stable, the hole in the wall, and the subterraneous vault" were "peopled with those who drank to the failure of prohibition." Enforcement everywhere was episodic, usually prompted by local prohibitionist or citizen pressure. In the local option town of Dickson, Tennessee, the inhabitants began an enforcement drive after a man was "run over by a freight-car and killed while lying on the railroad track in a state of beastly intoxication." Despite such sporadic cleanups, temperance workers had to confront the sad truth that prohibition was not prohibiting.[4]

The national dry organizations responded in typical radical prohibitionist style to this lax enforcement of liquor laws. The Prohibition party portrayed the prohibition state officials' lack of vigor as evidence of the domination of the established, rum-soaked political parties. Consequently, they argued that, as regular party members would not enforce dry laws, the only way to implement these laws was to fill government offices with Prohibition party members. Nonenforcement, therefore, became a rationale for supporting the party; if elected, its members would staff the enforcement positions and not "violate the sacred trust imposed upon them by the people." Indeed, this theme became central to the Prohibition party's program and lasted through the era of national prohibition.[5]

The WCTU also saw officials as the problem. As one noted, "Even Maine has not reached that blessed stage when every officer elected does his whole duty unflinchingly." On the other hand, the white ribboners argued that even partial enforcement was better than high license or local option. A *Union Signal* article invoked a Mosaic conception of law in explaining how drys should view nonenforcement. It asserted that law had an educational "design which transcends the penal one." Thus, a prohibition law "that is not enforced" was better than enforced laws that legitimated the liquor evil because it pointed the people in the proper direction. An 1894 editorial in the same paper reiterated these themes when it compared local option to unenforced prohibition laws and found local option lacking: "The deadliest sin of local option is that it substitutes expediency for the 'shalt nots' of God's law." Local option had "no cleansing power to make black white." It did not lead the people but bewildered their moral sense. Nevertheless, fewer and fewer people heeded the radical prohibitionist message.[6]

During the 1890s other social and economic issues pushed prohibition from the center of political debate and weakened the Prohibition party as well as the radical dry appeal. The crises in American farming and later the depression of 1893 brought to prominence plans to restructure the nation's economy, to control corporations, and to alter the monetary system. As early as 1893, the *Lever* admitted that "upheaval on economic questions" made prohibition a "rather neglected" issue. A new political party, the People's party, or the Populists, became champion of these reforms. The rise of Populism weakened the pulling power of the Prohibition party by coopting economic reforms that had frequently appeared in the party's platforms. In 1892 the popularity of the People's party eclipsed the Prohibition party; while the prohibitionist total vote reached 264,133, the People's party earned over a million votes. Their issues, especially monetary reform, not prohibition, became the dominant political topic of the decade.[7]

The Prohibition party disintegrated over how best to meet the challenge of Populism. The party's first impulse was to attempt to ride the wave of new issues. For instance, some drys spoke favorably of the Populist subtreasury plan for agricultural products. In 1891 and 1892 drys—led by Frances Willard—tried to fuse with the Populists and the Knights of Labor into a grand reform coalition. These efforts failed and the Prohibition party contented itself with the adoption of a broad, general reform platform. However, this path aroused fears that prohibition would be lost among the other issues. The success of the Populists in the 1892 election strengthened the hand of those within the temperance movement calling for the Prohibition party to focus only on the prohibition issue. The divisions in the party led to vicious infighting; John G. Woolley later noted "the deepest scars I bear . . . were got in open war with dirt and demagogy within my own party." The wrangling between broad-gauge and single-gauge prohibitionists simmered for four years, finally boiling over during the 1896 party convention. After the adoption of a single-issue platform the broad-gauge faction bolted to form the National party. Two prohibition parties did no better than one.[8]

For drys, the 1896 election confirmed the *Union Signal's* assessment that "politically our country is in the 'mixed-upedest' condition it has been for many a year." The issue of free silver and the person of William Jennings Bryan captured the nation's attention. The partial fusion of Democrats and Populists left little room for the drys. The two prohibition parties of 1896 gleaned fewer votes than the single party had gained in 1892. Even worse for radical prohibitionists, the defectors from dry ranks followed Bryan into the Democratic party, the protector of the saloon and "personal liberty."[9]

The broad-gauge and narrow-gauge fracture in the Prohibition party was only one of several divisions that destroyed the cohesiveness of the movement's leadership. Even before the decade opened, the WCTU split over support for the Prohibition party. As early as 1884, J. Ellen Foster—leader of the Iowa WCTU—had questioned the wisdom of the third-party approach. For five years the national conventions were upset by her "perennial protest" and internal dissension, which became increasingly bitter. Frances Willard maneuvered Foster into an untenable position during the 1889 national convention, and Foster left the organization to form the Non-Partisan Women's Christian Temperance Union.

Willard's commitment to the party proved embarrassing when it failed to live up to her dreams, ultimately dissolving over the course of the decade. The stress on Willard exhausted her and compelled her virtually to abandon the leadership of the white ribboners. She went to Europe to convalesce, where she spent nearly all of 1892 and 1893 and much of 1895 and 1896. Her absence opened the doors for others to turn crises into power plays for control of the WCTU. Without firm leadership other circumstances accelerated the dissipation of the movement's energies.[10]

The panic and resulting depression disrupted every radical prohibitionist venture that required capital. The completed Women's Temple opened to a depressed economy and could not fill its office space. The depression bankrupted the East Tennessee Land Company, forcing the drys to abandon community building in Harriman. In trying to save these projects prohibitionists poured good money after bad and investors lost heavily. Only Prohibition Park did not fail; it remained an important center for temperance reform and political debate. However, hopes that the park would become a model dry community died as the depression ended its expansion.[11]

The financial crisis divided the leadership of the Prohibition party and the WCTU. As the losses mounted, rancor grew. Debts incurred by the Woman's Temperance Building Association turned the Women's Temple into a drain on the mother organization. The temple's condition dominated discussion at meetings, and efforts to make it solvent monopolized WCTU fundraising efforts. During the mid-1890s temple finances became a subject of division and debate. A powerful faction within the organization mounted an insurgency against the temple, Willard, and its other backers. The supporters of the temple held off moves to disaffiliate the WCTU from the temple until Willard's death in 1898, but only at the cost of increasing division in the organization.[12]

In the Prohibition party the collapse of the East Tennessee Land Company paralleled the temple episode in the WCTU. Party prohibitionists and other drys who had lost money directed much of their anger at publisher Isaac K. Funk, chief sponsor of the enterprise. Charges of watered stock and poor investments deepened hostility between broad-gaugers and the narrow-gauge group that Funk headed, contributing to the 1896 split of the party. Thus, by mid-decade, because of political realignment, depression, division within the movement, and a pause in prohibition progress, the radical temperance movement was in shambles. It was ill suited to meet the challenge of an innovative alternative to the saloon.[13]

In the early 1890s other options for controlling liquor emerged in the United States. These proposals repudiated the radical idea of divorcing saloon from state, replacing it with the notion that the government take over the trade. The genesis of this idea lay in the Swedish Gothenburg plan (adopted in the town of Gothenburg in 1865 and implemented in Norway in 1871), a system of municipal ownership and control over liquor selling. Complete government control, it was argued, would remove the profit motive from liquor selling, assure Sunday closing and limited hours, and guarantee the purity of the liquor. In 1891 the utopian thinker Edward Bellamy proposed eliminating the saloon by nationalizing liquor retailing. Only the national government through publicly run stores would dispense alcohol. Many Populists supported this plan, which dovetailed with their ideas for regulating the economy. This type of proposal, so visionary and hard to implement on the national level, quickly became a reality on the local level.[14]

In October 1891 the people of Athens, Georgia, displeased with the ineffectiveness of prohibition by local option, replaced it with a municipal dispensary. Authorized by a state law drafted by the leading lawyers of Athens, the system took aim at abuses of the saloon trade. The law forbade operation on Sundays, holidays, and election days; it also prohibited liquor by the drink and sales to minors. Liquor was purchased in bulk, chemically analyzed to insure its palatability, and sold in pint and larger bottles for a profit that was split between city and county. Others took notice. A similar plan was proposed for Sioux Falls, South Dakota, and citizens of Boston queried the Athens officials about their system. "Pitchfork" Benjamin Tillman, the new governor of South Carolina, found the program appealing and in 1893 created a statewide dispensary system. The South Carolina plan copied the main features of the Georgia law, except that it divided the profits between county and state; it also prohibited the manufacture of distilled spirits in the state. The adoption of the dispensary in South Carolina sidetracked state prohibition. In an advisory referendum, held in the same year that brought Tillman to the governorship, a majority of the state's voters voted for prohibition. Thus, dispensaries were a true challenge to prohibition, turning the only dry victory in a state in the period into a defeat.[15]

The rise of the dispensary further divided the temperance movement. The radicals could not rally dry forces to defeat what they saw as a threat, but they persisted in attacking it. Some prohibitionists found the dispensary an acceptable means to a prohibitionist end. In early 1893 the *Union Signal* pointed out the advantages of the dispensary. It destroyed saloons and made liquor drinking uncomfortable. "No more wine parties or champagne suppers in magnificently appointed rooms." It also weakened the brewing and distilling "syndicates." A large group in the Prohibition party saw Bellamy's nationalization scheme and Tillman's state dispensary as tools for building a large temperance coalition. Such a group of voters, these prohibitionists argued, would redirect the political system, bringing the liquor issue to the foreground. Tillman, attracted by an opportunity to develop a national constituency, debated leading prohibitionists at Prohibition Park in 1894 and 1895. In each debate Tillman "produced a bottle of dispensary liquor for his text," assaulted prohibition as unenforceable, and praised the dispensary as the means of promoting temperance by destroying the saloon. The demoralization of prohibition radicalism was so advanced that in the juried 1895 debate, Tillman won.[16]

Drys loyal to radical ideas refused to abandon their "fundamental principles" to countenance stronger bonds between the state and the liquor traffic. Eventually the radical organizations came out strongly against the dispensary. In July 1893 the *Union Signal* asserted the typical radical critique that the dispensary did not go far enough: "It is the liquor we want to get rid of, not the dealer." The *Lever* condemned it as a "murder mill" and "most gigantic fraud." The *Voice* decried the proposal for making the government "directly and solely responsible for the entire traffic." But the dispensary's supporters in the temperance ranks defended the system and tensions heightened. After the last of Tillman's speeches at the park, two prominent prohibitionists, the Reverend William H. Boole and Charles H. Haskell, began a shouting match on a New York train that ended in blows. A movement whose leaders engaged in fisticuffs in public was in poor condition to lead drys into the promised land of a liquor-free nation.[17]

By mid-decade a leadership vacuum existed in the dry crusade, and prohibition progress was stalled, if not in retreat. External forces, internal divisions, and the failure of its political and legal methods had brought about the collapse of the radical temperance movement. A new organization filled the leadership gap, the Anti-Saloon League. The league introduced innovations in political and legal methods that revolutionized the prohibition movement. The Anti-Saloon League's approach fulfilled the prohibitionists' dreams of drying out the whole nation.

In 1893 Howard Hyde Russell, unhappy with the prevailing means of fighting demon rum, had launched a new organization: the Ohio Anti-Saloon League. Two years later the league declared itself a national organization, the Anti-Saloon League of America. The league differed dramatically from the Prohibition party and the WCTU in its organization, political style, and legal approach. Where the Prohibition party and the WCTU were democratic and open, the league was bureaucratic and secretive; where they were uncompromising and visionary, it was opportunistic and pragmatic. Yet the league shared with the older organizations a fundamental goal—national prohibition. The league grew slowly in the 1890s; not until well into the first decade of the twentieth century did it dominate the temperance movement. After that point its control of the movement, in part, determined the shape of national prohibition.

Dissatisfaction among nineteenth-century drys with the predominant radical prohibitionist solutions to the liquor problem provided the straw for the bricks that would build the Anti-Saloon League. Chief among critics of the old methods was J. Ellen Foster. As early as 1884, Foster saw as impractical the call for drying out the nation by immediate adoption of a national constitutional amendment. Instead, she advocated acceptance of what radicals disdained as "compromise measures," local option and high license. Other drys agreed; a letter to the *New York Times* pointed out that while the power of Tammany Hall assured the hopelessness of passing a New York state prohibitory law, the liquor traffic in the state could be controlled by enforced Sunday closing laws, local option for rural areas, and high license for wet enclaves. Foster also asserted that the third-party path led only to failure; she argued that its demands for purity of purpose and primacy for the prohibition issue limited its appeal with voters. She asserted that nonpartisan methods could effectively pressure one of the major parties into sponsoring temperance reform. As the Prohibition party disintegrated and as prohibition successes halted, the nonpartisan and limited-means ideas gained strength. Howard Hyde Russell made them the cornerstone of the Anti-Saloon League.[18]

Although the son of an Episcopal minister, Russell showed little religious enthusiasm in his youth. After experimenting with cattle driving and teaching, Russell settled in Corning, Iowa, to pursue a career in law. After joining the bar in 1878, Russell assured his quick rise in local legal circles by marrying Lillian Davis, the daughter of his law partner and patron, Judge Francis Davis. Like many lawyers, Russell dabbled with politics. He was a lifelong Republican; despite his father-in-law's long advocacy of the Prohibition party, that organization held no allure for him. In 1883 Russell underwent a religious conversion and abandoned his flourishing law practice to train for the ministry. Thus in 1884, at the age of twenty-eight, he entered Oberlin College in Ohio. In general, Russell's career (and also that of his most important disciple, Wayne Wheeler) followed the outlines of a "progressive" life theorized by Robert Crunden. The only variation was that Russell (and Wheeler) never rejected his religious upbringing.

While studying at Oberlin, Russell entered temperance work, and these early experiences foreshadowed the course he would set for the Anti-Saloon League. In 1887, as pastor of a Congregational church in Berea, Ohio, Russell mobilized his congregation, the local WCTU, nearby college students, and the Methodists into a "small committee for law observance." Educational lectures, public rallies, and a campaign of liquor law enforcement compelled the town's saloons to obey Sunday closing and other regulations; they eventually built enough prohibition sentiment to make the town dry. The next year, as the Columbus lobbyist of the Oberlin Temperance Alliance, Russell helped persuade the Ohio legislature to adopt a township local option law. Two years later, while a minister in Kansas City, Missouri, Russell set up the Anti-Liquor League of Missouri. This organization drew its strength from the Protestant churches and advocated a piecemeal drive for state prohibition. Russell did not stay to follow through on this plan. He went to the Armour Mission in Chicago and, for two years, took a break from his temperance work. But in 1893, believing that he had received a divine call to battle the saloon, Russell returned to Oberlin. There, with the assistance of members of the Oberlin Temperance Alliance, he founded the Ohio Anti-Saloon League.[19]

Russell conceived of the Ohio Anti-Saloon League, and the national organization, as a "temperance trust" and ordered it along business lines. The Ohio organization was the model league and the training ground for the league's leaders. "Graduates" of its program carried its structure and methods to the rest of the nation. Although its organization changed and evolved over time, in general, democratic ways and volunteerism had little place in the league. Its officers were salaried, and its rank and file were workers guided from above. It was a rigidly hierarchical organization that vested most power in a small, permanent, and self-appointed committee. This committee elected its own officers, who ran the league, hiring and directing superintendents, speakers, and other workers. Local leagues duplicated this form. A committee, usually selected by a state league official who was representative of the spectrum of community prohibition sentiment, ruled the local leagues. Like a business, the league separated its functions into various departments. Each department ran independently under its own administrator in a coordinated plan set by the ruling committee.[20]

The Anti-Saloon League, like the radical prohibitionists, proposed to rebuild America along dry lines, but its methods, like its organization, diverged from the radicals' pattern. The league outlined its main means as agitation, legislation, and law enforcement. It downplayed its program of political pressure. Yet the league's policy of omni-partisan politics was unique and inseparable from all it did. It favored legislators and officials, regardless of party affiliation, who would support league plans. Invariably the league worked almost exclusively with the two major political parties. According to league theory, agitation increased the league's political purse, which was quickly opened to purchase more restrictive liquor laws or better enforcement. Advances in dry legislation and enforcement efforts, in turn, increased prohibition's appeal and contributed to the league's political power.[21]

Russell believed that agitation, or education, was "the bedrock of the temperance reform"; it built favorable local public support for liquor restrictions. The Anti-Saloon League's educational program centered on publications and speakers. In the early years these propagandizing efforts often turned into organizational or fund-raising drives for local or state leagues. Eventually the league devoured forests to publish its tracts and newspapers and kept an army of speakers in the field. By 1915 the circulation of the *American Issue*—the league's banner paper—and other league periodicals neared 16 million. Between 1909 and 1919 the league's press—the American Issue Publishing Company of Westerville, Ohio—printed over 1.4 million books, 4.3 million pamphlets, and 67 million leaflets. Agitation was important in creating and mobilizing support for the dry cause. The league's leaders knew the value of such moral suasion. In 1903 they founded the Lincoln Legion (later renamed the Lincoln-Lee Legion during the league's entry into the south) as a branch of the league to educate American youth about temperance. In the league's view, the Lincoln Legion made the league a "well-proportioned" organization, balancing its many legislative and law enforcement activities with a moral suasion division.[22]

The creation of new laws restricting liquor traffic and the enforcement of all liquor regulations were the most public of the league's goals. In both cases league action served two purposes: to limit liquor sales and to arouse temperance sentiment by further educating the people. In the league's view, existing liquor legislation, "though it may be defective, is better enforced than trampled under foot." In the early twentieth century, the league promoted a program of "putting on the lid." This policy entailed enforcing legal restrictions on big-city saloons, such as Sunday closing, midnight closing on weekdays, and no sales to minors. In these campaigns the league resembled a communist popular front; it cooperated with any group willing to work toward a common goal—in this case, suppressing the saloon. But always the league focused its eyes on the ultimate goal of total prohibition. Enforced laws, the league argued, led to harsher restrictions on the saloon.

One particular halfway measure, local option, was the league's favored legislative means. Most league workers would have agreed with W. A. Pierson, who characterized local option as "a species of prohibition." From 1896 to 1908 the league publicized widely both its efforts to influence the Ohio legislature to adopt local option and its campaigns to defeat wet politicians. Local option swept the nation; by 1900 thirty-seven states had local option laws. Although the league had little to do with the passage of most of these laws, it was identified with the local option policy and took credit for the expansion of the nation's dry areas. Local option was never the final goal; it was but a stepping-stone to building public sentiment and political pressure for state and then national prohibition.[23]

Creation of a new organization and adoption of new methods did not guarantee that the Anti-Saloon League and the prohibition movement would prosper. Not until the first decade of the twentieth century (just when the movement experienced a revival of its fortunes) did the league become strong enough to gain dominance within the temperance crusade. League finances were always precarious and limited the group's power. The Anti-Saloon League spread slowly from its birthplace. Often it worked by affiliating itself with an existing state organization, like the Kansas State Temperance Union. At the third annual convention, held in January 1898, only seven state or territorial organizations formed the league, including the two original leagues of the national organization, those of Ohio and the District of Columbia. By 1904 the parent organization had recognized over forty state and territory leagues, although some were mere paper structures. Part of the league's problems derived from its tendency to overreach. For instance, before the turn of the century it attempted to penetrate the southern states without adequate spadework; and in 1899, although lacking funding and only partially organized in most states, the league founded a national legislative office in Washington.[24]

From inauspicious beginnings the Anti-Saloon League's national office grew into a powerhouse and became a key force in shaping national prohibition. In late 1895 Russell organized the Anti-Saloon League of America to preclude other organizations, especially the National Temperance Society, from preempting the role of director of national prohibition legislation. The founding of the national legislative office followed a similar pattern. In the league's lean years it did nothing at the national level. Others filled the gap. In 1898 the WCTU and Benjamin Tillman (who had moved into the Senate) stole the league's limelight by sponsoring bills of interest to all drys. The next year, to assert the league's importance, Russell appointed Edwin C. Dinwiddie as superintendent of national legislation. Dinwiddie, a former minister and lobbyist for the Ohio league, proved an exceptional leader in Washington. Within ten years he had won dry legislative victories. The Washington office became a showpiece, adding to the league's prestige and giving coordination to its piecemeal plan to make the nation dry.[25]

Yet the league was slow to gain prominence in prohibitionist circles because existing temperance organizations opposed it. In 1894, at the National WCTU's twentieth annual convention, Frances Willard attacked the league's approach. She argued that its "half-way measures" blurred the "straight line of ethical perception" and thereby set back the temperance movement. Willard claimed only "out-and-out methods" would produce results. The WCTU would settle for nothing less. "The WCTU is the Old Guard that never surrenders. It isn't beguiled by high licenses, or tax, by the Iowa Mulct law or the South Carolina dispensary, by non-partisanism or the Scandinavian System." These methods only served "politicians" and dimmed the "vision of well meaning but non-expert workers." Although invited to do so, the National WCTU refused to send representatives to the 1895 organizing convention that formed the Anti-Saloon League of America.

The Prohibition party was even more hostile to what it characterized as the "Into-Saloon League." League methods, in particular local option and high license, remained anathema to the party. The *New Voice* alleged that the Buffalo, New York, Anti-Saloon League conspired with city officials to establish a red-light district, pronouncing this tactic "Not a compromise but a surrender." The party was most upset about the league's political approach. Its papers published articles "exposing" the " 'omni-partisan' failure" of the league. Still, the fading fortunes of the party—it had become in the words of its own newspaper a "rainbow chaser"—and the failure of radical measures encouraged members of the older organizations to embrace the league's methods and eventually the league itself.[26]

Despite the rhetoric, both the Prohibition party and the WCTU cooperated with the league, and the league drew strength from this support. The party vacillated from conflict to cooperation. This pattern persisted through the era of national prohibition. But as time passed, the party became tied to the league. As an organization, the party became increasingly less important, existing chiefly as a haven for the few who could not accept all the league's programs. The WCTU, on the other hand, shifted its allegiance from the party to the league. In a pair of February 11, 1897, *Union Signal* editorials,

Frances Willard pointed the way to cooperation with the league. She stuck to her radical ideology, praising Henry Blair and the party for the educational efforts on behalf of prohibition, and she invoked the "precedent of the despised abolition movement" to assure her readers that prohibition would be "enshrined in the Constitution." However, as "the presidential campaign [was] over," she abandoned partisan means to secure that goal. Instead she challenged the Anti-Saloon League to lead temperance "forces if it can and will" to place prohibition before "every legislature of the land where it does not prevail already." She promised white ribboner support through petitions, literature, and mass meetings. Willard's death in early 1898 removed a strong radical prohibitionist influence from the leadership of the WCTU and opened the door to further cooperation. In 1901 the WCTU dropped its long endorsement of the Prohibition party and accepted the election of its national president to the Anti-Saloon League governing committee. But cooperation did not guarantee success.[27]

In its early years, temperance progress was critical to the league's survival. It needed victories to extend its influence in the prohibition movement. Bereft of any real progress, the Anti-Saloon League touted every new restriction on the liquor trade, whether sponsored by the league or not, as another league step toward national prohibition. League papers showed prohibition progress in the simplest of terms by publishing wet and dry maps of the United States—dry areas in white and wet areas in black. By 1908 this practice permeated the prohibition movement; the *Union Signal* printed similar maps, and one white ribboner even wrote a song, "Make the Map All White." When a prohibition revival occurred in 1907 and 1908, turning Alabama, Georgia, Mississippi, and North Carolina into prohibition states, the league claimed credit. In truth, the league had little to do with securing prohibition for those states. Nevertheless, the league rode the wave of prohibition renaissance to dominance within the movement. Before the southern sweep whitened the maps, the Anti-Saloon League maintained its image of prohibition progress by chronicling its legal successes.[28]

The league's view and use of law was critical to its success; yet it operated with a curiously divided legal culture. In their writings league leaders continued the Mosaic traditions: the obsession with positive law (statutes and constitutions); the assumption that natural law stood behind man-made law; and the belief that law was in essence moral commands. In various publications the league expanded the body of law that drys used to expound their moral statements against liquor by harnessing the common law to their cause. As the league perpetuated the goal of law as a statement of morality, it also continued earlier campaigns for new legislation. At the same time, the league developed a pragmatic and functional approach to law. This view of law came from the league's experiences in attempting to enforce liquor laws in localities and states. It rejected the notion that laws merely restricting the liquor traffic needed to be removed. Rather, it sought to enforce all liquor laws as a practical program of attacking the liquor evil. These pragmatic methods of thinking obscured the traditional dry view of law. The intellectual tension between the league's various legal cultures did not become a problem until the final drive for national prohibition.

Two works, the first by Howard H. Russell and the second by Wayne Wheeler, show the presence and persistence of the Mosaic legal culture in the league. Russell's book, *A Lawyer's Examination of the Bible*, published in 1893 for the Sunday school trade, contains elements of the Mosaic conception of law. Russell dedicated the book to his father-in-law, Francis M. Davis, commending him for his "Faith in the Code of Codes." This phrase was more than a literary allusion to scripture; it encapsulated a whole view of law. Russell applied a legal term—and it is no accident that he used "code," a phrase of statutory law—to the values of Christianity, implying the common Mosaic idea that lesser codes were also God-given and aspired to morality. By citing the work of John F. Dillon, president of the American Bar Association, Russell made this connection clear. "Moral law," which held dominion over all people "by divine ordination . . . and from which evasion or escape is impossible is the eternal and indestructible sense of justice and of right, written by God on the living tablets of the human heart, and revealed in his Holy Word." Thus God's law stood behind all human law. Moreover, Russell argued that the "Code of Code," God's moral law, shaped society. He asserted that the effect of Christianity improved the conduct of rulers from Roman to modern times. Whereas the Romans' "profligacy was open and notorious," today the wealthy class was no longer "selfish, gluttonous and sensual." In Christian nations they were mostly "upright" and "generous." And vice, insofar as it "is indulged in today . . . is not open but secret." As a consequence, society is improved: the "public school is in reach of the children of the humblest"; slavery is ended; infanticide is a thing of the past, as orphans are supported; and women's lot is improved. In addition, under Christian influence, more advances were coming; for instance, the "bloodthirsty games and shows" of Rome have disappeared. "The recent widespread sentiment of disgust throughout Christendom when an event of the prize ring was brought to public notice, indicates how radical a change of thought has come even within a few decades." Clearly when Russell created the league, the Mosaic ideas of law were in the founder's mind.[29]

Meanwhile, Wheeler's compilation, *Federal and State Laws Relating to Intoxicating Liquor*, written twenty-four years later, revealed the longevity of the Mosaic values in the league. The two compilations concerning liquor, published in 1917 and 1918, continued the Mosaic tendency to focus on statute, as opposed to common, law. According to the preface, the league wanted to meet "a need for general information" with these volumes, providing the public with "complete up-to-date information." In the foreword of the second edition, the league announced that it had "hoped to print with each section a digest of the principal decisions construing it." But as this "would make the book too large for general distribution," it promised that, in the future, it would prepare such a publication of "the Court's construction of the laws." Wheeler's volumes were merely collections of all the state and federal liquor laws and constitutional provisions. Meanwhile, the league directed interested people to obtain information on court decisions from the league's general counsel. But no work exploring the judicial construction of liquor laws came off the Westerville presses. Thus, the league, in attempting to reach a large audience, offered only one part—the part that Mosaic thinkers thought key—of the vast body of liquor law: statutory law.[30]

Sandwiched between these two works, parts of the Mosaic conception of law flourished and grew under league auspices. For instance, the tendency to conflate law with moral statements became a staple of Anti-Saloon League arguments. Three works fully delineate the league's perpetuation and expansion of the Mosaic conceptions: Lemuel D. Lilly's *Bench vs. Bar: Or Judicial Answers to Saloon Arguments*; Ervin S. Chapman's *A Stainless Flag*; and Eli F. Ritter's revised edition of *Moral Law and Civil Law: Parts of the Same Thing*. Each of the authors was a league worker. Lilly, a committed dry from his college days at Ohio Wesleyan, worked for thirteen years as a Sunday speaker for the Ohio league. He was a member of the Columbus bar as well as a member of the Board of Trustees of the Anti-Saloon League. Ritter, also an attorney, first enunciated his Mosaic view of law in a brief before the Indiana Supreme Court for the Anti-Nuisance League. After that, he moved from Republican ranks into the Prohibition party and eventually to the league. He was a founder of the Indiana league, that organization's consulting attorney in its early years, and author of Indiana's injunction and abatement law— which was later the model for the similar provision in the Volstead Act. In 1898 Chapman retired from the ministry (he served in United Brethren and Presbyterian churches) to become state superintendent of the California league as well as editor of its newspaper. The pamphlet *A Stainless Flag* grew out of an address Chapman delivered on an East Coast speaking tour for the Anti-Saloon League. It proved so popular that the California league published 135,000 copies, which were distributed nationwide. The American Issue Press published the other two works, and all three were advertised widely in league papers. Without a doubt, these works reflected league orthodoxy.[31]

In 1910 Eli Ritter revised his 1896 book, *Moral Law and Civil Law: Parts of the Same Thing*, perpetuating some of the earlier dry legal culture while omitting other parts of it. His revision for the most part merely expanded points made in the first work. For instance, the volume's list of statute topics supporting morality grew over four times as long as its predecessor's list. Ritter continued to assert that morality was the fundamental principle of law and that the only goal of law was to promote morality and suppress immorality. Law that did not foster morality would fail and disappear. In his expansion, Ritter bolstered his discussion of the moral foundation of common law by adding a chapter citing the "highest authorities" who, he argued, agreed with him. Moreover, he piled precedent upon precedent in support of his argument that the liquor trade was an immoral business not deserving legal support. But absent from the new work was his earlier argument for repeal of license laws. Through this change, Ritter reflected the league's pragmatic position of supporting existing liquor legislation. Ritter's views were similar to those of Samuel Lilly.[32]

Lilly's pamphlet reflected the Mosaic conception of law in a number of different ways. First, it saw morality as a key part of American law; citing George Washington's farewell address, Lilly asserted that "morality is a necessary spring of popular government." Second, in true crusading fashion, he contended that "no moral wrong . . . can acquire any legal rights. Whatever attributes of political power the wrong may manifest are usurpations. Vice has no rights." This stand should have prepared him to launch a higher-law assault against current law. But Lilly did not develop such an argument; rather, he attacked wets who advocated a higher law of personal liberty as holding views contrary to the "sacred traditions of the majority rule." He advocated instead the creation of new legislation or pushed for voting dry in local option elections. The legislature has "fullest authority to promote general welfare," including building public morals through legislation. The government has such a right "because immorality has no right to existence or toleration, and because vice impairs the strength of the community." Beyond that, the right of the state to protect itself against crime and misery was a law of nature—as "fundamental as the right of self-defense in the individual." To accomplish this end, the government relied on states' police powers. Like the radical prohibitionists, Lilly had little fear of the legislature; it required strong powers to accomplish its ends: "Government rests upon the necessity of putting even inherent rights under such control as is essential to their preservation." Thus, encouraging new temperance citizens to vote their districts dry and to vote for prohibition legislation became Lilly's goals.[33]

Lilly's proposed means of achieving that end differed from those of the radicals. He turned to the decisions of appellate courts as his main source, and this focus shows the spread of a Mosaic conception to case law. He used "a multitude of judicial opinions" to refute the arguments of wets. He believed that utterance of the "impartial" and "intelligent" judiciary would impress people more than the voices of "ministers and women" advocating the same thing: "These high judicial authorities ought at least to be persuasive to the average citizen seeking guidance on a serious subject of public importance." Lilly drew on various judicial utterances to discredit such wet arguments as infringing on personal liberty, depriving workers of their jobs, interfering with vested property rights, and eliminating necessary liquor tax revenue. League workers, like Lilly, hoped that these kinds of statements would help to build public sentiment in favor of their policies.[34]

Chapman's *A Stainless Flag* went further than Lilly's work in attempting to transform U.S. common law into a series of Mosaic moral statements. To do so, it drew on Christian interpretations of higher law. As befitting a minister, Chapman began with scripture rather than with law books. He focused on the passage, naming officials as "God's ministers" who were commanded to punish "evil doers" and praise "well doers." Civil government, in pursuing these ends, "has not the slightest liberty of choice as to its attitude toward good and evil"; it must follow divine law. Human law—whether, executive, legislative, or judicial—must follow the higher law: the "supreme and unwritten mandate" of God. An official was "no more a law-maker than an astronomer is a planet-maker. The task of each is not to make, but to make known" their discoveries. Legislatures should strive to make earthly law conform to God's "immutable law of good and evil." To support these statements, Chapman marshaled a host of legal authorities: Justinian, Blackstone, and the Declaration of Independence among them.[35]

Chapman's work paralleled that of Lilly, but he went further than Lilly by diminishing the role of representative assemblies and granting the judiciary a key role. Like Lilly, he cited various court pronouncements against the liquor industry to show that it was morally indefensible. He also advanced a more sweeping view of the judiciary's role in the reform. Enunciating a higher-law justification for judicial review, Chapman asserted that judges, "men of superior ability and learning, with large experience, of extended tenure in office and far removed from distracting influences," had the duty to invalidate "all acts of the legislature in conflict with immutable law." In his view, the courts became "the infallible judicial touchstone" that upheld the nation's morals. Furthermore, he argued that given the higher law, "not even by a unanimous popular vote can that which is morally wrong be made legally right." In establishing civil government people "covenant with the higher powers of the universe," agreeing that their laws shall conform to "supreme, immutable law." Chapman held out hope that the Supreme Court "in strict accordance with the imperative demand of that obligation" would place "its brand of outlaw" on the "beverage traffic in strong drink."[36]

Chapman concluded his argument by postulating that "civil government is constantly in a process of transformation into more perfect accord with the requirements of immutable law." He traced this "rapid and undeviating trend" by pointing to the various practices deemed immoral and in violation of God's law. Confusing both legislative and judicial measures, he listed the ending of the African slave trade, the prohibiting of lotteries in the United States, the banning of prizefights by the states, and the ending of slavery in Britain through the Somerset case of 1770 to support his contention. Pointing to the Supreme Court's upholding of various state restrictions on and prohibitions of liquor, he concluded that the rulings "like the solemn and confident utterances of the old Hebrew prophets . . . have startled the nation by their majestic and unexpected proclamations of fundamental truth." The Court would continue to "lead in the magnificent march of humanity." It would pronounce a "final imperative sentence of death" on the liquor traffic, thus giving America a stainless flag.[37]

Chapman's hope of national prohibition through Court action reveals the limits of the extension of Mosaic tradition to case law. This idea was far from practical. It was unlikely that the Court would ever make such a ruling; and it was unlikely that the league would push the judiciary in that direction. The league was not a precursor to the NAACP Legal Defense Fund; it was not a pressure group designed to bring about legal change through adjudication. Moreover, these ideas of Mosaic law rested on a weak foundation. In elevating judicial decisions as compelling statements of morality, Chapman overlooked the fact that these utterances came in cases reviewing prohibition legislation. Legislation came first, the statements of the courts followed in its wake. Thus Lilly, who marshaled the common law for the purpose of creating more and better legislation saw more clearly the purpose of the moral truths spoken by the courts.

Lilly's approach also coincided with the practical approach to law and prohibition that the league espoused. When it came to appellate court opinions, the league did not just see them as Mosaic statements of law, of course. As pragmatists, they saw court rulings as functional law, as markers that would determine how far their legislation—in all sorts of fields—could go. Thus, it is no surprise that Dinwiddie, the league's legislative agent in Washington, possessed a copy of the Court's decision in *Champion v. Ames*, the case upholding the federal act banning lottery tickets in interstate trade. Later in the league's history it would avidly wait for Supreme Court review of legislation it had helped create. And one of the high points of league attorney Wayne Wheeler's career was his arguing the constitutionality of the Webb-Kenyon Act and the Eighteenth Amendment.[38]

Another league leader and lawyer espoused similar conceptions of law and linked them explicitly to the league's law enforcement activities. Oscar G. Christgau, who had trained at the Chicago Law School, was a master of law, a teacher at the Hamilton College of Law in Chicago, and long a power in the Illinois organization. In a speech praising lawyers, Christgau asserted that "with the progress of the centuries the eternal principles of justice written by God in the hearts of men found expression in human law." Thus, in modern times, "right is determined by these laws," and all good people should admit that the "warrior of the present age" is the lawyer who has the "courage to enforce the people's law regardless of threats" of violators of law. Thus Christgau linked the league's idealistic view of law with its practical attempts to enforce liquor legislation.[39]

Its law enforcement program reflected the pragmatic part of the Anti-Saloon League's legal culture. From its inception to its demise, the Anti-Saloon League was a law enforcement organization. To the league, "the enforcement of law" equaled in importance "the enactment of law." By 1908, according to one account, the league had participated in over 31,000 cases of liquor law enforcement. The league announced guidelines for its law enforcement efforts in a plan that combined league lawyers, government officials, private detectives, and antiliquor volunteers into a coherent system. This law enforcement agenda was important to the early history of the league because it provided the league with an important tool that could bring needed victories. With varying success, the league attempted to adhere to this program throughout the era of national prohibition.[40]

Essentially the league's enforcement program attempted to enforce dead letter laws—existing laws that were unused. At the time the league was experiencing its first successes with the program, the pioneering political scientist Arthur Bentley assessed the merits of such a law enforcement approach. Speaking in general about the dead letter laws as exemplified by prohibition of Sunday sale of milk, he described "a track or a technical means by which milkselling on Sunday can be suppressed without the issue passing through the legislature." A "vigorous anti-milk-selling group" could "push its activity with fewer obstacles than if the old blue law had been repealed.... We observe as fact that just as an easier technique is provided for changing a statute than for changing an article of the constitution, so an easier technique is provided for making law in the field of dead-letter law than for making law in the ordinary legislative field."[41]

Given its obvious benefits, the league made law enforcement a key component of its program from the very beginning. The proceedings of the first Ohio Anti-Saloon League meeting in 1893, the resolutions of the first and second Anti-Saloon League of America conventions in 1895 and 1896, and the program of the first annual conference of superintendents of the Anti-Saloon League held in 1898 announced liquor law enforcement as one of the league's primary goals. Even the letterhead of the early league's stationary reflected this orientation. It read: "Our four departments: Agitation, Legislation, Enforcement, The Anti-Saloon Army." The founder of the league, Howard Hyde Russell, thought of law enforcement and lawyers as essential to the league's work. He believed that Providence guided him to the "law and the ministry and to Oberlin" so he could foster "the needs of such a unique movement" that combined law, Christianity, and reform. Divine Providence aside, Russell was trained in law, had prosecuted in 1878 at least one case of illegal liquor sales for the "Corning church people," and was deeply committed to the rule of law. A Corning friend of Russell's characterized him as a "lawyer-preacher."[42]

The public perception of the league, especially in its early days, turned on its law enforcement activities. Potential converts to the league method saw it in these terms. For instance, the *Christian Observer*, a "Presbyterian Family Newspaper" published in Louisville, Kentucky, contained two different columns: one entitled "Temperance" and another "Anti-Saloon League." The column on Anti-Saloon League activities did not cover moral suasion or legislative activities (it left those topics to the "temperance" section) but rather focused exclusively on enforcement issues. The paper believed the league's efforts were "directed chiefly to the enforcement of laws as they are, until better laws can be secured." The league fostered such views when, in its "suggestions" to speakers, it told them to "1st. Make a distinctively Anti-Saloon League, and not an old line Temperance Address." To do so they need to stress the league's "*programme* for immediate action," which included agitation, "*Legislation*," and "*Law Enforcement*."[43]

The emphasis on law enforcement infused the Anti-Saloon League and persisted throughout its history. In 1915, while addressing the Anti-Saloon League superintendents' conference, Russell described the prohibition movement as a huge arch, the capstone of which would be national prohibition.

One archstone, a "homely, but necessary" boulder, was what Russell, quoting an old temperance rhyme, called "prison suasion for the statute-breaker." Other leaders of the Anti-Saloon League, William H. Anderson, Boyd P. Doty, Edward J. Moore, Eli F. Ritter, and Albert E. Shoemaker, were lawyers and deeply involved in the enforcement program. But only one man other than Russell, Wayne Wheeler, was instrumental in formulating the league's law enforcement strategy. Hired in 1894 as an organizer, in 1898 Wheeler became the Ohio Anti-Saloon League's attorney, and in 1916, general counsel of the national organization. Interestingly, when Wheeler was hesitant about joining the league, confessing his ambition to become a lawyer, Russell told him, "Our League would very much need some good lawyers."[44]

Lawyers were necessary to wield the league's legal weapons, for without effective law enforcement temperance reform would falter. To prohibitionists who espoused the "new fangled gospel of gush" and were "too pious to enforce the law," the league quoted St. Paul: a "ruler should be a terror to evil doers." The "strong arm of the law" was "absolutely necessary" in controlling the "large proportion of our citizens who have no authoritative moral teacher." Law would be their educator; the "law must go before the gospel, Mt. Sinai before Mt. Calvary." Vigilant law enforcement created "a more intelligent respect" for law and "reverence for the sovereign rule" of the people. The call for legal work never faded; on the eve of national prohibition Russell argued that future Anti-Saloon League law enforcement work would help "copper-fasten and clinch" the dry amendment to the nation.[45]

The league promulgated rules to govern its law enforcement actions. Russell and Wheeler summed them up in frequent articles and in a "catechism" in the *American Issue*. The essence of the league program was simple. The league must work to make public sentiment for enforcement. League workers should not relieve public, regular officers of their job but rather "stimulate" them to act. Local leagues should aid "proper officials" in enforcing the liquor laws. "Beyond all this, on rare occasions," private law enforcement—through use of detectives or private prosecutions—could be utilized, especially if it jarred officials into doing their duty. Procedure in all legal matters should be determined by "an expert in the law," a league or hired lawyer. The Rhode Island league printed a pamphlet, called *Stop, Look, and Listen*, for its local leagues that repeated these rules and gave suggestions on how to proceed against liquor law violators. In a phrase, the leagues were "to enforce the law through local officials or in spite of them."[46]

Inclination, experience, and expediency directed the Anti-Saloon League to this method of law enforcement. The law enforcement agenda paralleled the league's preferred political tactic of omni-partisan pressure. Moreover, the league needed to set itself apart from the Prohibition party's policy of bringing about law enforcement by electing prohibitionists to office. Unlike the party's means, the league's program required no disruption of the political system and promised quick results. The league grew by swallowing law-and-order and citizen council groups that had taken law enforcement into their own hands and found it hard to manage. At the first and second Ohio Anti-Saloon League conventions in 1894 and 1895, Washington Gladden and Howard Hyde Russell spoke against extralegal methods. Russell contended that "the law and order system of hiring detectives and lawyers and conducting prosecutions is obsolete, or ought to be." Five years later, in 1900, the Rhode Island league concluded that "the experience of the past year has shown that the effort to enforce the law by private prosecutions must bring some disappointment."[47]

But old habits proved hard to shed. Anti-Saloon League pamphlets drew blueprints on how to go about private prosecutions, guiding temperance workers in hiring detectives and attorneys and in finding and preparing witnesses. The *American Issue*, in an article on the nature of state Anti-Saloon Leagues, listed the securing of detectives and the furnishing of attorneys for liquor law violation prosecutions among the state leagues' main functions. Several state leagues clung to the "law and order" methods; for example, the New York league ran up a debt of $15,000 through private prosecutions and the hiring of detectives. When the *American Issue* published Wheeler's "catechism" and drew it to the "particular attention of all Anti-Saloon League superintendents, law enforcement committees, and officers of Leagues," it admitted that the rules had "no binding authority." Rather, the paper hoped that other leagues, state and local, would "profit by" attorney Wheeler's experience in Ohio. The history of the Anti-Saloon League law enforcement program told of the tension between this plan of making officials act and the tendency of league workers to degenerate into vigilantes.[48]

To enforce the liquor laws, local and state leagues considered a lawyer "an imperative requirement." Attorneys were "needed as specialists" to explain liquor laws, to direct "temperance people," and to assist "well-disposed public officers" in enforcement campaigns. Permanent counsel was necessary—either league representatives or retained lawyers who would "devote all their time" to law enforcement—because the "liquor dealers invariably secure the best attorney available to defend them" and because of the "disinclination" of many lawyers "due to political and other influences" to prosecute liquor sellers. William Anderson in the league pamphlet *The Church in Action against the Saloon*, the so-called blue book (named after its paper cover) of the movement, emphasized the role of permanent attorneys: "Such an attorney" prepared "an annotated pamphlet of the liquor laws of his state." He could aid in preparing local legal cases for trial and in carrying "test cases upon important mooted points to the courts of last resort." For instance, the North Carolina league followed the league blueprint by hiring lawyers and using their knowledge to monitor elections, draft statutes, and enforce existing laws. In the estimation of dry workers, a strong legal program was central to Anti-Saloon League success; without one, the league "would be but a crippled affair." Lawyers made for an especially effective law enforcement division. In the period from 1900 to 1906, at least seven state leagues (Alabama, Indiana, Illinois, Michigan, Nebraska, Ohio, and Rhode Island) retained attorneys who vigorously pursued saloon keepers in the courts.[49]

As in so much of the Anti-Saloon League's history, the Ohio league's experiences proved the template for other leagues to copy. These local leagues were urged to assign an officer to the "enforcement department," which was to "look after the enforcement of law, swear out warrants, if necessary, for arrests for infraction of law." These local officers were to coordinate their activities with the state office. In Ohio, at the state level, Wayne Wheeler's activities as counsel revealed the promise and perils of lawyer-directed liquor law enforcement efforts. Wheeler, paid by the state league, was available to local leagues for consultation on liquor law questions and, if they paid his hotel and travel expenses, to prosecute cases. By his and Russell's estimate, he averaged one prosecution per day during his five-year (1898–1903) tenure. Although it hired a full-time assistant and retained two other lawyers, the Ohio league's law enforcement office could not keep up with the demand for services. Calls flooded the league's central office asking for legal aid. In 1903 requests came from over 750 different places, so there was "not enough Mr. Wheeler to go around." In the press, the league's rule of resorting to private prosecutions only as a means of last resort fell by the wayside. In 1900 only one-quarter of the Ohio league's prosecutions involved assisting government officers' efforts; the remaining three-quarters were local league-sponsored prosecutions. Wheeler and the Ohio league seldom lost a case.[50]

This success captured the attention of other temperance workers and helped to make Wheeler's reputation, but it also obscured the importance of relying on regularly constituted officials to enforce the law. All drys knew that "laws never enforced themselves" but needed officials to implement them. By law, the burden of enforcing state and local liquor regulations fell to public officers: governors, sheriffs, mayors, marshals, police, and prosecutors. These officials invariably found themselves between warring groups of citizens: prohibitionists clamoring for vigorous prosecutions and wets desiring lax or no enforcement of laws that they believed infringed on their "personal liberty."

Often drys won legislative victories, only to see them become dead letters through official indifference or inaction. Some officers argued that the liquor laws were unpopular and therefore unenforceable. On the issue of Sunday closing, Mayor Martin Behrman of New Orleans typified the officials' response. He claimed to have no official knowledge of infractions "as I have always been very busy on Sundays, or out of town or at home with my family." The implication of his statement was that others, including reformers, should also mind their own business and let "unobtrusive nonobservance" continue. Other officials deliberately sabotaged enforcement; for example, in Ohio mayors who presided at mayoral courts, where many liquor cases were prosecuted, left town to block proceedings, refused to convict on the basis of "spotters" (paid informants), or prohibited local police from going "undercover" to catch saloon keepers in violations of liquor laws.[51]

When faced with such official nullification, the Anti-Saloon League fought back. League papers like the *California Issue* told its readers to "demand that your officers enforce the law." The Anti-Saloon League's method to compel reluctant officials to serve "the people by enforcing the law" boiled down to the rewards and punishments of public pressure. In its newspapers, the league vilified as "backless bipeds" and "weaklings" those officials who refused to pursue actively illegal liquor sellers. It reminded them that President Theodore Roosevelt's career began with his "courageous" enforcement of the Sunday closing law in New York City. In other cases the league tried to force resignations, resorted to impeachments, or worked against officials' reelection. On the other hand, the league rewarded officials who enforced liquor laws. The prohibition press hailed them as heroes, as "brave" and "fearless."

League rewards to "officials favorable" to prohibition law enforcement could also be more tangible. The league could help prosecutors by securing evidence through the use of detectives and by lending legal counsel experienced in liquor law cases. The league could supply crusading mayors and police chiefs with men to fill out "hatchet parties." Indeed, officers sometimes became dependent on Anti-Saloon League assistance. In Oklahoma City "a conscientious officer," when impaneling a grand jury, first selected the president of the city's Anti-Saloon League "and with his advice" filled the rest of the seats; forty-five liquor law indictments quickly followed. In 1917 the prohibition commissioner of Virginia asked the Anti-Saloon League of America for a recommendation for a detective to hire.[52]

The Anti-Saloon League's friendly relationship with well-disposed officials could blur the line between the prohibition movement and the government, so much so that the drys could come to believe that the government needed to be staffed with ardent prohibitionists. This tendency was reminiscent of the Prohibition party's position on law enforcement: only staunch prohibitionists would enforce prohibitory laws. The most notable example of the Anti-Saloon League's support of "one of their own" in the government was the *American Issue*'s coverage of William E. "Pussyfoot" Johnson. Johnson began his career as a reporter and publisher of Prohibition party papers in which he revealed his abilities as an investigator of criminal activity. Appointed by Theodore Roosevelt as special federal agent to suppress the liquor traffic in Indian Territory, Johnson's exploits from 1906 to 1911 captured the drys' imagination. Johnson and his hand-picked deputies arrested 5,473 men and attained convictions for 4,400 of them. His tactics bordered on warfare. The stories of smash-and-run campaigns, midnight raids, and near brushes with death—eight of his deputies were killed while working—made for thrilling copy in the prohibition press. The coverage reinforced drys' tendencies to have only prohibitionists enforce the liquor laws or to take the law into their own hands.[53]

The league guidelines on law enforcement attempted to check the prohibitionist predilection for citizen enforcement of liquor laws. Before the league's founding, extralegal action was an established part of the temperance crusade. Individual prohibitionists, dry organizations, various churches, and some ministers routinely raised money to pay for the hiring of detectives, to reward informers, and to press private prosecutions. At other times, temperance workers themselves entered saloons to gather evidence of illegal activities. In 1888 Howard Hyde Russell guided such a campaign in Berea, Ohio. In 1896 and 1897, after the establishment of the league, Russell, Henry Faxon, some hired detectives, and other temperance workers toured the saloons of Haverhill, Massachusetts, to investigate illegal practices. Russell aired their findings in a speech to the town's citizens in hopes of generating pressure to spark city officials into better enforcement of the laws.

The Haverhill experience typified the league's conception of the role of private action in enforcement work. It was not an isolated example. For instance, in Oklahoma a 1911 league-approved law even provided that the people should direct their officials. It allowed any citizen to require the county court to issue subpoenas "for people having knowledge of the violation" of liquor laws. Thus, a citizen "who [knew] where liquor" was being sold could compel officials to investigate it. Private action never disappeared from the league program. In 1916 in Virginia, five hundred league and white ribboner volunteers worked as informers to the state's commissioner of prohibition. For many league supporters direct action could become an end in itself—or a means to support other methods, such as private prosecutions or reliance on detectives. When used indiscriminately, these methods undercut the league's law enforcement policy.[54]

Paid detectives, considered by league policy to be a means of last resort, in practice proved to be a common law enforcement aid. Certain detectives, like Louis Wien, were famous for their liquor law work. State leagues routinely recommended detectives for local leagues to hire. In fact, the public mind identified the league with detective work and rightly so. When officials refused to act and "the situation demands immediate action," league workers were justified in using detectives. The league admitted that detectives had many advantages. Often they were the only ones who seemed to be able "to penetrate the haunts of the saloonist and uncover his dark devices." Detectives could "ingratiate themselves with the sellers and drinkers of liquor"; they could enter lower-class saloons, black bars, and other places where the average temperance worker stood out like a sore thumb. Detectives gathered much evidence of illegal liquor selling in prohibition territory or violations of other liquor laws. They were indispensable to the enforcement program.[55]

The use of detectives also raised serious problems for the league. They were expensive and often aroused public opinion against prohibitionists. Detectives depleted some local leagues' treasuries, sapping their ability to agitate and to promote legislation. For many, detectives were despicable: "The American people look upon a spy with contempt." Sometimes jurors refused to convict on the basis of detective evidence; one Rhode Island jury announced that they would "rot in their chairs before they would find a verdict of guilty on 'spotter' evidence." While admitting the usefulness of detectives, the leading treatise on liquor law reflected the common view. It argued that judges were not bound to instruct juries that detective testimony should be received with "distrust," but endorsed limited cautionary remarks on the potential bias of a witness paid to discover crime. Some temperance workers shared this antipathy toward the use of detectives. These external and internal assaults forced league workers to defend detective work. Typically, the *American Issue* denounced prohibitionists who questioned the use of detectives as "super sensitive, overly-good" souls or as "Miss Nancys." They pointed out that the federal government used detectives to ferret out tax evaders; if detectives were a suspect means, "then the entire system of American government, in so far as the Criminal Code is concerned, is questionable." The chief defense rested on the grounds of expediency. In the words of Henry Faxon, "When you go fishing for the devil you need not be too particular about the net you use, if you only catch him."[56]

Such expediency could lead the league into perversions of the purposes of its law enforcement program. Ideally, law enforcement was supposed to help convince people that prohibition and liquor restrictions were good and workable ideas; it was meant to build favorable public sentiment as well as restrict the sale of liquor. But in practice it could lead to coerced support for prohibition. For example, in 1900 the Anti-Saloon League superintendent for New Hampshire, Michael J. Fanning, hired two Pinkerton detectives. These detectives visited speakeasies in a Vermont town frequented by "many leading citizens." These bars illegally sold liquor to college students. Disguised as students, the detectives induced leading merchants to drink with them at the town's many speakeasies. Then Fanning prosecuted one of the barkeepers, calling a merchant as his "principal witness." The man denied that he had visited the place, but on the testimony of the two detectives he was subsequently convicted of perjury and jailed for six months. Fanning then announced twenty-five more proceedings and threatened to call other businessmen to the witness stand. This blackmail prompted the town's leading lights to arrange guilty pleas by the liquor sellers and to close the town's saloons. This kind of drive, where any means were deemed legitimate to reach the dry end, made enemies for the league and prohibition. Enforcement success brought about by such chicanery was a hollow victory.[57]

The Anti-Saloon League program of law enforcement, for all its contradictions and deficiencies, was a success. Although it never worked as designed, it limited liquor sales, aroused temperance interest, and provided the league with needed victories before it built its political influence. Beyond that, it honed the legal skills of the league's officers. The enforcement program also embodied a pragmatic part of the league's approach to law. In day-to-day affairs the league rejected the Mosaic conception of law along with the radical's political methods. Thus in part of the league program law appeared to be nothing more than a tool to be used to achieve an end. But in its literature the league kept the Mosaic values alive. The divided nature of the league's legal culture served a purpose. By maintaining the Mosaic legal culture, the league maintained its links with the prohibitionist past. Works like Chapman's and Ritter's, and the occasional banners in league papers citing appellate courts' moralistic language, worked to inspire the faithful and inspire new conversions to the dry fold. Duality had its advantages.

Ultimately the drys' transformation of legal culture under the Anti-Saloon League reflected the changed means being employed by the movement. These changes came about in part because of the interaction with the polity. Most states rejected prohibition and kept liquor regulatory and tax systems. The federal government, through its tax policy and through interpretation of the interstate commerce clause, undercut prohibition where it existed. Under this pressure, drys went from abolitionist-styled solutions toward a more regulatory approach. But they never fully embraced regulation; rather, they tended to use it as an expedient that they hoped would bring about progress toward a dry nation. Similarly, their legal culture added a new layer of pragmatism to its Mosaic foundation. Given the success of the league in using regulatory means and pragmatic legal culture, it might be presumed that all reforms to succeed in this period needed a similar a transformation of their legal culture and means. This was not the case.

We do not know much about the legal cultures of other reforms, as the necessary research has yet to be done. But as means and legal culture both derive from the ideas and nature of the movement, it is a safe assumption that they were linked. So an examination of changing means in social reforms will give hints about changing legal culture. A survey of reforms shows that there is a spectrum—ranging from no change to total transformation—of means change and presumably a transformation of legal culture in the progressive era. Two key attributes determined where a reform fell on this spectrum. First, the differences in the nature and means of social reforms, in part, account for the pattern. Second, the contingencies of reformers in their interactions with the structures of the polity partially established where the reform would end up on a spectrum of changed means and legal culture. Comparison with the case of prohibition further helps to show how reforms and the polity interacted to produce different patterns.

Neither regulation-styled reforms nor reformation-styled reforms underwent a transformation of legal culture or means as the prohibitionists did. Obviously regulation reforms could not do so, as they started with a more pragmatic view of law. Logically, it is possible that regulation reform could change into an abolitionist reform. But logic did not shape reform histories. The interplay of ideas and structures did; structurally it was difficult for regulationist-style reform to change its means or legal culture. Consider for a moment the implications of a reform that has built within the polity a bureaucracy aimed a curbing abuses in some social practice through regulation. To shift to the abolitionist means and adopt a Mosaic legal culture would make the regulatory agency unnecessary. Instead of intimate scrutiny, the polity would seek only enforcement of the ban. The latter is a different task, better carried on by law enforcement officers rather than regulators. Similarly, to change to a reformist means would require a recasting of either its already existing agency within the government or proposals for one. Thus, bureaucratic inertia probably determined that no such change occurred in the progressive period.

Reformationist reforms, for different reasons, also did not experience a transformation toward regulation or abolition. The reformationsts' interactions with the polity were limited. A reformationist movement constructed within the polity an insular sphere of activity. For example, juvenile justice— beyond convincing various jurisdictions that they needed such a system— had little interaction with law or the polity. Once separately established (except, of course, for funding and staffing battles), the struggle was over for the reformers; they carried on their reformation in private. The insular nature of the reformationist reforms protected them from the pressures of the polity, unlike abolitionist and regulatory reforms. And to change their reform agenda from reformation to regulation would tie the reformers into the rest of the government and weaken their institutional autonomy. Moreover, the chasm in thinking between the scientifically cloaked reformationists (their efficiency) and the religion-inspired abolitionists (their morality) made unlikely a transformation to a Mosaic legal culture. Finally, reformationist systems needed subjects to remake (by manipulating their environment) into a desired model. But the Mosaic form of law assumed free will—that people would choose the proper path once the law declared it; no special structures needed to be built to help them. Reformationists, if they embraced an abolitionist approach, would erode the very justifications for the institutions they were dedicated to creating. Thus, the changes in reformers' means and legal culture in the progressive period occurred exclusively in abolitionist reform ranks, and they filled the spectrum of change.[58]

A number of abolitionist reforms (for example, those targeting gambling and obcenity) never shifted their means or legal conceptions. They had no need to do so. Antismut crusaders typified the pattern. Before the progressive era they won laws against obscene materials. These laws were bans, not regulations; states did not create inspection services to review printed media to set content level equivalent to pure food laws. While the enforcement may have been imperfect, dirty books were swept from the shelves by the states and from the mails and commerce by the federal government. No state regulated or taxed obscenity. The polity itself did not challenge these reformers, and no powerful social group attempted to undo their work; so they continued to use the existing means and legal culture to reach their ends.[59]

Even abolitionist reformers who did not find as easy a path in the polity as anti-obscenity reformers did not have to change their predominant means and legal culture. Antiprostitution, for instance, as a movement never went as far down the path of pragmatism and regulation as the prohibitionists. While governing bodies could, and did, turn abolitionist laws against prostitution into de facto regulatory systems (and a few jurisdictions did regulate prostitution through formal law), the reformers persisted in calling for a wiping out of the trade in sexual services. Stymied by local and state action or inaction, the antiprostitution reformers went national. Helped by the wave of hysteria (generated in part by their propaganda) over white slavery, they won passage of the Mann Act, which penalized interstate and international commerce in women. When this law proved more symbolic than effective, they tried a new state weapon: abatement laws. These laws closed brothels down as public nuisances and replicated the attempts of radical prohibitionists—like Ely Ritter—to do the same against the saloons. But the reformers did not prevail until the First World War allowed the crusaders to mobilize the federal war powers against red-light districts. Throughout the crusaders never abandoned a pure solution for regulation. Their successes in using the federal power and limiting the locales that adopted legal regulation of prostitution apparently gave them enough of a base to preserve their abolitionist style of reform.[60]

Others reforms (most notably the antitrust and pure food movements) saw a complete transformation in their means from abolition to regulation. Thus the most far-reaching changes in legal subculture probably came in these reforms. Such reforms were remarkably broad movements that drew support from all across society. Their amorphous nature allowed people in the polity to play a disproportionate role in shaping the reform agenda. Their diffuse nature and the predominance of policymakers in setting their course make it difficult to determine a coherent ideology or legal culture and to trace any such changes within these reforms. But a brief sketch of one—antitrust—shows the clear shift in means. While the nation's antitrust policy vacillated from the 1880s through the progressive era (and beyond), the overall thrust of change was a move away from abolition toward regulation.[61]

Antitrust was a widespread but inchoate social reaction to the rise of big business. The advocates of antitrust included a wide range of individuals and groups. Despite its diversity, abolitionism tinged the antimonopoly movement that emerged in the 1880s and 1890s. The many appeals against monopoly presented the new giant corporations as a threat to individuals' and the nation's liberty, equality, and fairness. Under this general pressure, and working on the assumption that trusts were "unnatural," the states and the federal government both acted to define as criminal many corporate (real or perceived) practices. The most important product of this early reaction to the rise of trusts was the 1890 Sherman Anti-Trust Act.[62]

The polity's response in the Sherman Anti-Trust Act was a Mosaic solution to the issue of trusts, but its clear prohibition did not remain so. The act declared illegal "every contract, combination in the form of trust or otherwise, or conspiracy, in restrain of trade or commerce." Typical of a Mosaic solution, the act did not create a regulatory agency—or indeed any machinery. Instead, it relied on the existing Department of Justice to implement the ban. The department failed to vigorously enforce the ban, and when it did act, the Supreme Court's interpretation of the Sherman Act significantly weakened the effect of the act. Indeed, the failure of the policy could be seen in the great merger wave of the 1890s. At the same time, a different view of the trusts began to emerge. This new view saw some monopoly as economically efficient and thereby beneficial to the nation. Even so, sentiment against the trusts remained strong enough to make "trust reform a pivotal and decidedly durable political issue."[63]

The state and federal governments—including the courts, executives, congresses, and bureaucrats—struggled with the issue, and their work led to the emergence of a regulatory antitrust response. The broad outlines can be seen in the three progressive-era presidential administrations. The Roosevelt administration attempted to balance these concerns in its efforts at revitalizing the Sherman Act. Its famous distinction between good trusts and bad trusts, and its attempts to use the Sherman Act to punish the bad trusts, perpetuated the absolutist ban. But its building of a fact-finding regulatory agency in the Bureau of Corporations turned the abolitionist law into a proto-regulatory system. The Taft administration's failed attempt to insure federal regulation of corporations through a federal incorporation law led it to use the abolitionist-styled Sherman Act with vigor. But this campaign faltered before the Supreme Court's "rule of reason." The Court limited the Sherman Act only to unreasonable restraints of trade, forcing parts of the government to make the regulatory decision (subject to the Court oversight) as to what was reasonable or unreasonable activity. The Wilson administration extended this conception in its revision of antitrust law in the Clayton Act and the creation of the Federal Trade Commission. The Clayton Act specified business actions that constituted restraint of trade while the new administrative agency mixed investigatory and regulatory functions in overseeing business activity. Its most powerful tool was the power (subject to judicial review) to issue cease and desist orders to corporations engaging in unfair methods of competition. Significantly, it could not destroy trusts, but it could regulate their activities.

Thus, by the late progressive era, the federal government (and the states in its wake as well as much of the antitrust movement) had turned away from abolition and toward regulation. Such a transformation of means was possible in every abolitionist social reform in the period. For pure-minded crusaders, like the prohibitionists, such a turn could be seen as little more than a defeat, as it permitted the evil to survive. Faced with the alternatives of defeat by transformation or defeat by failure, drys reacted creatively, embracing a pragmatic political strategy and reorienting their legal culture. Significantly, they only went part way: their legal culture, like their propaganda arm, always kept alive the absolute position. Mosaic values survived in the Anti-Saloon League era.

This evolution of dry legal culture was made possible by the collapse of radical prohibition in the 1890s. After the league's political successes established its dominance in the movement, its conception of law shaped prohibitionist policy. In particular, the league's pragmatic legal policies reacted with renewed interstate commerce issues and the persistent problems of the federal tax system. The polity continued to challenge the prohibition movement. But with their new political tools, the drys tamed the federal system. The successes of the league made the once unimportant contradictions in dry legal culture critical. During the campaign for national prohibition, these divisions over the meaning and use of law caused problems for the crusade. How the drys solved these problems, as well as their solutions to the problems of federalism, helped to determine the shape of the Eighteenth Amendment.

THE LIQUOR TAX AND THE PRAGMATIC

PROHIBITIONISTS

CHAPTER

The policies of the Internal Revenue Office, a part of the emerging administrative state, angered all drys, but the actions drys took to remedy the problems created by the agency changed over time. Most drys, at least before 1900, hoped for abolition of the tax. When abolitionist-style solutions began to fare badly, prohibitionists developed proposals for using the tax system to achieve temperance goals. The rise of the Anti-Saloon League brought to the fore these alternatives for dealing with the liquor tax implicit in some prohibition circles. But the league, which had been constructed as an instrument to pressure political parties, had difficulty in directly influencing the bureaucrats. As the parties still dominated the executive and legislative branches, however, the league was able to exert indirect pressure on federal tax officials. Thus, the league's political power won legislation from Congress and concessions from federal bureaucrats. These victories gave the league credibility within the temperance movement, helping to establish it as the predominant prohibitionist organization.

The federal Internal Revenue Office's belligerent policies toward prohibition were a key reason for the radical prohibitionist denunciation of the liquor tax. Throughout the 1880s and 1890s radicals cited tax auctions, settlement of tax evasion cases out of court, and especially restrictions on the use of federal tax lists as evidence of how the tax protected the liquor industry. Again and again they recounted these facts to bolster the case for repeal of the tax; but the hopelessness of implementing abolition led radicals to less drastic solutions to the problems created by the tax. These proposed methods helped lay the groundwork for the Anti-Saloon League's pragmatic policies.[1]

In keeping with their abolitionist heritage, the radical prohibitionists determined that if they could not purify the whole nation by repealing the tax, they should try to assure the sanctity of the jurisdictions that had implemented prohibition. They pressed Congress for "an adjustment between state and national laws." In the 1880s radical prohibitionists began advocating two different types of bills to accomplish this end. The first simply prohibited the federal government from issuing "licenses" in dry areas. The second proposed that the government issue its special tax receipt only to those who could prove that they had met the requirements of state liquor laws. These proposals shared the premise that the federal government should not interfere in the states' affairs. Neither proposal required the national government to take an active hand in suppressing the liquor traffic. The central government merely supported the policies of the dry states.[2]

The WCTU and the Prohibition party lobbied Congress for such legislation. In supporting these ideas, neither organization abandoned the idea of abolishing the liquor tax altogether. The radicals saw these proposals as "one of the most necessary means for the enforcement" of prohibition. They assumed that other states would fall in line when they saw how well the system worked without interference. Equally important was their belief that the enactment of such bills would be accomplished easily. A letter to the *Union Signal* urged drys to press Congress into passing "a law prohibiting the granting of liquor licenses in any state, town or county . . . which is under prohibitory law." Drys believed that they could build wide support for "such a just and common sense effort." The WCTU circulated many petitions in support of each type of bill. They called on every "white ribboner to speak her mind to Uncle Sam." Their national conventions endorsed such bills; and their lobbyist in Washington, Margaret Dye Ellis, did her best to find support for these measures. Through her column in the *Union Signal*, Ellis kept the faithful informed of the progress of various bills incorporating these proposals.[3]

Bills to restrict the collection of the special tax on retail liquor sellers only to those permitted by local laws to engage in that trade had been introduced in Congress as early as 1884. In 1887 the Kansas legislature passed a memo-rial instructing the state's senators to introduce and work for the passage of such a measure. The WCTU and the Prohibition party stood squarely be-hind these measures. As one correspondent wrote to the *Union Signal*, "Very few could venture to oppose so moderate and reasonable a petition." Radicals believed that this type of bill would "succeed where more radical measures would fail." But they continued to press for more sweeping plans.

In the same decade, radicals proposed bills intended to restrict the federal government from collecting the liquor tax in dry areas. This more complete measure had its first serious hearing in 1896. In that year, Congressman Denny of Mississippi introduced a bill that made it unlawful for the Internal Revenue Office "to grant or issue" liquor licenses "in any state, county, or parish where, under the laws of such state, county or parish, the sale of . . . intoxicants is prohibited." But radical temperance agitation was not strong enough to overcome constitutional and practical objections that congressmen and others found in this and similar bills.

The Denny bill was referred to the Committee on Ways and Means, which returned a scathingly adverse report. Written by Representative Evans, it denounced the bill's use of the word "license," explaining the meaning of "special tax" to the author of the bill. Evans also hinted that the bill, even if its practical defects in enforcement could be overcome, would be "obnoxious" to the constitutional provision that excises be uniform through-out the nation. The report concluded that, if passed, the bill would create "a judicial anomaly to hold that because a person had engaged in a business made unlawful by the local laws he therefore could escape from tax under the internal revenue law."[4]

Despite the hostile reception Denny's measure and other similar bills received in Congress, prohibitionists persisted in proposing them. The bills were popular because they addressed a common problem—lax implementa-tion of local liquor laws. According to one legislator who proposed such a bill, its purpose was "to effect the enforcement" of state liquor statutes. As late as 1906, the Prohibition party wrote such a measure into its platform. Committed radical temperance advocate and lawyer Finley C. Hendrick-son, who was the Prohibition party chairman for Maryland, questioned this course.

Hendrickson was convinced that these Denny-style measures would all break up on the rock of the uniformity clause. The Constitution (Art. I, sec. 8) stipulates that federal taxes be uniformly levied throughout the United States. In the 1890s the Supreme Court used the uniformity clause to strike down the federal income tax and made it a current topic of debate. Hendrickson's analysis was correct. Nearly a generation later, Congressman E. Yates Webb explained to a friend, "We would have passed long ago a law forbidding the issuing of revenue license to persons in dry states" save for the uniformity clause; it, he said, had "been the stumbling-block." To get around this uniformity problem, Hendrickson championed the other legislative alternative of the radical drys: that of requiring individuals applying for federal "licenses" to have proof that they had met the state's laws. Such a federal law would be uniform in principle, even if its application would vary between prohibition and license states.[5]

No matter how hard they worked, the radical prohibitionist agitation was fruitless. Frank Clark, a legislator who introduced these kinds of tax bills, summed up the experience. All such bills were "referred to the Committee on Ways and Means," he remarked in 1906, where they "peacefully slumbered" forever. Even the indefatigable Hendrickson was forced to admit that "Congress chloroforms in committee" most of the measures. A concerned party, the Vigilance Committee of the United States Brewers' Association, noted that these bills "appeared promptly and regularly at every session of Congress . . . only to be relegated quite as regularly and somewhat more promptly to the rubbishheap of discarded measures. They were never taken seriously." These proposals fared so poorly because, if enacted into law, they would have perpetuated an absurdity. The Vigilance Committee clearly and forcefully portrayed the result of their enactment. Passage "would mean, that while the honest dealers in all the states throughout the country must pay this tax, the lawbreakers, doing business in a prohibitory state, should enjoy perfect immunity in this and every other respect." In their drive to achieve legislation, the drys had forgotten that the federal government imposed the tax to raise a revenue, not to aid the states in their attempts to control liquor.[6]

Drys did not just seek legislation to end the collection of the liquor tax in dry areas. They also asked various presidents, through administrative action, to end the practice. But they were no more successful in these efforts than they had been in Congress. For instance, Matthew E. O'Brien wrote to President Roosevelt asking for an end of licensing in dry territory. The letter was submitted to Attorney General Bonaparte and never heard of again. In the next administration, Governor Haskel of Oklahoma and his assistant, Fred Caldwell, wrote President Taft and asked for the cessation of the collection of liquor taxes in Oklahoma. Attorney General Wickersham replied for the president, refusing the plea. And two years later John. H. Doddridge, pastor of a Methodist Episcopal church in Indiana, urged such a course on President Wilson. His letter was referred to the Treasury Department, which invoked a 1913 ruling of Commissioner Royal E. Cabell. This ruling, relying on previous rulings of the courts and commissioners, stated that there was "no authority vested in any administrative officer" to "waive the tax or decline to collect it." Despite this record of failure, the attempt of drys to bring federal tax power into line with state prohibition is in itself significant.[7]

As the *Union Signal* predicted, such proposals were "an entering wedge to a new era of federal action of tremendous and far reaching possibilities." By helping draft and support such measures, the prohibitionists moved closer to the idea that the states and national government could work in concert to suppress the liquor traffic. Despite the failures of these proposals, the agitation for their passage opened prohibitionists' eyes to the idea "that the federal government may work in harmoney [*sic*] with the state." Comity between the laws of nation and state became an important theme in the prohibition newspapers. Hendrickson became particularly adept at pointing out instances in which the states cooperated with the national government. He compared the federal government's action to a hypothetical case of states supporting smuggling. He also praised the states for not prohibiting Japanese children from attending public schools because of their obligations under federal treaties. This cooperative vision would blend together with a practical conception of the tax advocated by the Anti-Saloon League to produce the prohibition movement's final perception of the liquor tax.[8]

The Anti-Saloon League shared the radical prohibitionists' aspirations but went beyond their idealistic methods. The league prided itself on being flexible, not dogmatic. In the matter of the federal liquor tax the league adopted a pragmatic program. Unlike most radicals, league supporters saw benefits in the tax, and they realized that its abolition was undesirable. The sweeping solution, repeal, was never a league option, but perhaps to gain support of other temperance groups the league adopted the radicals' proposed legislative restrictions on the tax system. The league also concentrated its energies on changing the workings of the tax in the states. Building on the idea of a cooperative federal government, the league asserted that the government should actively assist the states and the prohibition movement by using its taxing power to augment state enforcement efforts. Although prohibitionists never fully converted federal bureaucrats into willing allies, they won enough concessions to make the federal tax system an effective enforcement weapon and a scheme worth preserving after the enactment of national prohibition.

The fledgling Anti-Saloon League coopted the existing temperance proposals for changing the liquor tax system. In 1899 Howard Hyde Russell told a league audience that "the government should cease everywhere, being a party to law breaking by collecting its liquor tax" in dry territory. Nine years later, the league endorsed letters (written by state officials close to the league) to Presidents Roosevelt and Taft that asked them to ban, by administrative action, the collection of the tax in prohibition areas. League workers even helped Finley Hendrickson by supplying him with information to formulate his arguments. But within the league some opposed limiting the collection of the liquor tax on the grounds that such plans would curtail the gathering of evidence in state liquor law violation cases by erasing the tax records. So the league, while verbally supporting bills restricting the collection of liquor taxes, in practice adopted a different approach to the tax system.[9]

In its publications the Anti-Saloon League portrayed the federal liquor tax, and indeed any liquor restriction, in a positive light. The league did not see the tax as a legitimating agent but rather as a badge of shame imposed on the liquor industry. "The putting of a tax upon" liquor manufacturing and selling did not bring these activities "into the same category of occupations as breadmaking or banking." Rather, the tax was levied "to defray the expense the traffic causes to the state, and also upon the theory that it is a dangerous or pernicious business which needs regulation." The famous prohibitionist congressman from Maine, Charles Littlefield, expressed a similar sentiment in an article in the *Union Signal*. He wrote that the federal liquor tax "is equivalent to a legislative declaration that the liquor business is not essential to the public welfare and may therefore properly be selected to bear a burden not imposed on other kinds of business." Reflecting league views, Littlefield argued that repeal was the wrong course. He believed that "it would be wise to make it more difficult to carry on the liquor business by increasing the tax." Littlefield's comments began a three-month debate in the pages of the paper, reviving all the old images of the federal tax pioneered in the 1880s and 1890s. Although some members of the Prohibition party and the WCTU still called for repeal of the federal tax, the debate revealed that many temperance workers wanted a new approach to the tax. The Anti-Saloon League would fulfill that wish.[10]

The league advanced views different from those of the radicals about the value of the statistics gathered by the Internal Revenue Office. For the most part, radical prohibitionists found federal tax officials and their statistics to be valueless. The 1893 *Cyclopaedia of Temperance and Prohibition* argued that officials were "responsible for many misleading representations that are eagerly repeated by the enemies of prohibition." The payment of the tax "by individuals in prohibitory states provides statistics that are deemed especially serviceable by unscrupulous anti-prohibition advocates." They used them to show that "state prohibitory laws are ineffective and farcical." According to the radicals, druggists and other legitimate sellers of liquor in dry areas were required to pay the tax and thus made the federal records "absolutely worthless as records of the number of persons actually engaged in the liquor traffic in a given state." On the other hand, the league found tax lists invaluable. Its official paper, the *American Issue*, claimed that "the truest test of the increase or decrease of drinking places in the state is gained by an inspection of the federal tax lists." In New Hampshire the Anti-Saloon League used the federal statistics to gauge the effectiveness of its enforcement agitation within the state.[11]

Indeed, law enforcement formed the foundation of the league's plans for the federal liquor tax. Because the Anti-Saloon League was more involved in liquor law enforcement than either the WCTU or the Prohibition party, it looked to the federal tax system as a means for perfecting dry enforcement efforts. For instance, prima facie evidence laws, like those of Maine and Massachusetts, were among the many liquor laws the league endorsed. Wherever the league agitated and wherever prohibition took root, prima facie laws followed. By 1917 twenty-eight states had enacted such laws. The Anti-Saloon League zealously lobbied for prima facie laws in many of these states and gleefully reported their passage and their testing in the courts. For the league the appeal of these laws was that they greatly aided "in convicting those engaged in selling liquor" illegally. Thus, the laws were one of the easiest ways of making local liquor laws effective.[12]

Prohibitionists proposing prima facie laws benefited from the unwillingness of judges to see such forced disclosures as violations of federal and state constitutional guarantees against self-incrimination. Passage of the early prima facie laws prompted the liquor industry to raise this constitutional issue. In his report to the 1888 United States Brewers' Association annual convention, Louis Schade, its longtime attorney and lobbyist, argued that the laws violated the Fifth Amendment and various state protections against self-incrimination. Schade based his argument on an analogous Iowa case, *State v. Smith*.

The facts of the Smith case were as follows. Under its prohibition laws, Iowa allowed druggists to dispense liquor under state supervision. Each pharmacist was required to submit monthly statements with the county auditor accounting for all liquor sold. J. R. Smith, an Iowa druggist, was indicted by a grand jury on the grounds that his reports revealed instances of illegal liquor dealing. The state district court quashed the indictment because it was based on evidences "which were illegal, in violation of the Bill of Rights and contrary to the Fifth Amendment of the Constitution of the

United States." Schade reported to the convention that the Iowa Supreme Court sustained the district court in its opinion and, by the same reasoning, the prima facie laws would be struck down.[13]

Unfortunately for liquor dealers in dry areas, the Iowa Supreme Court had reversed the lower court. In *State v. Smith* the court did not see the pharmacist's reports as a means of compelling Smith to testify against himself. Rather, it ruled that druggists' accounts were public records because they were "verified and deposited with the auditor." Public records were, in the court's words, competent evidence "to establish any fact in issue for judicial determination." Despite liquor dealers' continued contentions that the prima facie laws were an unconstitutional means of forcing people to testify against themselves, the idea flourished that records for payment of federal liquor taxes were competent evidence.[14]

In 1907 a North Dakota law carried the idea to its logical (and absurd) conclusion. In prohibition North Dakota payment of the federal liquor tax was, by law, prima facie evidence of liquor selling. In an attempt to improve enforcement, the state extended this law. Under penalty it required every holder of a federal "license" to publish for three successive weeks in local papers an official notice containing the name of the persons who held the tax receipt, a description of where the receipt was posted, and the name of the owner of the property where the receipt was posted. The liquor dealer was further required to file a copy of this notice with the local auditor, who was commanded to publish a complete list of such returns for the area. Wets challenged this law in the North Dakota Supreme Court on the grounds that it violated protections against self-incrimination guaranteed by the state constitution. While admitting that the law was passed "solely to furnish knowledge in the enforcement of the statute against the unlawful traffic in intoxicating liquors," the court dismissed the self-incrimination issue. It claimed, with no further elaboration, that it was "unable to see any force to this contention." Such judicial attitudes strengthened the hand of the drys advocating prima facie laws.[15]

In the right circumstances the prima facie laws could become a "very powerful agency" in the crusaders' enforcement arsenal. For example, in 1900 and 1901, the Anti-Saloon League of then dry Vermont mobilized its 1888 prima facie law to wreak havoc on the liquor sellers in the state. The league in Vermont was particularly active because federal officials there apparently did not hinder their actions. The league boasted of having complete lists of the license holders, and it used these lists effectively. In some counties every license holder was enjoined from further liquor selling. Violators of the injunctions were speedily prosecuted for contempt of court and were usually convicted. The Vermont league's superintendent, Reverend G. W. Morrow, proclaimed the prosecutions based on the tax lists a victory. He reported that one of the state's prosecutors praised the work, saying, "It is rather laughable to see how you have been pummeling the holders of the U.S. licenses." The effectiveness of the league's approach provoked Vermont wets to attempt unsuccessfully to "take out the teeth" of the enabling law. Eight months after the prima facie campaign began, 20 percent of the Vermont dealers, trying to avoid state use of the records, had canceled their federal "licenses." In short, because gathering evidence had become such a simple task, Vermont courts were "doing some royal work."[16]

Besides serving as the basis for prosecutions under state prima facie laws, the league could put the tax system and its records to other uses. For instance, the Virginia Anti-Saloon League, before that state passed a prima facie law, combed the tax records to "secure the names of all persons" who paid tax and sold liquor. The league published this list of liquor sellers in local newspapers, presuming that community pressure, suasion, and maybe even citizen-sponsored prosecutions would curtail illegal liquor sales. A few years later, after the state had adopted a league-drafted prima facie law, the league worked the process in reverse. It informed federal tax officials of liquor retailers who, out of fear of state prosecution, had not paid the tax or had failed to post their tax receipts as required by federal law. These liquor sellers were hauled before federal courts, and upon conviction they paid back taxes, assessed fines, and court costs. Thus, in the league's hands the tax could become a valuable and double-edged enforcement weapon.[17]

In 1906 various drys debated the league's approach to the tax in the pages of the *Union Signal*. Charles Littlefield argued the Anti-Saloon League case. He asserted that the tax receipt, as it "furnished very convincing proof of intent to sell," was "a very valuable aid in the enforcement of the statutes prohibiting the sale of liquor." Littlefield argued that, for this reason, the tax should not be repealed or altered. Other writers, especially Finley Hendrickson, mocked these views, delighting in pointing out that the tax did not then work as an enforcement aid because the government prohibited its officials from testifying. The final article in the series, a "summing up" by the prohibition judge Charles A. Pollock of North Dakota (himself a member of the Anti-Saloon League), gave the Anti-Saloon League's position full support. Pollock concluded that the regulations of the Internal Revenue Office and the Treasury Department were not final and that changes in personnel in Washington could bring about modifications in these regulations. Prohibitionists should work for changes in the federal government. In other words, "the general government ought to give friendly aid" to the states "by furnishing proof, whenever called upon, as to all persons who have paid the government tax."[18]

As the arguments waxed and waned in the *Union Signal*, Congress passed an act that changed some of the Internal Revenue Office's policy toward the prohibition movement. The Anti-Saloon League took credit for this act, the 1906 Certified List Law, which advanced its plans for using the tax as an enforcement aid. What the league's connection was to its drafting and passage remains unclear. William Anderson asserted that the league's department of legislation had secured its passage, but Reverend Edwin Dinwiddie claimed that the league "had charge of the campaign" for the measure "outside of Congress." But whatever its origins, the law reflected league thinking about the tax and marked the ascendancy of the idea that the federal liquor tax should be used to aid state prohibition.[19]

The bill that became the Certified List Law was one of several introduced in Congress. In the early twentieth century the spread of the prohibition movement into the south increased calls for such legislation, and newer southern congressmen succumbed to prohibitionist requests to sponsor liquor tax legislation. Members willing to introduce temperance measures drew few distinctions between various dry positions. For example, one congressman introduced both a bill designed to make it easier for drys to use tax materials in liquor law prosecutions and a bill to restrict the government from issuing licenses in dry areas. The bill of Benjamin Humphreys, a second-term representative from Mississippi, differed from his colleagues' bills in one way. It was the only bill on the subject to be reported out of the House Committee on Ways and Means. The debates in Congress over the measure underscored the confusion within the temperance camp and revealed congressional opposition to an active federal role in enforcing liquor laws.[20]

Humphreys's initial bill sought to amend the revenue code so that each collector "shall make and preserve a duplicate of the tax receipt or receipts issued" and "upon application of any person he shall furnish a certified copy thereof, as a public record" for a nominal fee. As drafted, it served two purposes: first, where state officials were eager to enforce prohibition laws, it secured them the needed evidence; second, the provision allowing "any person" to request a certified record reflected the league's strategy toward local officers. The Anti-Saloon League expected officials to do their duty, and if they would not, the league would force them to do so. Armed with tax list evidence, temperance workers could pressure local officials into enforcing liquor laws; the bill let prohibitionists easily direct law enforcement.[21]

In 1906, no one group—if any—directed the temperance forces in Congress. Thus, drys as well as wets attacked the bill. Representative Humphreys defended his bill from congressmen promoting more sweeping prohibitionist plans. For instance, Frank Clark, a first-term congressman from Florida, pressed for the adoption of a ban on licenses in dry areas. Clark's proposal gained little support as other legislators friendly to the temperance movement, like Humphreys and Littlefield, argued that it was unconstitutional. Most congressmen apparently agreed with Humphreys when he argued that his bill avoided the constitutional questions implicit in the more sweeping proposals while accomplishing the same goal, limiting federal hindrance to state prohibition policies. When questioned about the evidentiary value of the certified material, Humphreys replied that his bill "will do whatever good the state legislatures see fit to make of it." His assumption that the state legislatures would implement the law through supplemental legislation foreshadowed what the league would do after the passage of the act.[22]

Other opponents to the Humphreys bill attacked it as an expansion of the federal government's role in liquor law enforcement. Representative James R. Mann of Illinois feared that, as a result of the proposed law, liquor dealers would refuse to pay their taxes. Then the internal revenue officers would "be put upon the work of doing the police work which ought to be done by the States." Representative David J. Foster of Vermont defended the current Internal Revenue Office practices. He contended, "The revenue laws of the national government should not be used in executing the criminal laws of the several states."

Supporters of the measure responded to these attacks by appealing to states' rights and the idea that the general government should work in harmony with the states. Opponents found the states' rights argument specious. States' rights, they contended, existed without the aid of national authority. Representative Mann ironically congratulated "my friends from the south, who have always advocated states' rights, in now coming to Congress and appealing to the general government to do police duty in their own states. Nobody else has ever gone that far." These reservations conveyed hostility toward using the federal government to aid states. This view raised federalism into a near-sacred legal formula and portrayed the pragmatic, results-at-any-cost approach of the bill's supporters as almost sacrilegious. Their stance strangely paralleled radical prohibitionist thinking on the nature of law. But like the radicals, they also failed to block the bill from becoming law.

Before passage, however, Congress rewrote the act, modifying Humphreys's language. To make its operation more efficient, Congress replaced the tax receipts in the original bill with the alphabetical list kept by the collectors. For a slight fee the collectors had to "furnish a certified copy" of the list to "any prosecuting officer of any state, county, or municipality." By substituting specified state officers for "all persons," it reduced the league's potential role. Nevertheless, the law strengthened the Anti-Saloon League's position within the movement by writing into law its approach to the tax system. In practice, by making the federal government a partner in liquor law enforcement, it put the illegal liquor sellers in dry areas, as Representative Humphreys expressed it, "between the devil and the deep blue sea."[23]

The differing responses of the three major temperance organizations to the passage of the 1906 Certified List Law revealed their positions on the use of the federal tax system as an aid to state law enforcement. For the Anti-Saloon League, the *American Issue* praised the law. The paper found it "useful in law enforcement matters especially in the introduction of testimony." The league's legislative lobbyist admitted that the law was flawed, but argued that it opened the door for further action. He wrote, "It may not be in just the form we preferred," but it did completely change federal policy. In the future "it will be easier to secure any needful amendment . . . than it has been to effect the passage of this bill." The Prohibition party, as represented by Finley C. Hendrickson, thought the act would "defer for a long time the efforts to induce the government to return to its historic policy of refusing to lay a permissive tax on any occupation declared illegal by the state laws." Hendrickson continued his agitation for bills to have federal "licenses" issued only to the liquor sellers authorized by state law, and he persisted in his calls for repeal of the liquor tax. The WCTU vacillated between these positions. In a speech to the 1909 convention, national president Lillian Stevens admitted that the 1906 law was useful in the prosecution of illegal sellers. Moreover, it was important because it kept the federal government involved with the suppression of the liquor traffic. At the same time, the *Union Signal* published Hendrickson's and other writers' call for repeal of the internal revenue system, or enactment of laws limiting the collection of the taxes to liquor dealers authorized by state laws. The differences in the prohibition ranks revealed the unsettled nature of the movement's attitude to the liquor tax, a situation that would not last long.[24]

After passage of the 1906 Certified List Law, the Anti-Saloon League turned its attention to the states. League workers sought to make federal law effective by shaping complementary state legislation. Between 1907 and 1918, league political influence helped secure the passage of such laws in twelve states. Each state amended its liquor laws, adding sections that made the certified lists prima facie evidence of liquor law violations. However, passage of such laws did not mean smooth sailing for prohibitionists. Some state courts vigorously limited the introduction of the certified lists. The highest court of Louisiana refused to accept the prima facie lists despite such a statute. On the other hand, implementation of the 1906 Certified List Law was possible without state enabling laws. The courts of five states (Illinois, Kansas, Kentucky, North Carolina, and Oklahoma) accepted the certified lists as competent or prima facie evidence at common law. In only one jurisdiction, Arkansas, did courts rule certified lists inadmissible as evidence because the state lacked a law allowing their introduction. Thus, the passage of the 1906 law, and the activities of the states in implementing it, made real the Anti-Saloon League's idea that the internal revenue system could be used to aid dry states.[25]

The 1906 law and supporting state efforts marked a watershed. The congressional victory claimed by the league inspired many supporters of other organizations, particularly the WCTU, to accept the pragmatic view of the tax. From 1906 to 1917 the league and other prohibitionists sought to extend this view. In this period prohibitionists worked to end obnoxious federal tax policies and to transform the liquor tax into a temperance tool.

For the league, encouraging the states to pass laws implementing the 1906 law was much easier than coercing cooperation from internal revenue officials. The strength of the Anti-Saloon League lay in its ability to influence publicly elected officials, not in persuading bureaucrats. The league had few levers to use against appointed federal officials. The Internal Revenue Office obeyed the letter of the 1906 law, but it also continued to obstruct prohibitionist plans. Four practices—the use of confusing abbreviations and phrases in keeping federal records, the auction of seized liquor, the automatic compromising of tax cases in dry territory, and the refusal by officials to testify— provoked the ire of twentieth-century prohibitionists. In two cases, however, the drys were able to force the Internal Revenue Office to reverse its stand, bringing it that much closer to the cooperative ideal. Both of these reversals of policy came in the Taft administration. The timing reflected the growing power of the prohibitionists. The earlier Roosevelt administration mollified drys by appointing William E. Johnson as special agent for the suppression of the liquor traffic in Indian Territory and ignored the tax problems. The Wilson administration did not face the tax issues because the Taft administration had settled some of them and because, by 1913, the prohibition movement focused on national prohibition and neglected other issues such as the complications of the federal liquor tax.[26]

It was common practice for collectors to keep their records in abbreviations. Various state courts had held that these abbreviations had to be explained before the lists would be admissible as proof. When the 1906 law eased introduction of the collector's tax lists into court, drys discovered that the collectors' abbreviation practices increased the difficulty of their task. In Georgia the collector went beyond the usual abbreviations, like "R.L.D." for "Retail Liquor Dealer." The certified copies of this collector included the phrases "said business" and "such business." In each case, the reference was to an unclear antecedent. These usages were nothing more than an impediment to the prohibitionists' use of the documents.

Drys, through Congressman William Adamson of Georgia, complained of the practice of using abbreviations and unclear language. Adamson wrote to the commissioner of the Internal Revenue Office and received a reply. It stated that from "the earliest times the use of initials . . . has been sanctioned by this office, and no sufficient reason is seen to vary from the practice of using such abbreviations." The 1906 law required the collector to "furnish an exact copy, and this office fails to see that it is incumbent on him to explain the meaning of the abbreviations used, which have a recognized meaning in the Internal Revenue Service." The commissioner's letter deliberately avoided the main point—that the abbreviations did not have meaning in many courts. His reliance on obeying the letter of the law in providing an exact copy overlooked the intent of the law, which was to aid dry states in the enforcement of their liquor laws. And the rule prohibiting collectors from testifying in court prevented the only competent witnesses from interpreting the abbreviations. Perpetuating the abbreviation system and condoning the actions of the Georgia collector hindered the use of the Certified List Law and revealed the bureaucracy's resistance to the prohibitionists' use of the tax system.

Unsatisfied, Adamson took the matter to President Taft, who referred it to Attorney General Wickersham. After an investigation, Wickersham determined that the practice of using abbreviations had to stop and that a collector's tax list should be kept in terms "so that the public can understand it." This stipulation reflected the original purpose of the 1872 disclosure law— that the tax list be open to prevent official fraud—while it made the list more useful to the drys. Thus, despite its opposition, the Internal Revenue Office was forced to change its ways. By appealing to elected officials, the drys compelled the office to cooperate more fully with the prohibition movement.[27]

But federal bureaucrats' obstructions took other forms. To the annoyance of temperance crusaders, the Internal Revenue Office did not jail liquor dealers in dry states who had not paid their tax. The *Union Signal* described the workings of this system in prohibition territory. When a "bootlegger was caught selling liquor without a government stamp, all he had to do to square himself with the revenue officers" was pay his tax due and a fine. The revenue officers "were ever ready to accommodate him by dating his stamp back to cover the period of his violations." Collectors in dry Kansas carried this "obnoxious" policy to the ridiculous length of touring the local jails and forcing arrested liquor sellers into paying their tax and penalty. The Internal Revenue Office was uninterested in prohibitionist complaints concerning this practice. In the face of the office's refusal to alter its policy, the prohibitionists again appealed to elected officials.[28]

Governor Walter Stubbs of Kansas, backed by the governors of other prohibition states and with the full support of the temperance organizations, appealed to President Taft. The drys wanted an end to this type of compromising of penalties that undercut state enforcement of liquor laws. President Taft again supported the prohibitionist view of the matter. His attorney general, bypassing the Internal Revenue Office, instructed U.S. attorneys to refuse to settle cases of tax avoidance and to "secure conviction and imprisonment . . . as a general policy." Prohibitionists expressed great delight in the growth of the new cooperative spirit. It is clear that the drys' increased political influence brought results. Appeals to elected officials reversed the obstructionist policies of the internal revenue officials. Apparently revenue officers did not fully obey the new regulations; two years after Stubbs's effort, Kansas county attorneys said that the old practice still prevailed.[29]

Even though the bureaucrats imperfectly implemented the cooperative policy, it had an effect on the liquor trade in dry states. Soon the Anti-Saloon League could boast that the federal government's policies were "a radical departure from former methods." The Taft and Wilson administrations implemented dry plans, and many collectors ignoring the directives were forced to mend their ways. In Kansas bootleggers failed to pay their federal tax in "self-defense" so as to avoid state prosecution. Federal officials then arrested and prosecuted them for nonpayment of taxes, refusing to compromise their cases. The *American Issue* gloated over the predicament of the illegal liquor seller: "He can take his choice"—pay the federal tax and risk state prosecution or not pay it and chance federal prosecution. Either way, noted the paper, "he's headed straight for jail."[30]

On the other hand, the prohibitionists were unsuccessful in the matter of auctions of seized liquor. Wet papers were only too happy to report the government's sales. "There is a spot in 'dry' Atlanta that one day in the year is as 'wet' as any saloon on earth." On that day "the Internal Revenue Department . . . conducts an auction of spirituous liquor captured in raids on the stills" in the state. The sales, advertised heavily and inevitably held on the front steps of U.S. Post Offices, beyond the reach of state officials, resulted in "spirited" bidding that raised significant revenues. Such sales continued until the advent of national prohibition. All drys seemed to be able to do against these auctions was to rail: "Nullification by the federal government must end." But the federal auctions were a minor inconvenience compared with the Treasury Department's rule prohibiting collectors from testifying in courts.[31]

After the passage of the 1906 act, the Internal Revenue Office preserved its rule, first laid down in 1888, that collectors would not testify about matters contained in their records and would not produce them in court. With the passage of the Certified List Law, officials grafted a new justification to the old rationales. There was no need for a collector to go to court because drys and state officials could get the same information by requesting certified lists. But for temperance workers, appearance was almost as important as substance. They wanted the federal government to appear to be fully in line with the policies of the dry states, so they continued to agitate for the termination of the practice. Perhaps because the certified lists filled most of their needs, only one confrontation over the testifying rule took place between enactment of the 1906 law and implementation of national prohibition. This one instance, however, escalated beyond any other that preceded it.[32]

In 1909 the Georgia-based Cureton distillery operated despite the state's prohibition law. It followed all federal rules, which of course meant that a federal official oversaw the premises. A Dade County grand jury, meeting in the town of Trenton before Judge G. W. Fite, investigated the matter and called government gauger Charles E. Stegal as a witness. Stegal refused to testify, citing regulations, and said he had been so instructed by collector Henry S. Rucker. Judge Fite confined him to jail for contempt. Rucker telegrammed the incarcerated Stegal: "District attorney advises you are not required to testify to facts that came to your knowledge solely by reason of your confidential relations with distillery as an officer." The same message was relayed to Judge Fite by a federal deputy attorney sent to represent Stegal. In response, Fite ruled Rucker in contempt of court and had him arrested by the sheriff of Fulton County. Before the sheriff sent from Dade County could remove collector Rucker to Trenton, the federal district court released him on writ of habeas corpus. Another writ was transmitted to Judge Fite, who refused to deliver up Stegal. Fite spoke to the Associated Press about the injustice of an officer "at a government wild cat distillery" defying a state court and protecting distillers whom "he is aiding and abetting in violating the state law." It was rumored that a cavalry troop would be sent to remove Stegal from jail. Using this threat of force, state officials compelled Judge Fite to release Stegal.

The successful removal of Stegal on habeas corpus did not alter the conflicting views of state and federal officials. The Dade County grand jury returned a true bill against George Cureton and called for a new federal law to prohibit federal officials from aiding in the violation of state prohibition laws. In the habeas corpus proceedings in federal district court the state's attorney general persisted in questioning Stegal about knowledge he could have derived only from his official duties. The assistant federal attorney objected on the grounds that this questioning merely repeated Judge Fite's proceedings and that the Internal Revenue Office and Treasury Department rules prevented Stegal from testifying. The federal judge sustained his objection, and the no-testifying rule survived another test. Collector Rucker rewarded Stegal by advancing him to the post of deputy collector, "quite a promotion." The federal government had not surrendered an inch, and prohibitionists had clear proof that more needed to be done along the lines of reforming the federal liquor tax system.[33]

A dry member of the Georgia Assembly, Seaborn Wright, utilized the Stegal example in his calls for a restructuring of the federal government's policy toward the prohibition states. In a speech to a northern Anti-Saloon League audience, he invoked Civil War imagery to denounce the government's "open and shameless nullification" of state prohibition laws. He cited as his key example the recent problems in northern Georgia. Wright claimed that "we people in the South are helpless" against such practices, and he exhorted his audience, when faced with "the black flag of nullification," to "fix bayonets and charge." Prohibitionists, he insisted, should adopt the slogan "On to Washington."[34]

In many ways Wright was advocating a frontal assault on a citadel already captured by stealth, as the prohibitionist campaigns from 1906 on had brought about changes in the tax bureaucracy. The Anti-Saloon League, despite the irritations of the no-testifying rule and tax auctions, was quite near its goal of transforming the tax into a prohibition enforcement device. For instance, some sympathetic federal workers "leaked" to drys information concerning the liquor industry's activities. In Birmingham, Alabama, the league worker Samuel Weakley announced that the local collector was "in full sympathy" with dry efforts to uphold liquor laws. In 1911 the *American Issue* published a statement made by the commissioner of internal revenue, Royal E. Cabell. He argued that "90 per cent of the prosecutions in prohibition or local option communities are based on information obtained" from the federal tax collectors. Without the federal liquor tax records "local officers would not know the names of the dealers. . . . The tax, in short, is a practical temperance measure." The vision of a federal authority helping the states enforce their local laws was one that the Anti-Saloon League had long advocated. In admitting that the tax worked as a temperance tool, Commissioner Cabell indicated how far the Internal Revenue Office had moved from its historic position. According to the commissioner, the Internal Revenue Office now fulfilled the drys' desires for the tax. But for the league, this was not enough. New plans were afoot.[35]

The league, not content with the concessions it had already wrung from the federal government, sought to make the liquor tax an even more efficient temperance tool. The 1915 Anti-Saloon League convention adopted a resolution calling for the passage of a law requiring "all applicants for federal liquor tax receipts to state in their application that it is not unlawful to sell intoxicating liquors as a beverage at the place named in their application." Furthermore, the league wished the laws "amended to require" federal officials "to furnish the evidence they receive against liquor law violators in prohibition territory to local and state officers to aid them in the enforcement of the law." The first section of this resolution did more than revive the old idea that the federal government should not collect the tax from dry areas. It transferred to the federal level the old dilemma of the taking out a special tax, making its holder liable for prosecution. Liquor dealers who lied on their applications would be subject to federal penalties. The second part of this resolution repudiated the no-testifying rule. In its entirety the proposal would have made the federal government a major enforcer of state liquor laws. Beyond this, Representative Richmond Hobson, a dry, asked President Wilson to raise the liquor tax on dealers so as to burden the industry and prevent it from flourishing in prohibition territory. Other drys, in private, wanted to go even further; some leaders of the league speculated about using the tax power to secure "prohibition by indirection"—that is, taxing liquor out of existence.[36]

Congress never considered these proposals, and the Anti-Saloon League did not vigorously pursue them. For instance, the resolutions of the 1915 convention remained mere proposals, and the private plans remained just plans, not because the league lacked the political strength to back them, but because it chose to use its considerable political influence elsewhere. In 1913 the Anti-Saloon League launched its campaign for national prohibition through constitutional amendment. Other issues became sideshows to what prohibitionists rightly considered the culmination of their long struggle. However, the lessons learned in the debates over the liquor tax were not lost. Prohibitionists believed that the federal taxing power would play a role in the new order created by a prohibition amendment.

The place of the liquor tax in the plans for national prohibition reflected the dominance of the Anti-Saloon League and its ideas over the temperance movement. The other temperance workers eventually embraced these views. William J. Bryan and other drys wanted applicants for federal license to advertise their intention in the local press, which would, in dry areas, "inform the officers of the law where to find [them]." In an address on the proposed national prohibition amendment, delivered to the 1916 National WCTU annual convention, Lillian M. Stevens argued that "Congress may prohibit any incidental phase of the traffic by a tax." As it "destroyed the phosphorous match industry by a prohibitive tax," it could do so with liquor. If, despite national prohibition, "any part of the traffic continues it could be destroyed in this way." The federal taxing power would be used "not to encourage the traffic but to carry out the prohibition policy and law enforcement." The rest of her speech made it clear that the burden of enforcement would fall to the states and that the federal government would render them aid. It would be "team work" on a grand scale. "It places a double power" behind absolute prohibition, Stevens argued. Thus, the two ideas so integral to early Anti-Saloon League proposals—cooperation between the states and the nation, which the league borrowed from the temperance radicals, and the federal tax as a "practical temperance measure"—were preserved in prohibitionist plans for national prohibition.[37]

The prohibition movement's evolving approach to the problems created by the liquor tax revealed the changing nature of the temperance movement and underscored how the reformers learned to manipulate the legal environment. From the 1880s to early in the twentieth century, the WCTU and the Prohibition party saw the tax as inherently evil and pressed for sweeping solutions: abolition of the tax system or banning collection of the tax in dry areas of the nation. This near-utopian approach was predicated on a Mosaic conception of law, in which definitive "thou shall nots" were to stand before the people and guide them to a land free of alcohol and its evils. Even though dry idealism dimmed in the light of repeated failures, the radicals, by championing the idea that the federal government could use its tax system to aid the prohibition states, contributed much to the resolution of the tax issues.

Facing the continuing challenge of federal tax policy, the Anti-Saloon League began with the radical cooperative idea as a base, and it adopted the idea of the tax as an enforcement aid introduced by prohibitionists working in the states in the 1880s and 1890s. The league wed the cooperative ideal with this practical conception of law and used its political power to compel the government to change the tax system to suit drys. The federal tax system became an important asset in the campaign to enforce local liquor laws. This practical view of the tax insured that the liquor tax would have a role in the era of national prohibition. Moreover, the changing solutions to the tax issue revealed the transformation of prohibitionist means; the loss of purity in position was offset by the increase in effectiveness. Drys followed a similar path in another area of conflict between dry states and nation, interstate liquor shipments.

INTERSTATE COMMERCE, PRAGMATIC PROHIBITIONISTS, AND FEDERAL POWER IN THE PROGRESSIVE ERA

CHAPTER

In a number of rulings, delivered in the last decade of the nineteenth century and the first decade of the twentieth century, the U.S. Supreme Court made it easier to import liquor into prohibition states. The "state of courts" contributed to the creation of a thriving interstate liquor shipping industry. This industry soon filled the prohibition states with beer, wine, and hard liquor. In response the prohibitionists, eventually led by the Anti-Saloon League, sought state and national legislation to curtail this trade. Operating within the parameters set out in judicial doctrines, drys wrote many state laws that restricted interstate liquor shipments and prompted new court cases. These laws and court rulings tended to reaffirm the custom of allowing interstate liquor shipments into dry territory, thus keeping the interstate commerce issues alive. The persistence of the interstate liquor problem led drys to seek new legislation from Congress after the turn of the century.

In turning to Congress, drys were joining the host of reformers seeking federal remedies for social problems. The reformers of the progressive era, aided by politicians willing to stretch and bend the shape of the polity, expanded the scope of the postal, tax, treaty, and especially commerce powers. Indeed, by the middle of the second decade of the twentieth century, the federal government had developed a de facto police power, based on constitutionally enumerated powers. Each of these powers became the subject of lively debate between proponents and opponents of reform. Given this new legal environment, drys seeking federal legislation could either adopt a purely national solution to the problem or maintain the system, created by the earlier court cases and the Wilson Act, of concurrent state and federal action against the liquor evil.

Following the passage of the Wilson Act in 1890, the Iowa legislature revived its law regulating the transportation of liquor in Iowa, which the Supreme Court had ruled unconstitutional in *Bowman v. Chicago and Northwestern Railroad*. The resurrected law penalized common carriers and their employees if they accepted liquor shipments and moved liquor from one point in Iowa to another without meeting certain requirements. The law required every person receiving liquor to present a certificate issued by state authorities that attested that the consignee of the liquor was authorized to sell liquor in Iowa. Without such a certificate the shipment was illegal. The Dallas Transportation Company, of Illinois, routinely shipped intoxicating liquor—packed in wooden boxes labeled as groceries—into Iowa on various railroads. In August 1891 John Rhodes, a Brighton station agent of the Burlington and Western Railroad, accepted a Dallas Transportation Company shipment that had been carried on the line from Burlington, Iowa. Rhodes moved the box from the platform to the warehouse, "about six feet." Within a day of its arrival state officials seized the liquor. The state indicted Rhodes for violating the Iowa transportation law; at trial he was convicted, and the Iowa State Supreme Court upheld his conviction.[1]

The railroad company carried the case, on writ of error, to the U.S. Supreme Court. Argued in 1898, *Rhodes v. Iowa* raised the issue of where and when under the Wilson Act alcohol ceased to be in interstate commerce and became subject to the Iowa law. Counsel for Rhodes argued that the seized liquor had been in interstate commerce. Furthermore, the Wilson Act did not provide "that the laws of Iowa should apply before the consummation by delivery." The state of Iowa contended that the phrase "upon arrival" in the Wilson Act meant that state laws went into effect the moment liquor crossed the state line.

The Supreme Court sided with Rhodes and the railroad company, ruling the Iowa law an unconstitutional infringement on Congress's power to regulate interstate commerce. Justice Edward White, who wrote the majority opinion, advanced a narrow construction of the Wilson Act. The meaning of the words "upon arrival," he held, could be understood only by considering "the entire context of the act." Another phrase in the law, "or remains therein for use, consumption, sale or storage therein," made it "impossible in reason to hold that the law intended the word 'arrival' should mean at the state line, since it presupposes the coming of goods into the state." Similarly, the phrase "original package" used in the act "would have no place or meaning in the act if its purpose was to attach the power of the state to the goods before the termination of the interstate commerce shipment." White remained reluctant to base the decision only on the "subtle significations of words and the niceties of verbal distinction." Rather, he forecast the effect of the Iowa law on interstate commerce if he allowed the state's contentions. He claimed that if the Wilson Act allowed Iowa law to begin operation at the state line, Iowa's law would gain "an extraterritorial operation." It would affect "persons and property beyond" the state's borders because shippers in other states would be required to obey the Iowa law. Such a construction would create commercial anarchy. Thus, the Court ruled that the Wilson Act did not "cause the power of the state" to reach liquor shipments "whilst the merchandise was in transit." States could not act "until its arrival at the point of destination and delivery there to the consignee." The U.S. Supreme Court, by narrowly construing the Wilson Act, ruled that the Iowa law violated Congress's control over interstate commerce.[2]

In a companion case, *Vance v. W. A. Vandercook Co.*, the Court applied the *Rhodes* construction to the South Carolina dispensary law. Like Iowa, South Carolina regulated liquor transportation; its law required analysis of samples in advance of liquor to be imported for personal use. This requirement paralleled the test carried on by the state in purchasing liquors for its dispensaries. The consignee needed to possess a state-issued certificate attesting to the purity of the liquor for the shipment to be legitimate. And state law authorized the seizure of any other liquor transported into the state. Speaking for a majority of six, Justice White contended that the South Carolina law was not a valid inspection law. Under the Constitution and the Wilson Act, he explained, the "right of the citizen of another state to avail himself of interstate commerce" could not be controlled by the South Carolina officials "issuing of a certificate." It followed that the state could not stop the interstate shipment of liquor for personal use; although under the Wilson Act, it could prohibit its sale in original packages.[3]

The majority opinions in *Rhodes v. Iowa* and *Vance v. W. A. Vandercook Co.* set the limits of what the Wilson Act conceded to state power. White's opinion in *Rhodes* raised the theme that Congress, in passing the act, did not surrender its control over an essential part of interstate commerce. Original package sales were "but an incident" of commerce, especially as sales in general were "usually subjected to control" of the states. On the other hand, "the right to contract for the transportation of merchandise from one state" to another "involved" the "very essence" of interstate commerce, "which necessarily must be governed" by the federal government. Similarly, his opinion in *Vance* asserted that the "right of persons in one state to ship liquor into another state to a resident for his own use is derived from the Constitution of the United States." While skirting the question of whether citizens possessed a right of personal use of liquor, the Court asserted that the freedom of interstate commerce implied the right to ship liquor into every state. This statement by the Court became the cornerstone in liquor shippers' justifications of their business, and for seventeen years prohibitionists did not use law to attack personal-use shipments.[4]

Shippers, liberated from state hindrance by the *Rhodes* and *Vance* rulings, deluged the prohibition states with intoxicating beverages, stimulating more court cases. At the turn of the century, both the Adams and American Express companies carried cash-on-delivery (COD) liquor shipments into dry Iowa. State officials seized American Express Company shipments as contraband and charged Adams Express Company with maintaining a nuisance by keeping a building—its station office—for the sale of liquor. After losing appeals in the highest state court, the express companies brought their cases to the U.S. Supreme Court. There they claimed immunity from such state actions because they were operating as mere common carriers in interstate commerce. In the 1905 cases of *American Express Company v. Iowa* and *Adams Express Company v. Iowa*, Justice White, for the Court, extended the interstate commerce clause's protection to COD liquor shipments. White argued that the right of parties to make a contract of sale in separate states "and in doing so to fix by agreement the time when the conditions of which the complete title should pass" was "beyond question." Clearly, shipments so made "constituted interstate commerce." Iowa's laws could not operate in another state to "invalidate a lawful contract as to interstate commerce." If Iowa, or any state, could stop such shipments, it would establish a principle that would "cripple if not destroy that freedom of commerce between the states which it was the great purpose of the Constitution to promote." The Court refused to consider the question of when a COD shipment became the consignee's responsibility, subjecting the consignee or the consignee's agent to risk. State practices varied: some declared risk attached when the shipment was delivered and paid for, others when it reached the hands of the carrier. The distinction is important, as the second interpretation could lead to effective state action against COD carriers.[5]

The Supreme Court's construction of the Wilson Act, extending interstate commerce protection to liquor shipments until they reached the hands of their consignee, created a flourishing interstate commerce in alcohol between wet and dry states. Liquor sellers in wet states used the channels of interstate commerce to introduce their goods into prohibition states and local option localities. The "right" of citizens to import alcohol for personal use provided the pretext for this industry, but much of this liquor was diverted into illegal sales. Various practices insulated the buyers and sellers of liquor from the effect of state laws. The railroads and express companies carried the booze into dry areas, and thus the express freight offices in prohibition territory often became little more than interstate commerce liquor package stores.

Large and small brewers, distillers, and wholesalers all engaged in the interstate liquor trade. Their legal counsel advised them to "avail themselves of the privilege" of selling by express to persons in dry areas. The liquor sellers advertised their trade in newspapers, sent out circulars, and employed drummers. The W. F. Seeba Company called itself "Florida's Foremost Mail Order House" in its newspaper ads. A circular of the "Hutchison Ice Company" informed the citizens of Kansas that their company could "supply the wants of thirsty Kansas" from Kansas City, Missouri, and that their large stock enabled them to "fill orders without delay." Prohibitionists admitted that the number of liquor-house circulars and postal money orders for liquor sales swelled the mailbags of dry areas. The nation's largest brewer, Anheuser-Busch, established a special mail order department that sent one dozen quart or two dozen pint bottles directly to consumers. One of its advertising circulars showed a farmer loading his wagon with crated beer from a rural railroad station. Other companies used less pastoral advertising. The reform agitator Wilbur Crafts complained of St. Louis whiskey sellers who marketed in the south "adulterated liquors of the very worst type . . . many of them accompanied by obscene pictures that almost drive" the consumer "to rape as well as intoxication."

Other firms relied on soliciting drummers to generate their business. Such agents took "orders for liquor in every nook and corner of prohibition states." Students and others were recruited to work for commissions of 50¢ per gallon and $1.50 per case. The carrying and sharing of "samples" constituted the drummers' chief legal danger, for drummers did not collect money or deliver the merchandise. They merely took orders; express companies carried the goods into dry areas where the customer paid for them on delivery. Some dealers formed their own shipping companies, like the Interstate Express Company of Fall River, Massachusetts. It dealt "almost entirely in beer and liquors" and supplied the dry towns of Massachusetts with these commodities from across the border in Connecticut. More common was the use of the regular channels of interstate trade: the railroads and express corporations.[6]

According to prohibitionists, the liquor industry "bulldozed" the railroads and express companies into carrying liquor into dry areas. But the transportation companies and their employees, especially around the turn of the century, were willing partners in the trade. A Dayton, Ohio, distilling firm used the agents of the United States Express Company, with no hindrance from the parent company, as a source of customer lists. In exchange for "a miniature stone jug filled with our thirteen year rye malt whiskey," the agents supplied a list of names of people who "buy by mail order and can appreciate a good, pure, medicinal household article." For the agent the direct payment of booze was followed by an increase in express business. Sometimes the receiver of the liquor would be generous. In Hodgenville, Kentucky, Richard Graham, upon opening an unsolicited gallon of whiskey, drank the liquor, sharing it with J. R. Langley, the agent at the depot. Out-of-state liquor firms paid commissions to some agents for the liquor sent to their office. Invariably this business was COD and created fees for the express companies.

The complicity of the express companies went further. They routinely, and probably knowingly, handled liquor shipments addressed to "people who had not ordered it" and allowed them to be picked up by other people. Many packages arrived addressed to fictitious consignees and were stored in the express warehouse, available to anyone who wished to "claim" them. In effect, many express offices in dry states operated simply as "retail liquor stores." Indeed, secrecy and fraud characterized the whole process. To avoid interference by prohibition officials, liquor was falsely labeled as coffee, arrived in "plain wooden boxes tightly sealed and without marks," or was shipped so that it looked "like a package of groceries." Firms warned agents to use discretion in notifying customers that their packages had arrived. Despite that advice, the express agent in the dry town of Bainbridge, Ohio, sent out postal cards that read, "Dear Sir—we are holding at your risk a package of books . . . and you should get them at once as they are leaking badly."[7]

The COD liquor shipments were ubiquitous; if the estimates can be believed, a startling quantity of alcohol reached residents in prohibition territory. In Kansas, a state with good records, it was estimated that 4.5 million gallons of liquor entered the state in 1914. Most shipments originated in six major wet enclaves located on major rail lines: Chattanooga, Tennessee; Jacksonville, Florida; Louisville, Kentucky; Cincinnati, Ohio; Baltimore,

Maryland; and New York, New York. In 1901 the Anti-Saloon League estimated that each month $500 worth of liquor entered the small, dry town of Tekamah, Nebraska. Holidays were the peak season for the trade. Before Christmas of 1909 authorities in dry Memphis, Tennessee, seized 10,000 sealed quart to two-gallon packages of whisky. Around the same time, the Frisco Railroad Company shipped to twenty-six men with federal retail liquor licenses in Scapula, Oklahoma, 187 barrels, 1,674 cases, and 217 boxes of whisky; 57 boxes, 608 cases, and 245 barrels of wine; and 28 railroad carloads of beer. Invariably the hard liquor proved to be poor quality, sometimes consisting of nothing more than water, coloring, and wood alcohol. But that did not deter "the drinking part of the population" in dry areas from rushing "almost en masse . . . to the express office" and "juglines."[8]

Despite its profitability, the COD trade was a poor defense against prohibition. It was a common assumption that the availability of interstate liquor only encouraged voters to support prohibition because, despite the dry law, they could still get their liquor. At best, it was a profitable sideline that proved the ineffectiveness of prohibitory policies. But more direct challenges by the liquor barons proved disastrous. In 1906 and 1907, hoping to capitalize on dissatisfaction with prohibition and believing that the lax enforcement in the state's cities typified the whole state, the major brewers—including Pabst, Blatz, Schlitz, Heim, and Anheuser-Busch—organized an "invasion" of prohibition Kansas. The companies financed over one hundred barkeepers, in some cases purchasing buildings in which saloons soon opened, and supplied their "fixtures"—that is furnishings, glassware, and beer. Large city mayors supported the return of the liquor trade. Most state officials did not share their enthusiasm; the attorney general turned to courts of equity. The brewers' saloons were condemned as nuisances. Injunctions and padlock orders were issued forbidding the brewers from violating the prohibition law and from removing their fixtures and goods from the state. Eventually court-appointed receivers disposed of the brewers' property. The brewers, in the words of the *American Issue*, met "their Waterloo." Prohibition's constitutional legitimacy and its array of legal tools protected it from such frontal assaults; and after 1898 the drys sought new means to guard against the infiltration of interstate commerce liquor.[9]

The *Rhodes* and *Vance* rulings initially provoked little reaction from prohibitionists. But in the twentieth century, as the implications of the rulings became clearer and as the Anti-Saloon League began to assert its dominance over the temperance movement, the prohibitionists sought to limit the COD liquor industry. They proposed action at both the state and national levels. In the states they quickly won various laws curtailing the COD trade. In 1907 and 1908 the U.S. Supreme Court struck down the most far-reaching of these laws, and drys turned to different state measures. In Congress action was long delayed; eventually Congress would pass legislation restricting the interstate commerce trade in liquor.

The state of the prohibition movement and the circumstances in the *Rhodes* and *Vance* cases caused the subdued dry reaction to the rulings. In 1898 the temperance movement was mired in turmoil. The death of Frances Willard had left the WCTU directionless; the Prohibition party had collapsed into warring and ineffective factions; and the Anti-Saloon League was barely born. Furthermore, *Rhodes* originated in Iowa, a state that had repudiated its prohibition policy by passing the Mulct tax, which instituted a de facto system of local option liquor taxation; and *Vance* came up from the hated dispensary state of South Carolina. Thus the rulings, in many prohibitionists' eyes, did not directly affect their interests. But by the first years of the twentieth century, the revived temperance movement greeted the 1905 *Adams Express v. Iowa* case as a "new Dred Scott." In any case, no matter what their awareness of the rulings, drys could not miss the jug or COD trade, and they appealed to their state legislatures to stop it.[10]

Prohibitionists did not take the obvious step to stop the COD trade, the banning of personal consumption of liquor. The logic of that step was inescapable: if there were no legitimate reason to possess alcohol, there could be no legal reason to import liquors—the consignees would always be liable to state law. But before 1915 no state went "bone dry" by banning liquor imports. Indeed, the Anti-Saloon League supported the perpetuation of the personal-use exemption to prohibition laws. It did so not because it had changed its mind about the effects of liquor; it bothered prohibitionists that the families of "sorry white men and negroes" needed the money wasted on interstate liquor. It was not just that "a few men" got "liquor for personal use" that troubled drys but that "many lawless fellows [got] it to sell." The league made "its war mainly" against the "open saloon," and the idea of personal use of liquor did not bolster the rights of the saloon. Besides, as a matter of tactics, the personal-use exemption aided the league. It pacified wets in dry areas; they could get their liquor and so had little reason to try to repeal prohibitory laws. Similarly, it made prohibition laws and local option laws easier to sell to the public. So the drys moved against the COD industry with less sweeping enactments.[11]

Prohibitionists driven by the idea that "the jug trade is almost as pernicious as were the saloons" convinced many legislatures to restrict the industry. By 1907 fifteen prohibition and local option states had adopted laws regulating the soliciting of liquor orders and the delivery of intoxicants in dry areas. Although the details varied from state to state, Massachusetts's experience typified the pattern in the creation of such laws. In early 1903 liquor dealers located in the wet town of Haverhill, using a state law that had been written before the Wilson Act of 1890 and that legitimated original package sales, flooded the state's dry communities with "bottles of Canadian ale." Prohibitionists in "a turmoil of excitement" pressured the legislature into repealing the original package law and replacing it with another that banned soliciting of liquor orders in dry areas as well as the intrastate shipment of liquor into dry areas.[12]

Although the state anti-COD laws varied in their provisions, the Kentucky and West Virginia statutes characterized the general outlines of such laws. The 1903 Kentucky law, part of the state's local option statute, declared that all COD liquor shipments into the state's dry areas were "unlawful and shall be deemed sales of such liquors at the place where the money is paid or the goods delivered; the carrier and his agents selling or delivering such goods shall be liable jointly with the vendor thereof." While the Kentucky law was a straightforward prohibition, the West Virginia law was more circuitous. It stipulated that anyone "carrying on the business of common carrier," operating without a state liquor license, engaging "in the traffic or sale" of intoxicating liquors, or "interested for profit in the sale thereof" would be guilty of a crime and liable to fines and imprisonment. Since in West Virginia's local option territory it was impossible to procure a state liquor license, the law prohibited the COD sale of liquor in dry areas.

The convolutions of the West Virginia law originated in the prevalent idea that the U.S. Supreme Court would rule unconstitutional direct prohibitions of the COD trade. This view rested on the language of the *Vance* ruling, which stated that the right to import liquor for personal use derived from the Constitution. But in 1904 the Anti-Saloon League argued that the phrase in the West Virginia statute, "interested in the traffic or sales" of liquor, equated express agents with "regular saloon keepers" profiting from liquor sales. It placed the agents under the state's authority, recognized by the Wilson Act, to limit original package sales. It would then be legitimate under the Court's previous rulings.[13]

Prohibitionists knew of the constitutional jeopardy of the state regulations of the COD trade. They studied Iowa cases against the Adams and American Express companies in which the lower state courts had ruled that the state law violated the federal commerce power and the state supreme court had reversed those decisions. The prohibition press followed the development of similar cases in Massachusetts, Michigan, and Texas. These state court decisions varied too much to be conclusive. On the other hand, while the U.S. Supreme Court had not spoken definitively, it seemed inclined to void the COD laws. The Court's decision in *American Express Company v. Iowa* avoided the point of sale issue, which was an important part of the Kentucky statute. The thrust of the ruling—that COD contracts were valid and that the states could not interfere with interstate commerce shipments before they reached the hands of their consignees—suggested that the COD acts would not stand constitutional scrutiny. Similarly, in a ruling that reaffirmed *Rhodes, Heyman v. Southern Railway Co.*, Justice White—for a unanimous Court—raised doubts about the point of sale laws. He wrote, "For whatever may be the divergent legal rules . . . concerning the precise time when the liability of a carrier as such in respect to the carriage of goods ends, they cannot affect the general principle" as to when interstate commerce ended. His statement implied that, if a state law fixed criminal liability for COD shipments before the interstate commerce of the liquor ceased, the law would be unconstitutional.[14]

The questionable constitutionality of these laws and their popularity in prohibition circles caused the Anti-Saloon League to alternate between boosting and condemning them. The league thought direct prohibitions of the COD trade unconstitutional. The *American Issue* argued that such laws ran "squarely up against the United States interstate commerce law" and that, until federal law changed, interstate liquor shipments would continue "under federal supervision and protection." In 1906 the league, in its laboratory state of Ohio, replaced a Kentucky-style antishipping provision in the Beal Law of 1902 with a law that banned the use of fictitious names in liquor shipments. On the other hand, the league claimed to have "secured" the passage of the West Virginia law, praised its operation, and touted it as the best law in the country. However, in 1907, when the National Anti-Saloon League sent William Anderson to reorganize the Maryland Anti-Saloon League, one of his goals was the passage of an antishipping bill similar to the Kentucky law. Perhaps the league, tired of "waiting for Congress" to revise interstate commerce law, decided to "curb the evil" through state laws.[15]

While it vacillated in its support of state legislation restricting the COD liquor industry, the Anti-Saloon League wholeheartedly supported an alternative strategy for taming the interstate traffic: levying the federal retail liquor tax against the carriers. Given the WCTU's and Prohibition party's view of the liquor tax in these years, it is significant that the *American Issue* was the only prohibition paper that advanced this strategy. From 1900 to 1906, the league actively promoted efforts to apply the revenue laws to the express companies that shipped liquor COD. While courts typically saw the companies only as common carriers engaged in their trade, the Internal Revenue Office perceived them as liquor sellers. In 1906 it directed U.S. attorneys to prosecute railroads and express companies as liquor sellers who failed to pay their federal tax. The league hailed as victories the companies' convictions and out-of-court settlements. In the league's economically unsound view, the collection of the tax and penalties would improve prohibition and local option as "it will no longer be profitable" for the common carriers "to keep the traffic up." Presumably the federal tax burden that the league wished to impose on the carriers could be simply added to the price of the liquor. So in action the policy would only raise the price. This might cut consumption or encourage outright bootlegging, but it would not stop the carriers from participating in the business by cutting into profits. However, other aspects of the COD trade caused carriers to reassess the practice.[16]

Beginning in 1905, the carriers began to change their attitude toward COD liquor shipments. This reassessment was driven by the costs of litigation and by the disruption of their conventional business as depots turned into "dives" where it was "impossible for a lady to approach . . . without an escort." Express corporations and railroads searched for a way to curtail the COD liquor trade. Arguing that a Kansas law against false labeling extended to the COD trade, Wells Fargo and American Express refused to carry such shipments into the state. Similarly, the Pacific and Southern Railroad limited its COD liquor trade only to bona fide purchasers. Other companies raised their rates to discourage the business. Drys pressured the railroads to make these changes, knowing that companies "very much dread the idea of having any liquor seized at the railway station." Prohibitionists crowed over the changes, as they desired to have the railroads and express companies on their side. When American Express refused to ship intoxicants into Mississippi, the *American Issue* gloated that it drove "another nail . . . in the coffin of interstate nullification of law." But the legal justifications supporting these refusals were weak, and in 1907 and 1908 the U.S. Supreme Court decided two cases that extended legitimacy to the COD trade.[17]

In 1904 the Adams Express Company and the American Express Company were convicted of violating the Kentucky COD law. Each had sold COD liquor that, according to the state, had not been ordered by the purchasers and so acted as sellers, not just carriers. The companies lost their appeals in the Kentucky Court of Appeals and in 1907 brought the issue, on writ of error, to U.S. Supreme Court. The companies claimed protection from state law because the COD sales were part of interstate commerce. The state contended that sales lay in its "absolute power." Since the law fixed only the place of sale, it did not interfere with interstate commerce.

In the 1907 case *Adams Express Company v. Kentucky*, Justice Brewer wrote the opinion for the majority of eight. Ignoring the dissent of Justice John Harlan, who wrote that these were not "cases of legitimate interstate commerce" but simply "devices or tricks" designed to "defeat the Kentucky liquor laws," Brewer flatly stated that the law was "obviously an attempt to regulate" interstate commerce and was "in conflict with the Constitution." The Court reversed the Kentucky court's decision and remanded the case back to that court. Brewer did leave an opening for dry states determined to choke off liquor sales. "We do not mean to intimate," he said, "that an express company may not also be engaged in selling liquor" contrary to law. Presumably if a carrier participated in illegal sales, it could be held accountable, perhaps under a law similar to the West Virginia statute. To reach such carriers, other states would have to restructure their laws. While this case climbed the appellate ladder, the Kentucky anti-COD law continued to operate, giving rise to new cases. In 1908 yet another case, *Adams Express Company v. Kentucky*, arising from virtually the same circumstances, reached the U.S. Supreme Court. Again the Court held the Kentucky law to be an unconstitutional infringement on Congress's interstate commerce power. This second ruling added impetus to the drys' drive for devising different types of laws to control the interstate liquor shipments.[18]

Even before these decisions prohibitionists, wary of constitutional limits, changed the kind of statutes they sought from state legislatures. The new laws focused on the areas where the Supreme Court had left the states room to operate. One open area was the regulation of liquor solicitors. In the March 1907 case *Delamater v. South Dakota*, the Court ruled that a state license tax levied on drummers for out-of-state liquor companies was not an interference with interstate commerce. Justice White reasoned, for the majority of eight, that since under the provisions of the Wilson Act the states could prohibit original package sales of imported liquors and since solicitation was a part of sale, it was therefore within the ambit of state authority, recognized by the Court in *Robbins v. Shelby Co. Taxing District*, to tax such drummers.[19]

Reflecting their awareness of the constitutional limits, drys wrote new laws. For instance, a July 1907 Alabama law prohibited the acceptance or delivery of liquor in dry areas and the soliciting of liquor orders, but exempted any shipment that fell under "any provision of interstate laws of the United States." The 1909 Texas and the 1907 Mississippi laws used the states' power to regulate corporations to justify the levying of heavy taxes on out-of-state companies that maintained businesses where "legally deliverable" liquors were sent COD. While these laws were designed to punish the individuals and corporations dealing in spirits, a 1908 Mississippi law took a different tack. It made it illegal "to remove more than 100 feet from the point at which it is delivered" any legally imported liquor. The law operated clearly in an area reserved to the states and was designed to keep liquor sent for personal use from being diverted into illegal sales.[20]

Liquor shippers continued to challenge state liquor shipment statutes, but no clear doctrine emerged. Courts in Arkansas, Georgia, Mississippi, and Texas upheld the constitutionality of sundry COD restrictions; courts in Kentucky and Alabama ruled similar laws to be unconstitutional infringements on Congress's interstate commerce power. Nevertheless, the prohibitionists had the upper hand; until a court ruling, state anti-COD laws could interdict the trade and disrupt the carrier's business. Thus, some shipping companies attempted to comply with the laws. For instance, Adams Express Company asked the Anti-Saloon League to provide it with a list of local option and prohibition areas so it could instruct its agents not to ship COD liquor packages into those areas. Other transport companies carried on their COD trade "in protest" as the courts had ruled that they could not discriminate against liquor shippers by denying them COD privileges. In general, most common carriers refused to carry such shipments into states where COD restrictions were upheld or where litigation was pending. This refusal forced the liquor interests to take action.[21]

Facing financial ruin, mail order liquor houses sought injunctions from the courts and rulings from regulatory commissions requiring transportation companies to carry their liquor. But various courts and regulatory agencies disagreed. The federal Interstate Commerce Commission and various state courts found the carriers' practice of refusing COD liquor shipments to be reasonable. The business burdened transportation companies with unclaimed packages and made depots unpleasant to other patrons, thereby creating losses for the corporations. The Missouri Corporation Commission and several courts ruled that the refusal to ship was discriminatory and ordered carriers to resume the trade. The Virginia State Corporation Commission split the difference, requiring carriers to carry the shipments of retail liquor sellers but not the packages of wholesalers. The commission reasoned that because private consumers living in local option territory required only small quantities of alcohol for personal use and since wholesalers presumably supplied retailers, wholesalers were using the common carriers as "aiders and abettors in their violation of the law." The court injunction cases spread across the country, and eventually one of them was appealed to the U.S. Supreme Court. The Anti-Saloon League awaited "the outcome with interest."[22]

The Kentucky anti-COD law prompted the Louisville and Nashville Railroad to discontinue receiving liquor consignments for local option territory in the state. The railroad began this policy before the Kentucky Court of Appeals, following the first *Adams* decision, ruled the law unconstitutional and before the U.S. Supreme Court struck down the law in the second *Adams* case. The F. W. Cook Brewing Company responded to the railroad's decision by seeking and winning injunctions in state and federal courts enjoining the railroad from refusing such shipments. The railroad appealed to the U.S. Supreme Court, contending that it was only obeying the Kentucky law, that injunctive relief was improper, and that the ICC should settle the matter.

In the 1912 case *Louisville and Nashville Railroad Co. v. Cook Brewing Co.*, Justice Horace Lurton, for an unanimous Court, ruled against the railroad. Lurton held that injunctions were a proper recourse and that the Kentucky anti-COD law "was most obviously never an effective enactment in so far as it undertook to regulate interstate shipments to dry points." Since the company was a common carrier, it had no right to refuse legitimate shipments. As an unconstitutional enactment, the Kentucky law was no defense and the injunctions stood. The Supreme Court, in upholding the brewing company's claim, handed the liquor interests a weapon—the injunction—that counteracted the prohibitionists' power over the carriers. The new balance weakened the dry states by shifting the burden of enforcing prohibition back on local officials. They would have to catch the liquor sellers in the act instead of relying on COD laws to keep booze out of the state. The decision was a wet victory.[23]

When the Court construed the Wilson Act in a way that undermined the effectiveness of the state prohibition and local option laws, it reopened the interstate commerce issues. When it gave legitimacy to the COD trade by wrapping it in freedom-of-commerce doctrines, it strengthened the wets' hand. Drys responded by seeking new state laws to stop of the flow of liquor. In crafting the laws, they showed a growing familiarity with legal means. In the injunction cases, liquor sellers proved again the effectiveness of the shield of federalism. But the equilibrium set in the *Cook* case did not last. Drys had long sought to redress the situation in the national legislature, and Congress would tip the scales in their favor.

That the drys would turn to Congress was natural, given the history of their movement, but this impulse received extra impetus from the successes of other reformers of the progressive period. Dry proposals for federal action no longer seemed so outlandish, as government responded to problems and demands by altering the rules that governed state and federal action. Thus, when the states failed to solve a problem, policymakers would sanction expansion of federal powers. Every federal power of significance—the commerce power, the postal power, the treaty power, and the taxing power—saw expansion in the period. Abolitionist and regulationist reforms, like anti–child labor, conservation, pure food, and antiprostitution, became subjects for federal action. Activist presidents, most notably Theodore Roosevelt and Woodrow Wilson, supported such expansion of the government's role.

Indeed, as Robert Cushman noted, in the early twentieth century the federal government began to develop a rudimentary, independent police power; but the old conception of dual federalism—of joint federal and state action—remained vital. While based on existing delegated powers of the Constitution, some of the new regulations were, in effect, laws enacted to improve the general welfare—the equivalent of the states' police powers. Thus, a prohibitive tax on phosphorous matches, a regulatory system for migratory birds (based on the treaty power), and the Pure Food and Drug Act (based on the commerce power) tended to supersede state efforts. But the use of the commerce power, postal power, or tax power often simply supplemented state laws. The bans of lottery and gambling equipment from the mails and commerce, the prohibition of taking women across state lines for immoral purposes, the taxing of colored oleomargarine, and the banning of prizefight films from the mails all fell into this category.[24]

The shifting rules of the polity and the nature of each reform helped determine which power reformers would use and to what extent they would invoke it. When Congress passed an act and the courts upheld it, or when Congress refused to pass one or the courts struck one down, the actions became signposts for other reformers to follow. Thus, at different times, prohibitionists learned from child labor reformers, from conservationists, from pure food and drug advocates, and from antiprostitution reformers. Moreover, there was a tremendous exchange of ideas and justifications among proponents and opponents of these reforms. For instance, one of the leaders in shaping dry interstate commerce legislation, Senator William Kenyon, was instrumental in promoting anti–child labor legislation based on the commerce power. Prohibitionists in the twentieth century benefited from the actions of others who pressed against and changed existing government arrangements. To set the drys' career in the polity in context, it is necessary to examine other reforms of the period, like the anti–child labor crusade.[25]

The history of child labor reform points to the range of options available to drys in the progressive era. With the development of the factory system and industrial growth, various states began to restrict child labor. Thus, by 1900 most industrial states had enacted some form of child labor legislation.

But the regulations were weak in the south, and in the factories of North Carolina, South Carolina, and Georgia the practice of child labor became entrenched. None of those states limited child labor. Southern humanitarians—led by the Alabama minister Edgar Gardner Murphy—formed the National Child Labor Committee in 1904, which worked toward ending the practice. The committee's plans for reform reflected the late-nineteenth-century concept of the power of the federal government and the states. Its stated goal was legislation in every state banning all children under the age of fourteen from work and regulating the working hours and conditions for those from fourteen to sixteen. The committee "disavowed federal legislation" as a means to its ends. While achieving success in two-thirds of the states, the movement faltered in the Piedmont states. Then one of the allies of child labor reformers, Senator Albert Beveridge, overturned their conceptions of government power.[26]

In a dramatic speech on the Senate floor, Beveridge attacked the sin of "child slavery" and proposed federal legislation as the only remedy. Beveridge saw before many others in the movement that the nature of the polity was changing. President Roosevelt seemed willing to use the central government to act against problems that were once perceived as exclusively in the states' domain, like child labor. So hoping to link up with Roosevelt's agenda, Beveridge argued that states were unequal to the task of controlling child labor, as they tended to pass lax laws because of the competitive pressures from "backward" areas that allowed the practice. Congress alone could provide a uniform law. Relying on the Supreme Court's broad language in *Champion v. Ames*, which upheld the ban on lottery tickets, Beveridge argued that Congress could ban from interstate commerce the products of manufacturing establishments that employed child laborers. The National Child Labor Committee refused to endorse this action; indeed, it withdrew its support from Beveridge, purged its members who supported his ideas, and persisted in its program of state action. But its cherished goal of strong uniform state legislation proved impossible to achieve, and under pressure from other reformers the polity continued to change. In 1913, after the Mann Act prohibiting the transportation of women across state lines for immoral purposes had been upheld in the Supreme Court, the committee turned toward a national solution.

A conclave of committee leaders, lawyers, state officials, federal officials, and other reformers drafted a new bill. The meeting debated which federal power to use, seeking one that would be both constitutional and effective. They narrowed the choice to the commerce and taxing powers. With the support of the Wilson administration, the reformers chose the commerce power; it had received more recent sanction from the Supreme Court and offered a better chance for success. Following extensive debates in which opponents assailed the bill as an unconstitutional extension of federal power, Congress passed it in 1916. As enacted, the Child Labor Act banned from interstate commerce the goods made in factories that employed child labor contrary to federal standards. It was administered by the federal government. It was quickly tested in the courts, and in the 1918 case *Hammer v. Dagenhart*, a closely divided Court found it to be an unconstitutional extension of federal power. The Court ruled that the law was not a legitimate regulation of commerce but an attempt to control manufacturing, which was a local matter subject to state control.[27]

After the defeat, child labor reformers and their congressional allies assessed other legislative solutions to the problem. One solution was to attempt to pass a constitutional amendment allowing the federal government to regulate child labor. Another approach, pushed by William Kenyon, was to pass a federal law based on the postal power. Or the reformers could try to pass a Wilson Act for goods made with child labor, which would strip them of interstate character at an earlier period of time, allowing state laws to operate. All these were rejected for being of dubious value or too difficult to achieve. So they turned to the taxing power, invoking the examples of the oleo and phosphorous matches taxes and the Harrison Narcotics Act. The reformers' congressional supporters passed a heavy tax on the profits earned by companies that employed child labor. In 1922 the Court struck down this law in *Bailey v. Drexel Furniture Co.* After the second defeat the reformers did not abandon their hope of a federal solution to the problem. They pushed through Congress (and won ratification in twenty-eight states) of an anti–child labor constitutional amendment. And some proponents of child labor laws considered pushing a law based on the treaty power. That the anti–child labor advocates would turn to the treaty power was not as strange as it first seems: the treaty power saw growth in the progressive period, thanks to the efforts of reformers, including conservationists.[28]

Similar to the action of anti–child labor forces, the work of conservationists faced problems of federalism and raised a potential remedy for the drys to emulate. In the late nineteenth and early twentieth centuries, a wide coalition of groups—including conservation organizations, sportsmen's associations, state game officials, and even the federal Department of Agriculture—worried that Americans were indiscriminately destroying plumage, game, and insectivorous birds. State laws seemed to be ineffective in protecting birds for two reasons. First, many bird species migrated and thus could go into states with no protective laws. Second, competition to insure that their state harvested its full share of birds tempted states to adopt lax rules. Federal action seemed imperative.[29]

In 1900, following the pattern of 1890 Wilson Act, Congress used the commerce power to establish a federal law designed to cooperate with state game regulation. The 1900 Lacey Act banned the interstate transportation of the feathers or carcasses of game birds killed in violation of state law. But the law had one major failing: it did not come into operation until after the bird was dead. So beginning in 1904 reformers and others pressed Congress to enact a more comprehensive law to protect migratory birds. They sought a law that would set limits on when and how birds could be shot. But they ran into two constitutional objections: finding a power to support this comprehensive federal law and meeting objections that such a law conflicted with the police powers reserved to the states.[30]

Dual federalism complicated the conservation reformers' hopes. Game protection and regulation had long been recognized as a subject for state action, and they were seeking a federal law to override state law. Their constitutional authority for such a law remained ambiguous. The commerce power did not seem the proper base, as it was questionable whether live migrating birds were subjects of commerce. The postal and tax powers clearly did not apply. The treaty power was a possible base—a treaty became supreme law of the land and overrode state law—but logically required a treaty. Casting constitutional doubt aside in 1913, Congress passed the Migratory Bird Act. It was quickly held to be unconstitutional in federal district courts in 1914 and 1915 because there was no treaty on the topic.

So supporters of further protection for birds called for a treaty with other American nations to protect birds. By 1916 a treaty with British Canada had established the constitutional foundation for federal action. Two years later Congress enacted a law implementing the Migratory Bird Treaty. It was a comprehensive federal law that prohibited, through the Department of Agriculture, the killing or shipment of birds covered in the treaty. In the 1920 case *Missouri v. Holland* the Supreme Court upheld the new law and an apparently broad treaty power. Indeed, until the constitutional revolution of the 1930s expanded the commerce clause, many federal conservation efforts rested on the treaty power.[31]

While the treaty power per se was unimportant to the prohibition crusade, the dynamic that characterized its growth in the first two decades of the twentieth century was the same dynamic that drys (and other reformers) faced in the polity. For example, the proponents of the prohibitive tax of phosphorus matches explored the possibility of uniform state laws and rejected it as ineffective. They considered and rejected the treaty power and the commerce power: they did not think the treaty power applied as their cause had no connection with international relations; they eschewed the commerce power because it could not reach to intrastate commerce and would require state laws to be effective. Similarly, the drys had alternative federal powers to invoke for their cause; that they focused on the commerce power reflected the nature of their reform, just as those interested in protecting birds turned to the treaty power or those who wished to protect workers from the dangers of phosphorous turned to the tax power. The machine of the polity had particular cogs that fit various reforms better than others. Imperatives within a reform could also shape the nature of legislation. Thus, when the pure food and drug movement sought federal legislation, the centrality of Harvey W. Wiley to the campaign helped to shape the kind of commerce power legislation that it achieved.[32]

Perhaps no reform tale from the progressive era is more familiar than the creation of the Pure Food and Drug Act of 1906. As business reorganized and restructured the food and medicine supply, introducing products, new means of production, and vastly different means of marketing, Americans of the late nineteenth century became troubled. Worried about being poisoned by what they consumed and led by reformers obsessed with purity, Americans began calling for action from the government to protect public health. The states responded with regulations and prohibitions but seemed unequal to the task. After the turn of the century, though, exposé journalism reformers caught the attention of the public and federal policymakers. The volume of calls for federal action increased dramatically. The businesses engaged in the various industries targeted for control quickly joined in the agitation for government action. The meat packers, the diary industries, the drug companies, and others sought to use the power of the polity to improve their competitive position. The goal of the reforms was to purify the drug and food supply, and to abolish dangerous substances from foods and drugs, through regulation. Thus, this movement had elements of the abolitionist mentality, but in the main it was dominated by regulationist ideas.[33]

Harvey Wiley epitomized both the abolitionist and regulatory nature of the pure food and drug movement. Wiley grew up in an Indiana family of a strict evangelical sect; his father was a lay preacher, and both his parents were Sabbatarians and abolitionists. After the Civil War, Wiley trained as a physician but, after receiving a medical degree, never practiced—instead, he became a chemist. As the Indiana state chemist, he became obsessed with additives to food. He transferred that interest to the federal level when he was named chief chemist in the federal Department of Agriculture. The more he studied food, the more concerned he became with adulteration.

Additives and mislabelings to him were moral frauds; he embraced a kind of "chemical fundamentalism," asserting that only natural products were fully safe. But he also understood the impossibility of prohibiting artificial products and additives; thus, he espoused a regulatory approach that compelled disclosure of contents to the consumers who could avoid the adulterated or imitation goods.

While in many ways a typical abolitionist-style reformer, Wiley was also something new in the polity—the state expert and administrator—and the progressive era's food legislation reflected his second role. Like Gifford Pinchot in conservation and like Benjamin Lindsey in juvenile justice, Wiley brokered his special knowledge, his mastery of public relations, and his skill in mobilizing interest groups (it speaks volumes about Wiley that he managed to cultivate good relations with both the WCTU and the straight-bourbon distillers) into a base of bureaucratic power far beyond his official duties. He used that strength to help write the Pure Food and Drug Act, further extending his influence. Wiley was instrumental in giving the central government a greater role in food and drug policy than initially envisioned by the sponsors of the proposals.[34]

The calls for a food and drug act in the 1906 Congress reiterated the familiar refrain that Congress needed to act to aid the states in controlling interstate commerce in food and drugs. While the states could and did act against adulterated products, federalism allowed the product to be introduced into the states in original packages. The original proposal in the House proposed that state officials be the ones to notify federal authorities about misbranded and adulterated products. But Wiley and his supporters intervened, seeking a broader federal role. Fitting the constitutional strictures of the day, they proposed that the government act only within its delegated powers—by banning the transportation in interstate commerce and mails or the manufacture in federal territory of adulterated, impure, and mislabeled foods and drugs. Instead of the allowing states to identify the affected food and drugs, Wiley's Bureau of Chemistry was essentially named the arbitrator of what should and should not be in food and drugs. Opponents countered this proposal with one that would have rewritten the 1890 Wilson Act to cover food and drugs. But as the Wilson Act had been gutted by the 1898 *Rhodes* ruling, this proposal was more a tactic than a real alternative. The Wiley-backed proposal became the 1906 Pure Food and Drug Act. For the next five years Wiley would attempt to set the purity standards at his abolitionist-style levels.

Wiley's help in drafting the law and his role in administering it tended to place food and drug regulation in the sphere of the national government, overshadowing the cooperative federalism that still lay at the foundation the law. But the drys had no such state expert and administrator in Washington to manage a similar potential bureaucracy. Moreover, the prohibitionists had invested far more effort into state action than pure food regulators, and hence the true cooperative view of the federal government tended to be stronger within their crusade. Nevertheless, the two reforms shared a tendency, because of the nature of the things they wished to control and because of the way the federal system treated their reforms, to seek the use of the federal commerce power. Indeed, the commerce power proved to be one of the most malleable of federal powers during the progressive era.

The reform group that most closely paralleled the drys in agenda, the antiprostitution reformers, used the commerce power. Prostitution in the United States came to the attention of reformers in the early nineteenth century. In the states, reformers quickly gained stricter laws against prostitution and more vigorous law enforcement against whores, pimps, and procurers. But these efforts seemed to make no difference; even direct campaigns by citizen and reform groups against the practice failed to stifle it. Indeed, by the latter part of the century, prostitution flourished in the cities and towns of the nation.[35]

The changing economy, rising immigration, and rapid urbanization all contributed to increased prostitution and fueled fears of the practice in the late nineteenth century. Across the nation, red-light districts—concentrations of brothels, gambling dens, and saloons—sprang up in the cities and towns, becoming to many the tangible sign of moral and physical disease. In the eyes of reformers and many others, prostitution threatened the nation; it threatened the morality and health of women directly and it endangered public health by spreading venereal diseases. In response to the outcry about the dangers of prostitution, municipalities turned to regulation. One regulatory approach, led by physician reformers, proposed health inspections of prostitutes to limit the spread of venereal and other diseases. Another approach was to establish segregated districts in which the business could operate relatively unmolested. The idea motivating this moral geography was to drive the business out of sight from those likely to oppose it. These regulatory responses energized abolitionist-style antiprostitution reformers to new efforts to ban what they labeled "the social evil."

In the last decade of the nineteenth century and the first decade of the twentieth century, using new means to mobilize public opinion behind their cause, abolitionist-style reformers called for an eradication of prostitution. For the most part, they failed to move municipalities that had adopted a moral geography solution to prostitution. So to overcome the local governments, they tried to reach the larger public. They used two means: muckraking publications and vice committee investigations. Together, the vice committees and the muckraking created a portrait of prostitution as "white slavery" controlled by an organized syndicate. According to the reformers, organized gangs imported women from abroad or transported them from one state to another and kept them prisoners in brothels. Mixing together fears of immigrants, of sexuality, of disease, and of moral corruption, the reformers managed to create a national hysteria over the issue. At the crest of the crisis from 1907 to 1910, reformers pressed for federal action to aid the states that were strengthening their laws against white slavery.[36]

In 1910 Congress acceded to the reformers' demands by passing two acts, the Immigration Act and the Mann Act. The Immigration Act built on earlier acts of 1875, 1903, and 1907 in denying known prostitutes entry into the country and authorizing the deportation of any alien associated with brothel keeping or prostitution. But a few months later this act was followed by the Mann Act, an omnibus federal antiprostitution measure named for its sponsor, Representative James R. Mann of Illinois. The act rested on both the treaty and commerce powers. To implement the White Slave Treaty of 1908, it required brothel keepers to file statements about the alien women they kept for immoral purposes, under penalty of a large fine. They could not be prosecuted for filing the information by the federal officials, but in providing the information they made it public record, available to the states to use as they saw fit. This provision of the act replicated the role of the federal tax lists following the 1907 Certified List Law. The federal government took a more active role against prostitution through the commerce power.

The domestic side of the Mann Act used the commerce power to ban prostitutes from interstate trade. It made it a felony for anyone to transport "for the purpose of prostitution or debauchery, or for any other immoral purpose" a woman or a girl. Supporters of the act saw it as a legitimate congressional enactment. They compared it to the Lottery Act, which had been upheld by the courts. It was neither a usurpation of the state's police power nor a misuse of the commerce power, they believed. But they did envision a larger public purpose behind the act. Women, like the pieces of paper banned under the Lottery Act, were not harmful in themselves, but because they were to be put to an evil purpose, they could be banned from commerce. While it was relatively ineffective against prostitution (indeed, reformers turned to the war power during the First World War to root out red-light districts), the Mann Act constructed a rudimentary federal police power through the commerce (and treaty) power, which worked in concert with state action.

The antiprostitution reformers' success with the Mann Act became a valuable example for the prohibitionists. In 1913 the Supreme Court upheld this use of the commerce power. Thus, it would become a precedent relied upon by drys seeking federal legislation, much to the embarrassment of Congressman Mann, one the drys' leading opponents in the House. The act also pointed to one of the functional benefits of federal action for the drys. By invoking federal aid, reformers could bypass local governments that refused to enforce state bans. Federal law based on the commerce power (or any other power) could be used to choke off the supply of the banned commodity to undermine permissive local governments. Thus, the efforts of other reformers expanded the ambit of possibilities for prohibitionists.

Despite the examples of other reformers using other constitutional powers, drys turned to the commerce power as their most likely justification for federal legislation. The history of the movement propelled them toward it; after all, it was interstate commerce shipments that eroded their policies. Moreover, the Wilson Act rested on the commerce power. Yet even within the sphere of the commerce power, drys faced alternatives. When they turned to Congress to redress the problems created by judicial interpretations, drys entered the thorny thicket of constitutional debate over the meaning of the federal commerce power.

During the progressive era, as many reformers rested their calls for federal action on the commerce clause, opponents to these reforms raised constitutional objections to expanded use of the commerce power. The meaning of the commerce clause became contested ground. When drys proposed new legislation, wets typically objected on constitutional grounds. And the wet positions paralleled the stand of conservatives against such diverse reforms as anti–child labor and the creation of federal incorporation laws. Drys drew upon other constitutional ideas to overcome these conservative objections. To understand the drys' choices, it is necessary to examine the spectrum of thought regarding federalism in the progressive period. The work of three constitutional thinkers—E. Parmalee Prentice, Albert Beveridge, and George Wickersham—illustrates the range of views on federalism.

Typical of the conservative views about the commerce power was the work of E. Parmalee Prentice. Prentice had the credentials of a true conservative. After earning both bachelor's and master's degrees at Amherst College, he studied law at Harvard Law School and embarked on a career as a corporate attorney in Chicago. At the turn of the century he moved to New York and became a partner in the firm of Murry, Prentice, and Howland. He soon married Alta Rockefeller, fourth daughter of John Rockefeller Sr., and went to work for Standard Oil. His social views were strongly conservative within the republican tradition. His greatest fear was of governmental encroachment on liberty. His essential conservatism was revealed in his statement that "the nature of man and the principle of government are" unchangeable. "The influences which endanger free government," he wrote, "if unrestrained lead to license of the mob or arbitrary rule, are present in our, as in all other, people."[37]

In two works, a 1906 book, *The Federal Power of Carriers and Corporations*, and a 1909 article, "Federal Common Law and Interstate Carriers," Prentice enunciated a conservative, states'-rights view of the commerce power. This conception denied the federal government authority to act to achieve general ends through the commerce power. He saw the Constitution as a document that had been crafted to preserve liberty and that carefully divided the powers of sovereignty, and gave each constituent authority the power to check the others. The Constitution, he argued, was "a historical document"; its meaning could "be determined only by" studying the "constitutional practice of states and Congress" in "connection with contemporaneous [eighteenth-century] conditions." Thus, he asserted, the commerce clause of Constitution had to be construed with other phrases of the document in mind, especially the clauses giving the general government the power to tax and conduct foreign relations. In Prentice's view, the power to regulate commerce was granted to help raise a revenue, to aid in conducting foreign relations, and to prevent imposition of duties by the states. Beyond those limits the states' power, the existing reality at the time of the drafting, limited the federal power.

The states' police power checked any use of the commerce power beyond the limits he deduced from the document. He argued that, since the right to engage in commerce was inalienable and guaranteed by their constitutions, the states naturally limited the federal power. As they had control of granting of corporations' charters, monopolies, and licenses, these things could not come under the federal commerce power. The commerce power was limited to controlling navigation. Since in the eighteenth century commerce was nearly synonymous with seagoing navigation (control of which was denied the states in the Constitution), Prentice argued that navigation was a proper subject of federal regulation. In sum, the federal power of commerce was exclusive, but commerce was a limited subject. Through this interpretation of the commerce clause, Prentice condemned various reform proposals, including anti–child labor legislation, extensions to the Sherman Act, and federal incorporation laws. Each, he argued, was a dangerous experiment in centralization that, by abandoning the balanced constitutional system, endangered the liberties of the people.[38]

Similar constitutional constructions were serious obstacles for drys, but they were not insurmountable. Two statements by William Jennings Bryan illustrated the source of dry optimism about overcoming constitutional objections. Bryan had once said that no matter what you wanted to do, some railroad lawyer would pull out a list of decisions and prove it could not be done on account of the Constitution. Later Martin Behrman claimed that Bryan humorously recast this statement. In the New Orleans Athenaeum Bryan said, "But now . . . all those things have been done and if you want to get a really fine flow of constitutional law you have got to tap a barrel of beer. My friends, there is more Constitution in a small barrel of beer than there ever was in the railroad systems of the United States. The very foam of it throws up fine points of constitutional law." Besides mocking the wet lawyers, Bryan's statement underscored the dry belief that the constitutional roadblocks could be avoided, as similar ones had in the case of railroad regulation.[39]

In general, the Congress had shown some inclination to use the commerce power to reach broad social ends. Within their own reform's history drys had seen the successful passage of laws resting on the commerce power; the Wilson Act following the *Leisy* ruling gave them a model to follow. Beyond their agitation there were a number of other laws based on the commerce power. And as time went by, the drys gained more and more examples to follow. The Interstate Commerce Act of 1887 established a system of national railroad regulation. The 1890 Sherman Anti-Trust Act attempted to control the large business corporation's domination of markets by declaring monopolies in restraint of trade to be illegal. The Anti-Lottery Act of 1895 reinforced the states' efforts to destroy gambling by banning lottery tickets from commerce. The Lacey Act of 1900 supported state efforts to conserve game birds by banning the interstate transportation of game or feathers taken contrary to state laws. The 1910 Mann Act cooperated with the states' crusades against "white slavery" by making it a crime to transport these "commodities" in interstate commerce. The 1906 Pure Food and Drug Act, while in theory supporting state action against adulterated products, actually replaced it with federal action. The pattern of legislation, whether sole national legislation or legislation designed to parallel state laws, clearly favored the drys. Yet there were perils in aping the approaches of other reformers.

The centralizing tendencies of many reformers, if followed, threatened to send the dry movement down the path of seeking prohibition only through national means. The constitutional justifications of some reformers were nationalistic in one way or another. When Senator Albert Beveridge argued for federal regulation of child labor, he was unabashedly nationalistic. Since child labor was national in scope and the states had proved incapable of dealing with it, he contended that national law was the only remedy. As part of its power to regulate commerce among the states, Congress possessed the discretion to ban any article from interstate commerce. He called for a ban from interstate commerce of goods produced by child labor. In essence, he argued that the Constitution allowed Congress to mold national powers to meet conditions unknown to the founders.[40]

Equally destructive to state power were the constitutional ideas of George Wickersham. As Taft's attorney general, he was the leading proponent of a federal incorporation law, under the commerce clause, to control trusts. But he differed from Beveridge in thinking that the government's control of interstate commerce was the foundation of the Union. Before the Constitution, the states damaged each other's businesses by erecting tariff walls. Commerce was "the life blood of a nation." Its flow could not be "obstructed but congestion sets in, disease develops, and healthy life is impossible." Thus the "wise men" of the Constitutional Convention of 1787 vested Congress with a broad, comprehensive power to regulate commerce. It also granted Congress power to make all necessary laws for executing its enumerated powers, while at the same time forbidding the states, without the consent of Congress, to levy any duties on imports or exports. Wickersham concluded that the framers had "placed in the hands of the national government the exclusive power to regulate commerce between the states . . . without qualification or restriction." In short, it was the power "to preserve national existence."

Looking at his own time, Wickersham was sure that the corporate giants threatened the nation. He saw corporations as creatures of the sovereignty that chartered them but believed that they had come to dwarf their creators. The states, which had the potential to control trusts through the exercise of the "vast reservoir of control" in the police power, had failed to control them. Even worse, in shaping legislation to regulate trusts they victimized many legitimate businesses. Thus, Wickersham thought, the general government needed to act by passing a national incorporation law. It would result in "undisputed and clearly defined protection" for legitimate-acting corporations and regulation of trusts that used "unethical and illegal means." As nationally chartered bodies, corporations would "be at liberty to transact their business . . . free from state interference." But the national government would subject them to reasonable restrictions. In brief, national government would expand at the expense of the state.[41]

Some drys would not shrink at the idea of expanding national authority to control liquor. For instance, some prohibitionists argued that Congress could "prohibit all" liquor transportation, "not waiting until states have passed prohibition laws." They saw the advantage of such an act: it "would confine the liquor business of a state strictly within that state." On the other hand, such a course denied the states a strong role in prohibiting liquor and seemingly made irrelevant many of the prohibitionist legislative victories. But the drys did not have to embark on such a course of nationalization to achieve their goal.

There was a middle ground of cooperative dual federalism. Given the model they began with, that of the Wilson Act, they saw that they did not have to abandon dual federalism to achieve congressional legislation to aid prohibition states. As a prohibition publication for college students explained, "Under our form of government the Constitution limits to certain spheres the power of the general government over such matters as the liquor traffic." Liquor fell "directly under their state police power." Congress could not interfere with the exercise of this power. Without a constitutional amendment, it could "neither regulate nor prohibit the sale in any state." But the federal government, through its delegated commerce power, could prohibit the liquor traffic in interstate commerce or "supplement the actions of states which have prohibited the sale." It had the advantage of avoiding the problem of arousing "much opposition by those who fear great centralization of power into the hands of the general government" because it preserved state police power. Given the range of options, the prohibitionists would have to choose which type of legislation they would seek from Congress—national control or federal cooperation.[42]

In the last decade of the nineteenth century courts limited the Wilson Act and thereby undermined the effectiveness of state prohibition. Thus, the interstate commerce doctrines enunciated by the federal courts continued to challenge prohibition policy. Drys, increasingly led by the Anti-Saloon League, confronted the problem of interstate liquor shipments by seeking better laws from both state and national governments. Drys were initially successful in the states, but their new laws were no more effective than the old ones. Federal action seemed imperative, and when they called for federal action, drys joined a chorus of reform voices. Under the pressure of reformers and activist presidents, Congress expanded the federal government's powers, but not without raising significant constitutional doubts as to the legitimacy of the federal action. Yet in the progressive era the federal government gained a form of police power, and thus the drys were given the opportunity to supplant the piecemeal state effort with a sweeping nationwide law. That they chose to remain with concurrent state and federal action reflected the internal constraints within the movement and the limitations of their allies in government; and that the drys were able to win interstate commerce legislation reflected their maturing political power.

COMMERCE, PRAGMATIC PROHIBITIONISTS,

AND CONGRESS

C H A P T E R

Before 1902 prohibitionists lacked much interest in attaining an interstate commerce law, but after 1903, reflecting the new realities of the polity, campaigns for a national law became central to the temperance movement. The passage of the 1909 COD Act and 1913 Webb-Kenyon Act, which regulated interstate liquor commerce, marked the political maturation of the prohibition movement. In Congress dry lobbyists, and the movement's political power, overcame wet opposition and constitutional objections to their measures. But the legislative products varied in the emphasis on the active agency of the polity. The COD Act followed the common reform trend of an active federal role, while the Webb-Kenyon Act continued in the path of limited federal assistance for state action, first set out in the Wilson Act of 1890.[1]

The WCTU's Margaret Dye Ellis and the Anti-Saloon League's Edwin C. Dinwiddie, the drys' lobbyists in Washington, played key roles in the long drive for legislation. Ellis and Dinwiddie cultivated legislators, kept the leadership and the rank and file of the temperance movement informed of events in Congress, helped to draft legislation, and coordinated dry political pressure. In 1895, at the age of fifty, Margaret Dye Ellis became the white ribboner "superintendent of the Department of Legislation." Her "tact of womanliness" made her popular with temperance-leaning legislators, especially Representative Charles Littlefield of Maine, Senator Jacob Gallinger of New Hampshire, Congressman Richmond Hobson of Alabama, and Congressman E. Yates Webb of North Carolina. Her socializing with the wives of legislators permitted her to enter into their inner circles; she knew "everyone in both legislative houses." Like any pragmatic prohibitionist, she admitted her focus on means: "The *Congressional Record* is in my hands constantly, I am studying it more than I am my Bible." Her weekly column in the *Union Signal*, "Our Washington Letter," gave her readers the chance to become familiar with dry plans for national legislation.[2]

In 1899 the Anti-Saloon League sent to Washington Edwin C. Dinwiddie, a former minister and experienced league legislative agent, to be national legislative superintendent. Part of Dinwiddie's task was to capture the leading role in directing national temperance legislation from Ellis, the unaffiliated agitator Wilbur Crafts, and the maverick U.S. senator Benjamin Tillman. He succeeded brilliantly by cooperating rather than fighting with other dry forces working in Congress. From 1899 to 1907 he served as the league's lobbyist. A less frequent contributor to the temperance press than Ellis, Dinwiddie used it most often to call on prohibitionists to bombard Congress with petitions, letters, and telegrams. He became intimate with the leaders of Congress and other influential figures in Washington, promoting his independence from the league's leaders. From 1907 to 1910 he broke with the Anti-Saloon League and worked as a lobbyist for various temperance groups, and virtually single-handedly gained the enactment of the 1909 COD Act. His reunion with the league in 1911 did not return him to the inner circle of the organization; he became just a captain, only implementing the policies set by others.[3]

Dinwiddie and Ellis solidified the connections between the prohibition movement and members of Congress by augmenting the established ties between drys and legislators. The links between temperance organizations and Congress flowed through two channels: regular contact with their local dry organizations and letters from interested individual prohibitionists. For instance, Congressman E. Yates Webb regularly corresponded with the superintendent of his state's Anti-Saloon League, Reverend R. L. Davis. They exchanged political information, worked out plans for state and national legislation, and plotted internal strategy within the movement. Webb also maintained contact with other people in other states' leagues; for instance, former Alabama Supreme Court justice Samuel D. Weakley became his regular correspondent.[4]

It is important to note that, despite its image as a powerful political pressure group, the dry lobby never fully controlled the legislators. The officials always maintained a sphere of autonomy, even as they worked with the drys. For instance, Hobson often proposed plans at variance with league practice, but he proved willing to compromise. Ernest Cherrington, in discussing one of these differences, wrote that "in the early part of the conference he [Hobson] gave some slight indication of a feeling of independence but before we had gone far he came across in the very best of spirits." There was an active give and take between the two groups. The legislators provided important services for the drys. They operated as broadcasters of prohibitionist propaganda—sometimes using the congressional frank to send out dry appeals or writing letters to dry activists explaining plans and programs—and recommended language for dry proposals to the prohibitionists. In return, the dry organizations gave them good publicity in their press, advised them on political strategy, supplied them with briefs and other material, and worked for their reelection.[5]

As the prohibitionist presence in Washington grew, they were able to push their agenda. No point was important than "federal cooperation." This cooperation was "imperative, if states, counties, or towns are to cope successfully with the liquor traffic within their borders." But the primacy of this view developed slowly in dry circles. In the late 1890s few took action in Congress to achieve federal assistance. From 1897 to 1900 the *Union Signal* printed a list of "moral measures in Congress"—which included bills prohibiting interstate gambling by telegraph and banning interstate transportation of pictures or kinescopes of "brutalizing shows" such as prizefights as well as a proposal to create a Wilson Act to cover cigarettes (banned in several states). But the list omitted an interstate commerce liquor bill. The prohibitionists' first victories in Congress came in symbolic areas. Ellis and Dinwiddie, working in tandem, won laws prohibiting the sale of liquor at immigration stations, at the Capitol, and "upon any premises used for military purposes by the United States." Drys did not even offer an interstate commerce bill before late 1902.[6]

In 1897 and 1898, however, Senator Benjamin Tillman proposed to amend the Wilson Act. Acting on the mistaken belief that the Wilson Act did not apply to dispensary states, Tillman wrote a bill to "restore" to South Carolina the power to control the sale of liquors in its own way. Tillman's bill passed the Senate without debate and earned a favorable report from the House Judiciary Committee, but was never voted on in the House. Even so, his bill got farther than most later dry bills. If Tillman's bill was drafted to right a nonexistent wrong, the dry and local option states suffered real blows with the 1898 *Rhodes* ruling; yet it took four years for prohibitionists to draft a legislative remedy. The U.S. Supreme Court's extension of the rights of liquor shippers in the COD and injunction cases added further reasons for drys to seek a congressional act. Once drys settled on this course of action, they never abandoned it. Thus, for the next decade the dry goal was, in the words of Wilbur Crafts, to "dam the liquor traffic at every state line!"[7]

In 1902, following in Tillman's footsteps, Representative Hepburn of Iowa proposed to amend the Wilson Act. In a clear attempt to reverse the *Rhodes* ruling, his bill replaced the words "upon arrival" in the Wilson Act with "upon arrival within the boundary." As written, the bill would have attached state law to liquor shipments before delivery—in effect, at the state line. With no backing from the prohibitionists and no opposition from the liquor interests, whose lobbyists did not notice it, the bill passed the House. In the Senate it was sent to the Judiciary Committee, which held hearings where N. W. Kendall and Robert Crain, the president and counsel respectively of the United States Brewers' Association, assaulted it as unconstitutional. The bill received a favorable report from the Judiciary Committee, but Congress adjourned before it came to a vote. The drys adopted the bill, calling it "one of the most important measures . . . for a dozen years." Drys began to popularize the idea of such legislation; for example, in 1904 the Intercollegiate Prohibition Association made it a topic for its sponsored debates. Drys decided, as Reverend Dinwiddie said, that "it will be our special aim to put this measure through next session."[8]

To do this, the prohibitionists needed to meet the constitutional objections to the Hepburn and other antiliquor shipment bills raised by wets. Industry spokesmen and congressmen from districts that produced liquor directed the fight against dry legislation. They were often unabashed in announcing their area's economic interest in the trade; for example, Representative Henry S. Boutell of Chicago asserted, "There are more brewers living in my district than any other." Liquor makers and sellers marshaled four constitutional arguments against the Hepburn bill and every other proposed prohibitionist interstate commerce measure. These arguments were several: the bills violated the freedom of commerce; they interfered with the constitutional right to import liquor for personal use; they granted extraterritoriality to state laws; and they delegated to the states Congress's power to regulate commerce.[9]

A basic liberal ideology linked the arguments concerning freedom of commerce and personal use. The brewers argued that "the interstate commerce law" was intended "to secure the absolute freedom of commercial intercourse" among the states. Echoing the nationalist ideas of George Wickersham, the brewers thought this freedom "indispensable to the prosperity, the progress, and the development of the nation." The Hepburn bill and its successors threatened to emasculate "this grand law" by abridging the freedom of commerce. They argued that Congress did not have the power to pass a Hepburn-type law. It could only regulate commerce, not destroy its freedom. On a more narrow ground, the liquor advocates constructed from the U.S. Supreme Court's opinion in *Vance v. Vandercook* a constitutional right for citizens to receive personal-use shipments. They argued that prohibitionist-proposed liquor commerce laws would obviously interfere with "the free and uninterrupted Interstate Commerce to which we are entitled and upon which rights we stand as 'free American tax paying citizens and business men.'" A whisky circular announced the "constitutional privilege of buying and receiving in Interstate Commerce." And in a petition sent to the House Judiciary Committee, the German American State Alliance of Kentucky pleaded with Congress not to pass a law that would allow their state to "prevent us from bringing a glass of beer or a bottle of wine to our tables." If Congress did, the "divine right of each to pursue his own good in his own way will be sacrificed" to "fears and fanaticism."[10]

In two ways the wets also turned to ideas of the specified and limited powers of government against the dry proposals. Invoking themes from the Court's liquor transportation decisions, the liquor industry argued that if the goods lost their interstate character at the border, state laws would operate outside their jurisdiction. Therefore, they would be unconstitutional because they would void laws in other states. Similarly, the liquor forces argued, the Hepburn bill would interfere with transshipment of liquor. It would make shipments of liquor from one wet state to another wet state across a dry state subject to the dry state's liquor laws, and that was manifestly an interference with interstate commerce. Their final argument was that the bills, by letting state laws set the terms of commerce, unconstitutionally delegated Congress's interstate commerce power to the states. This reservation recalled earlier congressional objections to the Wilson Act and ignored the Supreme Court's ruling in the *Rahrer* case, which portrayed the Wilson Act as a complete enactment by Congress and not a delegation of power.[11]

Taken together, these four objections did not make a coherent whole. The freedom of commerce doctrine implied that Congress could not act, while the other arguments assumed that the states could not act because the power was reserved to Congress. This inconsistency did not concern representatives of the liquor industry. They sought to recruit congressmen with different constitutional ideas into their camp; thus, the constitutional scattergun approach was more effective than a clearly aimed, consistent argument. Though their arguments failed to win over the Senate Judiciary Committee in 1903, they remained the basis for objections to the prohibitionist interstate commerce bills until the passage of the Webb-Kenyon Act in 1913. And these constitutional reservations stimulated the drys into paying "particular attention to the verbiage" of their bills.[12]

From 1903 to 1910 the drys fine-tuned their bills' language and honed their constitutional arguments. In 1904 they met the transshipment objection to the original Hepburn bill by changing "transportation" into the state to "consigned" into the state. This change preserved the right of carriers to transport liquor across dry territory. Later proposals explicitly exempted through traffic from penalties. The prohibitionists strenuously opposed the personal-use amendments proposed for their bills, fearing that such exceptions "would add to the difficulties" in state enforcement or, in the words of Webb, "would practically emasculate the bill." They argued from a close reading of the Court's opinions that there was no "inalienable right" to import liquor for personal use. After all, they theorized, the state police power was plenary over liquor, and therefore it included the power to ban personal use. A congressional act recognizing the personal-use importation "right" would therefore shift control of liquor policy away from states to Congress.[13]

Prohibitionists sought analogies to disprove the argument that Congress could not pass an interstate commerce law affecting liquor because it would impair the freedom of commerce. They pointed to congressional acts, upheld by the Supreme Court, that prohibited the transportation of obscene materials and lottery tickets. The drys also drew strength from other reformers' efforts to use the interstate commerce power to remedy wrongs. They favorably quoted the proponents of bills prohibiting the interstate transportation of goods made with child and convict labor and of prizefight films. They traced the path of the Mann Act, which banned the interstate transportation of women for immoral purposes, from its earliest proposals to its enactment. Always the drys' arguments concluded by pointing out that if Congress could ban a commodity in interstate commerce, it could take lesser steps against it. Indeed, some in the movement, like Wilbur Crafts, continued to lobby for a total ban of liquor from interstate commerce.[14]

The drys also struggled to meet the argument concerning delegation of congressional power. They tinkered with various versions of their proposals "so as to make it show more clearly what it actually is, namely, a complete enactment by Congress itself and not an attempt at the delegation of its power to the states." On the other hand, the drys turned this attack into an asset by boasting of the states'-rights aspects of their interstate commerce bills. This stand gained the prohibitionists valuable southern supporters like Senators Edward Carmack of Tennessee and Alexander Stephens Clay of Georgia. It was a successful tactic that coincided with the prohibition movement's impressive gains in the south, but it did not bring about the quick passage of a federal interstate commerce law.[15]

By 1909 the Anti-Saloon League, through a process of trial and error, arrived at the essence of a bill, "most carefully drafted" by Wayne Wheeler, that met the delegation argument. Introduced by Representative James Langley, this bill prohibited the interstate shipment of liquor into states or areas where "transportation of such liquors can not legally be made from one point to another within such state." In the league's view, the bill established a uniform national rule: liquor could not be sent into states where transportation of liquor was banned. No federal power was delegated; the enforcement was left in the central government's hands. Of course, the nature of this proposal made it hard to portray it as a states'-rights measure, and this threatened to deprive the league of the support of some southerners. More attention to the verbiage was needed.[16]

Even while they changed the nature of their proposals, the Anti-Saloon League and the WCTU directed much of their attention to achieving the passage of any interstate commerce liquor law. They divided the necessary tasks of political pressure between themselves. The Anti-Saloon League focused on directly influencing legislators. It queried candidates, and those who supported the drys' measures got favorable press and reaped the reward of league support in elections. The league organized its efforts in Congress, usually choosing one congressman and senator each session as leader of the dry forces—a tactic that added status to the member chosen. For instance, in 1909 the league told other legislators that Representative James M. Miller of Kansas was "looking out for some legislation for us" and that "anything that he presents has the endorsement of our organization." The WCTU, on the other hand, managed huge petition, letter-writing, and telegram campaigns supporting each bill. They buried Congress with paper. The dry methods effectively built support for a federal interstate commerce liquor law.[17]

But dry pressure and arguments did not sway the Republican Speaker of the House, Joseph Cannon. Cannon thought the prohibitionist plans unconstitutional. He sent the prohibition bills to committees staffed with members "inimical" to the bills, where they were routinely smothered. Cannon punished members of his party who favored prohibition legislation, reassigning them from choice committees to less desirable posts. His intransigence caused prohibitionists, led by the Anti-Saloon League, to work against his reelection. These plans to "dislodge the 'Key log'" failed and further deepened Cannon's hostility to the league and its interstate commerce bills.[18]

In 1909 Congress ignored the Anti-Saloon League's proposals and passed a compromise measure, the COD Act. After his split with the league, Dinwiddie returned to Washington as lobbyist for other temperance groups. He used his connections with Cannon and other legislators, many of them league supporters—Representatives James Miller of Kansas and Benjamin Humphreys of Mississippi, for instance—to maneuver the COD Act through Congress. Many proponents of this bill intended to "rob" the leadership of the temperance forces from the league. Speaker Cannon and others hostile to the league, like Olin James of Kentucky, supported the act in hopes that it would curtail the clamor for a more sweeping law. Their plans backfired. The league simply claimed credit for the act and intensified its efforts to gain more comprehensive interstate commerce legislation. And the Anti-Saloon League took steps to insure that the COD law would work.[19]

The COD law required all liquor shippers using interstate commerce to label their packages clearly "on the outside cover" with the name of the consignee and the nature and quantity of its contents. Under penalty of a $5,000 fine or two years in jail, it prohibited common carriers and their agents from delivering liquor to anyone but a bona fide consignee and from collecting the purchase price on liquor orders. Since no enforcement mechanism was set out, this duty fell to the hands of federal marshals and attorneys. The Anti-Saloon League viewed the act, in "connection with the state legislation which it makes possible," as "a decisive gain for the prohibition movement."[20]

The league pushed states into adopting their own COD laws. These laws sought to guarantee that carriers brought in only bona fide shipments and did not engage in illegal sales. At the prompting of the league, New Hampshire in 1909, Virginia in 1910, and Oklahoma in 1911 passed such laws. Later Tennessee, Alabama, Utah, and California also enacted similar laws. In some cases the lawmakers merely copied the language of the federal statute. The Virginia law was typical. It prohibited the solicitation of liquor orders in dry areas and required that all liquor packages be marked "plainly on the outside" with a description of the contents and the name of "bona fide consignees." It also banned the delivery to "any persons other than the persons to whom" the package was shipped and stipulated that common carriers keep a separate book available to public officials recording information about liquor shipments—the amount, date received, date delivered, and the person who claimed the package. These laws restricted the COD trade, penalized shippers if they violated the law, and made the common carrier a valuable source of information about who received liquor in prohibition territory. The transformation of the carrier into an agent of law enforcement paralleled the method the league used in dealing with the federal liquor tax: a liability was turned into an asset. But these laws were not enough for most drys.[21]

Neither the league nor the WCTU intended the COD Act and its supporting state legislation to be the final word on the subject. League worker Heriot Clarkson wrote to Webb that it was not "the type of bill that is desired, but until we can get a better bill we will have to be satisfied." Similarly, Ellis considered it a "step in the right direction" and announced a campaign for more "comprehensive legislation." Indeed, prohibitionists and the liquor industry were surprised that the law did at times limit the COD trade. The league portrayed the passage of the act as a recognition of a "principle long contended for" by the league—namely, that the national government could and must aid the states in curtailing liquor shipments. The league also argued that it created "an implied obligation to go farther." At the next Congress the Anti-Saloon League pressed for a broader interstate commerce bill.[22]

In pressing for a new interstate commerce law the prohibitionists were not attempting to shift all liquor legislation to the national level. The decade's agitation over interstate liquor shipments had fixed in the minds of most leaders of the league and the WCTU the idea of concurrent exercise of state and national governing powers over liquor. The league's legislative superintendent for 1909, William Anderson, asserted that the league sought an interstate commerce bill so that the federal government could "use its power over interstate commerce in such manner as to aid the states." Once accomplished, "the center of the fighting will again shift back to the states." The states, "unhampered by the federal government," would make great progress in controlling liquor and "awakening civilization."[23]

By 1910, in the prohibitionists' plans, no other tangible goal equaled in importance the passage of a federal liquor interstate commerce law. Drys delighted in the spread of prohibition; by 1913 Alabama (which later returned to local option), Georgia, Mississippi, Oklahoma, North Carolina, South Carolina, and West Virginia had joined the ranks of prohibition states. Yet the flow of interstate commerce liquor kept these dry areas in reality "semi-moist." Although the drys saw liquor control as primarily "a state question," they also believed that "absolute prohibition" for the dry states was impossible "until Congress so amends the interstate commerce law." Thus, the "success or failure" of prohibition depended "upon the attitude of the general government." The key to changing the federal government's position was the passage of an interstate commerce law. Drys crossed this "last ditch" with the Webb-Kenyon Act of 1913.[24]

No dry act, after the Wilson Act and before national prohibition, was more important for the dry crusade than the Webb-Kenyon Act. It prohibited "the shipment or transportation" of liquor from one state or territory into any other state or territory where those alcoholic beverages were "intended by any person interested therein, to be received, possessed, sold or in any manner used, either in the original package or otherwise in violation of any law" of the receiving state. The law did not stop all shipments; for instance, if state law recognized the right to import liquor for personal use, then such shipments would be legal. It lacked provisions for setting out means for federal enforcement because drys always intended that the states would enforce it. The Webb-Kenyon Act implemented the prohibitionist idea of concurrent exercise of national and state power against liquor, and its passage awakened drys to the possibility of enacting national prohibition.[25]

The Webb-Kenyon Act grew from the prohibitionists' revival of their interstate commerce program after the passage of the 1909 COD Act. In 1910 and most of 1911 the drys made little progress on this front. Political miscalculations by the Anti-Saloon League hindered the league's program. Ironically, the league decided to work with Speaker Cannon and the regular Republicans right before the party lost control of Congress. Divisions between Dinwiddie and his supporters and the Anti-Saloon League weakened the prohibition movement's political power. Perceptions that the COD Act deserved a fair test before Congress proceeded further also worked against the prohibitionists.

By the opening of 1912 the situation was much more favorable for the drys. The Democratic party, now in control of Congress, had a strong rural southern wing. Many of these Democrats supported dry legislation. In late 1911 the federal Interstate Commerce Commission revealed the extent of the liquor shipping trade. It estimated that express companies carried over twenty million gallons of intoxicating liquors into dry areas across the nation. Despite the restrictions of the COD Act and state laws, eager customers could devise the means to get liquor. For instance, in North Carolina wets, in order to receive all the liquor they could, forged orders "in the name of other innocent parties," including "dead men" and "little children." On another plane, Dinwiddie rejoined the league and thus reunited the prohibitionist forces. To seal the dry union, the Anti-Saloon League sponsored a Washington, D.C., convention for all interested prohibition organizations and state officials. The stated purpose of this conference was to write an interstate commerce bill. The proposal of this well-attended conference eventually became the Webb-Kenyon Act.[26]

The December 1911 convention accepted a proposal for an interstate commerce bill drafted mostly by Fred S. Caldwell, an ardent dry and the former Oklahoma special counsel to the governor for prohibition law enforcement. Stripped to its essentials, the bill banned the interstate transportation of liquor into areas where it was to be used in violation of state law, and its second section declared contracts for such transactions to be void. The new form borrowed from the Langley bill, written by Wayne Wheeler. It did not seek, like the various incarnations of the Hepburn bill, to divest liquor of its interstate character at an earlier time than usual. It instead deprived liquor of its commerce clause protection only in certain instances. Caldwell's proposal differed from Wheeler's effort by leaving the matter mostly in the states' hands. It prescribed no penalties because enforcement was to be left up to the states. This form grew from the Anti-Saloon League's unhappiness with the Justice Department's implementation of the COD Act and the Internal Revenue Office's refusal to aid the prohibition states. The states, in the league's experience, could be pressured more easily into taking prohibitory action. The proposed law would permit the states to act through an in rem proceeding; a jury or judge would decide in each case whether the liquor that the state had temporarily detained was intended to be used to violate the state laws. If so, it was confiscated and destroyed. In dry areas or states where the law declared set amounts of liquor as prima facie evidence of intent to sell illegally, all large shipments would fall under the ban. In short, the Caldwell proposal would restore to the states the ability to stop the flow of liquor before it reached the hands of the consignee.[27]

The Anti-Saloon League persuaded Senator William S. Kenyon of Iowa and Representative Morris Sheppard of Texas to introduce the Caldwell-drafted bill in their respective houses. (With no prompting but eventually with league aid, Congressman E. Yates Webb of North Carolina, a vigorous dry, also introduced the same bill.) Through this dual track the league hoped to assure quick passage by overcoming a bottleneck in one house. League strategy called for no amendments to Caldwell's language. But the House Judiciary Committee struck out the contracts prohibition as redundant (at common law, contracts for illegal products are unenforceable); and the Senate Judiciary Committee grafted the language of the Hepburn bill onto the new bill (probably a wet attempt to make the bill constitutionally unpalatable), declaring that state police power attached when liquor crossed the state line. Caldwell agreed with the removal of the contracts clause, as he thought it was "very largely . . . declaratory." But he was worried about the return of the Hepburn language, voicing "very serious doubts" as to its constitutionality. The Senate addition defeated the purpose of Caldwell's careful drafting and increased the potential that the houses would pass separate measures and then fail to agree on a compromise version. Nevertheless, most debate focused on the initial form of the bill, a shape that raised the issue of unconstitutional delegation of congressional power to the states.[28]

In the press, before congressional committees, and on the floor of Congress, opponents of the Webb-Kenyon bill attacked it as a delegation to the states of Congress's power to regulate interstate commerce. They argued that the bill did not "prescribe the rules" governing interstate commerce, but rather adopted various and varying state laws. "The extent and measure and duration of the regulation" was wholly dependent on state action, and therefore the power was delegated to the state. The lack of federal penalties exacerbated the issue; presumably punishments for the illegal act of shipment would vary from state to state. The Anti-Saloon League debated this point, arguing that there were no punishments to the shippers other than the confiscation of the liquor. To remedy this perceived potential wrong, Congressman John W. Davis of West Virginia—who steadfastly opposed the bill in subcommittee, committee, and on the floor—proposed an amendment along the lines of the COD Act, adding federal penalties. The Davis amendment turned the Webb-Kenyon Act into Wheeler's Langley bill. Prohibition party members also thought the bill (and later the act) deficient on similar grounds. W. G. Calderwood, for instance, believed that the lack of the penalty would lead to confusion and lax enforcement, as it "opens the way for each state to provide its own penalty." But the drys, led by the Anti-Saloon League, so fixed on the one conception of joint sovereignty that they engineered Congress's rejection of Davis's amendment.[29]

The Anti-Saloon League met the delegation argument directly. Dinwiddie contended that the bill was "purely a regulation by Congress, full and complete in itself." Furthermore, the drys argued that Congress's power over commerce was plenary, extending to total bans, and thus included the means to pass lesser regulations. If it passed the bill, Congress would establish one rule: no liquor could be shipped into a state in violation of its law. Drys reinforced this position by pointing to Congress's interstate commerce enactments that had stood the test of time: the 1895 Anti-Lottery Act, the 1906 Pure Food and Drug Act, and especially the 1900 Lacey Act, which banned the interstate transportation of the feathers or carcasses of game birds killed in violation of state law. To drys, the Lacey Act, which had stood for a dozen years, was the perfect analogy because it did for birds what they wanted to do for liquor.[30]

Before the House Judiciary Committee, Lawrence Maxwell of the National Wholesale Liquor Dealers' Association and former solicitor general of the United States, attempted to defuse the Lacey Act analogy. He argued that it dealt with "an article which was not an article of commerce." At common law, wild animals were *fera nature*, a species of thing in which there was "no right of property . . . except by the authority of the state." Thus Congress, through the Lacey Act, had merely prohibited items that were not "an article of commerce" from interstate trade. But Congressman Webb caught Maxwell's fallacy. If, as he contended, wild animals were not an article of commerce, where did Congress get the power to regulate them? Webb also pointed out that congressional debates on the act focused on the commerce power and that a federal circuit court had upheld the act as a legitimate regulation of commerce. Thus, the prohibitionists built a constitutional defense against the delegation argument.[31]

The opponents advanced a second major constitutional argument against the Webb-Kenyon bill: that it infringed on the people's constitutional liberties. They argued that it would interfere with a citizen's right to import liquor for personal use and a church's right to acquire sacramental wine. They feared that the states would pass laws outlawing these practices and that the Webb-Kenyon Act would prevent federal intervention. Congressman Davis and Senator James O'Gorman proposed amendments that would have restrained the states from enacting laws restricting importations for personal use or communion use. The Anti-Saloon League, while not conceding that the states lacked the power to ban the personal use of liquor (though some allies like Senator Kenyon thought such bans were unconstitutional), assured legislators that temperance sentiment in the states had not proceeded far enough to allow such a ban. Indeed, in the 1912 Texas legislature, the league stifled a bill against personal use. The league also argued that no state would ever interfere with religious liberty by banning the use of sacramental wine. It characterized these amendments as devious plots to continue the illicit interstate liquor trade under a new guise. League political pressure assured the amendments' defeat in both houses.[32]

Some interested parties raised practical objections to the bill. For instance, George Brown, a whisky shipper, feared that it might make "the most innocent purchaser for his own use, liable to persecution from some vile enemy." L. P. Larson, the president of the Nebraska Wholesale Liquor Dealers Association, echoed the potential misuse of the law; anyone could "by alleging a possible intent of violation of some state law, so harass the transportation company handling the goods as to practically stop the traffic." Charles A. West, the chairman of National Wholesale Druggists Association, in a series of thoughtful letters to Webb, worried about "endless confusion and interference with legitimate commerce." He cited such examples as liquor shipments "for use in the manufacture of flavoring extracts" or compounding medicines. West wished to protect legitimate interstate commerce from interference by the states and thus attacked one of the strongest props of the bill, its appeal to states' rights.[33]

The language of the Webb-Kenyon bill made it easy for its proponents to portray it as a states'-rights measure. Thus, it could meet the cry common in the south that, under "the pretext of interstate commerce," the rights of the sovereign people of the southern states were violated. In arguing for the bill, Dinwiddie said he was a "northern man" with "enough of the principle of states rights" to see the necessity for this proposal. The bill, he argued, simply restored to the states the part of their police power unjustly removed by the *Bowman* and *Leisy* rulings; it returned liquor regulation to the status quo of the 1847 *License Cases*. Others, like Representative Robert Lee Henry, a Texas Democrat, appealed for its passage because it would "maintain the integrity of state law, state governments, and the right of local self-government." Wilbur Crafts asserted that the bill would end "the greatest national conspiracy for the overthrow of states' rights that this country has ever seen, in which the local speak-easies are only the tools of the great brewers and distillers." Webb saw his bill as the means to achieving that end. He claimed that it "never professed to make the federal government enforce the local prohibition laws." Rather, it granted something "we have always clamored for . . . the removal by Congress of the shackles which were heretofore on the states' action, so that the states could act" to control "the whole subject." In a Congress dominated by Democrats, and with southerners in key positions (chairmanship of both judiciary committees and the Speaker's chair), the states'-rights arguments fell on receptive ears. But the constitutional debates did not determine the passage of the Webb-Kenyon Act; they swayed few. Prohibitionist political pressure and power brought about passage.[34]

From its first committee hearings to its final passage, the Anti-Saloon League and the WCTU organized an unrivaled campaign of political pressure for the Webb-Kenyon bill. For fifteen months beginning in January 1912, the dry press made the bill its focal point. Readers were urged to write, telegram, or visit their representatives and senators. Beyond this, the *Union Signal*, *American Issue*, and *New Republic* reproduced letters by politicians and other prominent Americans—including labor leader Samuel Gompers, reformer Jane Addams, and juvenile justice proponent Benjamin Lindsey—testifying to their support of the measure. The organizations paraded nearly one hundred speakers before congressional committees. The Anti-Saloon League convened a national conference in Washington, from December 16 to December 19, 1912, for leading temperance figures, officials from dry areas, and leading businessmen, who all supported the bill. The political pressure led one congressman to denounce the league as "a clever and persistent lobby." Others in the body cheered antileague statements. Despite such sentiments, the drys' attempts at influencing Congress were successful, in part because they pressured an audience predisposed to accept their message.[35]

The new prohibition and local option territory created in the twentieth century had brought to Congress politicians amenable to the dry message. For nearly a decade the Anti-Saloon League had worked to build a Congress that would pass an interstate commerce law. By 1912 they had made significant progress in achieving that goal. The league's influence reached far. For instance, the opposition House managers called only sixteen speakers to attack the bill. Yet of this select group three voted for it. One of them, Davis, admitted that he voted for the bill to satisfy his constituents. And the lameduck members in the House, taking into account their high absentee rate, supported the Webb-Kenyon bill in proportions similar to the other members. Congressmen and senators seemed inclined to follow the lead of Congressman William R. Rucker of Colorado. An attorney turned out in the last election and thus bound "for one bar or another," he advised his colleagues "to go along the lines of least resistance and vote for this bill."[36]

While the temperance forces were powerful, the liquor interests, weakened by internal divisions, had made few converts in Congress. The base of their support remained representatives from wet districts, especially those with large liquor-producing plants, and probusiness senators who feared further congressional regulation of commerce. Moreover, their lobbying against the Webb-Kenyon bill was pitiful. Some of their speakers before the House Judiciary Committee did not even know the nature of the legislation they were opposing. The high point of their pressure came after the bill was docketed in both houses, not at the more vulnerable time of committee meetings. They published their most telling arguments against the bill after it became law. Not surprisingly, the league and its congressional allies maneuvered the bill through Congress. They defeated all crippling amendments offered on the floor, overcame the wets' delaying tactics, and delivered overwhelming majorities for the bill in each house.[37]

On February 8 the House version of the Webb-Kenyon bill passed the House, and on February 10 it passed the Senate. It read as follows:

> The shipment or transportation of any spirituous . . . or other intoxicating liquor of any kind from one state, territory, or district of the United States . . . or from and foreign country into any state . . . which said liquor is intended by any person interested therein, to be received, possessed, sold, or in any manner used, either in the original package or otherwise, in violation of any law of such state . . . is prohibited.

Thus, the act still embodied the league's original intentions. It earned widespread support. In the House over 63 percent of the Republicans and 68.1 percent of the Democrats voted for the measure. In the Senate over 71.1 percent of the Democrats and 60 percent of the Republicans supported it. Supporters came from all areas of the nation, but the strongest group consisted of the members of Congress from the prohibition states, 84.9 percent of whom voted for the bill. Only representatives of wet, urban districts opposed the bill as a solid group. By all accounts the league and the prohibitionists had won a major victory. All they needed to secure it was the president's signature on the bill.[38]

President William Howard Taft—a lame-duck president with no political future and therefore with little to fear from the prohibitionist lobby—vetoed the bill. His veto message, relying heavily upon Attorney General Wickersham's formal opinion on the bill, argued that the Webb-Kenyon bill "is in substance and effect a delegation by Congress to the states of the power of regulating interstate commerce." To Taft, such a delegation destroyed the central purpose of the Constitution, which was to relieve the nation's commerce "of the burdens which local state jealousies and purposes had in the past imposed upon it." Without a system of unified commerce, the nation would become fragmented. Taft admitted that the U.S. Supreme Court had not ruled on the theory underlying the bill, but he argued that the president had a duty to exercise the "principles of proper constitutional construction." He sent his message to Congress on the last day of February.[39]

Public reaction to the veto varied. The veto gathered much of the nation's press behind the opponents of the bill. For example, the *New York Times*, on March 2, 1913, praised the veto message, commended congressional critics of the bill for their "expression of principle," and hoped that the veto would be sustained. The dry press, on the other hand, pilloried both Taft and Wickersham, attacking their reasoning and implying that they acted only to pay off a campaign debt to the brewing interests. The *New Republic* published an article alleging that each man's son, then in law school at Harvard, thought their fathers' constitutional stand to be wrong. Dry papers also ran satirical pieces in which "Bathhouse John" (a reference to Chicago's infamous Irish machine politician John Coughlin) and "Judge Uriah Gump" defended the "proud coladium of our liberties, the star spangled constitooshun."[40]

Constitutional arguments figured in the two brief debates following the president's veto, as the opponents of the legislation pressed home his arguments. On the floor of the Senate, Thomas H. Paynter asserted the "importance of maintaining a constitutional government" against the assaults of "frenzied enthusiasts who waver oblivious" to the contents of the Constitution. He drove home this theme by having the clerk of the Senate read a poem by Daniel Parks, "Stand by the Constitution." Suffice it to say, the poem did not clarify the meaning of the document, but neither did the debaters in Congress. Along the same lines, Representative Richard Bartholdt of Missouri added the barb that "Mr. Dinwiddie and the Lobby which is now crowding the corridors of this Capital have not sworn by a solemn oath to support the Constitution. I have." Representative Augustus R. Stanley, invoking the nationalistic spirit of Daniel Webster and John Marshall, argued that the nation was absolutely dependent on the operation of the national commerce power; without it, the union would collapse.[41]

The proponents of the Webb-Kenyon bill were not constitutionally defenseless. They built on the earlier states'-rights framework as they sought to override the veto. In the House Representative Henry Clayton directly attacked the administration's contentions. He argued that the commerce clause was not one of the great compromises of the Constitution, nor was it "one of the reasons for the formation of the federal union." The police power preceded the Union and was recognized in the "inspection law" clause of the Constitution. All the Webb-Kenyon Act would do, he concluded, would be to restore to the states the proper level of police powers.[42]

Circumstances also favored the bill's defenders. Just a week before, the U.S. Supreme Court, in the case of *Hoke v. United States*, had ruled constitutional the Mann Act. The proponents argued that if Congress could prohibit this trade—interstate transportation of women for immoral purposes—through the commerce power, it could also prohibit the transportation of liquor in certain instances. To meet this challenge, the opponents called on the services of Representative James Mann, author of the act. He argued that the Mann Act provided an imperfect analogy because it did not delegate congressional authority to the states. But the wet attack did not change enough votes. Both houses voted by more than the required two-thirds to overturn the veto. On March 1, 1913, the bill became law.[43]

The course of the Webb-Kenyon Act testified to the league's influence and its opponents' weakness in Congress. The league asked congressmen and senators to support the bill, suppress amendments, and override the veto. In the Senate 42.1 percent and in the House 46.7 percent did just that. Only 11.5 percent of the representatives and 11 percent of the senators followed the diametrically opposed pattern of supporting amendments concerning personal and sacramental uses, voting against the bill and sustaining the veto. Moreover, winning over two-thirds of both houses' support in the veto vote awakened the league to the extent of its power in the national legislature. Indeed, it is likely that the next Congress, which had even more members that the league considered favorable to its program, would have passed a similar law if the Congress had sustained the veto. It is significant that the drys used this power to ask the government to lend its commerce power to the states. Prohibitionists did not intend to extend the federal government's role in controlling liquor.[44]

The drys' retreat from a purely national solution, embodied in the COD Act, was not an anomaly in the progressive era. Under pressure from reformers Congress created other laws that operated like the Webb-Kenyon Act. For example, in 1915 a federal postal law was created to be used in conjunction with state plant quarantine laws. States with inspection of plants informed the government of the plants it inspected, and all packages containing such plants sent through the mail were diverted to state officials for inspection before delivery to the addressee. Furthermore, after the Court of the 1920s became more restrictive in allowing expansion of federal powers, various other groups turned to Webb-Kenyon solutions. Thus, from 1922 to 1931, banking reformers unsuccessfully sought a federal law prohibiting the mailing of information about certain speculative securities where state laws prohibited dealing in such securities. But as with many reforms, legislation was just part of the struggle. While drys had secured the federal government's cooperation with the Webb-Kenyon Act, they still had to implement it in the states.[45]

The Webb-Kenyon Act worked a revolution in state prohibition policies and practices, and this new reality in the states helped to shape national prohibition. Most historians of the prohibition movement have viewed the drive toward national prohibition as the next step in the Anti-Saloon League's campaign after the Webb-Kenyon Act and have missed the important developments in the states. The act made effective state action against the interstate liquor industry. It revitalized old laws and stimulated prohibitionists to turn quickly to new tactics, including new state liquor transportation regulations, prohibitions of liquor advertising statutes, and personal-use bans—so-called "bone dry laws." When the U.S. Supreme Court upheld the constitutionality of the Webb-Kenyon Act and various state regulations, the dry triumph over the interstate liquor trade was secure.[46]

Once the Webb-Kenyon Act became law, both liquor dealers and prohibitionists began to ask, "How will it work?" For instance, the proprietors of George D. Tattingly and Company, distributors of wholesale liquors in Owensboro, Kentucky, thought there was "much misunderstanding about the matter." So they wrote Webb and asked him to explain the intricacies of personal-use shipments. Webb's answer summarized the state of the law: "You can ship whiskey into any state, provided the delivery, receipt or possession of same is not forbidden by the laws of the state into which you ship it. The bill . . . makes unlawful the shipment of whiskey, when it is intend to be used in violation" of the receiving state's law. While confusing, the Webb-Kenyon Act was also flexible.[47]

From 1913 to 1917 the nature of the Webb-Kenyon Act allowed state implementation to evolve. Initially the law worked simply through its symbolic existence. The Anti-Saloon League trumpeted its passage, even printing its text on a pamphlet card, implying that the federal government was now the drys' ally. Some liquor dealers panicked; one wholesale company announced, "*Forced Sale*, the Webb law has forced us out of business." Some railroads and transportation companies seized upon the law as a justification for ridding themselves of the troublesome jug trade, either by refusing to carry any liquor into dry areas or by limiting shipments to quantities suitable only for personal use. A mere month after its enactment, the Topeka freight agent for the Rock Island Railroad estimated that receipts for "bottled goods" ran 20 percent of the rate for the same period in the previous year. In its first year the act ended the tradition of the Fourth of July "Milwaukee Way" in dry areas.[48]

Beyond symbolism, the Webb-Kenyon Act suddenly expanded the scope of existing state regulations, reversing old rules that had governed the interstate trade in liquor. State laws that regulated commerce could now be expanded to interstate liquor shipments. In Iowa and Maine, for example, liquor was seized while still in the carrier's possession, long before it reached the consignee. Iowa justified such seizures on the grounds that the Webb-Kenyon Act revitalized the state's long-dormant liquor-shipping certificate system. Drys also invoked the Webb-Kenyon Act before the courts to reverse standing injunctions that blocked railroads from refusing liquor shipments into dry areas. Similarly, they used it to stop the issuing of new mandamuses requiring the common carriers to ship liquor into prohibition territory. This type of action brought results. For instance, not until this campaign did the Wells Fargo company issue, in July 1914, instructions prohibiting the handling of COD liquor shipments.

Drys based many attempts at stopping carriers from introducing liquor into dry areas on state point-of-sale laws. These laws made the place of delivery the point of sale; drys argued that since the place of sale was dry territory, liquor shipments into such areas were intended to be used in violation of state laws prohibiting liquor sales. In many states, most notably in West Virginia, liquor interests went to court, arguing that such laws were unconstitutional in an attempt to return to the old status quo. Their actions brought the issue of state regulation of interstate liquor shipments to the U.S. Supreme Court, which then set the limits of state action under laws existing before the Webb-Kenyon Act.[49]

In another Adams Express case, *Adams Express Company v. Kentucky*, which was decided on June 14, 1914, Justice James McReynolds—who as Wilson's attorney general had studied the Webb-Kenyon Act and had assured the Anti-Saloon League that he would intervene in the first good test case—explained the limits of the act. For a unanimous Court, McReynolds ruled that the act did not surrender the federal government's power over liquor commerce: "The subject-matter of such interstate shipment is left untouched and remains within sole jurisdiction of Congress." He cited its text to show that it prohibited liquor shipments only when a "person interested [in such shipments] intends that they shall be possessed, sold or used in violation of any law of the state wherein they are received." Turning to the facts of the case, McReynolds contended that, since the shipment in question was intended for personal use and since the 1907 Kentucky law recognized such use, "the liquor was not to be used in violation" of the state law. Thus the Webb-Kenyon law had "no application." If the prohibitionists wanted more, they needed new state laws.[50]

Some of the first state laws adopted in the wake of the Webb-Kenyon Act were actually remnants of previous agitation. In 1913 Texas and Delaware, both local option states, passed laws prohibiting the intrastate shipment of liquor into dry areas. Personal use, sacramental use, and interstate shipments remained exempt. These laws did not reach the interstate liquor shipments. Yet the common perception was that these state laws, combined with the Webb-Kenyon Act, prevented "the shipment of liquor from points outside the state into a prohibition community within the state." Because they were effective in stopping the intrastate trade, they received much credit. The Texas law, according to both wets and drys, choked off the illegal barrooms in dry parts of the state. For the Adams Express Company, the Christmas liquor-shipment business in Texas fell from $200 per day in 1912 to nearly nothing in 1913. Thus, the prohibitionists could argue that the Webb-Kenyon Act was "a good gun" but that "it must be manned" with more legislation. And the legislation was soon forthcoming. An attorney in a dry North Carolina county wrote to Webb saying, "On the strength of what I had seen of your bill in the papers" he had written a state bill making persons who deliver liquor in dry counties party to the sale and thus liable. It was bills like this, not personal-use bans, that the league supported.[51]

State bans on the personal use of liquor were one type of legislation that the Anti-Saloon League and other drys did not initially envision as a method of enforcing the Webb-Kenyon Act. The view of many legal experts and the liquor industry was that legislation forbidding the keeping of liquor for private use "where it is without injury to the public" would be unconstitutional. The league thought otherwise, but for the practical reason that it was far easier to pass a prohibition law if some liquor were available, it took great pains to point out that the Webb-Kenyon Act did "not prohibit one from getting liquor for personal or any other legitimate use." The league applauded Maine officials when they seized large shipments of liquor and let pass those intended for private use. The league wanted the Webb-Kenyon Act to stop shipments to illegal sellers, not to restrict shipments to private consumers; the new state laws were aimed at preventing the wholesale trade.[52]

Prohibitionists, under Anti-Saloon League leadership, turned the idea that personal-use shipments should be small into a yardstick designed to curtail liquor shipments headed for speakeasies in dry areas. A league-promoted 1913 North Carolina law—adopted two days after Webb-Kenyon—typified this use of the personal exemption. The law made possession "at any one time" of more than small amounts of liquor—one gallon of spirituous, three gallons of vinous, or five gallons of malt liquors—or the delivery of more than five gallons of hard liquor or twenty gallons of beer or wine within a month to one person or firm—prima facie evidence of violation of the state's law against liquor sales. All transportation companies were required to deliver only to the consignees or prenamed agents and to keep a "separate book" recording shipment information "open for inspection to any officer or citizen." This book listed the dates liquor was received and delivered, the size and amount of each shipment, and the name of the consignee and receiver. In addition, everyone who picked up a package of liquor was required to sign the book. The record was admissible in all state courts, and any firm that violated these terms was subject to a fine.[53]

To the league, the North Carolina law, coupled with the Webb-Kenyon law, had many benefits. Under it, large shipments of liquor were seized because the liquor was intended to violate state sales laws. The law hurt the business of Virginia border distilleries, as many of their best customers were illegal North Carolina speakeasies. On the other hand, it maintained the popular idea that citizens could get liquor for their own use. The law built a system similar to the states' use of the federal tax receipts and internal revenue collectors' records to enforce prohibition. It made the job of state officers easier. They did not have to pursue lawbreakers, as others—in this case, the transportation companies—would gather the information for them. If officers would not act, "citizens"—committed drys—would use the same sources to start private prosecutions. By 1918, with refinements and varying stipulations on the amount of liquor that would constitute a reasonable allotment for personal use, the system spread to virtually every prohibition and local option state. This system proved effective: in Kansas, for example, records generated by such a state law indicate that the per capita liquor consumption rate for the state ran under 15 percent of the national average. But some drys wanted to go farther, and West Virginia pushed through in 1915 a law that forbade the transportation of liquor within the state, the introduction of alcohol into the state, the reception of transported liquor, and the storage of transported liquor.[54]

A case arising from the 1915 West Virginia statute was added to the pending U.S. Supreme Court cases, *Clark Distilling Co. v. Western Maryland Railroad Co.* and *Clark Distilling Co. v. American Express Co.* These cases had come about from the transportation companies' refusal to carry liquor into West Virginia because its point-of-sale law made such shipments liable to seizure. The central issue in the *Clark* case was the constitutionality of the Webb-Kenyon Act; the legitimacy of the West Virginia law was secondary. The liquor spokesman Lawrence Maxwell and others argued for Clark Distilling Company that the Webb-Kenyon Act unconstitutionally delegated Congress's commerce power to the states. Furthermore, Maxwell contended, citing the 1914 case *Adams Express Company v. Kentucky*, the act did not give the state power to regulate the interstate shipment of liquor for personal use or to make the place of delivery the place of sale. Wayne Wheeler for the Anti-Saloon League and the West Virginia attorney general, Fred O. Blue (a dry and later the state's prohibition commissioner), asserted that the Webb-Kenyon Act was no delegation of Congress's power but a proper regulation of commerce; they also argued that state laws fixing the point of sale and state bans on personal-use shipments were legitimate police power enactments adopted to aid the state's liquor policy.[55]

On January 8, 1917, Chief Justice White, for a divided Court, delivered the opinion in *Clark*. The chief justice sustained the West Virginia law banning personal-use shipments by determining that the state police power to "forbid manufacture and sale" of liquor included the right "to restrict the means by which intoxicants for personal use could be obtained even if such use was permitted." There was no constitutional right to receive personal-use liquor shipments; and so presumably, though the Court did not say so, point-of-sale laws were legitimate. White also concluded that Congress had the power to pass the Webb-Kenyon Act and that it was not a delegation to the states of Congress's authority to regulate interstate commerce. Thus, the operation of the Webb-Kenyon Act and the West Virginia law did prohibit the shipment of liquor into the state. Common carriers could refuse such shipments, and courts could not force them to accept such shipments.[56]

Wets and drys disagreed as to the meaning of the decision. Wets saw the decision as a way to fend off national prohibition. They argued that it removed a compelling reason for national action, that state laws were not allowed to work. They also believed that it would slow down state prohibition because now many states would be trying to go bone dry and people would refuse such an extreme policy. On the other hand, the Anti-Saloon League and the WCTU considered the *Clark* decision a major victory, and they broadcast the opinion widely. Wayne Wheeler wrote to Congressmen Webb praising the "sweeping and far reaching" ruling, which sustained "every contention made for the law by its friends." Before the official version was printed, the Anti-Saloon League provided copies of the opinion to attorneys prosecuting transportation cases; the white ribboners arranged to have it printed as a Senate document and sent out under the frank. A cartoon in the *Union Signal* summarized the dry view of the decision. The Supreme Court—a policeman armed with a nightstick labeled "Webb-Kenyon Law"— ran the tramp "old John Barleycorn" out of a settlement of dry states. John muttered, "I can see my finish." Indeed, many drys saw the *Clark* decision as a key step to total prohibition. In the words of Wheeler, the ruling cleared "the decks for action for the final overthrow of the beverage liquor traffic."[57]

In the first decade of the twentieth century, interstate commerce in liquor, legitimated by various Court rulings, threatened prohibition's success. Like many reformers who ran afoul of court decisions, drys—eventually under the leadership of the Anti-Saloon League—worked to limit the damage caused by these rulings. The COD Act and the Webb-Kenyon Act (and the state legislation that it made possible) marked their victory over the interstate liquor trade. At first, following the centralizing trend so prevalent in the progressive period, the drys adopted a national solution in the COD Act.

Under it, the federal government regulated liquor shipments, supplanting state efforts. But by 1913 the drys had returned to the cooperative conception of the federal system. The Webb-Kenyon Act put control of interstate liquor in the hands of the states. Indeed, just as they had transformed the federal tax bureaucracy into a temperance tool, the pragmatic prohibitionists turned the federal and state powers over commerce to their advantage. Later dry legislative draftsmen used this system of joint state and federal action as a blueprint for the Eighteenth Amendment and the Volstead Act—but only after they again experimented with a predominantly federally centered system of national prohibition. The failure of their first effort also revealed that the pragmatism that had proved instrumental in their earlier successes became as much a hindrance as an asset.

CHAPTER

In 1913 the Anti-Saloon League turned its attention to enacting a national constitutional prohibition amendment, but the process soon left the path that the league had planned. Using its organizational muscle and political clout, the league brought its drafted amendment to the floor of Congress. This first effort, the Hobson resolution, failed; and its demise revealed the limits of the league's practical approach and the political indefensibility of a central-government system of national prohibition. Furthermore, the progress of state antiliquor laws and the prospect of achieving national prohibition reinvigorated the old absolutist ideology within the temperance movement. "Bone dry," the banning of all liquor shipments into a state or the personal ownership of liquor, became the new byword in prohibitionist circles. At first the Anti-Saloon League resisted the return of radical ideas and refused to abandon its pragmatic policies. Nevertheless, division in dry ranks and the momentum of the absolutist ideas led the league to get on the bone-dry bandwagon. And by the second decade of the century, the league had developed the tools to manipulate the polity into granting its goals. The league was able to use the commerce power almost to its fullest and write a national amendment. Moreover, the crisis of the First World War allowed the drys to mobilize the war power for their cause. Thus, radical temperance ideas combined with the league's practical predilections to shape the drys' final congressional enactments: the Reed Amendment to the Postal Appropriations Act, the Eighteenth Amendment, and the Volstead Act.

Early in 1913 the Anti-Saloon League launched its campaign for national prohibition. Its annual convention, held that year in the league's home city of Columbus, Ohio, focused almost exclusively on plans for making the nation dry. After the impassioned speeches, the temperance forces appointed a special committee of one hundred to draft a dry amendment; they also called another special convention of leading temperance figures to meet the next winter in Washington. On December 10, 1913, three to four thousand prohibitionists from that special convention formed a "human petition" and marched down Pennsylvania Avenue to the Capitol. There they asked their chosen Democratic legislators, Senator Morris Sheppard of Texas and Congressman Richmond Hobson of Alabama, to press for debate of the prohibition amendment, which in May had been introduced into Congress. The drys' timing was quite good. In its first congressional term the new administration of Woodrow Wilson would push through a number of reform proposals, including tariff reform, the Federal Reserve Act, and the Clayton Anti-Trust Act. Moreover, although Wilson had expressed doubts about prohibition, favoring a local option solution to the liquor issue, he did endorse national solutions for social evils like child labor. Thus, the drys' decision to turn to the reform-minded Democrats seemed promising.[1]

The two Democratic dry leaders, Hobson and Sheppard, were quite different; their roles in shaping national prohibition followed their personalities. When he first entered the Senate to finish out the term of Joseph Bailey, Sheppard announced his progressivism. He maintained this adherence; in the 1920s he voted for American Federation of Labor–backed proposals 100 percent of the time and for Conference for Progressive Political Action–supported bills 99 percent of the time. As he saw liquor as a danger to the nation, prohibition always topped the list of his progressive reforms. He was more than publicly dry, having forsaken coffee, tea, and tobacco while a Yale law student. He excelled at legislative draftsmanship and in the mastery of parliamentary procedures. His political savvy and "diligence" in serving his constituents assured his long stay in Washington; he served either as a congressman or senator from 1902 to his death in 1941.[2]

Hobson, on the other hand, was a fiery fanatic who labeled liquor a poison and the "great destroyer." He captured national attention as a captain during the Spanish-American War and made his reputation as a spellbinding speaker on the Chautauqua circuit. As a manager of bills, he proved quite ineffective. He seemed unwilling or unable to overcome his political differences to establish working relationships with other members of Congress. For instance, when asked by drys to give an opinion of Congressman Mann to be used against his reelection, he characterized Mann as an "obstructionist" who allowed "expediency" to "determine his course." Hobson's public thrashing of his enemies, his tireless self-promotions (he wrote at least one anonymous article praising himself), and his squabbling with Oscar Underwood over a senatorial seat angered other legislators. When he lost his bid for the Senate, he faded from all but temperance politics and ended up as a paid speaker for various temperance organizations.[3]

Hobson and Sheppard worked closely with the league, and thus people within the temperance movement, not legislators, initially drafted the prohibition amendment proposals. A group of league members and lawyers, including Wayne Wheeler, Fred Caldwell (author of the Webb-Kenyon Act), W. A. Covington, former Indiana governor J. Frank Hanly, Judge W. A. Campbell, John F. Burke, and national Anti-Saloon League superintendent Purley Baker, wrote the Hobson and Sheppard amendments. Many of the subsequent revisions came out of similar but less advertised conclaves.[4]

The form of the Hobson Amendment, as it came to be called, reflected the Anti-Saloon League's pragmatic step-by-step approach and its inexperience in amendment drafting. The joint resolution for the amendment began with a long preamble that denounced alcohol as a "narcotic poison" and as a blight threatening "the very life of the nation." Its major provisions "forever prohibited" in the United States "the sale, manufacture for sale, transportation for sale, importation and exportation for sale of intoxicating liquors for beverage purposes." It gave Congress "power to provide for the manufacture, sale, importation, and transportation of intoxicating liquors for sacramental, medicinal, mechanical, pharmaceutical or scientific purposes, or for use in the arts" and "to enforce this article by all needful legislation." This proposal died in the Senate Judiciary Committee, but in early 1914 the House Judiciary Committee reported the resolution, with no recommendation, to the full House. The House debated the measure in December of that year, marking prohibition as a national issue.[5]

Prohibition became a national issue not just because of congressional debate, but because the language of the initial amendment's enforcement section shifted responsibility for liquor control to the national government. Why the dry draftsmen worded the Hobson Amendment as they did remains a mystery. They could have been mindlessly copying enforcement clauses of the Civil War amendments. Or as two of the authors, Wheeler and Hanly, favored national solutions, thus following the trend of expanding central authority during the progressive period, they could have truly meant to transfer power over liquor to the federal government. In any case, prohibitionists defended this form. According to dry spokesmen, the power to enforce the prohibition amendment needed to rest in Congress's hands. Senator Sheppard (and also Senator Borah) argued, echoing Senator Beveridge on child labor, that since the liquor traffic was national in scope and "so firmly entrenched" in the country, national action was necessary "to exterminate it." Admitting that states had handled liquor in the past, he asserted that the danger alcohol posed to the republic required that the states make a new delegation of power through a constitutional amendment to the central government.[6]

Many critics within and outside the movement—including liquor defenders, states'-rights advocates, and conservatives—focused on the Hobson Amendment's enforcement clause, where this national system was set out. For instance, former president William H. Taft spoke out against the amendment's expansion of the national government's sphere of activity. Taft argued that this growth would "destroy the balance of power between central government and the state government." He portrayed the enforcement clause as a "direct blow at local self-government," asserting that under it "a horde of federal officials" would descend on every "hamlet and town in the country," trampling the rights of the people. The *Baltimore Sun* extended Taft's argument by contending that this "great army of officials . . . would build a permanent political power base and oppress" the people.[7]

Another conservative, former senator Joseph Bailey of Texas, thought the Hobson Amendment's national solution to a social problem a dangerous precedent. He worried that other "misguided reformers" would seek to fulfill their desires through similar means—such as national marriage laws. He warned that if the precedent of prohibition stood, "there will not be a square foot of territory in the United States where it will be unlawful for negroes and white people to intermarry." The amendment, by erasing "state lines," would result in the "utter subversion of this republic." The *New York World* thought that national prohibition would so consolidate the government in Washington that it would become "a fairly accurate imitation of the ruling power at Petrograd." In short, according to John C. Trice, prohibition was "the favorite spawn of the paternal government idea."[8]

Before the Hobson Amendment reached the House floor, bona fide states'-rights advocates attacked it as subversive of local power. In a minority report from the House Judiciary Committee, Representative Henry Garland Dupree, a Louisiana Democrat, called the amendment a direct threat to state authority and local autonomy. He asserted that the liquor question belonged to the states alone and was best "handled by them." He feared that the amendment would create a tyranny of a majority of states, which would be "unwilling" to let the people of his state determine their own internal policies. He also pointed out that it was unnecessary, as the Webb-Kenyon Act "cured" the evil of national interference in state control of liquor. That act, he argued, preserved the important principle of leaving as much as possible, including liquor policy, to the states. This use of the drys' most notable legislative victory became a staple criticism of all versions of the prohibition amendment.[9]

In public drys directly confronted the states'-rights critique, while in private they planned to change their amendment to meet the criticism. Senator Sheppard dismissed such attacks as "almost blasphemous." According to drys, states'-rights protection could not be extended to so palpable a wrong as liquor sales. They argued that "the modern knowledge of the nature of this poison" destroyed the right of the states "to authorize its manufacture or sale." But prohibitionists saw the seriousness of this states'-rights threat. It could cost their proposal important support in both Congress and with President Wilson, who at this point still expressed his admiration of states' rights. So behind the bluster drys moved to accommodate those concerned with states' rights. The amendment proposal, before the House debate, had "gone the rounds of most temperance and prohibition organizations," which made modifications to "remove all objections from the standpoint of states' rights." In a subcommittee of the Senate Judiciary Committee, temperance workers and some senators worked out new language for the enforcement section. This wording granted "the Congress or the states" the "power independently or concurrently" to enforce prohibition "by all needful legislation." Another change of language, proposed by the representatives and approved by the Anti-Saloon League and other dry groups, conferred power on both the states and central government "within their respective jurisdictions" to enforce the prohibition amendment. A third dry version, written to assure that the federal government not "supplant" the states but cooperate with them, gave Congress the power to enforce the amendment "only in concurrence with the states." Clearly, drys designed these new wordings to meet the states'-rights objections to the Hobson Amendment.[10]

Drys contended that these new forms guaranteed that the federal government would not encroach upon the police powers of the states, and they defended them as strongly as they had their earlier nationalistic version. Hobson insisted that the recast second section left the states "entirely free to exercise all of their police powers for the prohibition and suppression" of the sale and use of liquors. In other words, the revisions reserved to the states "all the police powers" they already exercised concerning liquor. He claimed that the modified proposal would not lead "to the enlargement" of federal powers "but a surrender of part of the taxing power" as the government would lose its right to tax liquor for beverage purposes. Other contended that the federal government gained no new powers. It merely cooperated with the states, exercising its other enumerated powers to suppress liquor. Pragmatic drys supported it strongly; for instance, WCTU president Lillian Stevens stated that "the WCTU stands for the Hobson Resolution in its amended form." Drys did not seem to understand that, in constitutional terms, Hobson's enumerated-powers argument undercut any need for an amendment. The federal government did not need an amendment to permit it to use its various numerated powers—commerce, postal, tax, treaty, and war—against the liquor traffic; it could already do so in theory and had done so in practice.[11]

Since the House Judiciary Committee reported the Hobson proposal with its original nationalistic enforcement clause and since the amendment's changes in the language (in part, thanks to Hobson's failure as a bill manager) were not voted on until the end of the debate, the opponents of the measure used the states'-rights critique against it. In the "ten mortal hours of speech-making" preceding the vote, opponents capitalized on the prohibitionists' failure to make clear their intentions on how the amendment would be enforced. Wets denounced the proposal as an attempt to "rob states of their jurisdiction over police matters." By portraying the amendment as corrosive of the "right of local self-government," opponents built a solid rhetorical criticism of national prohibition.[12]

If the drafters of the Hobson Amendment erred in writing its enforcement section by pioneering a new path, they made the mistake in focusing on sale and thus preserving the personal-use exemption to liquor prohibition. In essence, they cobbled together a federal amendment that followed state practice. Clever liquor spokesmen seized this provision and used it as the basis of strong attacks during the Hobson Amendment debates. And the preservation of personal use ran counter to the nation's tendency toward increasing aridness. Thus, the first section of the Hobson Amendment proved as controversial as its enforcement provisions.

As one prohibitionist noted, "Anyone who understands the English language can readily see" that the amendment "would not prohibit" the importation, storage, or even manufacture of liquor for personal use. Indeed, some prohibitionists (like most wets) believed that there existed no legal way to prohibit "importation for use on the part of citizens." They assumed that the liquor advocates were right in their assertions of "personal liberty"—that is, that the fundamental rights of citizens included the right to drink what they pleased. This idea gained much support from the Supreme Court's 1890 ruling in *Crowley v. Christensen*, which ruled that saloon keeping was not an inherent right or a privilege of a citizen. Many read this ruling as meaning that ownership was such a right. However, there are also indications that many dry supporters did not share these ideas and urged a personal-use exception to the amendment on practical grounds. Hobson, for example, claimed that the proposal left "regulating or prohibiting the use" in the hands of the states. He therefore assumed that the states could ban personal use. He left the matter there because he did not want give the impression that the drys intended "to do violence to the institutions founded on real individual liberty and the sanctity of the home." If that was the strategy in creating the "for sale" language, it failed miserably.[13]

In Congress, and in the press, liquor defenders attacked the Hobson Resolution's personal-use provisions. J. M. Gilmore (president of the National Model License League), Congressman Richard Bartholdt of Missouri, and other wets pointed out that, by preventing only manufacture for sale, this "adroit measure" put legitimate, tax-paying distillers out of business. Permitting manufacture, storage, and transportation for personal use, they argued, would encourage moonshiners, who already made untaxed spirits, to increase their production. Moreover, they predicted that the amendment, as worded, would fail to reduce liquor consumption and concentrate it in the home, where liquor would be made. It was, therefore, "a bill to promote home drunkenness" masquerading as a "so-called" prohibition measure. They proposed to alter the amendment, striking out the "for sale" provisions and thus making it a bone-dry constitutional amendment.

The wets drew much of their ammunition for their attacks from the utterances of drys, mostly members of the Prohibition party, who considered the Hobson Amendment a "half-leavened loaf." Eugene W. Chafin, the party's 1912 presidential candidate, denounced the proposal as a "foolish and impossible" waste of effort. Radical drys feared the "sudden chill of compromise" in the amendment. They argued that prudence dictated that the prohibitionists hold out for total prohibition; any halfway measure would only legitimate part of the liquor evil and put off their "ambition and hope—the complete overthrow of the liquor curse."[14]

Supporters of the Hobson Amendment defended it from these internal and external assaults. By the end of 1915 the drys had honed their arguments for a national prohibition amendment. The definitive defense was stated by Wayne Wheeler, Edwin Dinwiddie, and James Cannon of the Anti-Saloon

League and by Anna Gordon, Margaret Ellis, and Ella Boole of the WCTU, who acted as subcommittee for the committee drafting of a federal prohibition amendment. They had been appointed by a 1914 grand convention of drys, which as a body adopted the text of the Hobson Resolution with a revised second section calling for independent and concurrent actions by the state and national governments. The statement of this subcommittee circulated widely among prohibitionists; drys were told to "keep for future reference" a copy of this argument. Even after the amendment's wording and circumstances changed, drys continued to reprint this statement and refer to it.

This prohibition subcommittee argued that the amendment was "not as far-reaching as the laws of the most advanced prohibition states" because its main purpose was "to free the federal government from the responsibility for and the partnership in the beverage liquor traffic." After its passage, the Constitution's supremacy clause would bar the states from licensing liquor selling. The states could "add to the prohibitions provided" by the amendment and subsequent congressional legislation. The concurrent grant of power gave the states and the national government "the same authority within their jurisdictions to . . . provide for all needful legislation." The amendment would "result in team work between the states and the nation in fighting a great evil." The subcommittee also invoked the Mosaic mentality when it talked of freeing the federal government from its partnership with the liquor traffic and when it quoted the U.S. Supreme Court in *Stone v. Mississippi*, the lottery case: "No state can bargain away the morals of the people."

Beyond description of how the amendment would work, the subcommittee outlined its benefits to wet and dry states. The wet states would be "the greatest beneficiaries" because the amendment would root out the liquor traffic within their cities. For the dry states it would overcome "our greatest difficulty," the disparity between the policies of the national government and the prohibition states. No longer would law enforcement efforts in the dry states "be handicapped" by "brewers, distillers and dealers" using the mails "and other agencies of interstate commerce." Dry states would "have power to go just as far as they desire." Moreover, the "patriotic appeal to uphold the nation's prohibition policy" would lead them into passing more stringent liquor laws and thus remove temptation from those inclined to drink. In general, they argued, "the whole government will be lifted to a higher level" by the passage of the amendment.[15]

The subcommittee and other drys argued, in true league fashion, that the saloon, not the drinker, was the focus of their amendment. Through it they would reduce the flow of liquor in the nation "from a great organized flow to driblets." It was, in Hobson's view, a "strategic advance" that would destroy the "national organized liquor interest." He asserted that while the amendment failed to "go into the question of use," it did not "interfere with a state doing what it pleased to stop the use" of liquor. The state police powers were equal to the problem of home distilling under the amendment. The revised Hobson Amendment, in its defenders' eyes, rested on the concept of concurrent action by state and national government; coincidentally it followed the league's policy of supporting absolute prohibition—that is, bone-dry prohibition—only where public sentiment demanded it. In effect, drys proposed to write prohibition into the Constitution with a personal-use exemption, but with the option of letting each state go bone dry if it wished.[16]

Yet the league lacked the political muscle to force this measure through Congress. While winning a simple majority in the 197–189 vote, it failed to attain the required two-thirds necessary for passage of an amendment. After the defeat of the Hobson Resolution, the Anti-Saloon League turned its attention to assuring the election of a House of Representatives—the league knew it already had enough supporting senators—favorable to a prohibition amendment. It achieved that goal in the 1916 elections. When Congress again took up the issue, circumstances had changed. An altered legal environment and wartime attitudes influenced the course and shape of the amendment.

The Webb-Kenyon Act, the drys' most notable congressional victory before national prohibition, had created new possibilities in state liquor legislation. It had changed the rules of the polity, and it took drys several years to realize the implications. Eventually the Webb-Kenyon Act altered prohibitionist goals by opening the door to more sweeping state laws that prohibited personal-possession or personal-use shipments of liquor. In 1917 Congress followed suit by banning liquor transportation to all prohibition states. Thus, the American governments turned toward increasing dryness, and the Eighteenth Amendment would become the culmination of that movement.

The Webb-Kenyon Act and the state laws enacted to implement it established the basis for state bone-dry laws. Since the early state laws subjected personal-use liquor shipments to limitations, by inference a similar state law could completely ban such shipments. By 1915 prohibitionists in the local option state of Idaho thought that their movement had made "such rapid strides" that they pressured their legislature into passing a bone-dry law. This law totally prohibited possession and transportation of "any intoxicating liquor or alcohol within a prohibition district." When at the end of the year the citizens adopted prohibition by referendum, this ban was extended over the whole state.[17]

The 1915 *Clark* ruling added impetus to the state bone-dry movement. A mere two weeks after the decision, a dry Methodist minister wrote to the editor of the *American Issue* that before the Webb-Kenyon law and Supreme Court ruling, "there was an excuse for states . . . to pass laws allowing a limited amount of liquor for private use, now there is no excuse for it." E. J. Richardson replied for the league that the banning of personal use of alcohol had to wait until public "sentiment stands behind that view." But the national league lagged behind public opinion on this issue and many of its state organizations. For instance, as early as February 1914 the North Carolina league (over the protest of one of its leaders, who thought "jumping to the top of the ladder all at once" risky) decided to push for bone-dry legislation. By the end of 1917, eighteen states had adopted bone-dry laws. These statutes either outlawed all transportation of liquor or the personal use of liquor. Bone-dry laws proved popular; for instance, Charles H. Brough, governor of Arkansas, estimated that his state's law had decreased crime by "fully one-half" and would "never be repealed." State referenda on such laws passed by impressive majorities. By the end of the year, the U.S. Supreme Court had ruled on the constitutionality of the bone-dry laws.[18]

On December 20, 1917, in an opinion written by Justice James McReynolds, the Court upheld the Idaho personal-use ban. In the case of *Crane v. Campbell*, a sheriff had arrested a man for mere possession of "a bottle of whiskey for his own use." Against the claim that the Idaho law violated the Fourteenth Amendment, the Court ruled that the state had the power to "prohibit manufacture, gift, purchase, sale, or transportation" of liquor because of its "well-known noxious qualities." Under the police power states could enact "reasonably appropriate" laws, such as a prohibition of personal use. McReynolds also ruled that the right to "hold intoxicating liquor for personal use is not" a fundamental privilege of citizens of the United States "which no state may abridge." He argued, accepting the Anti-Saloon League's long-held view of the matter, that if such a right existed, no state could prohibit the manufacture, transportation, or sale of liquor. Despite its far-reaching nature, this case went almost unnoticed, for a new federal law made state bone-dry laws virtually irrelevant.[19]

In March 1917 Congress passed the Reed Bone Dry Amendment to the Postal Act, which prohibited the introduction of liquor into dry territory. This law grew from prohibitionist attempts to control liquor advertising in local option and prohibition states. Before 1917, under the umbrella of the Webb-Kenyon Act, most states directed their transportation laws at the wholesale dealers in liquor; since many states recognized the personal-use exemption, interstate liquor shippers turned to supplying what they called the "family user." Since state law made illegal the personal solicitation of liquor orders, in many dry areas dealers resorted to flyers and newspaper ads. When Oregon joined the dry ranks, liquor dealers opened a "string of depots . . . just over the California line" and supplied them with cheap booze and "30,000 stencils for the purpose of solicitation by circular letter." Every dry area was "besieged" by liquor ads and circulars. To the drys, these publications were a "nefarious pest" that tarnished prohibition's reputation.[20]

Drys responded to this flood of paper by passing state laws prohibiting liquor advertising in dry areas. By 1918 eighteen states had adopted anti-liquor advertising laws. The Alabama law typified these statutes, although its enforcement was more vigorous than average. It banned all advertisements of liquor within the state in newspapers, circulars, or signs. It also prohibited the sale of out-of-state papers carrying alcohol ads. In Jefferson County, which included the city of Birmingham, the sheriff launched an "active crusade" against liquor ads on buildings, billboards, fences, and vehicles. Liquor sellers were inventive in attempting to avoid this prohibition; one company had placed over its door "a whisk broom and a metal key"; another printed the following across its window: "We have it for sale, but the state won't let us tell you what it is." The county's young and ambitious solicitor, Hugo L. Black, an ardent dry and later a U.S. senator and Supreme Court justice, successfully sought injunctions banning these firms from advertising liquor. Some Alabama newspapers objected and were forced by court injunctions to refuse ads for liquor. Compliance was more common; out-of-state newspapers—the *Commercial Appeal* of Memphis, for instance— with large circulations in Alabama either refused to accept liquor advertisements, published special Alabama editions in which the ads were omitted, or allowed local news dealers to blacken or cut out objectionable ads.[21]

Prohibitionists thought the state laws effective in limiting the advertising but knew they could not choke off all avenues of liquor ad penetration. A *Union Signal* cartoon revealed the typical dry attitude. It showed booze advertising being kicked over the "state line" along with its "daddy," thus "completing the job." But the laws could not reach the mails. One wet magazine pointed out the laws' limitations by printing an edition for dry areas that carried, in the space left by deleted liquor ads, this statement: "If you want to know what this vacant space means subscribe for the paper" and "receive it through the United States mails. We are still on good terms with Uncle Sam." But use of the mails for mass solicitations by shippers provoked unfortunate results. For instance, one company, apparently working from the Birmingham city directory, sent its literature out "by street number without regard to the name of the owner or resident." Its flyers ended up in the homes of Methodist ministers, superintendents of the Anti-Saloon League, and even Samuel Weakley, author of the Alabama antiliquor advertising law. In North Carolina a mill manager complained about the effect of such circulars on his reputation: "It look bad for me when my help know that I receive from three to four circulars" per week. It was not just the ads themselves, but their content that often outraged drys. For instance, Congressman Webb was disgusted by an ad that Weakley had received; it was described as "attractive to our negro population and citizens of that character." The ad was perhaps sexually suggestive. Earlier Weakley had been angered by "the nude pictures of White Women on Whiskey Bottles. . . . These, with their vile suggestions sold only to the brutish negroes!" To completely prohibit this sort of liquor advertising, drys needed the help of the federal government.[22]

Through congressional legislation, the drys proposed to solve "the crime of newspaper liquor advertising" being sent through the mails. Individual prohibitionists, dry states, and the Anti-Saloon League pushed for bills that prohibited the mails from carrying liquor advertising into "prohibition territory in violation of state law." These proposal extended the formula of the Webb-Kenyon Act to advertising liquor by mail. In 1915 drys settled on a bill that subjected to federal penalties any person who sent liquor ads into dry areas with state laws prohibiting liquor advertising. In 1916 the House passed such a bill, proposed by the lone Prohibition party congressman, Charles H. Randall of California; in February 1917 a similar proposal—introduced by Senator Wesley Jones—was pending before the Senate as an amendment to the Postal Appropriations Act. During the Senate debates, wet senator James Reed of Missouri caught the drys by surprise when he proposed an amendment to the bill. It banned the interstate transportation of liquor, except for sacramental, medicinal, or mechanical uses, into all prohibition territory. With little discussion it passed the Senate by a vote of 45 to 11.[23]

By his amendment Reed hoped to embarrass the Anti-Saloon League and thereby "retard the cause of prohibition." It put the Anti-Saloon League in a difficult position, as the resolutions of the 1915 convention of the Anti-Saloon League called for barring liquor from interstate commerce, although the league had taken no action on this proposal. On the one hand, Reed's proposal advanced the league's ultimate goal: prohibition of the use of alcohol. On the other hand, the league, for pragmatic reasons, publicly denounced the passage of bone-dry laws if local public opinion did not demand them. The amendment to the postal act would impose the bone-dry policy on every prohibition state. The league also feared that such a nationalistic course would weaken southern, states'-rights support for the league program. Richmond Hobson warned dry leaders of the danger of going "too fast and being too drastic in bone dry legislation." Fearful of the effect in the south of this "stratagem of the enemy," he asked Dinwiddie to "put on brakes" in Congress.[24]

After the Senate approved the amendment, the league had to decide whether to oppose or support the bill. The league's congressional managers were equal to the challenge. They sent a letter to the members of Congress telling them to vote their conscience. At the same time, prominent southern league workers told congressmen that if they could vote on the floor, they personally would support the measure, since for them prohibition came before states' rights. Thus, the league neither publicly supported nor repudiated the bill. Among hand clapping, cheering, and cries of "bone dry, bone dry," the House passed the measure in a vote of 321 to 72. President Wilson—who at this point in his presidency supported local option and state prohibition, not national solutions to the liquor problem—signed it into law to keep the mails moving. The Anti-Saloon League and the WCTU applauded its passage. They also rejoiced in the discomfiture of the liquor interests and Reed—"the Senator unexpectedly found himself a Reed shakened by a strong prohibition wind." With the passage of the Reed Amendment and the Court's sustaining of it, the best the brewers could manage was to argue, just as they did when the Webb-Kenyon Act passed, that the act removed the "sole valid argument for national prohibition."[25]

It is important to note that the passage of the Reed Bone Dry Amendment did not lead the prohibitionists into adopting a strictly national approach to the liquor evil. Rather, they continued to advocate cooperative operation of state and national laws. At the national level the drys focused on ensuring that the act was enforced by the postal authorities and that the prosecutions were well managed by the Justice Department. At the state level drys argued for increased action. To the common contention that the Reed Amendment made state bone-dry laws unnecessary, drys replied, "To insure securing the full advantage of the federal law every prohibition state should have a law in harmony with the federal 'bone dry' statute." State laws were required to set the limits of the federal exceptions for medicinal, mechanical, and sacramental importations. Backed by such laws, state officers—more numerous than federal officials—could better enforce the policy. Consequently, after the passage of the Reed Amendment, two states, Michigan and North Dakota, through dry pressure, adopted bone-dry prohibition laws. Despite the temptation of a quick national solution promised in the Reed approach, drys maintained their adherence to concurrent exercise of state and national power.[26]

The passage of the Reed Amendment to the Postal Appropriations Act revealed much about the state of the temperance movement in 1917. It showed the prohibitionist victory through the exercise of concurrent state and national power over the problems posed by the federal interstate commerce doctrines. It exposed the Anti-Saloon League's mastery of political skills and the disarray and desperation of the wets. Finally, it revealed the potency of the bone-dry idea, an idea that repudiated the policy of pragmatism endorsed by the league. These circumstances all helped to shape the Eighteenth Amendment.

As the nation mobilized for war in December 1917, Congress passed the Eighteenth Amendment, sending it for ratification by the states. The amendment's three sections mixed two temperance traditions. The first section, by prohibiting all beverage use of alcohol, reflected the reemergence of radical temperance ideas encapsulated in the phrase "bone dry." The second and third sections, which set up a system of concurrent state and national enforcement and which mandated a time limit on ratification, embodied the pragmatic program so typical of the Anti-Saloon League. The welding together of these two strains came about during the sporadic and brief debates on the amendment.

The frenzied emotions of war mobilization carried over into the drive for national constitutional prohibition. The prohibitionists draped their political pressure tactics in patriotic bunting. The war made it easy for drys to portray the predominantly German American brewers as subversives, if not traitors. Under the guise of food conservation, and building on the air of sacrifice that surrounded war preparations, drys successfully urged wartime bans on distilling and brewing. The government prohibited the manufacture of distilled spirits on September 8, 1917, the manufacture of beer and wine on May 1, 1919, and the sale of distilled, malted, and vinous liquors on June 30, 1919. Like antiprostitution reformers, drys discovered that the war power was a handy tool to use against their enemies. The emergency surrounding war mobilization precluded long debate on the prohibition amendment.[27]

In 1916 and 1917 congressional consideration of the merits of national prohibition did not reflect the importance of the issue. Congress held no committee hearings on the subject. Little time was set aside for discussion of the matter. The House devoted less than six hours for debate on the proposed amendment, and the longer Senate deliberations centered on the side issue of a ratification time limit. In Congress Senator Sheppard and Representative

Webb (who had replaced Hobson as the lower house's dry champion) led the dry charge. Webb served in Congress for a decade and steadily rose in the party hierarchy. He was an able legislative draftsman and popular with other legislators. He was personally friendly to wets in the body. Indeed, James Mann, smarting from Anti-Saloon League attacks, asked for and received a statement from Webb that Mann was not the leader in the fight against the Hobson Amendment. As a floor leader, Webb managed to guide the resolution through the House debate.[28]

In general, the character of the debates in both bodies were as desultory as they were nearly one-sided. The brewers and distillers were hopelessly and bitterly divided; wet spokesmen in Congress appeared leaderless and lost. In the House dissenting members to the Judiciary Committee's favorable report on the prohibition amendment merely copied the objections of the previous session's minority report, which dealt with a different form of the amendment, instead of crafting new arguments against national prohibition. Some liquor advocates predicated many of their arguments against the proposal—such as a compensation plan and a time limit for state ratification—on the belief that the amendment would pass Congress. This defeatist attitude put the drys in the driver's seat and allowed them to guide through Congress an amendment of their own design.[29]

The intermittent debate over the amendment stretched over two sessions of Congress and nearly a full year, and in that time the form of the amendment changed. As late as March 1917, the Anti-Saloon League still pushed a measure that banned only liquor manufactured, transported, and stored for sale. It coupled this Hobson-like language with a concurrent-powers enforcement clause. Although out of office, Hobson argued for the preservation of this form. He believed that the concurrent division of enforcement had "already sunk into the consciousness" of the public and so opposed new "half-baked undigested" enforcement proposals. Furthermore, he thought the "for sale" provisions would defuse the charge that the drys wished to "invade the field of individual and domestic regulations" that "belonged to the police power of the state," thus arousing the ire of southerners "jealous about their organic law." Yet during the course of 1917 the league altered key aspects of the proposal; it replaced its narrow prohibition with stricter provisions, allowed the grafting of a time limit on ratification, and permitted a grace period of a year before implementation after ratification. But it refused to modify the enforcement clause, and after the Senate struck out the concurrent-powers clause, the league's congressional allies had it reinserted in the House. Thus, when the proposed amendment went to the states, it read as follows:[30]

Section 1. After one year from the ratification of this article, the manufacture, sale, or transportation of intoxicating liquors within, the importation thereof into, or the exportation thereof from the United States . . . for beverage purposes is hereby prohibited.

Section 2. The Congress and the several States shall have concurrent power to enforce this article by appropriate legislation.

Section 3. This article shall be inoperative unless it shall have been ratified as an amendment to the Constitution by the legislatures of the several states, . . . within seven years from the date of submission. . . .

The league saw two of these changes in the amendment as useful parliamentary strategies and thus acceded to them. First, the league defended the year's deferment of the implementation of national prohibition after ratification as a compromise measure offered to counter the wets' desires for a two-year grace period. In Congressman Webb's words, this provision gave the "legitimate at present" liquor distillers, brewers, and barkeepers a "fair and just" period "to wind up their business." It incidentally also undercut wet calls for compensation. Second, the league portrayed the seven-year ratification period as a means of making the ratification struggle fair. Suggested initially by Senator Warren Harding as a four-year period, it was perceived by many as a last-ditch attempt by the liquor interests to delay ratification long enough to defeat the amendment. But Wayne Wheeler, Ernest Cherrington, and the other leaders of the league had already calculated that, if they had not won ratification by 1920, reapportionment in the states would probably end their hopes. By agreeing to Harding's proposal—extending it to seven years—in return for a concession by the wets that there would be only a one-year (not a two-year) grace period before prohibition took effect, the league gave away nothing. Yet their action swung seven senators' votes to the amendment. But the change to a more sweeping liquor ban and the proposal to substitute national for concurrent enforcement went beyond legislative maneuvering.[31]

By preserving the Hobson for-sale formula, the Anti-Saloon League permitted its opposition the luxury of using against the new amendment all the arguments they had used against the old one. Liquor interests pointed out that, by focusing exclusively on sale and by permitting home manufacture for personal use, the measure worked a "discrimination against a legalized liquor traffic in favor of an illicit liquor traffic." It also did not "control the personal use" of liquor, including "unbridled" use of "powerful and noxious" spirits. Furthermore, the amendment failed to promote temperance, to protect "erring" individuals, or to establish safeguards for minors. In short, it was hypocritical.[32]

When Senator Thomas Hardwick of Georgia proposed to add banning use of liquor to the amendment, the league managers worked against him. Drys, under the direction of Congressman Sheppard, attacked the proposals and defended the Hobson language. Senator George Norris's contentions typified dry efforts. He asserted that use was deliberately not included in the ban to encourage buyers of illegal spirits to testify against sellers. This argument ignored the likelihood that purchasers of bootlegged booze would not testify unless forced to do so and that the threat of prosecution for use would open many mouths. It also overlooked the fact that the states had long used specified amounts of liquor to establish prima facie evidence of sale. Despite such dubious defenses, Hardwick's suggestion to change the language earned only four votes. Other forces, operating on Congress and prohibitionists, would lead to the broadening of the amendment's scope.[33]

The prohibitionist success in taming the federal system proved a hindrance in the quest for passage of a national amendment, especially one that allowed personal use of liquor. The dry laws—the Wilson Act, the COD Act, the Webb-Kenyon Act, and the Reed Amendment to the Postal Appropriations Act—became an embarrassment of riches. Wets and others pointed out, and quite rightly, that these enactments and the court cases sustaining them solved a major issue that drys used to justify a national amendment—the introduction of imported liquors into dry territory. As Oscar Underwood expressed it in the Senate debate, there was no need for a Hobson-like amendment as Congress had passed "every law that the most extreme prohibition advocate has demanded to enable the states to enforce their laws at home." Others argued that the *Clark* ruling sustaining the Webb-Kenyon Act and that passage of the Reed measure "clearly made unnecessary" submission of an amendment.[34]

This argument forced drys to develop a new justification for national prohibition. They could not easily claim that these laws were ineffective; if they did, they would denigrate over a generation of prohibitionist effort. Instead, they portrayed the legislation as incremental steps toward national prohibition. As Robert Woods noted, Webb-Kenyon gave state prohibition a "fair chance" leading to a "follow-up to ordinary prohibition," bone-dry legislation. It also pointed the way to national action to "eliminate entirely the risk" of out-of-state supply. The Reed Amendment moved in that direction, and a constitutional amendment would complete the trip. Webb amplified this argument on the floor of Congress. He asserted that the liquor problem was "bigger than a county or a state." It was "a national problem" beyond "local regulations," which incidentally had done a great deal in "curbing the evil." A series of statutory steps by the federal government had improved the situation, but final destruction of the traffic could come only through an amendment.[35]

Similarly, the final character of the struggle for national prohibition also transformed the dry approach and program. Because the issue had become, as William Anderson wrote, "amendment or nothing" and "national morality" or corruption, pragmatism gave way to reemerging temperance radicalism. This reversal appeared in the arguments used to call for passage of the amendment. For example, Representative John Tillman of Arkansas revitalized all the absolutist arguments and the Mosaic conception of law. In advocating passage, he condemned licensing of liquor selling as a "timid surrender to wrong" and declared local option "a cowardly yielding to expediency." He concluded by stating that "a law that sanctions wrong is a legislative crime." Law, especially a federal constitutional amendment, should be a "great civilizer and a great persuader." The temperance radicals' favorite analogy, the battle against the slave power, made a comeback. Senator Sheppard, invoking the famous phrases of Seward and Garrison, called the clash between liquor and prohibition "an irrepressible conflict" and declared that if it did not become "an anti-whisky constitution," then it was "still a covenant with death and an agreement with Hell." Even William Anderson, one of the most practical of the Anti-Saloon League's members, asserted that "the prohibition issue is inherently akin to the slavery question." These statements were more than bombast; they compelled prohibitionists to make their amendment more encompassing to live up to its supporting rhetoric.[36]

By portraying all their legislative victories as a march toward the dry millennium and by embracing the reawakened temperance radicalism to avoid the criticism heaped on the Hobson Amendment, the Anti-Saloon League destroyed the validity of a limited amendment. Such a proposal appeared in 1917 as a backward step because it sanctioned home manufacture of liquor. Many radical drys had made this point repeatedly: if the national constitutional prohibition amendment was to lead by example, it could not be a compromise measure. Thus, the league's own successes contributed to making the amendment an absolutist measure. John Woolley stated the process most clearly when he wrote, "Led by the logic of its own motive and forced upward by the lateral pressure of its own environment, it stands pledged . . . to the cardinal plank of the seven national Prohibition party platforms." In the Senate Judiciary Committee league workers encouraged the broadening of the amendment to ban manufacture, importation, transportation, and sale of alcohol "for beverage purposes." The new language reached to home manufacture and made the measure a "bone dry federal amendment."[37]

While the league conceded to the absolutist spirit in defining national prohibition, it refused to surrender its joint state and national enforcement ideas. When introduced in the Senate in 1917, the proposed amendment contained language that the league thought would implement their conceptions of cooperative teamwork between nation and states. It granted enforcement power to the nation but stipulated that "nothing in this article shall deprive the several states of their power to enact and enforce laws prohibiting the traffic in intoxicating liquors." Senator Sheppard explained that this language made "plain what was really an existing condition": that of federal and state cooperation in controlling liquor. The Senate Judiciary Committee, however, found this language unnecessary. Members of the committee argued that a national amendment would not deprive the states of their police power, which included "the power to enact and enforce laws prohibiting" liquor. They "did not deem it advisable to place" such a disclaimer in the amendment. Senator Sheppard accepted their judgment and argued that, without or with the clause, cooperation would characterize enforcement. Even so, loss of this language opened the amendment to attacks that it threatened to undermine states' rights. Many senators justified their opposition by standing on their "Jeffersonian principles" of a limited federal government. They feared, like Oscar Underwood, that the expansion of federal "police powers" would destroy state boundaries and result in the "abolition of state governments."[38]

The reopening of the states'-rights wound—in a body controlled by Democrats—apparently worried the league and prompted the return of the cooperative formula. The House Judiciary Committee, through Webb's efforts, recast the enforcement section, giving it its final form. It conferred "concurrent power to enforce" the amendment "by appropriate legislation" to both Congress and the states. The particular wording was the committee's, but the thinking that lay behind the words reflected the league's position. Webb's explanation of the language followed dry justifications of earlier cooperative enforcement clauses. He contended that the new wording was designed as a "reservation" to the states "of power to enforce their prohibition laws." He argued further that "nobody" desired sole national enforcement or wished to see the creation of "10,000 new federal officers" with expensive salaries. He contended that more plentiful state officials, "willing" to enforce the law, would do a better job at a lower cost. Webb also compared the concurrent-power clause to the operation of laws against counterfeiting. While a "peculiarly" national offense, "nearly all the states" had statutes "condemning and punishing" the crime. The states had the right to enforce these laws because Congress gave them jurisdiction. To implement a similar system over liquor, the amendment "set forth and granted" concurrent power to the nation and to the states.[39]

The switch in enforcement emphasis caught many wets off guard. Some of their congressional supporters continued to attack the amendment as a nationalistic steamroller that would "populate" the states with "federal spies" and bring about the "ending of state authority." The House Judiciary Committee's minority report, copying an earlier report, mistakenly contended that "all the state police powers and its agencies would be done away with." Given that they had already met these criticisms by inserting the concurrent-powers clause, drys did not bother to refute these attacks. Yet they could not resist pointing out that some of the opponents who defended states' rights in regards to prohibition had limited credentials for protecting the states, having advocated in the past the expansion of the national police power over labor relations. But not all wets focused on the states'-rights theme; a few saw the implications of the new enforcement language.[40]

Before passage of the amendment, opponents—echoing comments made earlier by drys—raised two questions about the meaning of the concurrent-powers clause. The Prohibition party leader Eugene Chafin in 1916 had asserted that a violator of national prohibition could not "be arrested by both" the federal and state authorities, as this would constitute double jeopardy. In debate Representative Arthur Dewalt picked up this theme and connected it to Webb's analogy to counterfeiting. Dewalt pointed out that even after state conviction for counterfeiting the federal government could "still" try and punish "the same offender" for the same act. Webb admitted that was law but disagreed with the analogy. He asserted that "one punishment ought to be sufficient" and that the power "getting jurisdiction first" should be the one to act. As a "supreme power," either the states' or nation's action would be final. This interpretation raised a serious question about the feasibility of joint enforcement that wets quickly seized upon.[41]

Critics brought up the willingness of the states to do their share of the policing. In the Senate Henry Cabot Lodge argued that "the states will, of course, cease to enforce prohibitory laws" after passage of the amendment. "They will only be too glad to get rid of the burden of the expense." His comments reinforced what the prohibition federal district judge Charles A. Pollock had asserted to Hobson in 1915. Pollock thought that under concurrent powers "it would be easy for unwilling legislators . . . to duck . . . responsibility. Would not some weak-kneed or positively vicious members of the legislatures . . . say: 'Let the General Government Act, they have the power'?" Following similar comments in the House, Webb admitted that such action might weaken prohibition "to a limited extent." But he argued that if states utterly refused to act, "the federal government will nab a man who has violated" federal prohibition law.

In the House Edward Denison took this issue in a different direction. He speculated about states acting in bad faith. He thought it would "defeat the operation of the law" in a state if that state "should provide very small penalties" for violators of liquor bans. Webb dismissed Denison's hypothetical case as ridiculous: "I am not afraid to trust the states" as "I never saw one that went counter to the United States Constitution, or whose law officers failed to enforce the law." Webb's disregard for history—surely he knew of state resistance to the fugitive slave law in the 1850s—went unchallenged. This thin discussion revealed the superficiality of Congress's discussions. As one commentator at the time noted, in the "brief debate that preceded" the vote on the amendment any realization of what Congress was doing "was conspicuously absent." Indeed, many of the critiques of the concurrent-powers clause came after passage by Congress and some after ratification by the states.[42]

On December 17, 1917, the amendment, in its changed form, passed the House by a comfortable margin of 282 to 128, with 23 not voting. A day later the Senate, with no debate, concurred with the House's changes by a vote of 47 to 8. The proposed amendment was sent to the states for ratification. During ratification "the result was never in doubt." Drys overcame the wets with superior organization, preparation, and generalship. Moreover, a popular wave of antialcohol sentiment fueled the process. Ratification "came with a speed and an avalanche like irresistibility" that surprised both wets and drys. On January 16, 1918, Nebraska became the thirty-sixth state to ratify, making national prohibition part of the Constitution. Eventually forty-six of the forty-eight states—only Connecticut and Rhode Island refused—ratified the amendment. Wets, led by the United States Brewers' Association, resorted to "desperation strategies" in attempting to block implementation of the amendment. They instigated a number of court cases to test the constitutionality of parts of the amendment and certain states' ratification proceedings.[43]

During the ratification struggle and in the courts, one of the main wet challenges to the amendment was to question the meaning of concurrent powers. Their arguments built on the views advanced during congressional debate on the amendment. Lawyers led the assault. A committee of the New York Bar Association, under the direction of George Wickersham, urged its legislature not to ratify. It argued that because of its "doubtful, dangerous, and mischievous" enforcement clause, the amendment would "induce a confusion of power and conflict of jurisdiction far-reaching in its consequences." It would, on the practical level, make national prohibition "meaningless and a mockery" as states would not do their fair share in insuring compliance. A committee of the Connecticut Bar Association also advised against the adoption because it viewed the second section as "clearly wrong." It feared that it would erase the lines dividing state and national authority by giving the states power over interstate commerce and the nation power over manufacture and individuals within the states.

On a different note, the Connecticut committee contended that concurrent powers required adoption of the same laws to be implemented. Citing the case of *Ex Parte Desjeivo*, which concerned a dispute between Oregon and Washington over the Columbia River and ruled that concurrent power required joint action, the committee argued that a lone enactment would have no force. This contention rested on the assumption that the states and the national government were equal sovereignties, just as Congressmen Webb had stated. Such a reading, while somewhat tortured, was not absurd. Exactly what "concurrent power" meant was open to interpretation. Many observers turned to their dictionaries to assign meaning to the phrase. Most rejected the argument that the words intended that state and national legislation "must agree to be authoritative." In its place, some supporters of national prohibition asserted that the amendment granted equal authority that "if exercised by one, [was] not usually assumed by the other." While the issue of the meaning of concurrent powers was before the courts, Wayne Wheeler turned to the source of the language, the House Judiciary Committee.[44]

In a series of letters to key members he inquired as to the "intention of the committee" in drafting the second section of the amendment. Wheeler enclosed with his letters his memorandum against New Jersey's proposal to license liquor sellers in an effort to help guide the congressmen in writing their replies. This memo reflected his advocacy of national solutions to the liquor question. It argued that "no state can legalize what the laws of the United States prohibit." The supremacy clause was not changed by the amendment; thus, when "Congress is given power over a subject matter its acts are supreme no matter whether the States have power over" the same subject. State laws that conflicted with the federal mandated standards of what liquor could be sold revived "the old discarded doctrine of nullification." For very practical reasons, Wheeler wanted the states to follow a uniform national liquor standard. He believed that the support of the states, with their "large number of officers whose duty it is to enforce criminal laws" and their greater experience in implementing liquor regulations, would be a prerequisite for effective national prohibition. He urged the passage of state enforcement codes consistent with the provisions of the Volstead Act. The letters he received from ranking Republican Andrew Volstead and Judiciary Committee chairman Webb were contradictory.[45]

In general, Volstead's reply ran along the lines of what Wheeler wanted to hear. At first, he vacillated a bit on the issue, arguing that concurrent power gave the federal government and the states "power to enforce the amendment independent of and irrespective" of what the other "might do." But this statement belied the thrust of his comments. He asserted that he, Webb, "and others interested" in passing the amendment had come up with the language and that concurrent power was "not a new idea." Volstead explained that the committee used the word "concurrent" in the Eighteenth Amendment with care, and its meaning was that the state and national authorities were "concurrent in time" and ran "side by side, though not necessarily equal in power." He further added, "It was not believed that any reason exists why" the supremacy clause "would not apply" to state and federal liquor legislation under the Eighteenth Amendment, "just the same as it now applies in other cases where legislation is enacted under such concurrent power."[46]

Webb's comments, contained in two letters, were probably far less pleasing to Wheeler. He wrote that the clause gave the federal and state governments "the right to enforce the constitutional amendment in their own way." For instance, a state might pass a law that prohibited liquor containing 3 percent alcohol, or six times more than the federal standard under the Volstead Act. Under concurrent powers "a person" within that state who sold the "3% beverage would be exempt from prosecution by the state authorities, but would be liable to indictment under the federal act." He admitted that some "wet states might not pass laws against the manufacture and sale of liquor," but thought that their "non-action" would not prevent federal enforcement. And, on the other hand, "some states" might pass laws more "drastic" than the federal statute, which would not give any "immunity from prosecution under state laws." Thus "each sovereign has the right, so far as its jurisdiction goes, to enforce this constitutional amendment in its own way." His interpretation would allow state laws to be less stringent than the federal law. Such a system, Wheeler thought, would mean that federal jails, not state jails, would be filled with violators of prohibition. Thus, key members of the body that created the enforcement clause's language disagreed; but the vagueness of the language allowed the drys to push the most stringent interpretation. Before the Supreme Court, Wheeler argued his, and Volstead's, view of the wording.[47]

In the June 1920 *National Prohibition Cases*, the Supreme Court settled the meaning of "concurrent powers." It dismissed the argument that federal and state enactments had to be identical to be effective. It denied the states, through action of the supremacy clause, the power of passing laws that conflicted with those of Congress on the subject. It also rejected the notion that the Eighteenth Amendment merely perpetuated limited federal powers (tax and commerce) and extended Congress's power to "intrastate trans-actions." The Court asserted that this power was not "affected by action or inaction" of the states. Wheeler considered the ruling a victory, as his and Volstead's conception of concurrent power, not the states'-rights doctrine of Webb, became the settled law. In practical terms, the states could not by legislation actively hamper national prohibition. But there was no constitutional requirement for them to enact supplemental prohibition codes. Before this ruling, the Anti-Saloon League simply dodged the issue when faced with a host of questions about concurrent power. In public Wheeler admitted that concurrent jurisdiction might create "confusion, litigation and even ineffectiveness in the enforcement" of the liquor ban. But he argued that clearing up definitions was less important than writing national liquor prohibition laws.[48]

Drawing upon nearly forty years of prohibitionist activity, the Anti-Saloon League implemented plans to have the Eighteenth Amendment enforced by federal, state, and private efforts. The league did not succumb to the popular idea that the "people will submit" to national prohibition "in a sportsmanlike and American way." The resolutions of the league conventions for 1918 and 1919 both underscored the "obligations" of Congress and the states "to enact the legislation necessary to put into effective operation" the dry amendment. Nor did the league draftsmen perceive the amendment, as later historians have, as merely a symbol, a "ceremonial enactment," a "ritual" law defining the nation's values. Moreover, the league linked enforcement to one of its larger goals, world prohibition. The league did not depend on "wizardry" or symbols but took steps to assure compliance to the national ban.[49]

The day after Nebraska ratified the amendment, Wayne Wheeler publicly announced the league's implementation proposals. He gave Congress "notice" that "it is its duty to enact a federal prohibition law." Similarly, the states should frame prohibition statutes "in harmony with the federal amendment." Finally, educational efforts and vigilance in "maintaining in office administrators and officers determined to enforce" the laws must continue. Keeping officials on the job and demanding state laws were familiar goals for the league, but the new ground—a national prohibition code—became the centerpiece of the league's plan.[50]

The federal prohibition code, named the Volstead Act after the congressman who introduced and perhaps wrote it, was designed as "a 1920 model of efficiency and speed." Despite a question over whether Andrew Volstead or Wayne Wheeler authored the law, it is beyond dispute that the measure was an Anti-Saloon League proposal. Soon after ratification of the amendment, Wheeler began the process of creating a national prohibition bill by collecting the various laws of the states and outlining the basic contours of the bill. Representative Volstead took Wheeler's original proposals and recast them, perhaps adding new substance. Each man claimed credit for the bill. Nevertheless, Congress forced a number of changes in the original, and thus the final act was a compromise. It is also important to note that, compared with other dry legislation—like the Eighteenth Amendment and the Webb-Kenyon Act—the Volstead Act was a rushed job. Previously they had years to refine their language.[51]

The Volstead Act had three major sections. The first section implemented the system of wartime prohibition. It went into effect the day the act was passed over the president's veto, October 24, 1919, long after the fighting had ended. It kept the nation from experiencing a wet spring during the tumultuous period of demobilization—when wartime bans would presumably lapse—before the coming of what most people thought would be a permanent dry spell. The third section laid out the regulations for the production and distribution of alcohol for industrial use. Even the most fanatical dry knew that alcohol was an indispensable solvent for science and industry and that it would still be manufactured. But fearing its diversion to illegal drinkers, the drys constructed a system of control over the production of alcohol and required its denaturing to render it unsafe for consumption. The second and most important section was the national prohibition code.[52]

The national prohibitory law closely resembled state prohibition laws. It outlawed the manufacture, sale, transportation, and possession of any intoxicating liquor "except as authorized in this act." Congress wrote two important exceptions into the act over Anti-Saloon League protests. These were the exception allowing the home fermentation of fruit juices—the so-called apple cider exception—and the exception allowing possession of liquors in "one's private dwelling . . . for use only for the personal consumption of the owner," the owner's family, and personal guests. These two exemptions stood outside the well-devised system the act constructed and proved to be major sources of enforcement problems.[53]

The act set out a detailed permit system, running to five pages in *Statutes at Large*, for the production and distribution of alcohol and the withdrawal from bond of existing liquor stocks for sacramental and medicinal use. The act was, in the words of Wheeler, "forged on the anvil of experience." It drew on time-tested state laws. With the aim of keeping alcohol from being diverted to illegal beverage use, it regulated the activities of church officials, doctors, druggists, manufacturers, and common carriers who would be involved in the legal industry. To curtail the illegal sale of intoxicants, the Volstead Act banned solicitation of liquor orders and prohibited liquor advertising. To further penalize liquor sellers, it instituted a system of barkeeper tort—that is, the collection of damages from the sellers of liquor resulting from the actions of intoxicated persons. It also condemned as a common nuisance any building or vehicle used in any aspect of the liquor trade and granted search and seizure powers to government agents. By dry standards, it was not perfect; for instance, Congress rejected more sweeping search powers proposed by the league. But to drys it seemed a workable system, not a mere symbolic enactment.[54]

The only truly symbolic part of the Volstead Act was also its most controversial aspect: its definition of intoxicating liquors. The act, at Anti-Saloon League prompting, set the level of alcohol defined as intoxicating at one-half of one per cent by volume. This limit, of course, forbade the manufacture of beer. As many thought it too severe, it sparked debate in Congress. In the dry view there was little choice. The federal law acted as a signpost for the states, compelling the adoption of a strict limit. According to Wheeler, a more lenient standard would cause confusion by overriding stricter state laws and encouraging "law breaking of state laws." And to restore, by federal law, some alcoholic beverages to legitimacy seemed an abomination to prohibitionists. They feared that if the national government recognized beer, the states would follow suit and in wet enclaves the liquor evil would survive.[55]

This was no phantom fear. Despite the federal alcohol limit, New York and New Jersey passed laws in 1920 legalizing the manufacture and sale of beer light in alcoholic content; Massachusetts's legislature passed a similar bill, but Governor Calvin Coolidge vetoed it. The governor of New Jersey proposed to permit the manufacture and sale of 50 proof liquors before the passage of the Volstead Act. In September 1920 Wheeler warned a league audience of such attempts to "cripple" prohibition enforcement. But, he continued, a remedy was at hand: "as long as Congress" set the "standard of effective enforcement legislation, the law will be fairly well executed in all the states." To insure this goal, the league must work to "harmonize" and "standardize" state codes with the national standard. The Supreme Court in the 1920 *National Prohibition Cases* agreed with Wheeler and halted state legalizing laws. It held that the amendment did not enable "the several states to defeat or thwart the prohibition" through legislation, "only to enforce it." Thus, state laws could be no wetter than the national prohibition statute. In practice, state laws could be stricter than the federal standard. The Anti-Saloon League insisted on an absolute solution reminiscent of the earlier radical temperance thinking. Nor it did not forget its long efforts to convert the federal tax into a dry weapon or its inclination to favor the appointment of malleable officials.[56]

The Volstead Act divided authority over national prohibition enforcement between the Justice Department and the Treasury Department. It vested the majority of federal power with the revenue officers. Drys turned to treasury officials because, according to William Anderson of the Anti-Saloon League, it would be "foolish" to construct "a new department, when there was already in existence" a bureau with the "experience, personnel, and equipment" that could be "converted" to new uses. The league thought, as Wheeler expressed it, that the internal revenue commissioner was "obviously the choice" for chief federal "law enforcement official" because his department had "dealt with the liquor traffic" for years. And it did not hurt that the commissioner was a dry. Since the "policy of the department" was "to cooperate with state officers in the enforcement of law," treasury officials would be the best federal administrators. The league added the Justice Department to the prohibition enforcement staff because it was the only part of the government competent to handle prosecutions. The initial budget, allocating $2 million for Internal Revenue and only $100,000 for Justice revealed the framers' intention that tax officials should carry the primary administrative burden. Since dry pressure had made federal tax officials an adjunct force in the enforcement of state prohibition laws, this arrangement seemed logical to prohibitionists.

Federal tax officials were empowered to implement all three sections of the Volstead Act, the temporary war time prohibition provisions, the permanent national prohibition code, and the regulations governing industrial alcohol and other legal forms of liquor. As befitting their role as tax officials, many of the revenue officers' duties involved oversight of the nation's legal supply of spirits. But the tax officers were more than mere regulators. The Volstead Acted vested the commissioner of internal revenue and his underlings with broad authority to investigate all violations of national prohibition. The tax officials' roles embodied prohibitionist, especially the Anti-Saloon League, conceptions of the proper role of federal bureaucrats. The league expected them to enforce one particular provision of the Volstead Act.[57]

In one section the league wrote its victory over the federal liquor tax into the national prohibition code. The prohibition act did "not relieve anyone from paying any taxes or other charges imposed upon the manufacture or traffic" in liquor. While "no liquor revenue stamps or tax receipts for any illegal manufacture or sale" would "be issued in advance . . . on evidence of such illegal manufacture or sale," double the current tax—"with an additional penalty of $500 on retail dealers and $1,000 on manufacturers—would be collected from "the person responsible for such" transactions. It also provided that payment of the tax gave "no right to engage in the manufacture or sale of such liquor, or relieve[d] any one from any liability, civil or criminal heretofore and hereafter incurred under existing laws." Thus, the tax machinery was left in place, but only to be used as a penalty aimed at those who were caught breaking the national prohibition law. The Volstead Act transformed the federal liquor tax into a mere temperance tool. But drys also believed that good laws required good officials to implement them.[58]

Thus, the federal law exempted "executive officers . . . and persons authorized to issue permits, and agents, and inspectors" from the civil service laws. This exemption was a deliberate strategy to assure that the federal bureaucrats would remain amenable to dry demands. In a letter Andrew Volstead explained why it was not a good idea to extend civil service law protection. He wrote, "Such a plan would be inadvisable because . . . it would make it mandatory on the Bureau to accept as agents men who might not be in sympathy with the law" and who would then be difficult to remove. The league, and especially Wheeler, planned to oversee federal enforcement, using the same pressure tactics it had long advocated in handling state enforcement officials. Some measure of the league's early control within the department was evidenced by how John F. Kramer, the first federal prohibition commissioner, envisioned the working of national prohibition. He said, "The matter of enforcing the law will be primarily in the hands of the local" authorities. County, city, and state officials should be "zealous in the performance" of this duty, and where they were not, the federal government would act to insure that the ban was obeyed. Kramer's remarks reflected league doctrine on the primacy of willing officials and state action.[59]

The league calculated that, under the concurrent-powers section of the Eighteenth Amendment, the states would actively enforce national prohibition. To assure a dry nation, the league set up the Volstead Act as a guide to their efforts. The league worked to make their scheme a reality by pressuring the states into adopting new prohibition codes modeled on the federal law. Wheeler argued that the states had "a greater moral obligation to enforce" the amendment as they had larger numbers of criminal law officers. Moreover, there were advantages, he contended, to passage of such laws, including discouraging lawlessness and the generation of "fines and forfeited bonds arising from the enforcement of the law." The main provisions of such laws adopted the federal alcohol limit; prohibited the manufacture, sale, transportation, and importation of liquor; and outlawed the soliciting and the advertising of alcoholic beverages. In particular, the league targeted populous and notoriously wet New York as a test state. The league contended that a "successful administration" of prohibition in New York would be "an answer for all time to those who say 'it can't be done.'" Ratification of the amendment came first, followed in late 1920 by passage of a prohibition law drafted by Wheeler and patterned on the Volstead Act. Meanwhile, the league formed a State Citizen League "to crystalize" dry sentiment behind state prohibition law enforcement. Through the early 1920s, under the direction of William Anderson—through the so-called Yonkers plan, which merely recast the league enforcement strategy for new times—drys pressured New York officials to enforce prohibition.[60]

The victory in New York, the adoption of the Eighteenth Amendment, and the passage of the Volstead Act caused many prohibitionists to "sound the jubilee." Indeed, drys had reason to celebrate; they had overcome all the obstacles raised by the polity and their opponents to their reform. But in their euphoria over their achievements, most drys failed to notice the limits of their victory. Prohibitionists, influenced by their predilections and thanks to various circumstances, constructed a system of nationwide prohibition that presumed cooperation between the federal government and the states in setting prohibition policy and enforcing the liquor ban. Drys did not reflect upon the implications of concurrent powers for national prohibition enforcement. While drys celebrated New York's conversion, few noticed that another wet state, Maryland, refused to accept either the league's model law or any other prohibition statute. Not many drys seemed to realize that the doctrine of cooperative exercise of state and national power over liquor, which had so long been a part of their movement, could lead to lax or no enforcement of the amendment and help to contribute to the collapse of national prohibition.[61]

CONCLUSION

THE RELATIONSHIP OF THE POLITY TO REFORMS AND THE LEGACY OF CONCURRENT POWER DURING NATIONAL PROHIBITION

The radical prohibitionist ideology of the 1880s and 1890s generated a Mosaic view of law that did not provide practical solutions for the problems posed by the federal system. But by the advent of national prohibition, drys had changed their approach to legal issues. The legal environment pushed prohibitionists into adopting the idea of joint state and federal action against liquor. From the 1890s temperance advocates struggled to make the federal commerce power aid prohibition states. By 1917 the Reed Amendment to the Postal Appropriations Act had fully mobilized that power for the dry cause. The rise of the Anti-Saloon League, with its more pragmatic view of law as a means to an end, transformed the legal strategy of drys, allowing them to take advantage of the federal system. For example, drys ceased to work for the abolition of the liquor tax and turned it into a valuable law enforcement weapon. But prohibitionists never gave up the idea of law as a moral statement. The drys, through the Eighteenth Amendment's concurrent-powers clause and the Volstead Act's provisions, wrote both conceptions of law into the nation's Constitution and statutes.

The drys sought a tremendous change in many Americans' drinking habits; by relying on their experience with the federal system as a guide, they constructed an enforcement system that contributed to the failure of national prohibition. The failings of enforcement, combined with economic, political, social, and cultural change, led to repeal of the Eighteenth Amendment. The past proved a blueprint not for success but for disaster. The debacle of national prohibition and the forty years of dry agitation that preceded it illuminate the rough parameters of polity and reform interaction in the progressive era. Brief surveys of three other contemporaneous reforms—

divorce, juvenile justice, and eugenics—help fill in the picture of the relationship between the polity and reforms.

As this work has shown, the structure of the polity shaped prohibition reform. The interaction of the reformers and parts of the polity combined to shape the legislative and constitutional means used by drys to achieve their goal. This relationship prompts the question of how other reforms fared in the machine of the polity. The answer varies according to a combination of factors: the means of the reform, the reformer's legal culture, the strength of the reform movement, the power of the movement's opponents, the configuration of the polity, and the nature of the particular legal environment. (Other factors, to be discovered only through reexamination of various reforms' histories, probably played their parts.) To date, there have been no studies of other reforms with this interpretation in mind. Yet in the secondary literature concerning three different reforms of the progressive era there are hints at the range of possibilities. The histories of the movement to amend divorce law, the crusade for juvenile justice, and the eugenics movement all illuminate factors shaping the interaction of the polity and reform. These stories of one regulationist and two reformationist reforms puts the prohibition crusade into context.

While a regulationist reform, divorce reform, like antiprostitution and antigambling, was a movement that shared many characteristics with the abolitionist prohibition crusade. The proponents of divorce reform, in the period from 1880 through the progressive era, came from the same social background and shared fundamental assumptions about society (and often membership) with their sister reformers. Yet divorce reform failed to follow the same pattern of federal aid to support state action that marked the other crusades. In part, this different course came from the way divorce interacted with the polity. While federalism undercut state efforts to set divorce policies, it never eroded away those policies. Thus, while reformers called for federal action, the polity saw little reason to respond. Moreover, the reformers were divided over what kind of divorce reform they wished the federal government to enact. So there was no federal divorce act or any serious attempt to pass a divorce amendment. Even the campaign to design uniform state laws came to little. For divorce reform the interaction of reform and polity followed a pattern different from that of prohibition, and an examination of the history of divorce with an emphasis on legal ideas, general social attitudes toward the practice, lack of cohesion in the movement, and relationship of federalism to the reform does much to explain this different pattern.[1]

Before the Civil War two competing forces, a restrictive tradition that virtually prohibited divorce and a popular desire for easier divorce, pulled the American polity in different directions over the issue; eventually liberalization won, but without changing the basic contours of the issue. Divorce for most of the country's history has been a moral question. Like most Christian nations, the United States saw divorce as an attack on the sacred nature of marriage. Thus, the polity acted to protect the morality of the people by making the practice difficult. The burden of setting and enforcing divorce policy fell to the states, as the framers of the constitution did not consider marriage and divorce suitable subjects for national government action.

The states of the new nation inherited an English legal heritage that severely restricted the grounds for and incidents of divorce. But divorce was not impossible in the American context. The states also borrowed from English law and practice a series of means to bypass the strict law. The two most practical means around the restrictions on divorce were, first, the court-ordered degree of divorce from bed and board, which prohibited the parties from remarrying and resulted in a permanent martial separation, and, second, divorce by a private bill of the legislature, which was absolute. Although it proceeded at different paces in various regions, by the time of the Civil War most states were expanding the grounds for divorce—adding causes such as cruelty, misconduct, or long imprisonment—and transferring jurisdiction over the matter to the courts. But some states, like South Carolina, which refused to recognize the legitimacy of the practice, and New York, which stipulated that adultery was the only grounds for divorce, refused to follow the liberalizing trend. Moreover, liberalization did not extend that far; the states in this period did not adopt the idea of mutual-consent divorce but rather upheld the notion that divorce was obtainable by a party if he or she were wronged by the spouse.

The new nature of divorce law spawned new problems, which persisted into the early twentieth century. First, since divorce proceedings were adversarial, those seeking a friendly divorce were forced to collude in perjury or to fake legal criteria for divorce. Second, the variations over grounds for divorce among jurisdictions led to migratory divorce, whereby citizens of a restrictive state would use the less vigorous laws of another state to terminate their marriage. From the 1850s through the 1870s, and then from the 1880s through the twentieth century, a series of western states (first Indiana, with Nevada the most notorious) with liberal laws became havens for those seeking divorce. Indeed, in this period western divorce lawyers opened New York offices to facilitate the process. Third, and most important for later developments, the wave of liberalization prompted the birth of a movement to restore the old restrictions on divorce.[2]

A wide array of groups in the late nineteenth and early twentieth centuries called for divorce reform, the most significant of which were the divorce reform societies. In 1881 critics of the liberal divorce laws formed the New England Divorce Reform League. Its first chief officer, the former president of Yale University, Theodore Woolsey, had in 1867 portrayed divorce as a danger to American civilization. He compared the United States to Rome and warned that the nation would repeat the empire's fate if it continued to allow "connubial unfaithfulness and divorce" to increase. Keeping "family life pure and simple" was the key to preserving the nation's "present political forms." Animated by such notions, Christian churches—not surprisingly—supplied the majority of the delegates to the organization. The organization thrived and pointed to its goal by renaming itself, four years later, the National Divorce Reform League; by the late 1890s it called itself the National League for the Protection of the Family. It was followed in its agitation by broader organizations that took up the issue, most notably the WCTU, the Farmer's Alliance, and the General Federation of Women's Clubs. Various churches (including the Methodist Episcopal and Episcopal churches) and certain state governments—especially Pennsylvania's—also embraced the cause. Such broad support guaranteed much activity but produced few results.[3]

The most positive results, from the reformers' perspective, came in the states, but they were less successful at the federal level. In the 1880s reformer pressure brought about the rollback of liberal laws in a number of states. Calls to create a federal law or constitutional amendment to set divorce parameters failed, however. In 1884 the first amendment was introduced into Congress, and for next sixty years similar proposals surfaced in nearly every session. Most never left committee, as Congress was not inclined to expand federal authority over marriage relations. Southern congressman, worried that the federal government might legitimate interracial marriages, refused to support a constitutional amendment and asserted that a federal law on the topic without an amendment would be unconstitutional. To quote a divorce reform conference report, passage of federal divorce legislation was not "feasible," and agitation for constitutional amendment, "futile." So the reformers turned to another course, uniform state legislation.[4]

From the 1890s through the first decade of the twentieth century, divorce reformers sought the creation of uniform state laws on the topic. This movement began in 1892, and its first fruit was a model law drawn up in 1901, which listed five grounds for divorce: adultery, desertion, extreme cruelty, habitual drunkenness, and conviction of a felony. But only two states adopted it in the following five years. In 1905 Theodore Roosevelt revitalized the movement for uniform divorce law by calling for a national congress on the topic. From this 1906 meeting another uniform law emerged, which added bigamy to the list of causes; this proposal allowed the states to have fewer causes for divorce and asserted that states did not have to recognize out-of-state divorces except for causes recognized in their own law. Yet only three states adopted this proposal as law. So a generation of agitation did not fundamentally alter the nature of divorce law in the United States.

Division in reform ranks, in part, accounts for the failure of the divorce reform movement. The writers of both uniform state law proposals and a federal amendment failed to build a consensus on what kind of divorce amendment they wanted. The divisions cut in several directions. For example, on the issue of migratory divorce, reformers from conservative New York sought to impose its strict standard on the rest of the nation, while other reformers from more liberal states asserted that restrictive laws were the real reason for migratory divorce and urged New York to bring its law into line with the majority of the states. Similarly, the WCTU wanted to end migratory divorce, but at the same time it wished to add intemperance as a legitimate grounds for divorce, contrary to other reformers' desire to make adultery the only acceptable grounds for the action. Beyond these divisions, the emergence of new psychology and the secularization of society not only undercut the religious justification for strict divorce laws and the reformers' call for restoration of the old laws but actually began a new movement for liberalization. Thus the divergent voices within the movement, and new forces outside of it, weakened its power to influence legislation, and the federal system worked to make reform less than a pressing necessity.

The U.S. Supreme Court, unlike its role in the prohibition issue, did not exacerbate the divorce issue. Indeed, in a number of cases decided in the first decade of the new century the Court allowed the states broad latitude in refusing to accept out-of-state divorces. Since the parties involved were almost the only ones who could bring the issue to the states' attention, the effects of the rulings were mixed. First, states could theoretically decide whether they would recognize migratory divorces or not. But the effect was to make the process merely uncertain—if both parties cooperated, the divorce was obtainable and would not be questioned unless the parties had a falling out or attempted to remarry in a restrictive state. Second, the rulings led to a proliferation of divorce-mill jurisdictions—some in the states, some in U.S. territories, and some in foreign countries—where migratory divorce became the basis for a tourist industry. These jurisdictions functioned as safety values for the states with strict standards. Because outlets were available, divorce reformers intent on preserving limited divorce could preserve the strict state laws. Thus, despite great similarities in the movements' constituencies, divorce did not follow the same path as prohibition. Divorce never became a national issue, nor did another reform of the progressive era, the juvenile justice movement.

The creation of juvenile courts was a reform of the progressive era, one of the many attempts in the period to remake the lives of children who had gone astray. Although the notions supporting the system were certainly widespread by the early 1890s, most scholars date the inception of the movement to the founding of the Chicago Court in 1899; by the end of the second decade of the twentieth century, juvenile court systems were well established across the nation. Indeed, by 1920 all but three states had some sort of separate juvenile justice system. This reform followed in the path of a host of other reforms that tried to save children from the dangers of modern life. Hence, it shared the same constituencies as other reforms of the period, such as those attempting to establish foster homes, limit child labor, construct playgrounds, and require compulsory schooling. Like many of their counterparts, juvenile justice reformers mirrored the progressive belief in morality and talked of their goal in religious terms. At the same time they embraced a particularly efficient means to save the child's "soul."[5]

A particular philosophy and certain means, reformers argued, were necessary to effect this goal. Philosophically, the creators of the systems believed that children were malleable and that through changes in their environment—physical and psychological—their character could be transformed. Furthermore, the proponents thought that the means of reformation should be the construction of separate juvenile institutions and procedures, including: courts, detention centers, reformatories, and probation. While these institutions and procedures paralleled the structures of the criminal justice system—courts, jails, prisons, and parole—different rules and purposes animated them. Indeed, many reformers preferred to have juvenile courts housed in a single-purpose building; they also insisted that juvenile records be kept distinct from all others. A 1920 study by the Children's Bureau identified three other aspects that marked the system: that the hearings were informal, not legal, in nature; that the court had the power to give mental and physical examinations; and that probation was one of the chief tools of the court.[6]

The court and its officers exercised these broad powers, with the guiding purpose of preventing children from becoming criminals. Its first function was diagnostic—to determine what caused the child to be brought to its attention. Informal procedures had an agent of the court—either the judge, a case worker, or a probation officer—examine the child, the family, and the neighborhood to discover the why of the particular delinquency. Once the cause of the delinquency was determined, the court shifted to its second function and applied various means to alter the child's character. A total change of environment could be ordered, placing the child in a juvenile reformatory for an indeterminate period. The reformers believed that an environment free from corrupting influences encouraged the natural good of the child to emerge. But the preferred means of reformation was probation. Proponents viewed probation as better adapted to the individual problems of troubled children. With the threat of the reformatory lurking in the back-ground, a indeterminate period began in which a probation officer became a regular presence in the life of the child, guiding both the child and the family to create an environment that would rehabilitate the child and eliminate the causes that led to criminal behavior.[7]

With broad support in society, experts in social work built the juvenile justice system. Reformers as prominent as Jane Addams, organizations as powerful as the National Congress of Mothers, and even the federal government—through the National Children's Bureau—promoted the juvenile court system's philosophy, methods, and staffing. At first self-proclaimed experts, like the charismatic "kids' judge," Benjamin Lindsey, dominated the system. But soon administrators from existing state and private child-centered institutions and school-trained social workers began to filter into the system. Operating essentially in a closed system, the reformers were able to put their full program—as far as practical and budgetary constraints would allow—into effect. They argued that the reforms had created an efficient system designed in such a way that experts could bring the power of the state to bear in the best interest of the child.[8]

Two legal doctrines, *parens patriae* and the best interest of the child, stood as the foundation of the juvenile justice system, even though lawyers played virtually no role in the system. *Parens patriae* gave the state guardianship power over minors when their parents—in the state's view—had been remiss in their duties. The related idea of the best interest of the child asserted that the state should act only with this one goal in mind. The designers of the system argued that friendly procedures with trained social workers—who could empathize with the clients—would best guarantee the goals of the state and the best interest of the child. Thus, lawyers with their traditions of advocacy, with their propensity for adversarial hearings, and with their panoply of legal rights were shut out of juvenile court. Indeed, lawyers were not necessary, the reformers argued, because the hearings were amicable and informal, aimed at securing the best interest of the child. And this exclusion of lawyers from the system prevented successful legal challenges to the juvenile justice system.

While a tremendous innovation in legal procedure, the juvenile justice system did not generate much controversy until the second half of the twentieth century. At the time of its inception, and for much of its history, few legal thinkers criticized the system. Moreover, there were no organized opponents (save police forces who thought it too lenient) to the system; no advocacy groups sought to limit its application or operation. The lawsuits that did emerge came from individuals ensnared in the machinery. Children and parents who fell under juvenile court jurisdiction found that the traditional legal system did not offer them any means of escape. When individuals asserted that the juvenile justice system denied them due process of law, trial by jury, right to appeal, or other legal procedures secured in state bills of rights, state supreme courts overwhelmingly denied their claims. The state courts agreed with the creators of the juvenile justice system, who contended the point of the proceedings was not to establish and punish guilt but to benefit the child. Therefore, there was no need for due process. And the defeats in the state courts were critical, for juvenile justice was a state matter, not a federal one.[9]

Until the Warren Court, America's federal government had virtually no role in the shaping of the juvenile court systems of the nation. The federal courts did not intervene in the system and Congress did not view it, except in limited areas, as the subject for legislation. The government's only involvement—until the rights revolution that came after the Second World War—was that of establishing juvenile courts for some its territories. Before the extension of the Bill of Rights to the states through the Fourteenth Amendment, there were no grounds for making juvenile justice a federal concern. The juvenile justice system raised no issues for the federal system equivalent to the problems posed by transportation of liquor contrary to state prohibition or even the development of migratory divorce.[10]

Thus, the history of interaction of juvenile justice reform with state and federal governments offers a stark contrast to the history of prohibition reform. Like the prohibitionists, the reformers who created the juvenile justice system were remarkably unified in purpose. And they were easily able to sway the states into adopting their programs. Indeed, as they had little opposition, they had far greater success than the drys ever did in the states. But the greatest difference between the reforms was in the reaction of the legal environment to their actions. Legal opposition to the new system of justice was minimal compared with the marshalling of legal talent against prohibition. Moreover, unlike the prohibitionists, the proponents of juvenile courts were not bedeviled by a federal system that allowed exceptions undermining state regulations.[11]

While juvenile justice has always been considered part of the progressive agenda, eugenics—like prohibition—was long denied such a place. Today eugenics is accepted by most scholars as a progressive reform, linked to famous reformers ranging from Theodore Roosevelt to Margaret Sanger. According to its proponents, eugenics was a Darwinian "science" of improving humanity through genetic manipulation. It shared the goal of many reforms, that of bettering society. Eugenicists believed that many problems, especially crime, stemmed from the genetic inferiors in the population. They asserted that through better breeding they could improve human stock and alleviate serious social problems. Eugenicists proposed to remake people through both positive means (the encouraging of the propagation of the "fit") and negative means (the limiting of reproduction by the "unfit"). Thus, eugenics is an example of progressive reform that sought to bring about changes through reformation of individuals. The person affected by the eugenic means would not be directly improved (though sometimes eugenicists claimed they would), but the "race's" offspring would be. Eugenics supporters saw their reform as an efficient solution to future social ills.[12]

Indeed, the eugenicists were perhaps the most efficient-minded of the reformers in the period. Their efficiency resulted from their "scientific" approach toward reform and the structure of their movement. Before 1910 the movement was centered in state institutions for dependents; the scientifically trained superintendents of these institutions pressed legislatures into restructuring their asylums along eugenic lines. Thanks to their inner track, they had some success, and the founding of a research center accelerated the movement.

After 1910 the core of the movement in the United States was the Eugenics Records Office, headed by Charles Davenport. This well-financed organization linked together field workers, professors, institutional superintendents, and committed amateurs into a cohesive network. Moreover, the Eugenics Records Office mapped in detail the course of the reform in seeking its goals and legal ends. Harry Laughlin's 1914 work, *Legal, Legislative and Administrative Aspects of Sterilization*, reviewed the existing and proposed laws, assessed the legal and practical difficulties, and proposed a model law and course of judicial testing. The Eugenics Records Office plan presumed that eugenicists and eugenically trained individuals would staff institutions to implement their plans for sterilization of the "unfit." (Indeed, Nicole Rafter views some of the movement's proposals as, in part, attempts to provide jobs for eugenicists.) The impact of the Eugenics Records Office can be seen when it is compared to its British equivalent; the British organization did not participate in shaping policy or mapping out a government program for implementing eugenics. This lack of coordinated action, in part, explains why Britain did not enact eugenic sterilization laws. With their clearly defined goals and tight organization, the eugenic reformers were successful in pressuring the polity to adopt their program.[13]

The nature of the American polity also helped the eugenicists. As Daniel Kevles pointed out, "British eugenicists marveled" at the success of "their American counterparts" in successfully writing "a comprehensive negative eugenics program onto the statute books." The federal nature of the American polity, which assigned the states the power of caring for the welfare of the people, aided the eugenicists. They were able, under the state police power, to pass laws limiting the procreation of people with "undesirable" heredity. With great shrewdness they targeted as subjects for sterilization groups already confined in state or charitable institutions. They encountered little effective opposition to their programs in the states. Indeed, the eugenicists themselves arranged the most far-reaching legal challenge to their sterilization program. In a colluded case they challenged the Virginia 1924 sterilization law as a deprivation of the Fourteenth Amendment's right to due process of law and equal protection of the law. The eugenics movement's victory in the U.S. Supreme Court case *Buck v. Bell* legitimated its state legislative program. By 1930 over half the states had adopted eugenic sterilization laws.[14]

But the states were not the only government the eugenicists used or sought to use for their cause. Eugenicists, with Harry Laughlin leading the way, asked the federal government to use its power over immigration to protect the nation from a flood of the unfit. Convinced that recent immigrants (the so-called new immigrants from southern and eastern Europe) harbored inferior genes, the eugenicists called for a halt to open immigration. Melding racism, nativism, and eugenic ideas, Laughlin helped convince Congress to adopt in the 1920s immigration laws that severely limited the number of immigrants coming into the country while favoring the immigrants from northwestern Europe. This use of the federal power to complement state action points to the eugenicists' mastery of the available tools of the polity. Indeed, they seemed always open to new means. For instance, in 1917 Laughlin wrote to Congressman Webb, who was guiding the prohibition amendment through the House. Laughlin suggested that the Congress change the language of the amendment so it would ban other "habit forming and racially dangerous poisons." He suggested including in this category opium, cocaine, and hashish. He argued that such a sweeping amendment would establish for "the American democracy the great principle of prohibition in its most fundamental aspect." Nothing came of Laughlin's proposal, but it indicates the flexibility of the eugenicists in dealing with the polity. Indeed, the very nature of the American polity aided the eugenics movement, and soon after the passage of the Eighteenth Amendment commentators assumed the same for prohibition.[15]

In 1923 the English statesman Lloyd George attributed the American adoption of prohibition to that key aspect of the American polity: federalism. Comparing the United States with his nation and its system of unitary government, he argued that the American federal system furnished the opportunity for experimentation in the states and that the drys took full advantage of it. As this work shows, George was partially correct; in state laws prohibitionists developed and tested almost every provision of the Volstead Act. Thus, the states did function as proving grounds for dry proposals. But the nature of the polity also undercut state action, prompting the prohibitionists to seek national government action. What George did not and, given his vantage point, could not see was that the polity—which contributed to the prohibition movement's triumph and was enshrined in the Eighteenth Amendment's concurrent-powers clause—would also contribute to prohibition's collapse.[16]

The doctrine of concurrent powers undermined national prohibition in two ways. First, it raised the question of whether the states or the nation would do the majority of the policing. Drys assumed that the states would do the lion's share of the work, and they built the national government's machinery accordingly. That the federal government had any role at all proved an excellent excuse for states to abdicate their law enforcement responsibilities. Some states were slow to enact prohibition laws. In 1921 Wayne Wheeler counted ten such states, two of which—Massachusetts and California—voted down such laws. Parsimonious state legislatures, even the ultra-dry Oklahoma General Assembly, refused to allocate sufficient funds for implementation of prohibition on the grounds that the national government should pay for enforcement. Officials in thirsty states did as little as they could and let federal officials bear the brunt of their constituents' hostility to the enforcement of prohibitory laws. In 1926 the state legislatures allocated eight times more to implement fish and game laws than to enforce prohibition.[17]

Second, concurrent power provided opponents of prohibition an easy way to nullify the policy in their state: repeal of a state's prohibition code. In 1923

New York repealed its version of the Volstead Act. Its action hurt prohibition by shifting the burden of enforcement to an already overloaded federal government and by serving "notice to the nation" of dissatisfaction with the system. Moreover, New York's conduct was contagious; for example, its repeal of the enforcement code sparked increasing criticism by the local mass media of prohibition in Michigan. In 1926 unsuccessful repeal campaigns took place in California (where 48 percent of the voters in a referendum voted for repeal), Colorado, Missouri, and Michigan. In the same year, Montana's citizens erased their prohibition laws. In 1929 the citizens of Wisconsin, in two advisory referenda, voted to repeal the state's liquor enforcement act and to modify it to permit the sale of beer. Thus, by preserving in the Eighteenth Amendment the status quo of divided government control over liquor, drys opened the door for wets. Opponents of prohibition followed the drys' path; they sought their goal first in the states. Thus, they were able to embarrass the drys and undermine the reality of the national prohibition.[18]

While the states' enforcement of prohibition varied from lackadaisical to nonexistent, the national government's efforts ranged from inefficient to corrupt. The conception of concurrent state and federal action that was integrated into the Eighteenth Amendment and Volstead Act diffused the power necessary for effective enforcement. Furthermore, the division of federal authority over prohibition between the Treasury Department and the Justice Department and the failure to extend civil service rules to most federal prohibition administrators weakened the government's enforcement efforts. Initially disagreements between Treasury and Justice hampered the government's operations. Moreover, meager allocations guaranteed only token federal enforcement, carried on by a skeleton force unequal to the task. The civil service exemption of the Volstead Act resulted in the appointment not of committed drys or officials susceptible to Anti-Saloon League pressure but of party hacks and patronage hunters. The National Civil Service League, along with many Americans, thought that most federal prohibition officers were at best incompetent and untrained and at worst venal and dishonest. Sensible reorganization began in 1925; at the same time funding rose, and in 1927 civil service rules were extended to the prohibition agents.

But reforms came too late, and the drys in the meantime had spent their political capital elsewhere. Tinkering with the federal enforcement machinery could not solve the problems of prohibition, as national prohibition burdened the whole federal establishment. In 1920, for example, 5,095 of the 34,230 cases in federal courts concerned violations of the Volstead Act. By 1929, there were 75,298 prohibition cases alone. In 1920 federal prisons held just over 5,000 inmates; a decade later that number had grown to 12,000.

Drys' attempts at stricter enforcement only promised greater increases. The 1929 Jones Five and Ten Law lifted the Volstead Act's maximum penalties from six months in prison and a $1,000 fine to five years of incarceration and a $10,000 fine. The government had to build new prisons to house the convicted violators of this law. Enforcement also demanded a huge increase in the federal government and federal expenditures; dry organizations had little inclination to demand such expansions. They feared what "10,000 federal officers," and the tax increase to support them, would do to their political coalition. Indeed, for much of the period drys fought rearguard actions to preserve their power in the federal establishment. For instance, they succeeded in helping to keep Congress from being reapportioned to favor wet urban districts; similarly, prohibitionist organizations helped to prevent the election of wet politicians, most notably Al Smith, to national office. But these efforts exhausted dry resources; although they lacked the means to repair the breakdown in enforcement, they continued to demand that the law be obeyed.[19]

The crisis in prohibition enforcement prompted President Hoover to form in May of 1929 an expert commission to study the nation's law enforcement. The National Commission on Law Observance and Enforcement, called the Wickersham Commission (after its chairman, George Wickersham), studied the problems of prohibition and law enforcement for a year and a half. Its report, issued in early 1931, confirmed what many observers had been saying: that prohibition was a failure. Its lengthy findings showed, according to historian David Kyvig, "widespread bootlegging and official corruption, overburdened judicial and penal systems, lack of state support for enforcement, and damaged respect for law." The individual statements attached to the report by the eleven commissioners reflected this data; five urged the adoption of a government liquor monopoly, and two urged repeal of the Eighteenth Amendment. Nevertheless, the commission's formal recommendations opposed repeal of the amendment, establishment of government monopoly, and legalization of wine and beer. Instead, as a body, the commission urged modification of the nation's law enforcement machinery—requiring extensive federal appropriations and increased cooperation of all the states—to achieve better law enforcement. The chasm between the findings (and the commissioners' individual views) and the formal recommendations made the work of the Wickersham (or "Wicked-and-Sham," as wets called it) Commission—and prohibition itself—a joke. Franklin P. Adams's poem, "Wickersham Report" captured this perception: "Prohibition is an awful flop. / We like it. / It can't stop what it's meant to stop. / We like it. / It's left a trail of graft and slime, / It don't prohibit worth a dime, / It's filled our land with vice and crime, / Nevertheless, we're for it." Thus, by the early 1930s many saw Hoover's so-called "experiment noble in purpose" as a failure, a view that contributed to the repeal of the Eighteenth Amendment.[20]

The failure of law enforcement—brought on, in part, by the system of concurrent jurisdiction—was only one of many causes for repeal of the national prohibition amendment. A cluster of factors, of greater importance than the collapse of law enforcement, brought about repeal. Changes in cultural values legitimated liquor consumption, eroding support for prohibition. Moreover, the strongest organization behind the amendment, the Anti-Saloon League, lost much of its influence just as effective wet lobbying groups emerged in the nation. And as World War I sped the adoption of the Eighteenth Amendment, the Great Depression, by destroying the dry claim that prohibition created national prosperity and by carrying predominantly wet Democrats into national office, assured the speedy demise of national prohibition.[21]

Prohibition, among other things, was a product of American culture in the late nineteenth and early twentieth centuries; as that culture changed, prohibition became less necessary in the eyes of many Americans. As Norman Clark argued, the "shifting moral and spiritual values" of the early twentieth century undermined the policy. In particular, a culture of "individuality and freedom" replaced the progressive-era culture focused on "moral sensitivity" to "urgent public questions." "Wants and desires" replaced "duties and obligations" as key aspects to many individuals' lives. Changes in technology, in psychology, and in demography fueled this cultural transformation. The increasing predominance of radio, automobiles, and urban life all worked to promote "modern individualism," which expressed itself not in the "quest for social justice" but in "the demand by individual men and women for individual civil liberty and want-gratification." Drinking—illegal drinking— became an acceptable social practice across the nation. Thus, prohibition became widely perceived as "simply inappropriate to the circumstances of life in the new society." Even a place as rural and Protestant as Kansas, as Robert Bader shows, eventually felt the influence of the cultural change. Fifteen years after national repeal, wet forces in Kansas mobilized urban and younger voters (all of whom seemed more likely to ascribe to modern individualism) to bring about repeal of the state's prohibitory policy.[22]

The changes in American culture in the 1920s coincided with the collapse—from internal divisions, outside assaults, and financial problems—of the leading prohibitionist organization, the Anti-Saloon League. As Austin Kerr shows, with the realization of its goal of a dry nation, the league naturally lost direction. Differences in approach toward temperance among league leaders, which had been submerged in the struggle for a national amendment, came into focus after the passage of the Eighteenth Amendment. Basically, the league divided into two camps distinguished by means. One group—headed by Wayne Wheeler until his death in 1927—favored law enforcement as the league's chief role, while the other group—led by Ernest Cherrington—thought that, with the amendment achieved, the league should focus on educating the public. The factional struggle for dominance within the organization kept the league from using its full influence outside the organization. At the same time the league was under attack. A congressional investigation into league methods generated much negative publicity; the bad impression intensified when two league leaders, James Cannon and William Anderson, were put on trial for financial misdeeds. Indeed, money became a problem for the league, as donations to the league began falling with the adoption of the amendment and continued to fall throughout the era of national prohibition. Thus, the Anti-Saloon League, in the national era, was not well equipped to do battle with the forces seeking repeal of the Eighteenth Amendment.[23]

Three antiprohibition organizations—the Association against the Prohibition Amendment, the Women's Organization for National Prohibition Reform, and the Voluntary Committee of Lawyers—reshaped the public debate over the liquor issue and reoriented the law on the topic. In the late 1920s the Association against the Prohibition Amendment (dominated by conservative businessmen) and the Women's Organization for National Prohibition Reform (a broadly based group) undertook extensive campaigns to persuade the public of the failure of prohibition and the necessity of repeal. As detailed by David Kyvig, they criticized national prohibition on many grounds; they asserted that it promoted hypocrisy, encouraged law breaking, destroyed the balance of power between state and federal authority, and impaired individual rights. In short, it was so flawed that repeal—by adopting another amendment—was the only acceptable solution. By the early 1930s, the Voluntary Committee of Lawyers had overcome the idea that repeal was a constitutional impossibility and channeled the impetus for change into workable channels. The Voluntary Committee fashioned the means for ratification of a repeal amendment, through special conventions in the states. Portraying such a process as democratic—almost as a referendum on the subject—the Voluntary Committee drafted a model bill for states to create such a special ratifying convention. The states followed the guidelines laid out in the bill: twelve adopted the model bill, and eight others used it with only small changes. But before the states could ratify, an amendment had to be proposed by Congress, and this came about thanks to the political realignment brought about by the Great Depression.[24]

In the heyday of the 1920s drys hitched prohibition to the carriage drawn by the horses of national prosperity and the Republican party. When the economy crashed and the party floundered, prohibition suffered severe blows. Throughout the 1920s drys pressured both parties to take a stand in support of prohibition. As the Democratic party divided bitterly over the issue, often adopting dry planks but running wet presidential candidates, the drys drifted into an alliance with the Republicans. While the Republicans proclaimed prosperity to be a result of their stewardship of the economy, drys insisted that prohibition contributed to the nation's affluence. When the economy fell into depression, this economic argument was stood on its head; wets and others portrayed repeal as a means to restore economic good times. Moreover, the Republican party was blamed for the economic crisis, just when wets won control of the Democratic party. Thus, in 1932, for the first time in the national prohibition era, a major party's platform promised repeal. The election of Franklin Roosevelt on that platform was "widely interpreted as a voter directive for repeal." In February 1933 the lame-duck Congress responded by passing the Twenty-first Amendment; in March the new Congress modified the Volstead Act to permit the sale of low-alcohol beer and wine. And in December of the same year, the thirty-sixth state ratified the Twenty-first Amendment, repealing the Eighteenth Amendment.[25]

From the wreck of the prohibition amendment drys rescued little; the most significant salvaged artifact was virtually unfettered state control of liquor. The second section of the Twenty-first Amendment stipulated that "the transportation or importation into any state . . . for delivery or use therein of intoxicating liquors, in violation of the laws thereof, is hereby prohibited." Embodying the thrust of the 1913 Webb-Kenyon Act, this clause guaranteed the sanctity of state liquor laws from intrusive interstate and foreign commerce liquor shipments. Never again would federal power disrupt state prohibition. But this clause was also the final defeat for drys. It deprived them of the ladder—the calls for cooperation between the states and the federal government—that they had climbed to place prohibition in the Constitution.[26]

SOURCES AND TEXTUAL CONVENTIONS

The main sources for this study of the interaction of a social reform with the legal system are government records and the papers, both published and in manuscript, of the prohibition movement. Public documents, including court cases, government reports, legislative debates, and especially the unfortunately fragmentary records of the Internal Revenue Office in the Treasury Department proved invaluable. The papers of Congressman E. Yates Webb, Congressman Richmond P. Hobson, and Congressman Andrew J. Volstead supplied inside information on the fashioning of dry legislation.

The prohibition crusade's sources are incredibly rich. The microfilmed Temperance and Prohibition Papers, including many of the leading dry newspapers—*Union Signal*, *Voice*, *New Voice*, *Lever*, *American Issue*, *American Patriot*, and *New Republic*—were heavily mined. Randall C. Jimerson, Francis X. Blouin, and Charles A. Isetts, eds., *The Guide to the Microfilm Edition of the Temperance and Prohibition Papers* (Ann Arbor, University of Michigan, 1977), is indispensable for use of this collection. In addition to these materials, I supplemented manuscript sources of the temperance movement by examining a number of other collections: Virginia Anti-Saloon League Papers, Edwin C. Dinwiddie Papers, Oscar G. Christgau Papers, and Heriot Clarkson Papers. Of equal importance is the large number of temperance pamphlets and book-length publications.

As the notes indicate, I have relied on the numerous secondary sources on the temperance movement. Beyond the works cited in the notes, interested scholars are directed to Jacquie Jessup's bibliography in *Alcohol Reform and Society: The Liquor Issue in Social Context*, ed. Jack Blocker Jr. (Westport, Conn.: Greenwood Press, 1979), 259–79, and to the frequent additions to that bibliography published in the *Social History of Alcohol Review*.

In letting the prohibitionists, liquor supporters, government officials, and others express their ideas in their own words, I have encountered several textual difficulties. There is the frustrating problem of late-nineteenth- and early-twentieth-century capitalization habits. Strictly preserving the capitalization within quotes became a nightmare, as no two writers emphasized the same words, so I have silently altered their capitalization to reflect modern conventions. The only exceptions to this rule are the rare documents—like the Constitution—in which the capitalization of certain words is familiar. The extensive use of short quotations also raised the perplexing issue of changing the case of letters at the opening of passages, and providing punctuation at the end of passages. I choose not to employ intrusive brackets, but rather have again silently altered the exact text. In no case do these alterations change the meaning. The rare insertions in the midst of quotes are set off in brackets, and any deletions are marked with ellipses.

To save space in the notes I have used two strategies. First, I have employed abbreviations wherever they proved practical. A guide to the abbreviations used is appended just before the notes. I have also adopted several condensed titles for certain proceedings, government documents, and law reports. Both the brewers and the prohibitionists either maintained great continuity in the publishing of their convention proceedings or included no publication data. For example, the brewers used the same company to publish their reports, the Economical Printing Company of New York City—which also published prohibition tracts—until 1898, when the organization took over the publishing of the reports, eventually including them in its annual *Yearbook* in 1909. Since the complete set resembles a serial, I have used, for the sake of brevity, serial-style citations. Thus, for instance, the United States Brewers' Association, *Report of Proceedings of the Thirtieth Annual Convention* (New York: Economical Printing Company, 1882), appears simply as USBA, *Convention Report* 30 (1882).

NOTES

ABBREVIATIONS USED

AJVP	Andrew J. Volstead Papers, Minnesota Historical Society
ASL	Anti-Saloon League
Cyclopaedia	*Cyclopaedia of Temperance and Prohibition* (New York: Funk and Wagnalls, 1891)
DATB	Mark Lender, *Dictionary of American Temperance Biography* (Westport, Conn.: Greenwood Press, 1984)
ECDP	Edwin C. Dinwiddie Papers, Manuscript Department, Library of Congress
EYWP	Edwin Yates Webb Papers, Southern Historical Collection, University of North Carolina Library
HCP	Heriot Clarkson Papers, Southern Historical Collection, University of North Carolina Library
HHRP	Howard Hyde Russell Papers, Series 15, Temperance and Prohibition Papers, Microfilm Edition (Michigan Historical Collections, Ohio Historical Society, and Woman's Christian Temperance Union)
JBP	Joseph Bailey Papers, Dallas Historical Society
NA58	Treasury Department, Internal Revenue—Record Group 58, National Archives
NA267	Records of Supreme Court, Record Group 267, National Archives
OGCP	Oscar G. Christgau Papers, Minnesota Historical Society
RPHP	Richmond P. Hobson Papers, Manuscript Department, Library of Congress
SEAP	Ernest Cherrington, ed., *Standard Encyclopaedia of the Alcohol Problem*, 6 vols. (Westerville, Ohio: American Issue Publishing, 1925–30)
TPP	Temperance and Prohibition Papers, Microfilm Edition (Michigan Historical Collections, Ohio Historical Society, and Woman's Christian Temperance Union)
USBA	United States Brewers' Association
VASLP	Virginia Anti-Saloon League Papers, Swem Library, College of William and Mary
WCTU	Woman's Christian Temperance Union

INTRODUCTION. REFORMERS AND THE POLITY

1. Carry A. Nation, *The Use and Need of the Life of Carry A. Nation* (Topeka, Kans.: F. M. Stevens and Sons, 1909), 134; see also Robert Lewis Taylor, *Vessel of Wrath: The Life and Times of Carry Nation* (New York: Signet Books, 1966), 113–17,

where this tale is retold but, with the association of the rocking chair campaign, McKinley is placed in a rocking chair. Robert S. Bader, *Prohibition in Kansas: A History* (Lawrence: University Press of Kansas, 1986), 133–55, provides the best coverage of Nation's career. A year after she published her autobiography, Nation urged repeal of "congressional" licenses in Nation to Hobson, November 20, 1910, box 126, RPHP.

2. Morton Keller, *Affairs of State: Public Life in Late Nineteenth Century America* (Cambridge, Mass.: Harvard University Press, 1977), 128–29.

3. William G. Anderson, "Progressivism: An Historiographical Essay," *History Teacher* 6 (1973): 427–52; Peter G. Filene, "An Obituary for 'The Progressive Movement,'" *American Quarterly* 22 (1970): 20–34; G. Edward White, "The Social Values of the Progressives: Some New Perspectives," *South Atlantic Quarterly* 70 (1971): 62–76; Louis Galambos, "The Emerging Organizational Synthesis in Modern American History," *Business History Review* 44 (1970): 279–90; Galambos, "Technology, Political Economy, and Professionalization: Central Themes of the Organizational Synthesis," *Business History Review* 57 (Winter 1983): 471–93; Daniel T. Rodgers, "In Search of Progressivism," *Reviews in American History* 10 (December 1982): 113–32, 114; and Don S. Kirschner, "The Ambiguous Legacy: Social Justice and Social Control in the Progressive Era," *Historical Reflections* 2 (1975): 88–100. Peter G. Filene, "Narrating Progressivism: Unitarians v. Pluralists v. Students," *Journal of American History* 79 (March 1993): 1546–62, 1550, divides the interpretation of progressivism in history textbooks into two large schools: the optimistic unitarians, who see progressivism as a "homogeneous, purposeful phenomenon," and the more skeptical pluralists, who portray "progressivism's varieties, fractures, and ambiguities." The context and typology approach used here places this work, roughly, in Feline's pluralist school.

4. Robert Stanley, *Dimensions of Law in the Service of Order: Origins of the Federal Income Tax, 1861–1913* (New York: Oxford University Press, 1993), shows how policymakers within the polity directed the course of a broad, weakly organized reform. His interpretation can be profitably expanded to other reforms, like the antitrust and (to a lesser extent) pure-food movements.

5. I thank Charles W. McCurdy for suggesting this typology of reformers. He is not responsible for my applications and extensions of his idea.

6. Theodore Roosevelt, "The Manly Virtues and Practical Politics," in *American Ideals: And Other Essays, Social and Political* (New York: G. P. Putnam's Sons, 1900), 75–92 (originally printed in *Forum* in 1894), and "Latitude and Longitude among Reformers," in *The Strenuous Life: Essays and Addresses* (New York: Century Co., 1903), 41–62. Allan M. Brandt, *No Magic Bullet: A Social History of Venereal Disease in the United States since 1880*, expanded ed. (New York: Oxford University Press, 1987), explores the interplay of efficiency and morality in one reform movement.

7. Ralph Milband, *The State in Capitalist Society: An Analysis of the Western System of Power* (New York: Harper, 1969); Peter B. Evans, Dietrich Rueschemeyer, and

Theda Skocpol, eds., *Bringing the State Back In* (Cambridge: Cambridge University Press, 1985); Charles Bright and Susan Harding, eds., *Statemaking and Social Movements* (Ann Arbor: University of Michigan Press, 1984); Margaret Weir, Ann Shola Orloff, and Theda Skocpol, eds., *The Politics of Social Policy in the United States*, Studies from the Project on the Federal Social Role (Princeton, N.J.: Princeton University Press, 1988).

8. Stephen Skowronek, *Building a New American State: The Expansion of National Administrative Capacities, 1877–1920* (Cambridge: Cambridge University Press, 1982); Richard L. McCormick, "The Party Period and Public Policy: An Exploratory Hypothesis," *Journal of American History* 62 (September 1979): 279–98, and *The Party Period and Public Policy: American Politics from the Age of Jackson to the Progressive Era* (New York: Oxford University Press, 1986); Herbert Hovenkamp, *Enterprise and American Law, 1836–1937* (Cambridge, Mass.: Harvard University Press, 1991).

9. McCormick, "The Party Period and Public Policy" and *The Party Period and Public Policy*, 3–7, 17–25, 197–227, 263–356; Keller, *Affairs of State*; Skowronek, *Building a New American State*; Morton Keller, *Regulating a New Economy: Public Policy and Economic Change in America, 1900–1933* (Cambridge, Mass.: Harvard University Press, 1990), 3; Charles C. Bright, "The State in the United States during the Nineteenth Century," in *Statemaking and Social Movements*, ed. Bright and Harding, 121–58. These works overstate the weakness of the late-nineteenth-century state; much of the governing was done by the states; see William R. Brock, *Investigation and Responsibility: Public Responsibility in the United States, 1865–1900* (Cambridge: Cambridge University Press, 1984). Daniel T. Rodgers, *Contested Truths: Keywords in American Politics since Independence* (New York: Basic Books, 1987), 145–213, examined the development of the idea of the state in the late nineteenth and early twentieth centuries among academics and lawyers.

10. Keller, *Regulating*, 3; see also 228–30. Morton J. Horwitz, *The Transformation of American Law, 1870–1960: The Crisis of Legal Orthodoxy* (New York: Oxford University Press, 1992), 3, argues that a fundamental shift in the legal order can take place "only when the intellectual ground has first been prepared." His work shows how "progressive legal thinkers" undermined the existing legal orthodoxy leading to legal realism, the New Deal, and the constitutional revolution of 1937.

The role of an autonomous state has yet to be fully explored for its influence on reform movements. William E. Leuchtenburg, "The Pertinence of Political History: Reflections on the Significance of the State in America," *Journal of American History* 73 (December 1986): 585–600, suggests the potential of the topic. In the allied field of labor history several recent studies examine the role of the state in shaping the labor movement and labor policy; these include Christopher L. Tomlins, *The Sate and the Unions: Labor Relations, Law, and the Organized Labor Movement in America, 1880–1960* (Cambridge: Cambridge University Press, 1985); William E. Forbath, *Law and the Shaping of the American Labor Movement* (Cambridge, Mass.: Harvard University

Press, 1991); Keller, *Regulating*, 115–47; Hovenkamp, *Enterprise*, 207–38; and David Montgomery, *The Fall of the House of Labor: The Workplace, the State, and American Labor Activism, 1865–1925* (Cambridge, Mass.: Harvard University Press, 1987).

11. Powell and Frankfurter quoted in Stephen B. Wood, *Constitutional Politics in the Progressive Era: Child Labor and the Law* (Chicago: University of Chicago Press, 1968), 291; Andrew C. McLaughlin, *A Constitutional History of the United States*, student's ed. (New York: D. Appleton-Century Co., 1935), 783–84. For the importance of federalism to McLaughlin's thought, see Herman Belz, "Andrew C. McLaughlin and Liberal Democracy: Scientific History in Support of the Best Regime," *Reviews in American History* 19 (September 1991): 447–49; *Bailey v. Drexel Furniture Co.*, 259 *United States Reports* (1922) 20.

12. Harry N. Scheiber, "Federalism and the American Economic Order, 1789–1910," *Law and Society Review* 10 (Fall 1975): 57–118; Charles W. McCurdy, "American Law and the Marketing Structure of the Large Corporation, 1875–1890," *Journal of Economic History* 38 (September 1978): 631–49; John P. Roche, "Entrepreneurial Liberty and the Commerce Power: Expansion, Contraction and Casuistry in the Age of Enterprise," *University of Chicago Law Review* 30 (1962–63): 680–703; William Graebner, "Federalism in the Progressive Era: A Structural Interpretation of Reform," *Journal of American History* 64 (1977): 331–57; Hovenkamp, *Enterprise*, 79–92, 105–68; Daniel J. Boorstin, *The Americans: The Democratic Experience* (New York: Vintage Books, 1974), 64–77.

The territorial power was of course of limited value, as it affected only the District of Columbia and the territories. The treaty power came from the Constitution's stipulation that treaties were part of the supreme law of the land—thus, laws made to implement a treaty had great reach. For an introduction to the treaty power, see Edward S. Corwin, *National Supremacy: Treaty Power vs. State Power* (1913; reprint, Gloucester: Peter Smith, 1965), 6:196–273; Charles A. Lofgren, *"Government from Reflection and Choice": Constitutional Essays on War, Foreign Relations, and Federalism* (New York: Oxford, 1986), 116–66. A combination of the treaty power, the territorial power, and the commerce power governed the federal government's relations with Indians—which included policies of liquor control and prohibition. These policies conflicted with state and local laws and practices; see William E. Unrau, "Indian Prohibition and Tribal Disorganization in the Trans-Missouri West, 1802–1862" (paper presented at the International Congress on the Social History of Alcohol, London, Ontario, May 13–15, 1993); Kathryn A. Abbott, "Citizens and Wards: Liquor, Law, and American Indians in Minnesota, 1906–1920" (May 1992, University of Massachusetts at Amherst, Department of History, photocopy). David F. Musto, *The American Disease: Origins of Narcotic Control*, expanded ed. (New York: Oxford University Press, 1987), 40–68, 221–29, shows that the major federal drug laws prior to World War II rested on the taxing power.

13. On social science and inebriate institutions and their relations to the temperance movement and the polity, see Thomas F. Babor and Barbara G. Rosenkrantz, "Public Health, Public Morals, and Public Order: Social Science and Liquor Control

in Massachusetts, 1880–1916," in *Drinking: Behavior and Belief in Modern History*, ed. Susanna Barrows and Robin Room (Berkeley: University of California Press, 1991), 265–86; Jim Baumohl and Sarah W. Tracy, "Building System to Manage Inebriates: The Divergent Paths of California and Massachusetts, 1891–1920" (paper presented at the International Congress on the Social History of Alcohol, London, Ontario, May 13–15, 1993).

14. Paul Aaron and David Musto, "Temperance and Prohibition in America: A Historical Overview," in *Alcohol and Public Policy: Beyond the Shadow of Prohibition*, ed. Mark H. Moore and Dean Gernstein (Washington, D.C.: National Academy Press, 1981), 130.

15. Jack S. Blocker Jr., *Retreat from Reform: The Prohibition Movement in the United States, 1890–1913* (Westport, Conn.: Greenwood Press, 1976); Ruth Bordin, *Woman and Temperance* (Philadelphia: Temple University Press, 1981); Harry G. Levine, "The Discovery of Addiction: Changing Conceptions of Habitual Drunkenness in America," *Journal of Studies on Alcohol* 39 (January 1978): 143–78; James H. Timberlake, *Prohibition and the Progressive Movement, 1900–1920* (Cambridge, Mass.: Harvard University Press, 1963). Works that neglect ideology include the following: Peter Odegard, *Pressure Politics: The Story of the Anti-Saloon League* (New York: Columbia University Press, 1928); Andrew Sinclair, *Era of Excess: A Social History of the Prohibition Movement* (New York: Harper and Row, 1962), 36–62; Joseph R. Gusfield, *Symbolic Crusade: Status Politics and the American Temperance Movement* (Urbana: University of Illinois Press, 1963); Norman H. Clark, *Deliver Us from Evil: An Interpretation of American Prohibition* (New York: W. W. Norton, 1976). In asserting that ideology was important in shaping dry legal strategies, I am following the work of Morton Horwitz and Robert W. Gordon on the general idea that legal ideas are important. Morton Horwitz, *The Transformation of American Law, 1780–1860* (Cambridge, Mass.: Harvard University Press, 1977), xiii; Robert W. Gordon, "Legal Thought and Legal Practice in the Age of American Enterprise, 1870–1920," in *Professions and Professional Ideologies in America*, ed. Gerald L. Geison (Chapel Hill: University of North Carolina Press, 1983), 70–110, 120–39.

16. Gusfield, *Symbolic Crusade*, 4, 107–8, 117–22, 120–21; Clark, *Deliver*, 118–39, 134; see Lawrence M. Friedman, *Total Justice* (Boston: Beacon Press, 1985), 140–41, for a discussion of the advantages and limitations of the "symbolic school." A similar approach to the symbolic and real issues in reform is Barbara Meil Hobson, *Uneasy Virtue: The Politics of Prostitution and the American Reform Tradition* (New York: Basic Books, 1987), 7, 140.

17. Friedman, *Total Justice*, 31–32, 38, 108; Friedman discussed the meaning of legal culture in several other works, most notably "Legal Culture and Social Development," *Law and Society Review* 4 (1969): 29. For a review of the literature on legal culture, see Austin Sarat, "Studying American Legal Culture: An Assessment of Survey Research," *Law and Society Review* 11 (1977): 427; see also the entire issue of the *University of Chicago Law Review* 55 (Spring 1988), which is devoted to the related topic of political culture and law.

18. Samuel P. Hays, *Conservation and the Gospel of Efficiency: The Progressive Conservation Movement, 1890–1920* (New York: Atheneum, 1980), first preface page (unnumbered).

CHAPTER 1. THE RADICAL PROHIBITION MOVEMENT
AND THE LIQUOR INDUSTRY

1. On the temperance movement in general, see Jack S. Blocker Jr., *American Temperance Movements: Cycles of Reform* (Boston: Twayne Publishers, 1989); Paul Aaron and David Musto, "Temperance and Prohibition in America: A Historical Overview," in *Alcohol and Public Policy: Beyond the Shadow of Prohibition*, ed. Mark H. Moore and Dean Gernstein (Washington, D.C.: National Academy Press, 1981), 127–81; and Norman H. Clark, *Deliver Us from Evil: An Interpretation of American Prohibition* (New York: W. W. Norton, 1976). For early alcohol habits, see W. J. Rorabaugh, *The Alcoholic Republic: An American Tradition* (New York: Oxford University Press, 1979); and Ian Tyrell, *Sobering Up: From Temperance to Prohibition in Antebellum America, 1800–1860* (Westport, Conn.: Greenwood Press, 1979).

2. Paul E. Johnson, *A Shopkeeper's Millennium: Society and Revivals in Rochester, New York, 1815–1837* (New York: Hill and Wang, 1978), 55–61, 79–83, 130–33; Ronald G. Walters, *American Reformers, 1815–1860* (New York: Hill and Wang, 1978); Jed Dannebaum, *Drink and Disorder: Temperance Reform in Cincinnati from the Washington Revival to the WCTU* (Urbana and Chicago: University of Illinois Press, 1984); Robert L. Hampel, *Temperance and Prohibition in Massachusetts, 1813–1852* (Ann Arbor, Mich.: UMI Research Press, 1982); and Sean Wilentz, *Chants Democratic: New York City and the Rise of the American Working Class* (New York: Oxford University Press, 1984), 147–48, 281–84, 306–14, 356–57.

3. The thirteen states that adopted prohibition were Connecticut, Delaware, Indiana, Iowa, Maine, Massachusetts, Michigan, Minnesota, Nebraska, New Hampshire, New York, Rhode Island, and Vermont. Ernest Cherrington, *The Evolution of Prohibition in the United States of America* (Westerville, Ohio: American Issue Press, 1920), 139; Dannebaum, *Drink and Disorder*, 156–75; Frank L. Byrne, *Prophet of Prohibition: Neal Dow and His Crusade* (Madison: State Historical Society of Wisconsin, 1961), 42–77.

4. J. S. Ezell, *Fortune's Merry Wheel* (Cambridge, Mass.: Harvard University Press, 1960); Henry Chafetz, *Play the Devil* (New York: Clarkson N. Potter, 1960).

5. James Harvey Young, *Pure Food: Securing the Federal Food and Drug Act of 1906* (Princeton, N.J.: Princeton University Press, 1989), 45–51.

6. Rorabaugh, *Alcoholic Republic*, 5–21; John Burnham, "New Perspectives on the Prohibition 'Experiment' of the 1920s," *Journal of Social History* 2 (1968): 51–68; Clark, *Deliver*, 14–67, the 1873 figure is from 50; John S. Billings, *Report of Social Statistics of Cities of the United States at 11th Census: 1890* (Washington, D.C.: Government Printing Office, 1895), 42; Norman H. Clark, *The Dry Years: Prohibition and Social Change in Washington* (Seattle: University of Washington Press, 1965), 54–63;

Perry Duis, *The Saloon: Public Drinking in Chicago and Boston, 1880–1920* (Urbana and Chicago: University of Illinois Press, 1983), 86–203; Elliot West, *The Saloon on the Rocky Mountain Mining Frontier* (Lincoln: University of Nebraska Press, 1979); Thomas Noel, *The City and the Saloon: Denver, 1858–1916* (Lincoln: University of Nebraska Press, 1983). By 1920 in many areas, the saloon had lost its important social functions; see Madelon Powers, "Decay from Within: The Inevitable Doom of the American Saloon," in *Drinking: Behavior and Belief in Modern History*, ed. Susanna Barrows and Robin Room (Berkeley: University of California Press, 1991), 112–31.

7. Richard Jensen, *The Winning of the Midwest; Social and Political Conflict, 1888–1896* (Chicago: University of Chicago Press, 1971); Paul Kleppner, *The Cross of Culture: A Social Analysis of Midwestern Politics, 1885–1900* (New York: Macmillan Free Press, 1970); Clark, *Deliver*, 88–117; Jed Dannebaum, "Immigrants and Temperance: Ethnocultural Conflict in Cincinnati, 1845–1860," *Ohio History* 87 (Autumn 1978): 125–39. Robert Smith Bader, *Prohibition in Kansas: A History* (Lawrence: University Press of Kansas, 1986), 111, shows that dry Kansas had a ratio of pietist to liturgicals double that of neighboring but wet Nebraska. In a larger sense, the prohibitionist revival was part of a general reform wave aimed at controlling behavior perceived as threatening to the social order; see Morton Keller, *Affairs of State: Public Life in Late Nineteenth Century America* (Cambridge, Mass.: Harvard University Press, 1977), 439–521.

8. David Leigh Colvin, *Prohibition in the United States* (New York: Doran, 1926), 61–64; Cherrington, *Evolution*, 163–64. For the National Temperance Society, see John. J. Rumbarger, *Profits, Power, and Prohibition: Alcohol Reform and the Industrializing of America, 1800–1930* (Albany: State University of New York Press: 1989), 47–50, 60–61. *Richmond Dispatch*, November 2, 1892, 1.

9. Colvin, *Prohibition*, 65–81; Paul S. Boyer, *Purity in Print: The Vice-Society Movement and Book Censorship in America* (New York: Charles Scribner's Sons, 1968), 3–15, 14, 20–26, 25; Michael Grossberg, *Governing the Hearth: Law and the Family in Nineteenth-Century America* (Chapel Hill: University of North Carolina Press, 1985), 176–78.

10. Clark, *Deliver*, 73–81; Colvin, *Prohibition*, 49–81; Cherrington, *Evolution*, 165–68; Samuel T. McSeveney, *The Politics of Depression: Political Behavior in the Northeast, 1893–1896* (New York: Oxford University Press, 1972), 20–25; John M. Dobson, *Politics in the Gilded Age: A New Perspective on Reform* (New York: Praeger, 1972), 36–38; Keller, *Affairs*, 548–49.

11. Ruth Bordin, *Woman and Temperance* (Philadelphia: Temple University Press, 1981), 15–33; Jack S. Blocker Jr., *"Give to the Winds Thy Fears": The Women's Temperance Crusade, 1873–1874* (Westport, Conn.: Greenwood Press, 1985); Norton Mezvinsky, "White Ribbon Reform, 1874–1920" (Ph.D. diss., University of Wisconsin, 1959), 3–70; Charles A. Isetts, "A Social Profile of WCTU Crusade: Hillsboro, Ohio," in *Alcohol Reform and Society: The Liquor Issue in Social Context*, ed. Jack Blocker Jr. (Westport, Conn.: Greenwood Press, 1979), 99–110; Dannebaum, *Drink and Disorder*, 180–230; Mother [Eliza Daniel] Stewart, *Memories of the Crusade*, 2d ed.

(1889; reprint, New York: Arno Press, 1972); Mary Earhart, *Frances Willard: From Prayers to Politics* (Chicago: University of Chicago Press, 1944); Bader, *Kansas*, 31.

12. Bordin, *Woman*, 50–135; Mezvinsky, "White Ribbon," 68–69; Earhart, *Willard*, 143–92, 210–26, 227–72; Anne Firor Scott, *The Southern Lady: From Pedestal to Politics, 1830–1930* (Chicago: University of Chicago Press, 1970), 144–50. In 1883 the WCTU had 73,176 members; seven years later, 149,527 members.

13. Clark, *Deliver*, 77; Bordin, *Woman*, 90; Earhart, *Willard*, 178–83.

14. Clark, *Deliver*, 73; Cherrington, *Evolution*, 176–80. The fourteen states were Arkansas, Connecticut, Illinois, Indiana, Michigan, Missouri, Nebraska, New York, North Carolina, Ohio, Oregon, Pennsylvania, Texas, and West Virginia.

15. S. H. Thompson, *The Life of John R. Moffett* (Salem, Va.: McClung and White for Pearl Bruce Moffett, 1895), 81.

16. *Union Signal*, October 29, 1884, 2–3; WCTU, *Convention Resolutions*, 176, in *Union Signal*, March 12, 1885, 1; see also Prohibition party platforms for 1876, 1884, 1888, and 1892 in *National Party Platforms*, ed. Donald B. Johnson (Urbana and Chicago: University of Illinois Press, 1978), 2: 52, 63–64, 77–79, 91–92; *Union Signal*, August 15, 1888, 9, October 10, 1889, 1, November 21, 1889, 5, July 21, 1891, 1; *Voice*, June 4, 1885, 2.

17. *Union Signal*, July 27, 1889, 8; *New York Times*, April 20, 1882, 4; *New York Times*, November 1, 1886, 4, July 24, 1884, 3; Henry W. Blair, "Prohibition," *North American Review*, January 1884, 50–59; Blair, *The Temperance Movement: Or the Conflict between Man and Alcohol* (Boston: William E. Symthe Co., 1887), 388; *Voice*, October 2, 1884, 2, February 12, 1885, 3, March 1885, 2, March 12, 1885, 2; *Union Signal*, December 6, 1888, 2–3.

18. National WCTU, *Annual Convention Minutes* 6 (1879): 17; *New York Times*, July 24, 1884, 3, March 3, 1887, 9; *Cyclopaedia*, 97; J. N. Stearns, *The Constitutional Prohibitionist* (New York: National Temperance Society and Publication House, 1889), 11.

19. *Voice*, April 30, 1885, 2; *Union Signal*, October 2, 1884, 8; Prohibition party platform for 1892, in *Platforms*, ed. Johnson, 91–92; National WCTU, *Annual Convention Minutes* 12 (1885): 44; Willard quoted in Colvin, *Prohibition*, 286; J. N. Stearns, ed., *Temperance Shot and Shell* (New York: National Temperance Society and Publication House, 1892), 78–84; Shattuck quoted in Edith Smith Davis, *A Compendium of Temperance Truth* (Milwaukee: Advocate Publishing Co, n.d.), 161, 168.

20. Frederic H. Wines and John Koren for the Committee of Fifty, *The Liquor Problem in Its Legislative Aspects*, 2d ed. (Boston and New York: Houghton Mifflin Co., 1898), 181, 226, 232–91; *Cyclopaedia*, 207–9, 212–13, 215, 218, 220; *Voice*, November 10, 1892, 4; John G. Woolley and William E. Johnson, *Temperance Progress in the Century* (London: Linscott, 1902), 177.

21. *Union Signal*, October 15, 1891, 3; *Voice*, April 23, 1885, 2: John H. Bechtel, ed., *Temperance Selections* (1892; reprint, Freeport, N.Y.: Books for Library Press, Granger Index Reprints Series, 1970), 7, 8, 66; *Cyclopaedia*, 167–69; Stearns, ed.,

Temperance Shot and Shell, 70, and see the six pages of antilicense statements, 68–74; Colvin, *Prohibition*, 188–89; John C. Burnham, "Medical Inspection of Prostitutes in America in the Nineteenth Century: The St. Louis Experiment and Its Sequel," *Bulletin of the History of Medicine* 45 (May 1971): 203–18.

22. Wines and Koren, *Liquor Problem*, 6–8, 226–30; *Cyclopaedia*, 390–400; *Union Signal*, August 15, 1889, 8; Colvin, *Prohibition*, 189.

23. *Union Signal*, February 6, 1890, 8; Party 1872 platform in *Platforms*, ed. Johnson, 45; see also: K. Austin Kerr, *Organized for Prohibition: A New History of the Anti-Saloon League* (New Haven: Yale University Press, 1985), 54–58, 65.

24. *Cyclopaedia*, 148; *New York Times*, October 19, 1881, 8; Keller, *Affairs*, 130–31.

25. *Lever*, June 16, 1891, 1; *Voice*, June 9, 1887, 1, October 2, 1890, 1; *Union Signal*, September 29, 1892, 3, October 31, 1889, 13.

26. Clark, *Deliver*, 73, 77; *New York Times*, June 12, 1890, 4, January 19, 1896, 4, January 14, 1892, 2, April 15, 1887, 6, January 9, 1889, 8, October 16, 1888, 5, October 31, 1888, 5, July 27, 1891, 1, December 1, 1891, 10; *Chicago Tribune*, September 10, 1886, 4; *Richmond Times*, February 7, 1892, 4; Jensen, *Winning*, 178–208.

27. National WCTU, *Annual Convention Minutes* 6 (1879): 4; *Voice*, January 27, 1887, 2, April 23, 1885, 1, August 29, 1885, 9; *Union Signal*, April 5, 1888, 3, 1; *Lever*, March 9, 1893, 1; Jensen, *Winning*, 89–121; Bader, *Kansas*, 36–62.

28. Bechtel, *Temperance Selections*, 29, 89; *Oquawaka Spectator*, December 10, 1890, 2, July 2, 1888, 2.

29. *New York Times*, June 15, 1881, 2, June 22, 1889, 4; *Voice*, April 23, 1885, 2, 4; *Union Signal*, December 15, 1887, 8, February 1, 1883, 3; Johnson, ed., *Platforms*, 27, 52; *Oquawaka Spectator*, July 2, 1888, 2.

30. *SEAP*, 1059, 1185, 1247; *DATB*, 129, 181; for other ventures, see Ray Hutchison, "Capitalism, Religion, and Reform: The Social History of Temperance in Harvey, Illinois," in *Drinking*, ed. Barrows and Room, 184–216, and Charles K. Landis, *The Founders' Own Story of the Founding of Vineland, New Jersey* (Vineland, N.J.: Vineland Historical and Antiquarian Society, 1903).

31. Bordin, *Woman*, 142–48.

32. *Voice*, July 19, 1888, 1, December 4, 1890, 4, December 18, 1890, 6, March 26, 1890, 10, December 24, 1892, 8, December 15, 1892, 8.

33. *Voice*, October 9, 1890, 5, April 23, 1891, 10, July 2, 1891, 5; Tennessee Session Laws (1887), 293. Jesse Ketchum pioneered the idea of deed restrictions in 1848 in Toronto; see F. Laurie Barron, "Damned Cold Water Drinking Societies," *Upper Midwest History* 4 (1984): 14. The practice was also used in Kansas during the 1850s; see Bader, *Kansas*, 15–17.

34. National WCTU, *Annual Convention Minutes* 1 (1874): 24; Ireland quoted in Paul A. Carter, *Another Part of the Twenties* (New York: Columbia University Press, 1977), 101; *Cyclopaedia*, 272; Blair, *The Temperance Movement*, 377, 385; Lori D. Ginzberg, " 'Moral Suasion Is Moral Balderdash': Women, Politics and Social Activism in the 1850s," *Journal of American History* 73 (December 1986): 601–22.

35. George Lee Haskins, *Law and Authority in Early Massachusetts: A Study in*

Tradition and Design (New York: Macmillan, 1960), 140, 115–24, 141–62; Robert M. Cover, *Justice Accused: Antislavery and the Judicial Process* (New Haven: Yale University Press, 1975), 154–59; Louis S. Gerteis, *Morality and Utility in American Antislavery Reform* (Chapel Hill: University of North Carolina Press, 1987), 44–48, Stewart quoted at 47; Lawrence J. Friedman, *Gregarious Saints: Self and Community in American Abolitionism, 1830–1870* (Cambridge: Cambridge University Press, 1982), 98–99, 112–19; Howard Jones, *Mutiny on the Amistad* (New York: Oxford University Press, 1987).

36. Perry Miller, *The Life of the Mind in America: From the Revolution to the Civil War* (New York: Harcourt, Brace & World, 1965), 187, 190, 197, 186–206.

37. On the fading of these ideas, see Cover, *Justice Accused*; William M. Wiecek, "Latimer: Lawyers, Abolitionists, and the Problem of Unjust Laws," in *Antislavery Reconsidered: New Perspectives on the Abolitionists*, ed. Lewis Perry and Michael Fellman (Baton Rouge: Louisiana State University Press, 1979), 219–37.

38. Elizabeth Clark, "Organized Mother-Love and the Obligations of the State in Late Nineteenth-Century America" (paper delivered at Harvard Law School, November 28, 1989), explores the themes of religious ideas and dry attitudes toward law and government.

39. Norman Pollack, *The Just Polity: Populism, Law, and Human Welfare* (Urbana: University of Illinois Press, 1987), 24, 27, 29, 162–65, 229, 243, and chap. 8; Boyer, *Purity in Print*, 10–11, quoting Frederick Allen. William R. Brock, *Investigation and Responsibility: Public Responsibility in the United States, 1865–1900* (Cambridge: Cambridge University Press, 1984), 24–29, makes clear the connection between theological ideas and law in relation to the good government reformers of the late nineteenth century. For a rare use of the Mosaic conception against prohibition, see William B. Weeden, *The Morality of Prohibitory Liquor Laws* (Boston: Robert Brothers, 1875), 6, 164–78, 179, 180.

40. For an early assessment of the drys' view of rights and individualism, see Charles Edward Merriam, *American Political Ideas: Studies in the Development of American Political Thought, 1865–1917* (New York: Macmillan Company, 1920), 349–50; for a suggestive view of prohibition and the regulation of morality by law, see Paul L. Murphy, "Societal Morality and Individual Freedom," in *Law, Alcohol, and Order: Perspectives on National Prohibition*, ed. David E. Kyvig (Westport, Conn.: Greenwood Press, 1985), 67–80, especially 67–71.

41. Duncan C. Milner, *Lincoln and Liquor* (New York: Neale Publishing, 1920), 82; for the drys' use of Lincoln, see Richard F. Hamm, "The Prohibitionists' Lincolns," *Illinois Historical Journal* 86 (1993): 93–118; Merrill D. Peterson, *Lincoln in American Memory* (New York: Oxford University Press, 1994), 247–51.

42. Eli F. Ritter, *Moral Law and Civil Law: Parts of the Same Thing* (New York: Hunt and Eaton, 1896), 18, 49, 52, 60, 77, 80, 82, 83, 86–87, 93, 101–22, 141, 168–69, 180, 185–87.

43. *Union Signal*, January 13, 1887, 9, February 17, 1887, 9, February 4, 1886, 2,

June 29, 1895, 3; for awareness of prominent legal writers like Thomas Cooley, see *Union Signal*, February 18, 1886, 3; *Voice*, February 4, 1886, 2.

44. *Cyclopaedia*, 85–86, 97–128, 272–360; Cherrington, *Evolution*, 176–80; Colvin, *Prohibition*, 135–44, 202–27; Foster quoted in Frances Willard, *Woman and Temperance* (Hartford, Conn.: Park Publishing, 1883), 274; on catechism, see Clark, "Organized Mother-Love," 22.

45. *Cyclopaedia*, 85, 86; Willard, *Woman and Temperance*, 274; Cover, *Justice Accused*, 232–38.

46. *Union Signal*, February 1, 1883, 1, December 10, 1885, 1, August 6, 1885, 1.

47. For Brewer's decisions, see *Kansas v. Peter Mugler*, 29 *Kansas* (1883) 152, *Kansas v. Walruff*, 26 *Federal Reporter* (1886) 178 (see also *Mugler v. Kansas*, 123 *United States Reports* [1887] 623); *Cyclopaedia*, 90–92; *Voice*, September 16, 1886, 2, February 4, 1885, 4, December 12, 1889, 1, January 28, 1886, 2; *Union Signal*, January 2, 1890, 1, February 1, 1886, 2. Drys also initially opposed the appointment of L. Q. Lamar to the bench, wrongly fearing that he was wet; *Union Signal*, October 27, 1887, 4; *Voice*, January 2, 1890, 2.

48. Hester M. Poole to the editor, *Union Signal*, February 13, 1890, 5. The relationship between the legal profession and the prohibitionists never improved; see Bader, *Kansas*, 167, for a telling example.

49. Jack Blocker Jr., "Modernity of Prohibitionists," in *Alcohol Reform and Society*, ed. Blocker, 158, 160, showed that the Prohibition party possessed a proportionally larger number of lawyers than the more legally oriented Anti-Saloon League; Jack Blocker Jr., "Politics of Reform, Populists, Prohibition and Woman Suffrage, 1891–1892," *Historian* 34 (August 1972): 618; Stewart quoted in Willard, *Woman and Temperance*, 443; *DATB*, 47–48, 175–76, 197–98; Edward T. James, Janet W. James, and Paul S. Boyer, *Notable American Women, 1607–1950: A Biographical Dictionary* (Cambridge, Mass.: Harvard University Press, 1971), 153–54, 651–52; Kathleen E. Lazarou, " 'Fettered Portias': Obstacles Facing Nineteenth-Century Women Lawyers," *Women Lawyers Journal* 64 (Winter 1978): 21–30; Terrence C. Halliday, "Six Score Years and Ten: Demographic Transitions in the American Legal Profession, 1850–1980," *Law and Society Review* 20 (1986): 53–78. The chart on 62 shows that, in 1880, 75 of 64,062 lawyers were women; in 1890, the number was 208 out of 89,422; Robert H Wiebe, "Lincoln's Fraternal Democracy," in *Abraham Lincoln and the American Political Tradition*, ed. John L. Thomas (Amherst: University of Massachusetts Press, 1986), 11–30, 27; Robert Stevens, *Law School: Legal Education in America from the 1850s to the 1980s* (Chapel Hill: University of North Carolina Press, 1983), 51–111; Robert W. Gordon, "Legal Thought and Legal Practice in the Age of American Enterprise, 1870–1920," in *Professions and Professional Ideologies in America*, ed. Gerald L. Geison (Chapel Hill: University of North Carolina Press, 1983), 70–110, 120–39.

50. Morton J. Horwitz, *The Transformation of American Law, 1870–1960: The Crisis of Legal Orthodoxy* (New York: Oxford University Press, 1992), 4–17.

51. *Union Signal*, September 27, 1883, 8, April 8, 1886, 9, November 16, 1893, 3; Nellie H. Bradley, *A Temperance Picnic* (New York, 1888), cited in Clark, "Organized Mother-Love," 38.

52. Willard quoted in Clark, "Organized Mother-Love," 59–60.

53. *Voice*, October 30, 1884, 2, October 27, 1887, 1–2; *Union Signal*, June 30, 1887, 8; *New York Times*, March 4, 1888, 1, March 5, 1888, 4; 101 *United States Reports* (1880) 819; Eli F. Ritter, *Is License Constitutional: A Brief . . . Before the Supreme Court of Indiana* (New York: Funk and Wagnalls, 1891), 5:41–42; Stearns, ed., *Temperance Shot and Shell*, 85–86; Samuel R. Artman, *The Legalized Outlaw* (Indianapolis: Levey Bros., 1908); *SEAP*, 209.

54. *Voice*, June 1, 1893, 5; see also *Union Signal*, March 2, 1893, 3.

55. Perry R. Duis, *The Saloon: Public Drinking in Chicago and Boston, 1880–1920* (Urbana and Chicago: University of Illinois Press, 1983), 15–83; William L. Downard, *Cincinnati Brewing Industry: A Social and Economic History* (Athens: Ohio University Press, 1973), 110–11; Vincent P. Carusou, *The California Wine Industry, 1830–1895: A Study of the Formative Years* (Berkeley: University of California Press, 1976).

56. William Downard, ed., *Dictionary of Brewing and Distilling Industries* (Westport, Conn.: Greenwood Press, 1980), xxii, xxiii, Appendix XI, 142; Duis, *Saloon*, 33; Amy Mittelman, "The Politics of Alcohol Production: The Liquor Industry and the Federal Government, 1862–1900" (Ph.D. diss., Columbia University, 1986), 46, 102–49.

57. Downard, *Dictionary*, 8, 62, 100–102, 213–14; *Union Signal*, February 19, 1891, 9; Mittelman, "Alcohol Production," 102–49; *Cyclopaedia*, 373.

58. The percentage is computed from Tun-Yuan Hu, *The Liquor Tax in the United States, 1791–1947*, Columbia University Monographs in Public Finance and National Income, no. 1 (New York: Graduate School of Business, Columbia University, 1951), endpiece. Miller to Cleveland, December 24, 1886, Grover Cleveland Papers, Library of Congress (microfilm edition).

59. On the importance of trade organizations, see Kerr, *Organized*, 31–34.

60. Ibid., 33–34; Downard, *Dictionary*, 127; Isetts, "A Social Profile of WCTU Crusade," 99–110; Blocker, *"Give to the Winds,"* 57–62; *Cyclopaedia*, 387–88. A typical distiller publication was Joseph Debar, comp., *Prohibition: Its Relation to Temperance, Good Morals and Sound Government* (Cincinnati, Ohio: n.p., [1910?]).

61. Stanley Baron, *Brewed in America: A History of Beer and Ale in the United States* (Boston: Little, Brown and Co., 1962); Thomas C. Cochran, *The Pabst Brewing Company: The History of an American Business* (New York: New York University Press, 1948); Downard, *Cincinnati*, 36–39; Ronald Jan Plavchan, *A History of Anheuser-Busch, 1851–1933* (New York: Arno Press, 1976).

62. All figures from Downard, *Dictionary*, Appendix X, 242–43, Appendix II, 229, lists the major brewing centers; Downard, *Cincinnati*, 3–46; Cochran, *Pabst*, 1–71; Plavchan, *Anheuser-Busch*, 2, 5–8, 30–31, 43–45.

63. *Washington Post*, July 20, 1890, 5; Plavchan, *Aneuser-Busch*, 52–70; Cochran, *Pabst*, 1–71, 126–28, 172; Downard, *Cincinnati*, 36–38, 40.

64. Cochran, *Pabst*, 50–51; Downard, *Cincinnati*, 49, 84; *Cyclopaedia*, 373.

65. Cochran, *Pabst*, 50–51; *Washington Post*, May 19, 1890, 8; see also USBA, *Convention Report* 22 (1882), 30 (1890), which were both printed in German. On labor policy, see Amy Mittelman, "'A Conflict of Interest': The United Brewery Workmen in the Nineteenth Century," *Contemporary Drug Problems* 12 (Winter 1985): 511–40.

66. For instance, the 1887 USBA convention sent $5,000 to Michigan brewers to finance propaganda against prohibition; typical of brewer propaganda was Percy Andreae, *The Prohibition Movement in Its Broader Bearing upon Our Social, Commercial and Religious Liberties* (Chicago: Felix Mendelsohn, 1915); USBA, *Convention Report* 27 (1887): 27, 37, 39–40; 25 (1885): 61; 21 (1881): 32, 38; 23 (1883): 45; 26 (1886): 17; Cochran, *Pabst*, 53, 176, 308; *Union Signal*, June 4, 1885, 1. The consensus among scholars that the brewers were slow to recognize prohibition and ineffective in fighting it fails to take into account their court efforts. Cochran, *Pabst*, 306–8; Plavchan, *Anheuser-Busch*, 115, Kerr, *Organized*, 31–34.

67. *Union Signal*, January 11, 1883, 2, May 29, 1884, 1, August 28, 1884, 1; *Voice*, June 4, 1885, 5, April 2, 1885, 1; *Foster v. Kansas*, 112 *United States Reports* (1884) 201–6; Bader, *Kansas*, 70–71; Jerry Harrington, "Bottled Conflict, Keokuk and the Prohibition Question, 1888–1889," *Annals of Iowa* 46 (Spring 1983): 593–617; Bader, *Kansas*, 52; USBA, *Convention Report* 21 (1881): 43; 23 (1883): 17; 28 (1888): 54–55, 65; 26 (1886): 15.

68. USBA, *Convention Report* 21 (1881): 20–22, 28, 70.

69. 13 *New York* (1856) 378, 384–86, 396.

70. Arnold Paul, *Conservative Crisis and Rule of Law* (New York: Harper Torchbooks, 1969); Benjamin Twiss, *Lawyers and the Constitution: How Laissez Faire Came to the Supreme Court* (Princeton: Princeton University Press, 1942); Sidney Fine, *Laissez Faire and the General-Welfare State: A Study of Conflict in American Thought, 1865–1901* (Ann Arbor: University of Michigan Press, 1964), 96–140; Horwitz, *Crisis*, 45; *Washington Post*, May 19, 1890, 8, May 21, 1890, 2, May 23, 1890, 1; Percy Andreae, *The Prohibition Movement*, 50, 51, see also 45–48, 50–56, 280–339; *License Cases*, 5 *Howard* (1847) 504; *Beer Co. v. Massachusetts*, 97 *United States Reports* (1877) 26.

71. 18 *Wallace* (1873) 129, 133, 136, 134.

72. The brewers paid Vest $2,500 for his work, but the prohibitionists claimed $10,000; USBA, *Convention Report* 23 (1883): 17, 44; 24 (1884): 25; see *Cyclopaedia*, 92; *Mugler v. Kansas*, 123 *United States Reports* (1887) 623–27; August Bondi to Governor George W. Glick (Kansas), quoted in James C. Mallin, "*Mugler v. Kansas* and the Presidential Campaign of 1884," *Mississippi Valley Historical Review* 34 (September 1947): 274–77.

73. *Union Signal*, February 4, 1886, 2, August 28, 1884, 1; *Voice*, May 21, 1885, 1, June 4, 1885, 5, December 15, 1887, 1, April 25, 1885, 1; USBA, *Convention Report* 28 (1888): 54; Walruff to L. W. Clay, May 22, 1882, quoted in Bader, *Kansas*, 73–74, see also 80–81.

74. *Voice*, June 4, 1885, 5: *Union Signal*, February 4, 1886, 2; USBA, *Convention Report* 26 (1886): 23.

75. *Union Signal*, February 25, 1886, 3–4, February 4, 1886, 2, July 15, 1886, 1: *Philadelphia Ledger*, May 30, 1886, 3; USBA, *Convention Report* 26 (1886): 15–16.

76. *Voice*, June 18, 1886, 2, February 4, 1886, 2, February 25, 1886, 3, January 29, 1887, 5, April 23, 1885, 2, January 28, 1886, 2.

77. USBA, *Convention Report* 28 (1888): 15; the brewers may have been unhappy with Vest's handling of the matter. At one point he could not remember the titles of the cases or when they would be docketed. Vest to Samuel Middleton, Clerk of Supreme Court, October 5, 1884, File 10986, NA267.

78. USBA, *Convention Report* 28 (1888): 15; *Union Signal*, October 20, 1887, 1, October 27, 1887, 1, 8–9, November 3, 1887, 1, November 10, 1887, 1, November 17, 1887, 8; *Voice*, October 27, 1887, 1–2, 4, November 10, 1887, 1–2.

79. *Mugler v. Kansas* and *Ziebold v. Kansas*, 123 *United States Reports* (1887) 629–33, 633–37, 645–53, 638–45; both Choate and Vest raised the issue that the Kansas law interfered with interstate commerce by prohibiting the manufacture of liquor for export from the state. The Court refused to hear this argument but settled the issue in favor of the prohibition states in the 1888 case *Kidd v. Pearson*, 128 *United States Reports* (1888) 1–26.

80. 123 *United States Reports* (1887) 623, 664, 669, 670–75; USBA, *Convention Report* 28 (1888): 54; Horwitz, *Crisis*, 16, 17, 27–28; Justice Field dissented on the Court's dismissal of the interstate commerce issue as not being raised by the record, and all the justices believed that the interstate commerce questions were important and needed to be settled. Drys also realized that the interstate ramifications were left open; see *Union Signal*, December 15, 1887, 9. The decision did not reach to the question of nuisance action at common law; see Henry Schofield, "Equity Jurisdiction to Abate and Enjoin Illegal Saloons as Public Nuisances," in *Essays on Constitutional Law and Equity* (New York: Da Capo Press, 1972), 2:863–92.

81. *Voice*, December 8, 1887, 1, 4; *Union Signal*, December 15, 1887, 8; USBA, *Convention Report* 28 (1888): 16–18.

CHAPTER 2. LIQUOR AND INTERSTATE COMMERCE

1. For other interpretations for the act's passage, see Peter Odegard, *Pressure Politics, The Story of the Anti-Saloon League* (New York: Columbia University Press, 1928), 130; Thomas C. Cochran, *Pabst Brewing Company: A History of an American Business* (New York: New York University Press, 1948), 315–16. The discussions in Congress about the federal commerce power and state police power during the Wilson Act debate reflected the ideas advanced in legal periodicals, the courts, and Congress over the trust issue; see William Letwin, *Law and Economic Policy in America: The Evolution of the Sherman Antitrust Act* (New York: Random House, 1965), 53–99, 143–66; Charles W. McCurdy, "The Knight Sugar Decision of 1895

and the Modernization of American Corporation Law, 1869–1903," *Business History Review* 53 (1979): 304–36.

2. 9 *Wheaton* (1824) 1; Lyndsy Rogers, "Interstate Commerce in Intoxicating Liquors before the Webb-Kenyon Act," *Virginia Law Review* 4 (December 1916): 174–95; R. Mason Lisle, "Note: The Original Package Case," *American Law Review* 24 (1890): 1016–26.

3. 12 *Wheaton* (1827) 419–50, 441–42, 448.

4. Ibid., 441–43, 449.

5. 2 *Peters* (1829) 245.

6. 5 *Howard* (1847) 504–633, 504, reporter's notes.

7. Ibid., 575, 581, 601, 608, 632, 624–25; Carl Swisher, *The Taney Period*, Oliver W. Holmes Devise History of the Supreme Court (New York: Macmillan, 1974), 5:35.

8. 12 *Howard* (1851) 299, 319; see also David P. Currie, "The Constitution in the Supreme Court: Limitations on State Power, 1865–1873," *University of Chicago Law Review* 51 (Spring 1984): 329–65; J. Willard Hurst, *Law and the Conditions of Freedom in the Nineteenth Century United States* (Madison: University of Wisconsin Press, 1956), 44–50.

9. 91 *United States Reports* (1876) 275; *Walling v. Michigan*, 116 *United States Reports* (1886) 446; see also Charles W. McCurdy, "American Law and the Marketing Structure of the Large Corporation, 1875–1890," *Journal of Economic History* 38 (September 1978): 631–49, 633–42; Harry N. Scheiber, "Federalism and the American Economic Order, 1789–1910," *Law and Society Review* 10 (Fall 1975): 57–118, 101–2; David Gordon, "Swift & Co. v. United States: The Beef Trust and the Stream of Commerce Doctrine," *American Journal of Legal History* 28 (1984): 245–79.

10. 70 *Otto* 25, 33–34; 123 *United States Reports* (1887) 674. In *Kidd v. Pearson*, 128 *United States Reports* (1888) 1–26, the Court denied that interstate commerce provided manufacturers the right to make liquor for out-of-state shipments only.

11. *Atlanta Constitution*, October 19, 1886, 1, 3; *New Englander*, September 1885, 707; *Voice*, January 29, 1885, 2, March 5, 1885, 1; *New York Times*, July 15, 1889, 3; *Union Signal*, February 25, 1886, 3, January 14, 1886, 1, January 21, 1886, 4–5.

12. *Voice*, March 26, 1885, 2, March 5, 1885, 7, February 12, 1885, 3; *Union Signal*, October 16, 1884, 9, September 11, 1884, 2, November 26, 1885, 3, December 6, 1888, 2–3; *New York Times*, July 24, 1884, 3; *North American Review*, January 1884, 50–59.

13. *New York Times*, July 15, 1889, 3; *Union Signal*, October 16, 1884, 9; *Public Opinion*, April 12, 1890, 7; Jerry Harrington, "Bottled Conflict, Keokuk and the Prohibition Question, 1888–1889," *Annals of Iowa* 46 (Spring 1983): 593–617, 596–600.

14. *Voice*, March 5, 1885, 5; USBA, *Convention Report* 28 (1888): 65.

15. 115 *United States Reports* (1885) 611, 613.

16. 125 *United States Reports* (1888) 465–524; *Voice*, March 22, 1888, 1; in the majority with Matthews were Justices Miller, Bradley, and Blatchford. Justice Field wrote a concurrence, and Lamar did not participate. Chief Justice Waite and Justices Harlan and Gray dissented.

17. 125 *United States Reports* (1888) 465–524; Justice Field's concurring opinion raised the sale issue in even stronger terms and appeared to show that he would support the original package doctrine. The Court's views were not lost on the drys. In response, the *Voice* wrote that it "shows clearly enough what the decision would be in a case taken to it on that one point." *Voice*, September 3, 1889, 3–4.

18. *New York Times*, March 21, 1888, 4; *Voice*, March 29, 1888, 1; USBA, *Convention Report* 28 (1888): 17–18; 29 (1889): 11.

19. *Voice*, March 29, 1888, 4; *New York Times*, August 7, 1888, 5; *Union Signal*, November 8, 1888, 8, July 27, 1889, 8; see also *Union Signal*, May 31, 1888, 2. The Kansas WCTU's proposal to ban transportation of liquor into states unless it was consigned to licensed sellers was very near the formula drys would later embrace in the 1913 Webb-Kenyon Act; *Union Signal*, February 28, 1889, 1.

20. *Cong. Rec.* 50th Cong., 2d sess., 1887; *Oquawaka Spectator*, December 11, 1889; *Voice*, March 29, 1888, 1; *Union Signal*, December 29, 1889, 1; of the four, John Ingalls of Kansas was a political trimmer least committed to the dry cause; he always kept liquor in his home and made his own wine; Robert S. Bader, *Prohibition in Kansas: A History* (Lawrence: University Press of Kansas, 1986), 116–18.

21. USBA, *Convention Report* 32 (1891): 16; *Voice*, September 3, 1889, 1, October 4, 1888, 4; Harrington, "Bottled Conflict," 608.

22. Harrington, "Bottled Conflict," 608, title page; 135 *United States Reports* (1890) 100–135; Bruce R. Leisy, *A History of the Leisy Brewing Companies* (North Newton, Kans.: Mennonite Press, 1975), 68–73; transcript, *Leisy v. Hardin*, 14, 16, File 10986, NA267.

23. *Voice*, October 4, 1888, 4; *Union Signal*, January 3, 1889, 9; Harrington, "Bottled Conflict," 597–601, 605, 612; Richard Jensen, *Winning of the Midwest: Social and Political Conflict, 1888–1896* (Chicago: University of Chicago Press, 1971), 104; *Voice*, April 16, 1885, 2.

24. *Union Signal*, May 2, 1889, 8, January 24, 1889, 1, February 28, 1889, 1, October 10, 1889, 1; at a late point in the proceedings, Leisy tried to add (unsuccessfully) Edgar G. Blum, who had helped argue the Bowmans' case, as counsel before the Court; see Edgar G. Blum to James McKenney, Clerk of the Supreme Court, January 9, 1890, Aldolph Moses to M. W. Fuller, May 9, 1890, File 13866, NA267.

25. 135 *United States Reports* (1890) 130–32.

26. Ibid., 109; Justices Blatchford, Bradley, Field, Lamar, and Miller joined Fuller in the majority; see also William L. King, *Melville Weston Fuller, Chief Justice of the United States, 1888–1910* (Chicago: University of Chicago Press, 1950), 167–69; David P. Currie, "The Constitution in the Supreme Court: The Protection of Economic Interests, 1889–1910," *University of Chicago Law Review* 52 (1985): 324–90, 359–60.

27. 135 *United States Reports* (1890) 109, 111.

28. Ibid., 124, 161–67.

29. *Voice*, May 29, 1890, 1, May 8, 1890, 1; USBA, *Convention Report* 31 (1891): 16–

17; *Washington Post*, May 22, 1890, 1; *New York Times*, May 18, 1890, 4; *Union Signal*, May 22, 1890, 1; *Oquawaka Spectator*, August 6, 1890.

30. *New York Times*, May 2, 1890, 4, June 26, 1890, 4; *Washington Post*, May 25, 1890, 3.

31. *Voice*, May 30, 1890, 2, June 5, 1890, 8; *Union Signal*, August 14, 1890, 12; *New York Times*, July 4, 1890, 5; *Washington Post*, June 6, 1890, 6, June 15, 1890, 2, May 18, 1890, 9; Joseph Shippen, "Original Packages and Prohibition," *Chautauquan*, July 1890, 456–60.

32. *New York Times*, July 4, 1890, 5; *Washington Post*, July 22, 1890, 4.

33. *Washington Post*, June 11, 1890, 4; *Atlanta Constitution*, July 3, 1890, 11. Contrary to some press accounts asserting that original package houses offered "big drinks and cheap ones," beer, based on sixteen-ounce servings, was 2.5 times the common price of the nickel beer. On the pervasiveness of nickel beer, see Perry Duis, *The Saloon: Public Drinking in Chicago and Boston, 1880–1920* (Urbana and Chicago: University of Illinois Press, 1983), 48; *Washington Post*, July 17, 1890, 1.

34. *Union Signal*, November 13, 1890, 4; *Washington Post*, May 18, 1890, 8; *New York Times*, July 4 1890, 4; *Washington Post*, June 26, 1890, 4; *Union Signal*, November 13, 1890, 5, July 10, 1890, 1; *Atlanta Constitution*, July 18, 1890, 4; *Washington Post*, May 18, 1890, 9, July 7, 1890, 5; *New York Times*, July 4, 1890, 5; *Union Signal*, July 31, 1890, 5; *Voice*, June 23, 1809, 1, July 3, 1890, 2; Bader, *Kansas*, 107.

35. *New York Times*, May 22, 1890, 4; *Atlanta Constitution*, May 23, 1890, 1; *Washington Post*, July 11, 1890, 4; *Atlanta Constitution*, May 24, 1890, 20; *New York Times*, July 1, 1890, 5, July 4, 1890, 5; *Voice*, July 3, 1890, 2, July 10 1890, 1, July 24, 1890, 1, July 31, 1890, 1; *Washington Post*, July 19, 1890, 1; *Union Signal*, July 31, 1890, 5; Bader, *Kansas*, 107.

36. *Oquawaka Spectator*, April 30, 1890, 1; *Voice*, May 8, 1890, 4, 1; *New York Times*, May 20, 1890, 4; Shippen, "Original Packages," 456–60; Duis, *Saloon*, 62.

37. *Washington Post*, June 14, 1890, 1, July 11, 1890, 4; *Voice*, June 5, 1890, 8, June 19, 1890, 1; *New York Times*, July 4, 1890, 5.

38. *Washington Post*, June 26, 1890, 4, June 16, 1890, 4, July 10, 1890, 4; see also *Atlanta Constitution*, May 25, 1890, 20, June 27, 1890, 4, July 17, 1890, 4, July 18, 1890, 4.

39. R. Hall Williams, *Years of Decision: American Politics in the 1890s* (New York: John Wiley and Sons, 1978), 19–41; Homer E. Socolofsky and Allan B. Spetter, *The Presidency of Benjamin Harrison* (Lawrence: University Press of Kansas, 1987), 47–76; *Union Signal*, April 2, 1891, 8, September 2, 1888, 8; *Voice*, January 12, 1883, 1.

40. *New York Times*, November 24, 1889, 11; *Washington Post*, November 17, 1889, 4, May 25, 1890, 4, May 29, 1890; *Voice*, October 2, 1890, 2.

41. Michael Grossberg, *Governing the Hearth: Law and the Family in Nineteenth-Century America* (Chapel Hill: University of North Carolina Press, 1985), 176–77, 188–89; James Harvey Young, *Pure Food: Securing the Federal Food and Drug Act of 1906* (Princeton, N.J.: Princeton University Press, 1989), 51–62; 135 *United States Reports* (1890) 110, 119, 125.

42. *Atlanta Constitution*, May 9, 1890, 3, 8; *Washington Post*, May 18, 1890, 4; *New York Times*, June 26, 1890, 4; *Voice*, May 1, 1890, 1, May 8, 1890, 1, 4; *Union Signal*, May 8, 1890, 1, 8, May 9, 1890, 8.

43. *Washington Post*, May 22, 1890, 7, May 19, 1890, 8, May 21, 1890, 2, May 23, 1890, 1; *Union Signal*, June 5, 1890, 2; *Voice*, May 29, 1890, 1.

44. *DATB*, 47–48; *SEAP*, 348–49; *Union Signal*, September 27, 1888, 8, August 23, 1888, 9.

45. *Union Signal*, May 15, 1890, 4, August 21, 1890, 3–4.

46. *Voice*, May 8, 1890, 8; *Union Signal*, May 8, 1890, 5.

47. *Union Signal*, October 30, 1890, 2–3, November 13, 1890, 3–4, June 5, 1890, 1, October 9, 1890, 5, July 3, 1890, 1, July 17, 1890, 1, July 31, 1890, 1; *Voice*, July 17, 1890, 1, May 29, 1890, 4, July 3, 1890, July 31, 1890, 1, August 7, 1890, 1.

48. *Union Signal*, May 27, 1890, 8, May 8, 1890, 8, June 5, 1890, 1, May 15, 1890, 8; *Voice*, July 10, 1890, 4, July 24, 1890, 4; *Atlanta Constitution*, July 15, 1890, 3, July 16, 1890, 4.

49. *Union Signal*, July 25, 1889, 2–3; *Cyclopaedia*, 439–42; *New York Times*, April 5, 1886, 4; *Voice*, May 8, 1890, 1; *DATB*, 50–51; *SEAP*, 354–55, 659–66, 1058, 2253–54; Henry Blair, *The Temperance Movement: Or the Conflict between Man and Alcohol* (Boston: William E. Smythe, 1888), 381.

50. *Chicago Inter-Ocean* and *Burlington Hawkeye*, cited in *Oquakawa Spectator*, April 30, 1890, 1; *Washington Post*, June 16, 1890, 1; *Chicago Daily News*, cited in *Union Signal*, May 8, 1890, 1; *Voice*, July 10, 1890, 4; *Washington Post*, June 1, 1890, 1, July 7, 1890, 4; *Atlanta Constitution*, May 24, 1890, 20.

51. *Cong. Rec.*, 50th Cong., 2d sess., 1888, 2882; see also *Voice*, May 8, 1890, 1.

52. *Cong. Rec.*, 51st Cong., 1st sess., 4960; see also *New York Times*, May 21, 1890, 1–2; *Washington Post*, May 21, 1890, 7, May 24, 1890, 1. The *Voice* agreed with Vest, but only to support the dry idea that liquor commerce be totally prohibited by Congress; see *Voice*, May 29, 1890, 4.

53. *Cong. Rec.* 51st Cong., 1st sess., 5324.

54. *Washington Post*, May 24, 1890, 1; *Union Signal*, May 22, 1890, 1; *Cong. Rec.* 51st Cong., 1st sess., 5437, 5439.

55. *Cong. Rec.* 51st Cong., 1st sess., 5324, 4955; *New York Times*, May 21, 1890, 4; *Atlanta Constitution*, May 18, 1890, 4.

56. *Cong. Rec.*, 51st Cong., 1st sess., 5325, 4958; Letwin, *Law and Economic Policy*, 89–90.

57. For example, Senator Joseph C. Blackburg, a Kentucky Democrat, showed his opposition to prohibition by voting for a title change, but he abstained from voting on the bill; *Union Signal*, June 5, 1890, 1; *New York Times*, May 21, 1890, 4, May 22, 1890, 4; *Atlanta Constitution*, May 10, 1890, 4, May 2, 1890, 4, June 2, 1890, 7. Strangely enough, Edmunds and George in the same year also agreed on the Judiciary Committee's wording of the Anti-Trust Act, despite George's earlier hostility. Letwin, *Law and Economic Policy*, 94.

58. *Cong. Rec.*, 51st Cong., 1st sess., 8231; Letwin, *Law and Economic Policy*, 98.

59. *Cong. Rec.*, 51st Cong., 1st sess., 8231. The Senate party and sectional break down on the Wilson Act was as follows:

	Nay	NV	Yea
Democrats			
Northern	5	6	0
Southern	5	17	5
Republicans			
Northern	0	16	29
Southern	0	1	0

Of Republican senators from states where the issue had been submitted to voters in the period from 1889 to 1891 (Pennsylvania, Massachusetts, Connecticut, Rhode Island, Washington, and Nebraska) and where prohibition was an active political issue, 13 voted yes and 9 were absent; of the remaining Republicans from states where prohibition was not so current, 15 voted for the bill and 8 did not vote.

60. The Republicans apparently based their strategy on the hope that the voters would reject the policy. In states like Iowa, where prohibition was written into law, the political backlash hurt the Republican party; Jensen, *Winning*, 89–121. The same Republican members of Congress also passed an Army Canteen Act, which prohibited liquor sales in army canteens—messes—located in the prohibition states. It short-circuited prohibitionist calls for a complete ban of liquor sales in all army canteens and pushed the issue back into the states. It passed with near-identical support as the Wilson Act; *Cong. Rec.*, 51st Cong., 1st sess., 7506; USBA, *Convention Report* 32 (1891): 17.

61. *Cong. Rec.*, 51st Cong., 1st sess., 826, 5477, 5485, 7495–98, 7427–7506, App. 492–93, 717.

62. *Washington Post*, July 24, 1890, 1; *New York Times*, June 26, 1890, 4; *Union Signal*, July 17, 1890, 1.

63. Letwin, *Law and Economic Policy*, 53–99, 143–66; McCurdy, "The Knight Sugar Decision of 1895," 304–36; *Union Signal*, July 17, 1890, 1; Dorothy G. Fowler, *Unmailable: Congress and the Post Office* (Athens: University of Georgia Press, 1977), 73.

64. *Cong. Rec.*, 51st Cong., 1st sess., 7521, App. 435–37, 482–83, 493–94. Senator Morgan raised a similar line of argument in the Senate, but that body did not pursue the point.

65. *Atlanta Constitution*, May 18, 1890, 4, July 21, 1890, 4; *National Democrat*, cited in *Washington Post*, June 3, 1890, 4.

66. *Cong. Rec.*, 51st Cong., 1st sess., 5513.

67. *Cong. Rec.*, 51st Cong., 1st sess., 7437, 7490, 7428, 5373, 7506, App. 483, letter of H. W. Holman of Independence, Iowa, App. 416; *Voice*, June 26, 1890, 1.

68. *Cong. Rec.*, 51st Cong., 1st sess., 7490, 7501, 7521, 8219, 8220, App. 495–98, 7487, 7511.

69. *Voice*, July 7, 1890, 2, July 24, 1890, 1, July 31, 1, June 19, 1890, 1; *Washington*

Post, July 21, 1890, 1, June 16, 1890, 4; *Atlanta Constitution*, May 10, 1890, 4, May 18, 1890, 4, May 2, 1890, 4, June 4, 1890, 7; Shippen, "Original Packages," 458.

70. The sectional and party breakdown of the vote on the House substitute was as follows:

	Nay	NV	Yea
Democrats			
Northern	18	26	21
Southern	13	37	38
Republicans			
Northern	7	41	108
Southern	0	7	11
Totals	38	112	177

A similar breakdown on the final version proposed by the conference committee showed this pattern:

	Nay	NV	Yea
Democrats			
Northern	38	26	1
Southern	43	42	3
Republicans			
Northern	11	39	106
Southern	1	7	9
Totals	93	115	119

States deemed Southern are the eleven states of the Confederacy plus Maryland, Kentucky, and Delaware. Two Union Laborite representatives have been included in the Republican total and in the breakdowns. One Independent Southern representative is not included in the sectional breakdown; *Cong. Rec.*, 51st Cong., 1st sess., 7562, 8216.

71. Letter from August Frolich, ibid., App. 717.

72. Ibid.; *Voice*, December 5, 1889, 1, January 12, 1888, 1; *Washington Post*, July 23, 1890, 2.

73. *Washington Post*, August 1, 1890, 4, August 7, 1890, 1; *Cong. Rec.*, 51st Cong., 1st sess., 8219, 7459.

74. *Voice*, August 21, 1890, 1, August 14, 1890, 1; *Union Signal*, September 11, 1890, 11.

75. *New York Times*, October 18, 1890, 1, October 19, 1890, 3, October 26, 1890, 3, October 28, 1890, 2, November 1, 1890, 3; *Voice*, August 14, 1890, 1; *Lever*, January 21, 1892, 4; Bader, *Kansas*, 107–8.

76. 140 *United States Reports* (1891) 545, 546–47, 551, 553–54; *Voice*, August 28, 1890, 1.

77. 140 *United States Reports* (1891) 563, 564, 561–62; David P. Currie, "The Constitution in the Supreme Court: The Protection of Economic Interests, 1889–

1910," *University of Chicago Law Review* 52 (1985): 324–90, 360–61. The Court's rulings in two other cases, *Christensen* and *O'Neil*, were just as bad for the liquor industry. In *Christensen* the Court denied that the Fourteenth Amendment's privileges and immunities clause protected the liquor-selling trade and labeled the profession a "danger to the community." In *O'Neil* the Court upheld the sentence of seventy-nine years at hard labor for a man convicted of breaking Vermont's prohibition laws. *O'Neil v. Vermont*, 144 *United States Reports* (1892) 323–71, *Crowley v. Christensen*, 137 *United States Reports* (1890) 86–95; USBA, *Convention Report* 32 (1891): 17; 33 (1892): 14–15; King, *Fuller*, 169–73.

78. Fowler, *Unmailable*, 73; *Union Signal*, January 22, 1891, 1, July 23, 1891, 10; *New York Times*, December 31, 1890, 1.

79. *Union Signal*, May 28, 1891, 1, June 4, 1891, 4–5, August 21, 1890, 3, 4, August 7, 1890, 2–3, 8; *Voice*, June 4, 1891, 4.

CHAPTER 3. THE FEDERAL LIQUOR TAX
AND THE RADICAL PROHIBITIONISTS

1. The study of the economic aspects of the liquor tax began with the work of the architect of the system, David Wells. Wells and subsequent scholars have been most interested in the theoretical and practical aspects of collecting taxes. Wells's views are summed up in one of his later works, *The Theory and Practice of Taxation* (New York: D. Appleton, 1900). For more on Wells's role and views, see Herbert R. Ferleger, *David A. Wells and the American Revenue System* (Ann Arbor, Mich.: Edward Bros., 1942). Other works explore various aspects of the liquor tax; see Frederic C. Howe, *The Internal Revenue System in the United States* (New York: Crowell and Company, 1896); Harry E. Smith, *The United States Federal Internal Tax History from 1861 to 1871* (n.p.: Hart, Schaffer, and Marx, 1914); Amy Mittelman, "The Politics of Alcohol Production: The Liquor Industry and the Federal Government, 1862–1900" (Ph.D. diss., Columbia University 1986); Wilbur R. Miller, *Revenuers and Moonshiners: Enforcing Federal Liquor Law in the Mountain South, 1865–1900* (Chapel Hill: University of North Carolina Press, 1991), 61–86; and Tun-Yuan Hu, *The Liquor Tax in the United States, 1791–1947*, Columbia University Monographs in Public Finance and National Income, no. 1 (New York: Graduate School of Business, Columbia University, 1951). Two other works are noteworthy for their failure to deal with the internal revenue tax on liquor: Sidney Ratner, *Taxation and Democracy* (New York: John Wiley and Son, 1967); and R. Alton Lee, *A History of Regulatory Taxation* (Lexington: University Press of Kentucky, 1973). Lee omits considering the liquor tax because its primary purpose is "to raise a revenue rather than to exert a regulatory effect" (x).

2. The funds generated by the liquor tax quickly tied the government to this tax. A joint resolution of February 18, 1879 "resolved . . . that a reduction of the tax on distilled spirits is inexpedient." 20 *Statutes at Large* 248. The fiscally insignificant tobacco tax was repealed in 1890. On the reforms and the Whiskey Ring, see Ross A.

Webb, *Benjamin Helm Bristow: Border State Politician* (Lexington: University Press of Kentucky, 1969), 187–212.

3. For the workings of the liquor tax system, see 12 *Statutes at Large* 432–84, 713–31; 13 *Statutes at Large* 14–17, 233–306; 14 *Statutes at Large* 469–87; 15 *Statutes at Large* 98–151; Mittelman, "Politics of Alcohol," 12–101, 152–73; Smith, *History*, 185–207, 212–23; Howe, *Internal Revenue*, 205–8. In practice, the rules of the Internal Revenue Office were equal to the statutes. For example, relatives of distillers, even distant cousins, were prohibited from being gaugers in the family's works. See E. C. Duncan to John Yerkes, Commissioner of Internal Revenue, January 31, 1901, Collectors Letters Concerning Alcohol Tax, box 173, NA58.

4. For examples of collectors' attacks on the prohibition movement, see *New York Times*, May 14, 1889, 4; *Voice*, July 2, 1885, 1; *American Issue*, May 31, 1907, 3. *Cyclopaedia*, 638–39; USBA, *Convention Report* 21 (1881): 12, 14; Report of Secretary of Treasury, *Internal Revenue Record* 33 (December 2, 1887): 390; for Raum's career, see Miller, *Revenuers*, 97–99, 159. At lower levels federal officials who oversaw plants occasionally left the service to become liquor makers; see E. C. Duncan to John W. Yerkes, December 31, 1900, Collectors Letters Concerning Alcohol Tax, box 173, NA58.

5. *DATB*, 98; William H. Armstrong, *National Internal Revenue Taxation: Its Relations to Temperance and Prohibition* (New York: National Temperance Society and Publishing House, 1889), 7. In President Cleveland's first term, eighty-four of eighty-five collectors were replaced; see Allan Nevins, *Grover Cleveland: A Study in Courage* (New York: Dodd, Mead, 1933), 251. The collectors often acted as political managers for an area. For example, see Thomas C. Crenshaw to Joseph S. Miller (telegram), March 22, 1888, Grover Cleveland Papers, Library of Congress (microfilm edition). During Cleveland's second term, the *New York Times* reported that the president exercised his control over the offices to punish the intraparty heretics, the fusion Democrats. *New York Times*, June 12, 1893, 4. Also in Cleveland's second term civil service protection was extended to storekeepers, gaugers, and deputy collectors; see Miller, *Revenuers*, 149. Atypical was the service of William H. Taft as a collector; Henry Pringle, *Life and Times of William H. Taft* (New York: Farrar and Rhinehard, 1939), 1:56–63.

6. The figures come from Hu, *Liquor Tax*, end piece. For government reliance on liquor taxation in emergencies, see 28 *Statutes at Large* 563, 30 *Statutes at Large* 448; Charles Gilbert, *American Financing of World War I* (Westport, Conn.: Greenwood Press, 1970), 26–27; *New York Times*, January 17, 1919, 12. Of course, this reliance was strengthened when the Supreme Court struck down the income tax; see Miller, *Revenuers*, 166.

7. "Rescind Internal Revenue Regulations, Re: the Branding of Whiskey" (transcript), April 7, 1909, 4, copy in Department of Justice Papers, National Archives, Record Group 60, 112, Straight Numerical Files, file 90766. I thank Richard J. Fiesta for pointing out this material; *Washington Post*, May 23, 1890, 1; Miller, *Revenuers*,

170; John G. Capers, "The Federal Internal Revenues," *Yale Law Journal* 23 (May 1914): 602–6 (Capers was a former commissioner of internal revenue).

8. USBA, *Convention Report* 37 (1897): 11–15; 44 (1904): 37; *Florida Times Union*, May 9, 1907, 8; *Union Signal*, July 7, 1904, 9, citing a lost circular; *New Republic*, January 24, 1912, 3; William S. Parry to A. J. Daugherty, November 24, 1900, Collectors Letters Concerning Alcohol Tax, box 173, NA58; M. Monahan, ed., *A Text-Book of True Temperance* (New York: United States Brewers' Association, 1911), 46–48; Mittelman, "Politics of Alcohol," 173–78; Mittelman, "Who Will Pay the Tax? The Federal Government and the Liquor Industry, 1880–1933," *Social History of Alcohol Review* 25 (Spring 1992): 28–38. The revenue argument appears constantly in liquor publications; see, for example, Henry S. Boutell, "A Congressman Denounces Prohibition" (address at Fiftieth Annual Convention of USBA, June 8, 1910), 5–7.

9. Gallus Thomann, *Liquor Laws of the United States; Their Spirit and Effect* (New York: Economical Press for the USBA, 1885); USBA, *Convention Report* 24 (1884): 36; *Cong. Rec.*, 48th Cong., 1st sess., 1024.

10. J. Ellen Foster, *Constitutional Amendment Manual* (New York: National Temperance Society, 1882), 33.

11. Percentages and figures on Atlanta's tax are derived from James M. Wright, *The License System of the City of Atlanta* (n.p.: Harper Printing Co., 1964), 237; for Portsmouth, see loose papers in Scrapbook box, ECDP. The alternatives to higher liquor licenses were of course higher property taxes, reduced services, or general license taxes. The experience of Birmingham, Alabama, reveals the perils of each; see Carl V. Harris, *Political Power in Birmingham, 1871–1921* (Knoxville: University of Tennessee Press, 1977), 96–175, 289; *Nation*, July 5, 1888, 5–6; *Union Signal*, August 21, 1884, 9; *Voice*, September 29, 1887, 9; John R. Kemp, ed., *Martin Behrman of New Orleans: Memoirs of a City Boss* (Baton Rouge: Louisiana State University Press, 1977), 157. See also *Union Signal*, September 3, 1886, 1, May 14, 1885, 2.

12. *New Voice*, December 22, 1904, cover; *Union Signal*, September 14, 1893, 16; *American Issue*, April 19, 1907, 1; *Union Signal*, October 19, 1899, 1, January 16, 1908, 1; *Cyclopaedia*, 168, 495; *New York Times*, July 25, 1884, 1; *Union Signal*, September 11, 1884, 8–9, August 23, 1900, 9.

13. *Union Signal*, June 4, 1896, 1; *Voice*, June 14, 1894, 1, September 29, 1887, 4, *Union Signal*, January 29, 1887, 2. For articles using similar language, see *Union Signal*, January 31, 1884, 9, July 7, 1904, 9; *New York Times*, October 13, 1884, 5. Gambrinus is the mythical inventor of beer.

14. *Union Signal*, September 11, 1884, 8–9. The longevity of this view is shown by the article on the liquor power in *SEAP*, 1328–30, which presented the 1890s view culled directly from the 1893 *Cyclopaedia*, 371, 148, 255.

15. *Arena*, February 1890, 310, January 1890, 19; John G. Woolley, *A Hundred Years of Temperance* (Westerville, Ohio: American Issue Publishing, [1909]), 11; see also *Union Signal*, July 21, 1887, 8–9.

16. *Lever*, September 22, 1892, 1; *Arena*, February 1890, 320; *Union Signal*, April 30, 1891, 4; *Lever*, December 8, 1892, 4; *Union Signal*, November 30, 1893, 2–3, February 23, 1888, 4. For a late use of the rhetoric of the antitrust movement, see the speech of Seaborn Wright reported in *Union Signal*, November 23, 1911, 2.

17. *Cyclopaedia*, 251. In a similar vein radical drys denied that the federal government had the power to levy a regulatory tax; see *Voice*, January 28, 1892, 1; *College Patriot*, March 1904, 55; *National Liberty Herald*, January 1914, 1.

18. *Voice*, July 14, 1887, 3; *Union Signal*, October 8, 1896, 8, February 15, 1883, 8, September 27, 1883, 8; J. N. Stearns, ed., *Temperance Shot and Shell* (New York: National Temperance Society and Publication House, 1892), 75–77.

19. *Voice*, January 21, 1892, 4; *Lever*, December 8, 1892, 4.

20. *Union Signal*, November 30, 1893, 3; *Voice*, January 21, 1892, 4. See also *Union Signal*, March 5, 1885, 2, January 26, 1888, 3; *Cyclopaedia*, 567; National WCTU, *Annual Convention Minutes* 9 (1882): 29.

21. L. Ames Brown, "National Prohibition," *Atlantic Monthly* 115 (June 1915): 745; *Cong. Rec.*, 63d Cong., 2d sess., App. 745, 508; *Cong. Rec.*, 65th Cong., 2d sess.; House *Report 1493*, pt. 2, 64th Cong., 2d sess., 5–6; House *Report 211*, pt. 3, 65th Cong., 2d sess., 4.

22. Armstrong, *Revenue Taxation*, 7.

23. *Union Signal*, July 5, 1888, 5.

24. *Union Signal*, August 28, 1888, 3, April 30, 1891, 4; Nevins, *Cleveland, Study in Courage*, 384; Wayne Morgan, *From Hayes to McKinley: National Party Politics, 1877–1896* (Syracuse, N.Y.: Syracuse University Press, 1969), 170–72; *Union Signal*, September 11, 1884, 1. The same image is used in *Proceedings 1896 Convention National Anti-Saloon League* (n.p.: American Anti-Saloon League, n.d.), 7.

25. *Voice*, October 23, 1884, 2; *Union Signal*, January 29, 1887, 2, April 30, 1891, 4; *Annual Report of Secretary of Treasury 1886, Finance* (Washington, D.C.: Government Printing Office, 1886), 1: 55–56; *Chicago Tribune*, September 10, 1886, 4.

26. *Union Signal*, November 5, 1914, 3, February 15, 1883, 8. *Voice*, March 27, 1895, 4. Hendrickson to Shoemaker, April 4, 1908, 2, TPP, ser. vi.

27. *Union Signal*, September 27, 1883, 8, April 5, 1906, 8. Some bills for repeal of the tax were introduced in the period 1880–1920 by legislators who were from distilling and tobacco-producing areas and thus unsympathetic to temperance.

28. Smith, *History*, 129–35.

29. 13 *Statutes at Large* 122; reporter John William Wallace, notes, *McGuire v. Commonwealth*, 3 Wallace (1866) 383; 5 *Wallace* (1867) 462, 472.

30. 5 *Wallace* (1867) 462. For state court decisions, two treatises are exceptionally helpful: Henry C. Black, *A Treatise on the Laws Regulating the Manufacture and Sale of Intoxicating Liquors* (St. Paul, Minn.: West Publishing, 1892), 600–601; and Howard C. Joyce, *The Law Relating to Intoxicating Liquors* (Albany, N.Y.: Matthew Bender and Co., 1910), 102–3, 727–28. For the action of the Internal Revenue Office in printing the disclaimer, see *Union Signal*, April 9, 1891, 10–11. The desire of liquor dealers to have the *License Tax Cases* rule overturned is evident in the number

of times they raised the issue. For examples, see *In Re Jordan*, 49 *Federal Reports* (1892) 238; *New York Times*, May 14, 1891, 4, February 22, 1891, 4; *Union Signal*, January 17, 1884, 5.

31. *Union Signal*, January 31, 1884, 5, January 17, 1884, 5, June 11, 1885, 8–9; *Voice*, July 14, 1887, 4. The expansion of the temperance movement compelled prohibition papers to repeat this type of information over and over. Citizens of newly dry area had to be educated about the delicate distinctions between license and special tax; *Union Signal*, February 7, 1884, 5, July 28, 1910, 4. Drys overestimated the instructional value of their newspapers. As late as 1899, citizens sought explanation of the tax system's licensing of illegal sellers; see Wilson to Lantham, 2 *Treasury Decisions* (1899) 809, 810. Following reorganization of the Treasury Department brought on by the increase in the number of taxes during the Spanish-American War, *Treasury Decisions*, which lump together Customs and Internal Revenue matters, replaced the semi-official *Internal Revenue Record*. The exchange between Wilson and Lantham prompted the drafting of a bill designed to prevent the federal government from issuing license in dry areas; see USBA, *Convention Report* 40 (1900): 71.

32. *Union Signal*, March 7, 1907, 3, April 26, 1906, 5; *New Voice*, December 22, 1904, 4.

33. *Union Signal*, July 24, 1902, 1, February 5, 1885, 2.

34. *Voice*, January 20, 1887, 4.

35. *Voice*, October 17, 1895, 2; see also *Chicago Tribune*, September 25, 1886, 3.

36. 17 *Statutes at Large* 401.

37. *Commonwealth v. Brown*, 124 *Massachusetts* (1878) 318; and *State v. Mellor*, 13 *Rhode Island* (1882) 66; Black, *Treatise*, 600–601; Joyce, *Law*, 102–3, 727–28.

38. *American Issue*, January 4, 1901, 4; *Voice*, April 21, 1887, 1, April 7, 1887, 2.

39. Morton Keller, *Affairs of State: Public Life in Late Nineteenth Century America* (Cambridge, Mass.: Harvard University Press, 1977), 128–29. The following account of the oleomargarine controversy is based on R. Alton Lee, *A History of Regulatory Taxation* (Lexington: University Press of Kentucky, 1973), 12–27, 48–57; and James Harvey Young, *Pure Food: Securing the Federal Food and Drug Act of 1906* (Princeton, N.J.: Princeton University Press, 1989), 71–92. See also Thomas A. Bailey, "Congressional Opposition to Pure Food Legislation, 1879–1906," *American Journal of Sociology* 36 (July 1930–May 1931): 52–64; J. K. Mallory Jr., "The Oleomargarine Controversy," *Virginia Law Review* 33 (1947): 631–41.

40. *State v. Addington*, 77 *Missouri* (1882) 110; *People v. Marx*, 99 *New York* (1885) 377; 127 *United States* (1888) 678.

41. The cases are *Plummley v. Massachusetts*, 155 *United States* (1894) 461; *Schollenberger v. Pennsylvania*, 171 *United States* (1898) 1; and *Collins v. New Hampshire*, 171 *United States* (1898) 31.

42. *State v. Intoxicating Liquors, James Key and Other Claimants*, 44 *Vermont* (1872) 207–9. My examination of the *Internal Revenue Record* for this period failed to turn up any notice taken of Crane's and Jewett's actions, or any evidence of a set policy on this subject during the 1870s. As late as 1885, the *Union Signal* claimed that the

commissioner of internal revenue ordered collectors to obey summons to bring their records into court; *Union Signal*, May 28, 1885, 1. However, I have found nothing corroborating this statement in the *Internal Revenue Record*. Perry Duis, *The Saloon: Public Drinking in Chicago and Boston, 1880–1920* (Urbana and Chicago: University of Illinois Press, 1983), 62, believing an assertion of prohibitionist Henry Faxon, implied that the federal government began to cooperate with the dry states far earlier than it did.

43. 9 *Federal Cases* (1876) 1158–59. Despite the strong statement of principle by the secretary, the policy remained confused. The clerk who delivered the secretary's note to the district court was willing to testify as to the contents of Anderson's letters. But his testimony was ruled hearsay by the trial judge.

44. Devens to John Sherman, Secretary of Treasury, October 12, 1877, *Internal Revenue Record* 23 (October 22, 1877): 341–42.

45. Devens to Sherman, May 31, 1878, *Internal Revenue Record* 24 (June 10, 1878): 178. The *Record* was privately published but treated as an official register. Congress appropriated money for the department to subscribe to the *Record*; see 13 *Statutes at Large* 195, 445. In *Internal Revenue Record* 19 (June 7, 1883): 177, all collectors were ordered to impress upon their subordinates the "duty of a careful perusal and preservation of the *Record*."

46. For an example of a collector hindering access to the list, see *Voice*, May 12, 1887, 2. For Crenshaw's remarks, see Josiah Carter to editor, *Chicago Tribune*, September 25, 1886, 3. The reprinting of the text is at *Internal Revenue Record* 32 (November 15, 1886): 358. The question as to whether this was official policy or Crenshaw acting on his own is nearly impossible to determine, as the evidence conflicts. The policy position is strengthened by the phrase "I have been advised." On the other hand, the emerging policy stressed resistance to court process, while Crenshaw asserts the opposite. Crenshaw was a rather independent and proud man with political aspirations. He boasted of being the first collector appointed by President Cleveland; he was quite capable of independent action. T. C. Crenshaw to David Lamont, January 17, 1889, Grover Cleveland Papers, Library of Congress (microfilm edition).

47. *Voice*, June 9, 1887, 4; *Union Signal*, October 7, 1886, 1, December 16, 1886, 2.

48. *Voice*, June 9, 1887, 4; for Miller's career, see Miller, *Revenuers*, 149, 167.

49. *Chicago Tribune*, September 3, 1886, 8; *Voice*, April 21, 1887, 12, May 12, 1887, 2, June 9, 1887, 4.

50. For the prohibitionist interpretation of the redistricting, see *Voice*, July 14, 1887, 7; *Union Signal*, September 1, 1887, 1. On the details of the reorganization, see *Internal Revenue Record* 33 (May 23, 1887): 157. Strangely, it is possible that a case could be made for such federal chicanery in the reorganization of the collection district of Iowa. Iowa was redistricted twice, once with the rest of the nation and again a few weeks later. But given the attitude of Commissioner Miller, such a scenario seems unlikely. *Internal Revenue Record* 33 (June 29, 1887): 189.

51. *Voice*, April 21, 1887, 1; *Union Signal*, September 1, 1887, 1; *New York Times* December 18, 1887, 4.

52. *Internal Revenue Record* 34 (August 20, 1888): 261.

53. Miller was on shaky ground. Most American lawyers agreed with the view that public records were admissible; see Francis Wharton, *A Commentary on the Law of Evidence in Civil Issues* (Philadelphia: Kay and Brother, 1877), 1:609–17. The public-policy exception originated in England and is explained in William Best, *The Principles of the Law of Evidence* (1875; reprint, Jersey City, N.J.: Frederic D. Linn and Co., 1882), 1:407–11, 2:979. The examples of such public-policy justifications were exclusively judicial in nature, so Miller was extending the doctrine to new areas.

54. *In Re Huttman*, 70 *Federal Reporter* (1895) 700, 701, 703. In this case the collector's counsel quoted Miller's exact language; *Voice*, October 17, 1885, 2; predictably the *Voice* found the decision unpalatable.

55. 74 *Federal Reporter* (1896) 928, 929, 931, 933. Judge Shipman cited the *License Tax Cases* and the congressional act setting out the policy that the special tax was not a license and did not confer any rights.

56. 82 *Federal Reporter* (1897) 729, 731–32, 732.

57. 1 *Treasury Decisions* (1898) 521.

58. Ibid., 593–94.

59. Ibid., 566–67, 710–11.

60. 96 *Federal Reports* (1899) 552; Miller, *Revenuers*, 147, 221 n. 1.

61. 177 *United States* (1900) 459, 469–70.

62. Circular 583, October 10, 1900, Circular 651, December 10, 1903, Collections of Circulars (loose-leaf volumes), NA58; also *3 Treasury Decisions* (1900) 311–12, 313, 583; Ballard to Yerkes, March 13, 1901, Collectors Letters Concerning Alcohol Tax, box 173, NA58; Letter to Hon. Charles H. Weisse, *Spirits Rulings and Letters 1891 On*, collected by R. E. Wilbur (bound volume), NA58.

CHAPTER 4. THE TRANSFORMATION OF PROHIBITIONIST MEANS

1. Jack S. Blocker Jr., *Retreat from Reform: The Prohibition Movement in the United States, 1890–1913* (Westport, Conn.: Greenwood Press, 1976), 44; David Leigh Colvin, *Prohibition in the United States* (New York: Doran, 1926), 140.

2. Louis Albert Banks, *Ammunition for Final Drive on Booze* (New York: Funk and Wagnalls, 1917); Robert H. Wiebe, *The Search for Order, 1877–1920* (New York: Hill and Wang, 1967); Louis Galambos, "The Emerging Organizational Synthesis of Modern American History," *Business History Review* 44 (Autumn 1980): 279–90; Samuel P. Hays, *Response to Industrialism, 1885–1914* (Chicago: University of Chicago Press, 1957), 48–70; Alfred D. Chandler Jr., *The Visible Hand: The Managerial Revolution in American Business* (Cambridge, Mass., Harvard University Press, 1977); Louis Galambos, "Technology, Political Economy, and Professionalization: Central

Themes of the Organizational Synthesis," *Business History Review* 57 (Winter 1983): 471–93.

3. Ernest Cherrington, *Evolution of Prohibition in the United States of America* (Westerville, Ohio: American Issue Press, 1920), 236, 242, 244, 246, 180; *Lever*, March 9, 1893, 1; USBA, *Convention Report* 32 (1892): 11–15, 36 (1896): 42–43; Frederic H. Wines and John Koren for the Committee of Fifty, *The Liquor Problem in Its Legislative Aspects*, 2d ed. (Boston: Houghton Mifflin, 1898), 127–40.

4. *Union Signal*, January 9, 1890, 8; *New York Times*, March 10, 1891, 5; *Lever*, May 11, 1893, 1. For a complete picture of Kansas enforcement, see Robert Smith Bader, *Prohibition in Kansas: A History* (Lawrence: University Press of Kansas, 1986), 106–32. See also *Lever*, April 6, 1893, 4; *Voice*, August 25, 1892, 1.

5. *Lever*, April 6, 1893, 2, May 11, 1893, 1; Blocker, *Retreat*, 147; Colvin, *Prohibition*, 605–41; *New Voice*, September 5, 1901, 8–9, October 24, 1901, 9.

6. *Union Signal*, August 27, 1891, 1, October 8, 1891, 3, February 24, 1894, 9; Bader, *Kansas*, 108–9, 112–13.

7. *Lever*, May 11, 1893, 3; *Union Signal*, January 4, 1894, 3; *New York Times*, July 2, 1892, 4; Colvin, *Prohibition*, 252; Blocker, *Retreat*, 39–99, 45; Morton Keller, *Affairs of State: Public Life in Late Nineteenth Century America* (Cambridge, Mass.: Harvard University Press, 1977), 548–49.

8. Blocker, *Retreat*, 39–128; *New York Times*, June 28, 1892, 2, June 29, 1892, 5, June 30, 1892, 5, October 19, 1895, 15, October 19, 1896, 14; *Union Signal*, July 31, 1890, 8, 9, December 15, 1892, 3–4, January 5, 1893, 3, January 19, 1893, 3, January 26, 1893, 2, February 16, 1893, 3, April 16, 1896, 1, April 23, 1896, 5, May 21, 1896, 4, June 11, 1896, 8; John G. Woolley, *The Wounds of a Friend* (Westerville, Ohio: American Issue Publishing, n.d.), 11.

9. *Union Signal*, July 16, 1896, 1; Blocker, *Retreat*, 119–20.

10. Ruth Bordin, *Woman and Temperance: The Quest for Power and Liberty, 1873–1900* (Philadelphia: Temple University Press, 1984), 123–30, 142; *Union Signal*, November 14, 1889, 2, November 21, 1889, 2; Mary Earhart, *Frances Willard: From Prayers to Politics* (Chicago: University of Chicago Press, 1944), 320–39.

11. Bordin, *Woman*, 144–48; *Voice*, December 1, 1892, 2; *Lever*, August 31, 1892, 1; *Voice*, November 16, 1893, 8, November 9, 1891, 3, November 9, 1894, 2.

12. Bordin, *Woman*, 142–48; Earhart, *Willard*, 345–52, 364–66, 373–77. See also Willard to Reba Butler, December 15, 1897, Frances Willard Papers, Misc. Manuscripts Collection, Library of Congress.

13. *Lever*, August 31, 1892, 1; *Voice*, November 16, 1893, 8, November 9, 1894, 2.

14. Blocker, *Retreat*, 52–53; SEAP, 218, 812–15, 1121–24, 2521–24; *New York Times*, April 1, 1893, 2.

15. E. Merton Coulter, "The Athens Dispensary," *Georgia Historical Quarterly*, 50 (March 1966): 14–33; *New York Times*, July 29, 1892, 1, July 30, 1892, 4, January 9, 1893, 3; John Evans Eubanks, *Ben Tillman's Baby: The Dispensary System of South Carolina, 1892–1915* (Augusta: n.p., 1950); Frederick M. Heath and Harriet H. Kinard "Prohibition in South Carolina, 1880–1940: An Overview," *Proceedings of*

the South Carolina Historical Association (Aiken, S.C.: University of South Carolina, 1980), 118–32; Ellen Alexander Hendricks, "The South Carolina Dispensary System," *North Carolina Review* 22 (April 1945): 176–97.

16. *Union Signal*, January 26, 1893, 8; Blocker, *Retreat*, 71–72; *Voice*, January 12, 1893, 4, January 26, 1893, 4; *New York Times*, June 5, 1894, 1, June 6, 1894, 1, 4, August 9, 1895, 5, August 10, 1895, 5.

17. The *Lever* always opposed the dispensary despite a pose of friendliness it sometimes assumed; see July 6, 1893, 4, June 22, 1893, 1, June 29, 1893, 1, July 13, 1893, 1, 5, August 3, 1893, 4, September 28, 1893, 4; *Union Signal*, July 13, 1893, 8, February 1, 1894, 3; *New York Times*, August 11, 1895, 1; *Voice*, February 11, 1892, 4, February 18, 1892, 4, March 9, 1893, 1.

18. K. Austin Kerr, *Organized for Prohibition: A New History of the Anti-Saloon League* (New Haven: Yale University Press, 1985), 67–73; *New York Times*, December 1, 1893, 9; Russell, impressed by Herrick Johnson's speech at the World's Temperance Congress held at Chicago's 1893 World's Fair, claimed that it inspired him to form the league. Russell "Autobiography," incomplete typescript, chap. 14, 1–4, folder 52, TPP, ser. xv. The idea of limited means spread and found its proponents within radical organizations. For instance, see the assertion of Illinois white ribboner Mary E. Metzgar in the *Union Signal* that "all states have some good laws upon their statutes books," a reference to Sunday closing and antibrothel laws. *Union Signal*, June 29, 1895, 3.

19. *DATB*, 424–25; *SEAP*, 2324–27; Kerr, *Organized*, 76–77; Blocker, *Retreat*, 156; Peter Odegard, *Pressure Politics: The Story of the Anti-Saloon League* (New York: Columbia University Press, 1928), 1–7; Russell, "Autobiography," chap. 9, 1–8, folder 51, and miscellaneous materials, folder 54, TPP, ser. xv; Robert M. Crunden, *Ministers of Reform: The Progressives' Achievement in American Civilization, 1889–1920* (Urbana: University of Illinois Press, 1984), 3–38.

20. Kerr, *Organized*, 80–82; Norman H. Clark, *Deliver Us from Evil: An Interpretation of American Prohibition* (New York: Norton, 1976), 94; James H. Timberlake, *Prohibition and the Progressive Movement, 1900–1920* (Cambridge, Mass.: Harvard University Press, 1963), 128–30; Odegard, *Pressure*, 5–15.

21. Timberlake, *Prohibition and Progressive*, 137, 140–44; Odegard, *Pressure*, 78–103; *Model Constitution for Local Anti-Saloon Leagues* ([New York]: New York Anti-Saloon League, n.d.); Russell, "The Anti-Saloon League Movement" (undated but clearly a twentieth-century New York recruiting speech), folder 28, TPP, ser. xv.

22. Timberlake, *Prohibition and Progressive*, 132, 139; *American Issue*, October 9, 1903, 9; Russell, "The Anti-Saloon League Movement," folder 28, TPP, ser. xv; Ernest Cherrington, *Report of the General Manager of the American Issue Publishing Company* ([Westerville, Ohio: American Issue Publishing], 1919), 5, 6; Blocker, *Retreat*, 161.

23. Gordon B. Moore to J. M. Johnson, October 8, 1903, folder 1, VAASP; *Addresses at Omnipartisan State Temperance Convention* (Indianapolis, Indiana: ASL, [1911]), 22; Kerr, *Organized*, 98–114; Odegard, *Pressure*, 97–98, Clark, *Deliver*, 97–

99. Virtually any issue of *American Issue* between 1904 and 1907 has a reference to "putting on the lid."

24. Kerr, *Organized*, 96–97, 215, 148–50; Bader, *Kansas*, 129, 192; Blocker, *Retreat*, 157–61.

25. Kerr, *Organized*, 18, 127–28; Odegard, *Pressure*, 127; *Union Signal*, February 18, 1897, 1.

26. *New York Times*, November 17, 1894, 3; Kerr, *Organized*, 89; *New Voice*, March 22, 1901, 4, January 24, 1901, 8, March 6, 1902, 1, January 4, 1900, 4, January 11, 1900, 3, January 18, 1900, 16, April 26, 1900, 1, May 31, 1900, 9, February 15, 1900, 1, February 22, 1900, 7, March 15, 1900, 1, September 5, 1901, 8–9, October 24, 1901, 9. Blocker, *Retreat*, 138–44, 176–92, points out that while the party refused to work for local option laws, it permitted its members to vote under the laws once they were adopted.

27. Blocker, *Retreat*, 138–47, 187; *New Voice*, February 2, 1905, 6–7, April 20, 1905, 9, May 11, 1905, 9; *Union Signal*, February 11, 1897, 10; Kerr, *Organized*, 155.

28. *California Issue*, August 1913, 3; Kerr, *Organized*, 86–87, 123–25; *American Issue*, December 11, 1903, 3, June 1900, 14, November 1900, 9; Blocker, *Retreat*, 199–202; Dewey W. Granthem, *Southern Progressivism: The Reconciliation of Progress and Tradition* (Knoxville: University of Tennessee Press, 1983), 160–77; *Union Signal*, January 23, 1908, 1, April 16, 1908, 3, October 15, 1908, 8, November 19, 1908, 1; the song about the white maps, written by Mable Dufford Pinkerton, was sung to the tune "The Wearing of the Green." Its refrain ran as follows: "Till we make the map all white, till we make the map all white; We'll work for prohibition till we make the map all white / We'll agitate and organize, and surely win the fight. We'll work for prohibition till we make the map all white." Anna Gordon, comp., *Popular Campaign Songs* (Evanston, Ill.: National WCTU Publishing House, 1915), 4.

29. Howard H. Russell, *A Lawyer's Examination of the Bible* (Chicago and New York: Fleming H. Revell Company, 1893), 14, 182–87.

30. Wayne B. Wheeler, comp., *Federal and State Laws Relating to Intoxicating Liquor* (Westerville, Ohio: American Issue Publishing, 1918), foreword, n.p.

31. Lemuel D. Lilly, *Bench vs. Bar: Or Judicial Answers to Saloon Arguments* (Westerville, Ohio: American Issue Publishing, 1910); Ervin S. Chapman, *A Stainless Flag* (Los Angeles: Times-Mirror P & B House, [1907]); Eli F. Ritter, *Is License Constitutional: A Brief . . . Before the Supreme Court of Indiana* (New York: Funk and Wagnalls, 1891); Eli F. Ritter, *Moral Law and Civil Law: Parts of the Same Thing*, rev. ed. (Westerville, Ohio: American Issue Publishing, 1910); *SEAP*, 480, 555, 1553, 2289.

32. Ritter, *Moral Law and Civil Law*, rev. ed., 65–115, 131–88, 264–65, 275–78.

33. Lilly, *Bench vs. Bar*, 3, 4, 5, 7, 9, 29; on the goal of voting dry, see 9, 46–47.

34. Ibid., 5, 11, 15, 21–44.

35. Chapman, *A Stainless Flag*, 4–7, 9, 10–12.

36. Ibid., 12, 13, 14, 16, 17; some party prohibitionists also embraced the idea that court decisions, especially Supreme Court rulings, could be used against contentions

of the liquor traffic; see John G. Woolley and William E. Johnson, *Temperance Progress in the Century* (London: Linscott, 1902), 170–76; paying particular attention to *Stone v. Mississippi* and *Crowley v. Christensen* (which they call "the crowning decisions of the series"), they assert that in the 1880s and 1890s the Court, despite "the corruption of the times," made a distinct advance in its attitude to the liquor traffic.

37. Chapman, *A Stainless Flag*, 18, 20, 22, 24, 26–28.

38. Given the Court's retreat into formalism in the middle of the nineteenth century, such a course was unlikely. See Robert M. Cover, *Justice Accused: Antislavery and the Judicial Process* (New Haven, Conn.: Yale University Press, 1975); William E. Nelson, "The Impact of the Anti-Slavery Movement upon Styles of Judicial Reasoning in Nineteenth Century America," *Harvard Law Review* 87 (1974): 513–66; Morton J. Horwitz, *The Transformation of American Law, 1780–1860* (Cambridge, Mass.: Harvard University Press, 1977), 253–66; Dinwiddie Papers, Library of Congress, loose papers in Scrapbook box; Charles Marshall Hogan, "Wayne B. Wheeler: Single Issue Exponent" (Ph.D. diss., University of Cincinnati, 1986), 171–78, 221–25.

39. Oscar G. Christgau, in "Speeches Undated, 1909–1943" folder, OGCP.

40. *American Issue*, August 1900, 12. This aspect of the league has escaped the notice of previous scholars who have examined the temperance movement; Odegard, *Pressure*, lacked a chapter on law enforcement in the league to balance the ones on finance, political methods, and congressional lobbying. Blocker, *Retreat*, 115, and Clark, *Deliver*, 113–14, referred to the league's enforcement activities in passing but missed its importance. Kerr, *Organized*, 220–24, talked of later enforcement issues, but not the early and shaping ones. Timberlake, *Prohibition and Progressive*, 143–44, is best and also provides the source of the estimate (218 n. 63). See also Lloyd Sponholtz, "The Politics of Temperance in Ohio, 1880–1912," *Ohio History* 85 (Winter 1976): 4–27, which presents a balanced view of league activity.

41. Arthur F. Bentley, *The Process of Government*, ed. Peter H. Odegard (1908; reprint, Cambridge, Mass.: Belknap Press and the John Harvard Library, 1967), 283.

42. First Ohio Anti-Saloon League Proceedings (1895), quoted in Odegard, *Pressure*, 4; *Proceedings National Anti-Saloon League* (1895), ii, and *Proceedings of National Anti-Saloon League* (1896), 59, TPP, ser. v; Scrapbook, 8, ECDP; Russell, "Mob and Law" (1886 college speech), 4, folder 61; Russell, "My First Case" (1878), Miscellaneous Writings, folder 30, Horace M. Towner to Samuel J. Fickel, August 7, 1936, folder 54, TPP, ser. xv; *SEAP*, 2326.

43. *Christian Observer* (Louisville, Ky.), March 1, 1905, 1, 22; Reverend John F. Brant, "Suggestions to Our Volunteer Anti-Saloon Speakers," Scrapbook, between 368–69, ECDP.

44. *DATB*, 5–6; *SEAP*, 837, 1817, 2289, 2434; *American Issue*, May 1, 1915, 3; Russell, "A Hasty Sketch Appreciative of Wayne B. Wheeler" [1916?], folder 28, Russell, "Address" (July 1915), 5, folder 35, TPP, ser. xv; Hogan, "Wheeler: Single Issue Exponent." The verse from the 1880s that Russell quoted runs as follows: "Mental suasion for the man who thinks / Moral suasion for the man who drinks / Legal suasion for the drunkard-maker / Prison suasion for the statute-breaker."

45. *American Issue*, August 1900, 13; Reverend A. P. Doyle, *American Issue*, December 22, 1905, 12, December 8, 1905, 2, 6; Russell, "Our League—Its Future" (speech delivered in Washington, D.C., December 1918), folder 35, Russell, "January 16, 1919," folder 59, TPP, ser. xv.

46. *American Issue*, October 17, 1902, 4, September 24, 1903, 2, May 29, 1903, 4, August 14, 1903, 9, July 1900, 2; *Stop, Look, and Listen*, ser. v, no. 6 (Providence: Rhode Island Anti-Saloon League, n.d.); *American Patriot*, May 1913, 37, 46, 47.

47. First Annual Congress Ohio Anti-Saloon League (1894), 16, Second Annual Report of State Superintendents (1895), 4, TPP, ser. v; *American Issue*, August 1900, 2, September 30, 1904, 8.

48. *Stop, Look, and Listen*, ser. v (Providence: R.I.: Anti-Saloon League, n.d.); *American Issue*, May 31, 1901, 1, May 29, 1903, 6; Blocker, *Retreat*, 159–60.

49. *American Issue*, February 5, 1904, 4, April 29, 1904, 11, May 1900, 3, March 29, 1901, 7, December 28, 1906, 4, January 8, 1904, 13, July 10, 1903, 4, March 3, 1905, 5. Anti-Saloon League attorneys included the following: for Ohio—Wayne Wheeler, Boyd Doty, Benjamin Moore, and two others (unnamed); for Nebraska—Thomas Darnall; for Indiana—Judge Benjamin F. Ibach, J. F. Lewis, Eli F. Ritter, Charles J. Orbinson (retained); for Illinois—William Anderson, J. F. Burke, E. A. Scrogin, H. L. Sheldon, F. B. Ebbert, and J. H. Collier; for Alabama—Samuel D. Weakley. See Volstead to Hinshaw, October 20, 1920, Secretary of Mr. Volstead to Wheeler, October 14, 1920, AJVP; W. A. Smith, *A History of Anti-Saloon League of Illinois* (n.p.: Anti-Saloon League of Illinois, 1925), 9; William Anderson, *The Church in Action against the Saloon* (n.p., 1907), 20; for North Carolina, see Clarkson to Cansler, Tillet, and Harris, February 5, 1904, Clarkson "The Drink Evil" (speech delivered in Wilmington, July 13, 1904), Poe to Clarkson, September 4, 1909, HCP; *Alabama Citizen*, May 1908, 2.

50. "Instructions to Our Superintendents" (undated), Scrapbook, ECDP; *American Issue*, July 17, 1903, 7, February 1900, 11. The raw number of total cases was 248, only 60 assisted by prosecutors. Of the 188 private prosecutions, the league won 170. For a typical case, see *American Issue*, April 3, 1903, 9; Justin Steuart, *Dry Boss: An Uncensored Biography of Wayne B. Wheeler* (New York: Fleming H. Revell Co., 1928), 48–49, 62–63; Russell, "A Hasty Sketch."

51. *Union Signal*, April 9, 1891, 1; *American Issue*, February 7, 1902, 3, June 26, 1903, 4, January 6, 1905, 4, May 1911, 6; John R. Kemp, ed., *Martin Behrman of New Orleans: Memoirs of a City Boss* (Baton Rouge: Louisiana State University Press, 1977), 156.

52. *American Issue*, January 25, 1901, 2, January 8, 1904, 10, August 1900, 12, August 15, 1902, 3, August 2, 1903, 7, June 7, 1906, 10, February 16, 1906, 16, November 6, 1903, 3, January 25, 1901, 2, January 6, 1905, 14; *California Issue*, August 1913, cover; Mayor J. A. White, *How Blind Tigers Were Captured in Barnesville, Ohio: or What a Mayor Can Do with a Speakeasy* (Columbus, Ohio: Ohio Anti-Saloon League, n.d.); J. Sidney Peters, Virginia Commissioner of Prohibition to Reverend E. S. Richardson, Anti-Saloon League of America, May 18, 1917, TPP, ser. vii.

53. On Johnson, see *DATB*, 262–63; *SEAP*, 1408–13; F. A. McKenzie, *"Pussyfoot" Johnson, Crusader—Reformer—A Man among Men* (New York: Fleming H. Revell Co., 1920); Woolley and Johnson, *Temperance Progress*, 156–70; *American Patriot*, March 1914, 9–10, 18; *American Issue*, September 28, 1906, 3, December 28, 1906, 12, August 9, 1907, 12; *Minnesota Issue*, April 30, 1910, 4; Richard F. Hamm, "Administration and Prison Suasion: Means and Ends in the American Temperance Movement, 1880–1920" (paper delivered at the International Congress on the Social History of Alcohol, London, Ontario, May 13–15, 1993).

54. *Voice*, July 31, 1890, 5, April 27, 1893, 2; *Union Signal*, May 18, 1899, 11; Henry Faxon to Russell, February 11, 1897, Russell, "Autobiography," chap. ix, folder 51, speech of December 6, 1897, reported in *Haverhill Gazette*, typescript copies in folders 32, 33, 52, 58, and 59, TPP, ser. xv; *American Issue*, May 1900, 8, August 1900, 14, January 18, 1901, 4, July 1911, 7; Clark, *Deliver*, 111.

55. Reflecting the official policy, the *American Issue* carried only one advertisement for a detective service in the period from 1900 to 1920. But the temperance press was filled with accounts of detective activity. *American Issue*, January 15, 1904, 5, 10, March 11, 1904, 10, May 25, 1906, 4, August 1900, 3, August 24, 1904, 12, September 1900, 7, August 1903, 3, May 10, 1901, 4; *Union Signal*, October 11, 1900, 2. C. E. Jones to Virginia Anti-Saloon League, August 24, 1908, VASLP; George M. Brown and Elisah A. Barker, comp., *Laymen's Primer on the Oregon Dry Law* (Portland: Anti-Saloon League of Oregon, [1914]), 12.

56. *American Issue*, February 2, 1906, 1–2, January 15, 1904, 5, March 1900, 4, September 18, 1903, 4, June 2, 1905, 14, September 28, 1906, 7, June 12, 1903, 9, July 1910, 8, March 15, 1901, 7; Henry C. Black, *A Treatise on the Laws Regulating the Manufacture and Sale of Intoxicating Liquors* (St. Paul, Minn.: West Publishing, 1892), 583. Bader, *Kansas*, 130, shows that the league-affiliated Kansas State Temperance Union had similar experiences with detectives; even the word "detective" carried a stigma. Thus, the federal government in 1872 changed the title of its detectives in the revenue service to agents; see Wilbur R. Miller, *Revenuers and Moonshiners: Enforcing Federal Liquor Law in the Mountain South, 1865–1900* (Chapel Hill: University of North Carolina Press, 1991), 68.

57. Russell, "Miscellaneous Writings," 2, folder 53, TPP, ser. xv. This account was written on March 9, 1933, long after the events described, and revealed Russell's failure to understand the limits of law enforcement.

58. For juvenile justice, see the works cited in the Conclusion, note 5.

59. Paul S. Boyer, *Purity in Print: The Vice-Society Movement and Book Censorship in America* (New York: Charles Scribner's Sons, 1968); Michael Grossberg, *Governing the Hearth: Law and the Family in Nineteenth-Century America* (Chapel Hill: University of North Carolina Press, 1985), 176–78.

60. This sketch is based on the works cited in Chapter 6, note 35. The St. Louis experiment in legally regulating brothels and the New Orleans practice of regulating prostitutes are famous; see John C. Burnham, "Medical Inspection of Prostitutes in America in the Nineteenth Century: The St. Louis Experiment and Its Sequel,"

Bulletin of the History of Medicine 45 (May 1971): 203–18. Less known but more important were the many cities that constructed de facto systems. For instance, St. Paul, Minnesota, used its state's ban to regulate brothels through a system of turning fines into license fees; see Barbara Meil Hobson, *Uneasy Virtue: The Politics of Prostitution and the American Reform Tradition* (New York: Basic Books, 1987), 47.

61. The literature on antitrust is huge, divided into various schools by ideology, and is generally focused on what used to be called political economy. This brief sketch is drawn from the following works: Tony Freyer, *Regulating Big Business: Antitrust in Great Britain and America, 1880–1990* (New York: Cambridge University Press, 1992); Herbert Hovenkamp, *Enterprise and American Law, 1836–1937* (Cambridge, Mass.: Harvard University Press, 1991); Morton Keller, *Regulating a New Economy: Public Policy and Economic Change in America, 1900–1933* (Cambridge, Mass.: Harvard University Press, 1990); Gabriel Kolko, *The Triumph of Conservatism: A Reinterpretation of American History, 1900–1916* (New York: Macmillan Free Press, 1963); Naomi R. Lamoreaux, *The Great Merger Movement in American Business, 1895–1904* (Cambridge: Cambridge University Press, 1985); William Letwin, *Law and Economic Policy in America: The Evolution of the Sherman Antitrust Act* (New York: Random House, 1965); Thomas K. McCraw, *Prophets of Regulation* (Cambridge, Mass.: Harvard University Press, 1984); Charles W. McCurdy, "The Knight Sugar Decision of 1895 and the Modernization of American Corporation Law, 1869–1903," *Business History Review* 53 (1979): 304–42; Martin J. Sklar, *The Corporate Reconstruction of American Capitalism, 1890–1916* (Cambridge: Cambridge University Press, 1988); David Thelen, *Paths of Resistance: Tradition and Dignity in Industrializing Missouri* (New York: Oxford University Press, 1986); Melvin I. Urofsky, "Proposed Federal Incorporation in the Progressive Era," *American Journal of Legal History* 26 (1982): 160–83.

62. McCraw, *Prophets*, 78; while later than most abolitionist-style efforts, those of Joseph Folk in Missouri epitomized the abolitionist origins of antitrust. Significantly, Folk also launched attacks on gambling halls, saloons, and businesses that operated on Sunday. Missouri's history also shows the general trend of moving from abolition to regulation in state trust policy. Thelen, *Paths*, 218–65, 354–65.

63. McCraw, *Prophets*, 79.

CHAPTER 5. THE LIQUOR TAX AND THE PRAGMATIC PROHIBITIONISTS

1. *Voice*, January 21, 1892, 4; *Lever*, December 8, 1892, 4; *Union Signal*, November 30, 1893, 3, March 5, 1885, 2, January 26, 1888, 3.

2. *Union Signal*, September 5, 1907, 5, March 19, 1896, 10.

3. *Union Signal*, February 27, 1896, 9, April 11, 1901, 6, December 12, 1907, 1; *National WCTU Convention Report* 29 ([1902]): 345; National WCTU, *Annual Convention Minutes* 32 ([1905]), 86; *National WCTU Convention Report* 35 ([1908]): 22.

4. The text of the Denny bill is reprinted in *Union Signal*, February 27, 1896, 8–9;

the Evans report is quoted in USBA, *Convention Report* 36 (1896): 19; *Cong. Rec.*, 48th Cong., 1st sess., 1554, *Cong. Rec.*, 49th Cong., 2d sess., 1601.

5. *American Issue*, September 7, 1906, 7; *New Voice*, June 28, 1908, 8; *Voice*, December 22, 1892, 2; Webb to Robins, May 7, 1913, EYWP.

6. *Union Signal*, February 28, 1889, 11, December 23, 1897, 3, April 16, 1908, 2, February 14, 1884, 1; USBA, *Convention Report* 44 (1904): 106; *Cong. Rec.*, 59th Cong., 1st sess., 2862, 1307, 1308, 60th Cong., 1st sess., 389.

7. O'Brien to President of the United States, March 31, 1908, VASLP; *Union Signal*, June 11, 1908, 2; *New Republic*, January 10, 1913, 4; Jimmie Lee Franklin, *Born Sober: Prohibition in Oklahoma, 1907–1959* (Norman: University of Oklahoma Press, 1971), 41–43; Doddridge to Wilson, January 25, 1915, Doddridge to Hobson, February 8, 1915, enclosing Fluther to Doddridge with enclosed Treasury Decision 8126, box 2, RPHP.

8. USBA, *Convention Report* 40 (1900): 72; *Union Signal*, February 27, 1896, 9, May 27, 1886, 1, June 7, 1906, 3, June 28, 1906, 3, May 27, 1909, 4. Whenever the theme of cooperation was raised, these tax proposals would revive. For example, during the 1913 debates over the Webb-Kenyon Act drys introduced as a companion measure restrictions on liquor tax collections in prohibition areas. *Union Signal*, April 24, 1913, 2; *New Republic*, January 10, 1913, 4; *Dallas Morning News*, February 7, 1913, 16.

9. Russell, "New Anti-Saloon Problems" (December 1899), 4–5, TPP, ser. vx; Hendrickson to Shoemaker, April 4, 1908, TPP, ser. vi. Matthew E. O'Brien to President of United States, March 31, 1908, VASLP; *Union Signal*, June 11, 1908, 2; *New Republic*, January 10, 1913, 4; Franklin, *Born Sober*, 41–43.

10. *American Issue*, August 1900, 5, August 14, 1915, 5; *Union Signal*, March 1, 1906, 5.

11. USBA, *Convention Reports* 36 (1896): 12, 40 (1900): 72; *American Issue*, January 1900, 3; *Cyclopaedia*, 257. In practice, the radicals inconsistently used federal statistics to show the size of the "drink bill," to bolster claims of dryness, to condemn Uncle Sam for his "profits" on his "partnership" with liquor sellers, or to point out that high license did not work. *Union Signal*, September 3, 1896, 2; *Voice*, April 16, 1891, 5, January 7, 1892, 5, March 16, 1893, 4, June 15, 1893, 4, December 22, 1893, 1; revealing of pragmatic drys' reliance on tax records were the copies in Representative Richmond Hobson's prohibition files, "Statement Showing . . . Internal Revenue from . . . Liquors . . ." and "Statement Showing the Collection of Internal Revenue . . . for Past Ten Years," enclosed in Cabell to Hobson, December 2, 1909, box 2, RPHP.

12. Alabama Session Laws (1915), 23; Alabama Code (1907), 3:770; Colorado Session Laws (1915), 285; Connecticut Code (1918), 851; Delaware Session Laws (1917), 24; Florida Session Laws (1901), 60, (1907), 201; Georgia Session Laws (1911), 180–81; Idaho Session Laws (1911); Indiana Session Laws (1917), 28, 33; Iowa Code (1897), 854; Kansas Code (1915), 1097; Kentucky Session Laws (1902), 41; Louisiana

Code (1915), 1497; Maine Session Laws (1887), 129; Massachusetts Session Laws (1887), 1078–79; Michigan Code (1915), 2600; Mississippi Session Laws (1900), 141; New Hampshire Supplement to Code (1914), 250; New York Session Laws (1909), 510; North Carolina Session Laws (1905), 361; North Dakota Session Laws (1890), 327; Ohio Session Laws (1906), 15; Oklahoma Session Laws (1913), 46; Oregon Code (1904), 1873; South Carolina Code (1912), 438; South Dakota Session Laws (1917), 537; Tennessee Code (1917), 5485; Texas Session Laws (1903), 55; Utah Session Laws (1917), 164; Vermont Session Laws (1888), 69; Virginia Session Laws (1910), 303; Washington Session Laws (1915), 7; West Virginia Session Laws (1913); 103–4; Arkansas did not have a law but accepted the evidence at common law; see 88 *Arkansas* 393, 93 *Arkansas* 23; for league support, see *American Issue*, March 8, 1901, 2, March 28, 1901, 6, August 14, 1903, 9, January 26 1906, 1; *Union Signal*, April 11, 1901, 1; Oregon Anti-Saloon League, *Laws Passed by Legislature*, Pamphlet 7 (n.p., [1913]); *What the Moral Forces Gained at the Legislature* (Seattle: Washington Anti-Saloon League, n.d.); "Minutes of Fourth Annual Convention of Virginia Anti-Saloon League," 9, VASLP; Alvin L. Hall, "The Prohibition Movement in Virginia, 1826–1916" (master's thesis, University of Virginia, 1964), 99–105.

13. USBA, *Convention Report* 28 (1888): 41.

14. 74 *Iowa* (1888) 580, 583; the Iowa Court also rejected the Fifth Amendment question, arguing that it related only to federal jurisdiction.

15. North Dakota Session Laws (1907), 307–8; *St. Ex Rel R. E. Flaherty v. O. G. Hanson*, 16 *North Dakota Reports* (1907) 347–55, 350, 354. Six years later Congressmen Webb wished to adopt the North Dakota system as federal law; Lusk to Webb, December 27, 1913, Webb to Lusk, December 31, 1913, EYWP.

16. *Voice*, April 7, 1887, 2; *New Voice*, October 25, 1900, 3, December 13, 1900, 13, *Union Signal*, May 21, 1891, 1; *American Issue*, March 1900, 3, December 28, 1900, 3, January 1900, 2, January 4, 1901, 4, March 8, 1901, 2. The success of the Anti-Saloon League in Vermont proved short-lived. The Vermont wets, aroused by the curtailing of the flourishing illegal trade, forced a referendum that repealed the prohibition law; *SEAP*, 2752.

17. Address of Reverend J. W. West, Annual Convention of Virginia Anti-Saloon League, February 1904, 4, Collector of Second District of Virginia to Reverend J. D. McAlister, June 11, 1904, B. G. Howard to Reverend J. W. West, February 5, 1906, Reverend James R. Laughton to ASL, September 8, 1908, J. R. Clark to ASL, May 5, 1911, typescript copy of Internal Revenue Laws, 1900, copies of various cases of federal tax evasion, October 3 and 12, 1906, VASLP.

18. *Union Signal*, March 1, 1906, 5, April 26, 1906, 5, May 24, 1906, 3, June 28, 1906 3, 16; *New Voice*, December 22, 1904, 4; National WCTU, *Annual Convention Minutes* 36 ([1909]): 20.

19. William Anderson, *The Church in Action against the Saloon* (n.p., [1907]), 31; *American Patriot*, May 1913, 11.

20. Sponsors of such legislation in the 59th Congress were all Southerners and predominantly new to Congress. B. Humphreys entered the 58th Congress (1903)

and served to 1923; Sydney Bowie (Alabama) entered the 57th Congress (1901) and served to 1907; John S. Little (Arkansas) entered the 54th Congress (1894) and served to 1907; Frank Clark (Florida) entered the 59th Congress (1905) and served to 1925. *Cong. Rec.*, 59th Cong. 1st sess., 200, 292, 309, 420, 481.

21. Ibid., 1307.

22. Ibid., 309, 481, 1306–8, 1309, 2861, 2863, 2914, 6346–48; Representative Clayton also proposed substituting a complete ban on issuing tax receipts in dry areas.

23. Ibid., 2913, 6348, 2862, 2914, 1309, 8307.

24. *American Issue*, August 3, 1906, 7, August 31, 1906, 6; June 1, 1906, 13; *Union Signal*, March 7, 1906, 3, July 12, 1906, 1, September 5, 1906, 5; National WCTU, *Convention Minutes* 33 ([1906]): 112, 36 ([1909]): 111.

25. Alabama Code (1907), 3:775; Florida Session Laws (1907), 201; Georgia Session Laws (1915), 85; Iowa Session Laws (1911), 104; Kansas Code (1915), 1097; Louisiana Code (1915), 1497; Oregon Session Laws (1915), 170; South Dakota Session Laws (1917), 537; Tennessee Session Laws (1909), 1366–67; Texas Criminal Code (1916), 321; Utah Session Laws (1911), 164; Virginia Session Laws (1910), 303; *State v. Wilson*, 137 *Louisiana* (1915) 19, and *State v. Wilson*, 141 *Louisiana* (1917) 404; Oklahoma, on the other hand, accepted a deputy collector's certification. *Billingsley v. State*, 4 *Oklahoma Circuit* (1910) 597; *People v. Barton*, 147 *Illinois Appeal* (1909) 185; *State v. Schaeffer*, 74 *Kansas* (1906) 390; *State v. Dowdy*, 145 *North Carolina* (1907) 432; *Hargrove v. State*, 8 *Oklahoma Circuit* (1910) 487; *Peyton v. State*, 83 *Arkansas* (1907) 102. By law, South Carolina took evidence from anyone who read the posted list of special taxpayers; South Carolina Code (1912), 2:148.

26. A federal Internal Revenue Office circular (No. 716), issued in 1907 and entitled "Revenue Officers to Cooperate with State Officers in the Suppression of Certain Violations of Law," probably set out the department's guidelines for cooperation under the 1906 act. Unfortunately, this circular—like many others—is missing from the Collections of Circulars in the Treasury Department records, NA58.

27. Examples of the practice and courts' insistence on the explanations are *People v. Barton*, 147 *Illinois Appeals* (1909) 185, and *State v. O'Connell*, 82 *Maine* (1889) 30. The facts of the Georgia example and the commissioner's letter are quoted in *Opinions of Attorney Generals* 28 (1909–11): 561–63.

28. *Union Signal*, February 10, 1910, 2.

29. *Union Signal*, March 3, 1910, 2, April 7, 1910, 2; National WCTU, *Convention Minutes* 37 ([1910]): 8, 63; *American Issue*, April 1910, 2; Robert Smith Bader, *Prohibition in Kansas: A History* (Lawrence: University Press of Kansas, 1986), 181.

30. *American Issue*, December 4, 1915, 1, July 1912, 11, September 25, 1915, 8.

31. *Beverage Trade News*, November 12, 1909, 6; *American Issue*, January 1910, 6, reprinted a liquor paper's words. In 1918 the U.S. Post Office solicitor ruled that the Reed Amendment ban on liquor advertising in dry territory did not apply to federal government ads for liquor auctions. *New York Times*, January 24, 1918, 16.

32. *New Voice*, June 21, 1906, 6, 7; *Union Signal*, March 7, 1907, 5, September 5, 1907, 5.

33. *Atlanta Constitution*, September 24, 1909, 2, September 25, 1909, 2; *New York Times*, September 26, 1909, 15. Why the prosecutor desired Stegal's testimony before the grand jury remains unclear. Perhaps a grand jury confrontation was the only way to bring the facts to official notice, as owner George E. Cureton was a "political quantity in North Georgia." *Atlanta Constitution*, September 30, 1909, 10; September 26, 1909, 4, September 28, 1909 1–2, September 29, 1909, 1, September 30, 1909, 10; *New York Times*, September 28, 1909, 4, September 29, 1909, 16. Stegal and the sheriff of Dade County were friends. See *Atlanta Constitution*, September 28, 1909, 2, October 2, 1909, 5, September 30, 1909, 10; on the other hand, relations between local officials and revenuers in the mountain South were often bad. See Wilbur R. Miller, *Revenuers and Moonshiners: Enforcing Federal Liquor Law in the Mountain South, 1865–1900* (Chapel Hill: University of North Carolina Press, 1991), 107–17, 171, 179.

34. *Union Signal*, December 19, 1901, 3, August 15, 1907, 4; E. J. Richardson, "Report" (September 1910), VASLP; *American Issue*, January 1910, 5–6; *SEAP*, 1084.

35. George B. Safford to Hobson, July 19, 1914, box 1, RPHP; *Alabama Citizen*, May 1908, 2. The editorial comment that attended Cabell's statement attacked him, disagreed with his conclusions, and assaulted the policies that the Anti-Saloon League had long endorsed. The commentary was directed toward advocating the passage of an interstate commerce bill, and its writer seemed quite unfamiliar with the liquor tax issues. The commentary also reflected Cabell's wet views. He opposed state prohibition; as commissioner, he refused to open tax files to drys beyond what was mandated by the 1906 act, and he used his position to gather information to argue against prohibition. *American Issue*, February 1911, 10; R. E. Cabell to editor, January 24, 1912, quoted in House Judiciary Committee, *Hearings on Interstate Traffic in Intoxicating Liquors*, 62d Cong., 2d sess., 76; Cabell, "No Decrease in Consumption," *National Liberty Herald*, June 1914, 5; Robert A. Hohner, "Prohibition Comes to Virginia," *Virginia Magazine of History and Biography* 75 (1967): 473–88, 477.

36. *American Issue*, July 24, 1915, 9, 11; Hobson to Wilson, September 30, 1914, Cherrington to Cannon, March 26, 1915, box 2, RPHP.

37. Bryan to Webb, April 19, 1916, December 20, 1916, Lusk to Webb, January 9, 1914, EYWP; National WCTU, *Convention Minutes* 43 ([1916]): 129–30, 131; various drys supported this view; see Harry Hayward to Hobson, January 7, 1915, box 2, RPHP.

CHAPTER 6. INTERSTATE COMMERCE, PRAGMATIC PRAGMATISTS, AND FEDERAL POWER

1. 170 *United States Reports* (1899) 412–38, 413, 414.

2. Ibid., 421, 426, 425, 422. Chief Justice Fuller and Justices Brewer, Shiras, Peckham, and McKenna, along with White, formed the majority.

3. Ibid., 438–68, 455, 456. There was a different majority in *Vance* as Justices

Harlan, Gray, Brewer, Brown, and Peckham joined White. In an earlier case, *Scott v. Donald*, the U.S. Supreme Court, in an 8–0 decision, ruled the whole dispensary law an unconstitutional barrier to commerce. This ruling implied that the Wilson Act did not apply to dispensary laws. The dissent in *Vance*, written by Justice Shiras for Justice McKenna and Chief Justice Fuller, again asserted this point. 165 *United States Reports* (1897) 58–107, 93, 101; 170 *United States Reports* (1898) 457.

4. 170 *United States Reports* (1898) 424, 452, 461–62. The dissenters in *Vance* saw no such distinction between shipments for use and shipments for sale.

5. 196 *United States Reports* (1905) 133–46, 147–48, 143, 146; only Justice Harlan dissented.

6. *American Issue*, July 1900, 9, May 1908, 12, August 8, 1902, 4, 7, February 1, 1901, 6; *Union Signal*, April 11, 1901, 9, January 12, 1905, 3; *Florida Times Union* (Jacksonville), April 2, 1907, 12; *Beverage Trade News*, November 26, 1904, 7; Anheuser-Busch circular, box 4, RPHP; Crafts to Kebler, December 19, 1911, box 3, EYWP; David Fogarty, "From Saloon to Supermarket: Packaged Beer and the Reshaping of the United States Brewing Industry," *Contemporary Drug Problems* 12 (Winter 1985): 556. Moreover, the rise of local option prohibition with few limitations on liquor shipping rights probably promoted some division within the brewing industry. For instance, Fogarty (557–60) shows that, in the vicinity of the southern, dry parts of California in 1911 and 1912, brewers bottled most of their beer, while in the wet San Francisco area the brewers relied on direct distribution through saloons. And as bottling was expensive, the southern brewers tended to be larger and more mechanized. His evidence suggests that a similar trend occurred across the nation.

7. *American Issue*, July 1900, 9, February 1, 1901, 6, January 2, 1902, 6, July 24, 1903, 3, February 12, 1904, 6, March 3, 1905, 11, September 27, 1907, 5, September 4, 1915, 7; *Union Signal*, January 12, 1905, 3; transcript, *American Express Co. v. Kentucky*, October Term 1906, File 20548, NA267.

8. *American Issue*, March 8, 1901, 3, May 1908, 12, January 1911, 8; *Beverage Trade News*, December 24, 1909, 13, 19; Robert Smith Bader, *Prohibition in Kansas: A History* (Lawrence: University Press of Kansas, 1986), 184.

9. *American Issue*, March 8, 1907, 9, May 3, 1907, 10; *Union Signal*, August 16, 1906, 2, 14, May 2, 1907, 12, May 16, 1907, 2, 14.

10. *New Voice*, January 12, 1905, 5.

11. *American Issue*, July 4, 1902, 1; Clarkson to Webb, December 23, 1909, Davis to Webb, May 18, 1910, box 2, EYWP; Norman Clark, *Deliver Us from Evil: An Interpretation of American Prohibition* (New York: W. W. Norton, 1976), 125.

12. *American Issue*, January 25, 1907, 11; *New Voice*, May 18, 1903, 1; Alabama Session Laws (1907), 488; Arkansas Session Laws (1891), 90; Florida Session Laws (1901), 62; Georgia Session Laws (1893), 115, (1897), 39; Iowa Session Laws (1888), 106, (1900), 59; Kentucky Session Laws (1902), 41–43, (1906), 321; Louisiana Session Laws (1906), 61; Massachusetts Session Laws (1903), 487, (1907), 517; Mississippi Session Laws (1906), 103–4; Nebraska Session Laws (1907), 294–30; North Carolina Session Laws (1905), 628–34; North Dakota Session Laws (1890), 327; Ohio Session

Laws (1906), 15–16; South Carolina Session Laws (1901), 706; West Virginia Session Laws (1903); 130–31; Bader, *Kansas*, 179–80.

13. Kentucky Code (1915), 1315. This law was passed to reverse *James v. Commonwealth*, 102 *Kentucky* (1897) 108, which held that the sale takes place in the county where the goods are delivered to the carrier. *American Issue*, February 12, 1904, 6; *Union Signal*, December 31, 1903, 1, 14.

14. *Union Signal*, December 21, 1905, 15, August 7, 1902, 1, November 6, 1902, 2, May 22, 1902, 1, January 21, 1904, 2, March 9, 1905, 14; *New Voice* May 22, 1902, 1; *American Issue*, July 4, 1902, 1, December 1902, 7, February 12, 1904, 7, December 16, 1904, 6; 196 *United States Reports* (1905) 133, 146, 143; *Heyman v. Southern Railway Co.*, 203 *United States Reports* (1906) 270–78, 276.

15. *American Issue*, June 19, 1903, 6, September 18, 1903, 3, September 25, 1903, 3, December 11, 1903, 3, January 21, 1904, 2, February 12, 1904, 6, April 12, 1907, 12, April 19, 1907, 14, January 26, 1906, 4; *Union Signal*, December 31, 1903, 1, 14; clipping enclosed in Theodore Alvord to Reverend J. W. West, February 12, 1904, VASLP.

16. *American Issue*, January 5, 1904, 4, April 1900, 16, November 9, 1900, 5, January 2, 1902, 6, July 24, 1903, 3, November 13, 1903, 8, February 19, 1904, 5, January 1909, 5, August 2, 1907, 3; see also Crafts to William, Southern Express Co., May 20, 1913, box 4, EYWP.

17. *American Issue*, May 11, 1906, 11, June 1, 1907, 10, July 6, 1906, 2, August 17, 1906, 4, April 5, 1907, 5, May 17, 1907, 14; *Union Signal*, May 9, 1905, 3, February 21, 1907, 4, May 16, 1907, 14; Crafts to Webb, May 20, 1913, box 4, EYWP; J. H. Gambrell, "Are Texas Railroads Friendly to Saloons?," *Home and State*, February 15, 1915, 7.

18. 206 *United States Reports* (1907) 129–41, 129, 131, 133, 141. See also USBA, *Yearbook* (New York: USBA, 1908); 214 *United States Reports* (1908) 218–23.

19. 205 *United States Reports* (1907) 93–104, 100–102; 120 *United States Reports* (1887) 489. Only Chief Justice Fuller dissented.

20. Alabama Code (1907), 772: *Union Signal*, September 12, 1907, 3–4, May 6, 1909, 3; Mississippi Session Laws (1908), 115; Mississippi Code (1915), 1137. For a full statement of one state's laws concerning liquor shipping, see Heriot Clarkson, *The Liquor Laws of North Carolina* (Raleigh: Mutual Publishing, 1909), 8–18, 25.

21. *F. W. Cook Brewing Co. v. Gardner*, 168 *Federal Reporter* (1909) 942; *Union Signal*, January 29, 1910, 13; *L. Crodock and Co. v. Wells Fargo*, 125 *Southwest Reporter* (1910) 59; USBA, *Yearbook* (New York: USBA, 1909), 55–62; *Commonwealth v. McKinney*, 131 *Southwest Reporter* (1910) 766; *Yearbook of the Anti-Saloon League* (Westerville, Ohio: ASL Publishing, 1908), 99–107; *Union Signal*, September 19, 1907, 8.

22. *Union Signal*, March 26, 1908, 2, February 1909, 2, 3, March 31, 1910, 13; *American Issue*, March 15, 1907, 13, May 1908, 15; USBA, *Yearbook* (1909), 63.

23. 233 *United States Reports* (1912) 70–84, 82; *American Issue*, June 21, 1907, 7, December 28, 1908, 14.

24. Robert E. Cushman, "The National Police Power under the Commerce Clause of the Constitution," *Minnesota Law Review* 3 (April 1919): 289–319, 3 (May 1919): 381–412, 3 (June 1919): 452–83, Cushman, "The National Police Power under the Taxing Power of the Constitution," *Minnesota Law Review* 4 (March 1920): 247–28, Cushman, "The National Police Power under the Postal Clause," *Minnesota Law Review* 4 (May 1920): 402–40; Dorothy G. Fowler, *Unmailable: Congress and the Post Office* (Athens: University of Georgia Press, 1977), 104, 126–27; R. Alton Lee, "The Eradication of Phossy Jaw: A Unique Development of Federal Police Power," *Historian* 29 (November 1966): 1–21.

25. Stephen B. Wood, *Constitutional Politics in the Progressive Era: Child Labor and the Law* (Chicago: University of Chicago Press, 1968), 28.

26. This account of the development of child labor reform is based on Wood, *Constitutional Politics*, 2, 4, 6, 10, 12, 13–16, 17–25; see also Elizabeth H. Davidson, *Child Labor Legislation in the Southern Textile States* (Chapel Hill: University of North Carolina Press, 1939); Raymond G. Fuller, *Child Labor and the Constitution* (New York: Thomas Y. Crowell Co., 1929), especially 236–85; Jeremy P. Felt, *Hostages of Fortune: Child Labor Reform in New York State* (Syracuse, N.Y.: Syracuse University Press, 1965); Walter I. Trattner, *Crusade for the Children* (Chicago: Quadrangle Books, 1970), 21–142, 163–86; and Thomas G. Karis, "Congressional Behavior at Constitutional Frontiers: From the 1906 Beveridge Child Labor Bill to the 1938 Fair Labor Standards Act" (Ph.D. diss., Columbia University, 1951). Arden J. Lea, "Cotton Textiles and the Federal Child Labor Act of 1916," *Labor History* 16 (1975): 485–94, presents the contrary view that industry seeking to rationalize costs was the driving force behind the movement to end child labor.

27. Wood, *Constitutional Politics*, 26–82, 154–59; *Hammer v. Dagenhart*, 247 *United States* (1918) 251.

28. Wood, *Constitutional Politics*, 186–97, 203–6; 259 *United States* 20; Charles A. Lofgren, *"Government from Reflection and Choice": Constitutional Essays on War, Foreign Relations, and Federalism* (New York: Oxford University Press, 1986), 161.

29. This account of the use of the treaty power is derived from Lofgren, *"Government,"* 116–66.

30. Lacey Act, 31 *Statutes at Large* 188; see Morton Keller, *Regulating a New Economy: Public Policy and Economic Change in America, 1900–1933* (Cambridge, Mass.: Harvard University Press, 1990), 166–67.

31. 252 *United States* (1920) 416.

32. R. Alton Lee, *A History of Regulatory Taxation* (Lexington: University Press of Kentucky, 1973), 95.

33. This account is derived from John Braeman, "The Square Deal in Action: A Case Study in the Growth of the 'National Police Power,'" *Change and Continuity in Twentieth Century America*, ed. John Braeman et al. (Columbus: Ohio State University Press, 1964), 35–80; Oscar Edward Anderson, *The Health of the Nation: Harvey W. Wiley and the Fight for Pure Food* (Chicago: University of Chicago Press, 1958); David M. Moyers, "From Quackery to Qualification: Arkansas Medical and Drug

Legislation, 1881–1909," *Arkansas Historical Quarterly* 35 (1976): 3–26; Margaret R. Wolfe, *Lucius Polk Brown and Progressive Food and Drug Control: Tennessee and New York City, 1908–1920* (Lawrence: Regents Press of Kansas, 1978); Gabriel Kolko, *The Triumph of Conservatism: A Reinterpretation of American History, 1900–1916* (New York: Free Press, 1963); Jack High and Clayton A. Coppin, "Wiley and the Whiskey Industry: Strategic Behavior in the Passage of the Pure Food Act," *Business History Review* 62 (Summer 1988): 286–309; James Harvey Young, *Pure Food: Securing the Federal Food and Drug Act of 1906* (Princeton, N.J.: Princeton University Press, 1989); James Harvey Young, *The Toadstool Millionaires: A Social History of Patent Medicines in American before Federal Regulation* Princeton, N.J.: Princeton University Press, 1961), 226–44; James Harvey Young, *The Medical Messiahs: A Social History of Health Quackery in Twentieth-Century America* (Princeton, N.J.: Princeton University Press, 1967), 3–65; Robert M. Crunden, *Ministers of Reform: The Progressives' Achievement in American Civilization, 1889–1920* (Urbana: University of Illinois Press, 1984), 164–99, 185 (source of "chemical fundamentalism"); Peter Temin, *Taking Your Medicine* (Cambridge, Mass.: Harvard University Press, 1980), 18–37; Richard C. Litman and Donald S. Litman, "Protection of the American Consumer: The Muckrakers and the Enactment of the First Federal Food and Drug Law in the United States," *Food and Drug Cosmetic Law Journal* 36 (December 1981): 647–68; Donna J. Wood, *Strategic Uses of Public Policy* (Pittsburgh, Penn.: University of Pittsburgh Press, 1986); Richard J. Fiesta, "Food and Federalism" (paper presented at the annual meeting of the Organization of American Historians, Philadelphia, April 2–5, 1987).

34. D'Ann Campbell, "Judge Ben Lindsey and the Juvenile Court Movement 1901–1904," *Arizona and the West* 18 (1976): 5–20; David J. Rothman, *Conscience and Convenience: The Asylum and Its Alternatives in Progressive America* (Boston: Little Brown, 1980), 205–35; M. Nelson McGeary, *Gifford Pinchot, Forester-Politican* (Princeton, N.J.: Princeton University Press, 1960); James Penick Jr., *Progressive Politics and Conservation: The Ballinger-Pinchot Affair* (Chicago: University of Chicago Press, 1968); Harold T. Pinkett, *Gifford Pinchot, Private and Public Forester* (Urbana: University of Illinois Press, 1970); Samuel P. Hays, *Conservation and the Gospel of Efficiency: The Progressive Conservation Movement, 1890–1920* (New York: Antheneum, 1980).

35. This sketch of the antiprostitution movement and the Mann Act is based on Barbara Meil Hobson, *Uneasy Virtue: The Politics of Prostitution and the American Reform Tradition* (New York: Basic Books, 1987); Ruth Rosen, *The Lost Sisterhood: Prostitution in America, 1900–1918* (Baltimore: The Johns Hopkins University Press, 1982); Mark T. Connelly, *The Response to Prostitution in the Progressive Era* (Chapel Hill: University of North Carolina Press, 1980); John C. Burnham, "Medical Inspection of Prostitutes in America in the Nineteenth Century: The St. Louis Experiment and Its Sequel," *Bulletin of the History of Medicine* 45 (1971): 203–18; John C. Burnham, "The Social Evil Ordinance: A Social Experiment in Nineteenth-Century St.

Louis," *Bulletin of the Missouri Historical Society* 27 (1971): 203–17; Neil Shumsky, "Vice Responds to Reform," *Journal of Urban History* 7 (November 1980): 31–47; Elizabeth C. MacPhail, "When the Red Lights Went Out in San Diego: The Little Known Story of San Diego's 'Restricted' District," *Journal of San Diego History* 20 (1975): 1–28; Eric Anderson, "Prostitution and Social Justice: Chicago, 1910–1915," *Social Service Review* 48 (1974): 203–28; Roy Lubove, "The Progressives and the Prostitute," *Historian* 24 (1962): 308–30; Paul A. Hass, "Sin in Wisconsin: The Teasdale Vice Committee of 1913," *Wisconsin Magazine of History* 49 (1966): 138–51; James R. McGovern, " 'Sporting Life on the Line': Prostitution in Progressive Era Pensacola," *Florida Historical Quarterly* 54 (1975): 131–44.

36. Rosen, *Lost Sisterhood*, 112–35, argues that white slavery was more than a myth. Hobson, *Uneasy Virtue*, makes the point that in effect regulatory and prohibitory solutions to prostitution functioned in the same way.

37. E. Parmalee Prentice, *The Federal Power of Carriers and Corporations* (New York: Macmillan, 1907), vi; for his life, see *New York Times*, April 13, 1900, 1, March 14, 1906, 1, December 17, 1955, 23; Arthur M. Johnson, *Winthrop W. Aldrich* (Boston: Harvard University Press, 1968), 45–49; *New York Times*, February 9, 1907, 84.

38. Prentice, *The Federal Power*, vi–viii, 22, 24, 29, 30, 32, 68–69; Prentice, "Federal Common Law and Interstate Carriers," *Columbia Law Review* 9 (May 1909): 375–96.

39. John R. Kemp, ed., *Martin Behrman of New Orleans: Memoirs of a City Boss* (Baton Rouge: Louisiana State University Press, 1977), 163; for the arguments against the child labor bill, see Wood, *Constitutional Politics*, 49–55, 58–62.

40. Wood, *Constitutional Politics*, 14–17, 28–38, 62–64; John Braeman, *Albert J. Beveridge: American Nationalist* (Chicago: University of Chicago Press, 1971), 112–21; Claude G. Bowers, *Beveridge and the Progressive Era* (New York: Literary Guild, 1932), 250–55, 264–66.

41. George Wickersham, "State Control of Foreign Corporations," *Yale Law Journal* 19 (November 1909): 1–16, 12, 13, 15; Wichersham, "Government Control of Corporations," *Columbia Law Review* 18 (March 1918): 187–207, 206; Wichersham, "Federal Control of Interstate Commerce," *Harvard Law Review* 23 (February 1910): 241–59, 241–42, 244; Wickersham, "The Police Power: A Product of the Rule of Reason," *Harvard Law Review* 27 (February 1914): 297–316. Comparing Prentice's, Beveridge's, and Wickersham's explications of *Gibbons v. Ogden* gives a good impression on how various progressive-era lawyers tended to read precedents to suit their own theories; see Albert J. Beveridge, *The Life of John Marshall* (Boston: Houghton Mifflin Co., 1919), 4:397–461; Wickersham, "Federal Control of Interstate Commerce," 241–43; Prentice, *The Federal Power*, 68–69; on the movement to give the central government regulatory powers over corporations through an incorporation law, see Melvin I. Urofsky, "Proposed Federal Incorporation in the Progressive Era," *American Journal of Legal History* 26 (1982): 160–83; Keller, *Regulating*, 26.

42. *College Patriot*, March 15, 1904, 55–56.

CHAPTER 7. COMMERCE, PRAGMATIC PROHIBITIONISTS, AND CONGRESS

1. Other scholars who have explored the temperance campaign for national legislation have slighted the legal dimensions of the process. See K. Austin Kerr, *Organized for Prohibition: A New History of the Anti-Saloon League* (New Haven, Yale University Press, 1985), 127–38; Peter Odegard, *Pressure Politics: The Story of the Anti-Saloon League* (New York: Columbia University Press, 1928), 126–34; James H. Timberlake, *Prohibition and the Progressive Movement, 1900–1920* (Cambridge, Mass.: Harvard University Press, 1963), 159–61. For a brief temperance history of the court decisions, their effects, and laws, see Wilbur Crafts, "History of Interstate Liquor Legislation," Undated Papers 1911, EYWP.

2. *SEAP*, 906; *Union Signal*, April 24, 1902, 5, December 1903, 2, February 5, 1903, 3, December 24, 1903, 2; Ellis to Mrs. Zelda Hobson, June 22, 1914, box 1, RPHP.

3. Kerr, *Organized*, 127–38; *American Patriot*, May 1913, 11–13; *SEAP*, 727–28, 806–9, *DATB*, 112–13, 138–39; *American Issue*, February 13, 1903, 6, February 27, 1903, 1, February 6, 1903, 1, February 29, 1903, 1, December 25, 1903, 1; Dinwiddie to Webb, August 9, 1915, EYWP; *Union Signal*, January 29, 1903, 2, February 19, 1903, 2; *New Voice*, March 12, 1903, 1.

4. Davis to Webb, April 11, 1911, Davis to Webb, February 5, 1909, March 18, 1910, May 18, 1920, Davis to Webb, May 29, 1912; Weakley to Webb, April 20, 1915, May 10, 1915, July 15, 1915; Webb to Weakley July 21, 1915, September 29, 1915, EYWP.

5. Cherrington to James Cannon, October 18, 1915, Cherrington Papers, TPP, ser. xiii; Dinwiddie to Hobson, October 13, 1915, Hobson to Dinwiddie, October 20, 1915, box 2, Stevens to Mrs. Hobson, February 16, 1914, box 52, Dinwiddie to Hobson (telegram), December 7, 1915, box 3, Ellis to Hobson, January 26, 1915, box 4, RPHP; Dinwiddie to Webb, November 18, 1912, Ellis to Webb, May 28, 1914, Davis to Webb, March 18, 1914, EYWP; Wheeler to Volstead, January 3, 1922, box 2, Gordon to Volstead, August 25, 1922, box 3, AJVP. After his defeat in the Senate race, Hobson's father-in-law advised him to maintain some autonomy from the league; see George Hull to Hobson, July 10, 1916, box 57, RPHP. Hobson tried to do this by trying to create his own temperance organization; see various letters in box 126, RPHP. The relationship between the league and Andrew Volstead was close; see Secretary to Wheeler, September 23, 1920, Dinwiddie to Volstead, October 25, 1920, Wheeler to Rudd, October 22, 1920, Secretary to Wheeler (telegram), October 14, 1920, Secretary to Wheeler (telegram), October 19, 1920, Volstead to Hinshaw, October 20, 1920, box 1, AJVP.

6. National WCTU, *Convention Minutes* 23 (1896): 36; *Union Signal*, April 1, 1897, 1, December 16, 1897, 4, February 24, 1898, 9, March 23, 1899, 4, June 14, 1900, 9; *American Issue*, May 15, 1903, 10; Timberlake, *Prohibition and Progressive*, 159; Odegard, *Pressure*, 129–30; Ernest Cherrington, *Evolution of Prohibition in the United States of America* (Westerville, Ohio: American Issue Press, 1920), 268–73.

7. The ruling in *Scott v. Donald*, 165 *United States Reports* (1897) 58, gave Tillman this idea; see also 80 *Federal Reporter* (1897) 786; *Cong. Rec.*, 55th Cong., 1st sess., 40, 1405, 1473, 2612, 2622, 55th Cong., 2d sess., 671; *Union Signal*, February 18, 1897, 1; Crafts to Webb, February 9, 1912, EYWP.

8. *American Issue*, February 13, 1903, 1, June 19, 1903, 6; *Union Signal*, January 29, 1903, 2; *College Patriot*, March 15, 1904, 55; House of Representatives, *Report 3377*, January 26, 1903, 57th Cong., 2d sess.; hearing partially reprinted in USBA, *Convention Report* 43 (1903): 34–45; *New Voice*, March 12, 1903, 1, 13; see also *Addresses at Omnipartisan State Temperance Convention* (Indianapolis: Indiana ASL, [1911]), 41–46, 65.

9. Henry S. Boutell, "A Congressman Denounces Prohibition" (address at Fiftieth Annual Convention of USBA, June 8, 1910), 3.

10. USBA, *Convention Report* 43 (1903): 35–40; 170 *United States Reports* (1898) 440; 165 *United States Reports* (1897) 58–107; German American State Alliance to Webb and Sloan to Webb, 1911, Stark to Davis, April 15, 1912, EYWP.

11. USBA, *Convention Reports* 43 (1903): 40, 44 (1904): 15, 33–37, 45 (1905): 30–31, 47 (1907): 41; *American Issue*, November 6, 1903, 1.

12. *American Issue*, March 9, 1906, 3.

13. *New Voice*, September 24, 2903, 1; *American Issue*, April 8, 1904, 9; Dinwiddie, "To Our Temperance Friend" and "To the Editor" (March 8, 1906), VASLP; Webb to Davis, February 12, 1908, Davis to Webb, February 8, 1908, EYWP.

14. *American Issue*, March 8, 1907, 6–7; *Union Signal*, July 16, 1903, 2, February 18, 1909, 3, 13, December 16, 1909, 1–2, January 20, 1910, 2, January 27, 1910, 2, May 19, 1910, 1, July 21, 1910, 8, August 4, 1910, 3; John Marshall, *Interstate Commerce in Intoxicating Liquors*, address at National Woman's Christian Temperance Union Convention, 1909 (Topeka: Kansas State Temperance Union, n.d.); Crafts to Webb, February 9, 1912, EYWP.

15. *American Issue*, February 2, 1906, 2, *Union Signal*, January 18, 1906, 3, May 14, 1908, 1–3.

16. Dinwiddie, "To Superintendents" (February 6, 1909), 2, and attached bill, VASLP; *Union Signal*, April 1, 1909, 2, June 3, 1909, 2; Charles M. Hogan, "Wayne B. Wheeler: Single Issue Exponent" (Ph.D. diss., University of Cincinnati, 1986), 90–91.

17. *American Issue*, July 7, 1905, 10, August 3, 1906, 10–11; *Union Signal*, January 28, 1904, 2, February 5, 1904, 1, February 11, 1904, 1, December 20, 1906, 2, March 12, 1908, 3; J. W. West to Campbell Slemp, August 29, 1904, Slemp to West, September 2, 1904, C. C. Carlin to Reverend R. H. Bennet, April 18, 1907, William Anderson, "To Superintendents" (January 20, 1909), VASLP; R. L. Davis to Webb, February 5, 1909, EYWP; Kerr, *Organized*, 158–59.

18. Kerr, *Organized*, 129–32; Odegard, *Pressure*, 127–29, 134–39; Blair Bolles, *Tyrant from Illinois* (New York: W. W. Norton, 1951), 111–13; George A. Pearre (Republican, Maryland) to Albert E. Shoemaker, Anti-Saloon League District of

Columbia Attorney, September 17, 1909, TPP, ser. vi; *American Issue*, August 1908, 4, June 1908, 4, May 1908, 5, April 5, 1907, 5; *Union Signal*, September 17, 1908, 4, December 17, 1903, 2, March 25, 1909, 3 March 24, 1910, 2.

19. USBA, *Convention Report* 49 (1909): 36; Kerr, *Organized*, 128, 133; Odegard, *Pressure*, 129; *American Issue*, March 1909, 6, May 1909, 22.

20. *American Issue*, March 1909, 6, May 1909, 22; Anderson, "To Superintendents" (February 6, 1909), VASLP.

21. Virginia Session Laws (1910), 307; Oklahoma Session Laws (1911), 158; Tennessee Session Laws (1909), 633; New Hampshire Supplement to Code (1914), 253; California Session Laws (1909), 3247; Utah Session Laws (1911), 164. This law allowed delivery only to private homes. On league support, see *New York Times*, September 2, 1909, 5; J. A. Robinson, "To All Superintendents" (May 8, 1909), W. J. Nelson to Reverend J. D. McAllister, May 17, 1911, Dunning to McAllister, September 2, 1909, William Anderson to McAllister, September 17, 1909, VASLP.

22. *American Issue*, May 1909, 22–23; *Union Signal*, January 29, 1910, 2, February 25, 1909, 2, March 4, 1909, 3, February 3, 1910, 4; *Beverage Trade News*, July 16, 1909, 5; Clarkson to Webb, December 23, 1909, EYWP.

23. *American Issue*, May 1909, 22–23. Dinwiddie shared the same ideas; see *American Issue*, January 1912, 10, December 1910, 6.

24. *American Issue*, February 1911, 8; *American Patriot*, April 1912, 17; *Union Signal*, June 27, 1912, 2; *New Republic*, January 3, 1913, 4.

25. While scholars have seen the importance of the Webb-Kenyon Act, many have misconstrued its nature. Andrew Sinclair, Joseph R. Gusfield, and K. Austin Kerr all captured the purpose of the act but failed to describe how the act worked. Norman Clark weakened his account by implying that its lack of "specific provisions for federal enforcement" made it a mere "noble" statement. Robert Bader erroneously argues that the act's questionable constitutionality "discouraged states from taking action." This error is even more egregious because, following the passage of the Webb-Kenyon Act, Kansas enacted a measure, the Mahin Law, to implement it. Timberlake, *Prohibition and Progressive*, 159; Odegard, *Pressure*, 139–48; Kerr, *Organized*, 137–38; Bader, *Kansas*, 183–85; Daniel R. Murrel, "Prelude to Prohibition: The Anti-Saloon League and the Webb-Kenyon Act of 1913" (master's thesis, University of Western Ontario, 1974); Joseph R. Gusfield, *Symbolic Crusade: Status Politics and the American Temperance Movement* (Urbana and Chicago: University of Illinois Press, 1963), 120; Norman Clark, *Deliver Us from Evil: An Interpretation of American Prohibition* (New York: W. W. Norton, 1976), 119.

26. Kerr, *Organized*, 136–37; *Beverage Trade News*, July 14, 1911, 2; *American Issue*, July 1910, 1, January 1912, 10, 11; *Union Signal*, December 28, 1911, 3, January 4, 1912, 3; Kirpatrick to Webb, July 13, 1911, H. Q. Alexander to Webb, April 23, 1912, EYWP.

27. House Committee on the Judiciary, *Hearings on the Interstate Traffic in Intoxicating Liquors*, 62d Cong., 2d sess. (1912), 1, 33, hereafter cited as House Committee *Hearings*; SEAP, 474–75; Jimmie Lewis Franklin, *Born Sober: Prohibition in Okla-*

homa, 1907–1959 (Norman: University of Oklahoma, 1971), 36–42; *American Issue*, January 1912, 10–11, February 1912, 4; *Union Signal*, December 28, 1911, 3, January 4, 1912, 3; *American Patriot*, December 1913, 72; *New Republic*, February 28, 1913, 3. Wheeler thought Webb-Kenyon was unconstitutional; see Justin Steuart, *Dry Boss: An Uncensored Biography of Wayne B. Wheeler* (New York: Fleming H. Revell, 1928), 81–83.

28. In Dinwiddie to Webb, October 31, 1911, EYWP. The league sent to Webb Caldwell's and Wheeler's view of legislation; Webb to Dinwiddie, November 4, 1912, Caldwell to Webb, July 31, 1912, EYWP; USBA, *Yearbook* (New York: USBA, 1912), 40; *Dallas Morning News*, February 11, 1913, 1; *American Issue*, August 1912, 11; *Union Signal*, February 29, 1913, 2, August 1, 1912, 2.

29. House Committee *Hearings*, 175–76. The fullest argument against Webb-Kenyon was John T. Beasley, *Brief: Concerning Proposed Legislation* (Terre Haute, Ind.: Viquesney Co., [1912]). On constitutional issues of Webb-Kenyon, see Lyndsy Rogers, "The Constitutionality of the Webb-Kenyon Bill," *California Law Review* 1 (September 1912): 499–512; Allen H. Kerr, "The Webb Act" (and accompanying note by G. E. Sherman), *Yale Law Journal* 22 (June 1913): 567–82; Winfred T. Denison, "States' Rights and the Webb-Kenyon Liquor Law," *Columbia Law Review* 14 (April 1914): 321–33. These works brought the liquor issues to the notice of the legal establishment, so much so that *Case and Comment* 20 (December 1913) was devoted entirely to liquor law, illustrated with pictures of Bacchanalian orgies.

30. *American Issue*, January 1912, 10, January 1913, 9; *American Patriot*, April 1913, 8, December 1913, 70–72; *Union Signal*, March 6, 1913, 3. For the Lacey Act, see 31 *Statutes at Large* 188. On January 22, 1912, the U.S. Supreme Court ruled on another case arising from the Kentucky 1906 COD law, *Louisville and Nashville RR Co. v. F. W. Cook Brewing Co.* This case was much discussed in the debates. The drys were able to prove that the case merely reiterated the rulings of previous cases. 223 *United States Reports* (1912) 70–84; *American Issue*, January 1912, 1; *Union Signal*, February 15, 1912, 2.

31. House Committee *Hearings*, 177 (Maxwell), 178 (Webb); *Rupert v. United States*, 181 *Federal Reporter* (1910) 87–91.

32. *American Patriot*, April 1913, 8; *New Republic*, January 3, 1913, 1; *Dallas Morning News*, February 11, 1913, 8; *Union Signal*, February 27, 1913, 1; Calderwood to Webb, April 15, 1913, EYWP.

33. Brown to Webb, February 1912, Larson to Webb, February 22, 1912, Webb to Webb, March 7, 1912, March 11, 1912, and March 21, 1912, see also Webb to West (misfiled), undated, 1911, EYWP.

34. House Committee *Hearings*, 24; *Cong. Rec.*, 62d Cong., 3d sess., 2793, 2787, 2792–94, 2806–7, 2793; Crafts to Webb, February 9, 1912, 3, Kirkpatrick to Webb, July 13, 1911, Davis to Webb, December 18, 1911, Dinwiddie to Mallory, enclosed in Dinwiddie to Webb, April 13, 1913, Webb to Moseley, May 28, 193, EYWP.

35. *Union Signal*, February 8, 1912, 1–2, February 22, 1912, 2, March 14, 1912, 2, December 5, 1912, 2, December 26, 1912, 2, 9; *American Issue*, January 11, 1912, 3,

January 18, 1912, 2, January 25, 1912, 2, 8, February 12, 1912, 7, March 7, 1912, 3, March 14, 1912, 8, March 21, 1912, 8, December 12, 1912, 2, December 19, 1912, 8, January 1913, 1, 6–7, February 1913, 3, 5, 11; *New Republic*, January 3, 1913, 4, January 17, 1913, 2, January 24, 1913, 1, February 2, 1913, 1, February 21, 1913, 1, March 21, 1; *Cong. Rec.*, 62d Cong., 3d sess., 2836, 2828, App. 68–69; William H. Harbaugh, *Lawyer's Lawyer: The Life of John W. Davis* (New York: Oxford University Press, 1973), 76.

36. *Cong. Rec.*, 62d Cong., 3d sess., 2838. In the House 64.3 percent of the members and 58.9 percent of the lame ducks voted for overriding the veto. This indicates the widespread support for the measure. Harbaugh, *Lawyer*, 77. Congressmen William Linthicum and Rucker are the other two House members besides Davis who talked one way and voted the other.

37. Kerr, *Organized*, 161–65, 173–84; House Committee *Hearings*, 42–45; *Union Signal*, February 21, 1913, 1; *American Issue*, February 1913, 4; *New Republic*, January 17, 1913, 1; T. M. Gilmore, *Harper's Weekly* 58 (July 19, 1913): 5; Timberlake, *Prohibition and Progressive*, 163. A typical pro-business senator opposing the bill was Sutherland of Utah; see *Cong. Rec.*, 62d Cong., 3d sess., 2903–11.

38. As there was no roll call on Webb-Kenyon in the Senate, support for the bill has been measured by counting those who voted for the Senate Judiciary Committee amended version on the grounds that senators believed that, if they passed it, they could later substitute House language; 37 *Statutes at Large* 699.

39. *Cong. Rec.*, 62d Cong., 3d sess., 2491–98.

40. *American Issue*, March 1913, 7, 10, 11, 15, May 1913, 6, 7; *New Republic*, March 7, 1913, 3, May 2, 1913, 1, 4; *Cong. Rec.*, 62d Cong., 3d sess., 4299, 4447; *Union Signal*, March 6, 1913, 2, 14; see also *New York Times*, March 7, 1913, 10.

41. *Cong. Rec.*, 63d Cong., 3d sess., 4291, 4292, 4296, 4444, 4435, 4438.

42. Ibid., 4434.

43. Ibid., 4291–99, 4433–48, 2809, 4334, 4443; *New York Times*, March 2, 1913, 6; *American Issue*, March 1913, 4; *American Patriot*, April 1913, 4; *Union Signal*, March 13, 1913, 8, February 27, 1913, 1; *New Republic*, February 28, 1913, 4.

44. For House and Senate votes, see *Cong. Rec.*, 62d Cong., 3d sess., 2922, 2924, 4299, 2866, 2867–68.

45. Dorothy G. Fowler, *Unmailable: Congress and the Post Office* (Athens: University of Georgia Press, 1977), 127, 135–37.

46. *American Issue*, March 1913, cover, 2; Odegard, *Pressure*, 148–62; Kerr, *Organized*, 138–59; Timberlake, *Prohibition and Progressive*, 165.

47. Mattingly and Co. to Webb, December 5, 1913, Webb to Mattingly and Co., December 11, 1913, Dinwiddie to Webb, January 24, 1914, with enclosures, Davis to Webb, January 26, 1914, Davis to Mebane, January 26, 1914, Brown to Webb, September 22, 1915, Webb to Brown, October 9, 1915, Webb to Dinwiddie, September 25, 1915, EYWP.

48. *Literary Digest*, 46 (April 12, 1913): 816; Virginia ASL, *Webb-Kenyon Act* (n.p.,

n.d.); *California Issue*, May 1913, 4. On the other hand, in Ashville, North Carolina, Wilbur Crafts discovered that the new law had not changed "the treatment of liquors" in interstate commerce; Crafts to Webb, May 20, 1913, EYWP; *New Republic*, June 19, 1913, 1, March 21, 1913, 1, July 11, 1–2, March 28, 1913, 1, April 11, 1913, 1, May 2, 1913, 2, May 16, 1913, 1 May 30, 1913, 1; *American Issue*, April 1913, 7; *Union Signal*, April 3, 1913, 9.

49. *American Issue*, September 4, 1915, 4, October 30, 1915, 2; *New York Times*, March 8, 1913, 1: *New Republic*, December 26, 1913, 4, July 11, 1913 1, 14; *American Issue* (Minnesota edition), May 1913, 12; Wells Fargo and Company Express, "Rules and Instructions," copy of company regulations provided by History Department, Wells Fargo Bank, San Francisco. How much of a revolution Webb-Kenyon worked in the states can be seen by comparing the reach of state authorities outlined in this paragraph with the rule in *Kirmeyer v. Kansas*, 236 *United States Reports* (1915) 568–73. This case came up on pre–Webb-Kenyon Act facts, and the Kansas transportation law was restricted from stopping liquor before it reached the consignee; see *Union Signal*, March 11, 1915, 8. The issue of whether new laws were needed was raised and settled in the affirmative in many states; see Bixby to Webb, June 30, 1913, Webb to Bixby, July 16, 1913, EYWP; West Virginia Code (1914), S. 1297, Act 1913, chap. 13 (February 1913). This law was passed before the Webb-Kenyon Act but was extended to all liquor shipments after the federal law went into effect; *American Issue*, July 1914, 4; *Union Signal*, March 18, 1915, 4.

50. 238 *United States Reports* (1914) 190–202, 199, 202; *New York Times*, March 19, 1913, 1; *American Issue*, May 1913, 10, April 3, 1915, 1; *New Republic*, May 9, 1913, 1. In his opinion McReynolds (201) quoted language of the Kentucky Court of Appeals, which argued that the state Bill of Rights protected citizens' right to own liquor, provided such owning did not directly injure society. This statement contributed to the idea that states could not prohibit the use of liquor. The author of this ruling, Judge John D. Carroll, sent a copy to Congressmen Webb. Webb replied, heaping praise on the opinion but demurring on the point that banning personal use was beyond the power of the states: "I do think that there are some states where such a state law would be held valid and the interstate law would apply." Webb to Carroll, August 1, 1913, Carroll to Webb, August 5, 1913, EYWP.

51. Texas Session Laws (1913), 125–26; USBA, *Yearbook* (New York: USBA, 1914), 24; Delaware Code (1917), 21–22; *Dallas Morning News*, October 2, 1912, 10, January 1, 1913, 13, February 8, 1913, 8, February 9, 1913, 13, February 21, 1913, 8, April 2, 1913, 1; Coman to Webb, January 23, 1914, EYWP. For a good example of how the league intended state laws to work under Webb-Kenyon, see George M. Brown and Elisha Baker, comps., *Laymen's Primer on the Oregon Dry Law* (Portland: Anti-Saloon League of Oregon, [1915?]), 6–7

52. Virginia ASL, *Webb-Kenyon Act*; *Literary Digest* 46 (April 12, 1913): 816–17; *New Republic*, May 30, 1913, 1, June 17, 1913, 1; Howard C. Joyce, "Legislative Regulation and Control of Intoxicating Liquors," *Case and Comment* 20 (December

1913): 443–47, 445, and *The Law Relating to Intoxicating Liquors* (Albany, N.Y.: Matthew Bender and Co., 1910), 104; *State v. Gilman*, 33 *West Virginia* 146; *American Issue*, July 24, 1915, 6.

53. North Carolina Session Laws (1913), 76; *New Republic*, April 18, 1913, 2; *American Issue*, May 15, 1915, 6; *American Issue* (Illinois edition), September 11, 1914, 3.

54. Arizona Session Laws (1917), 95–96; Arkansas Digest of Statues (1916), 1436–37; Colorado Session Laws (1915), 275–79; Delaware Session Laws (1917), 1925; Florida Session Laws (1913), 71–77; Georgia Session Laws (1915), 76–108; Idaho Session Laws (1917), 104; Iowa Session Laws (1915), 170–71; Kansas General Statutes (1915), 1100; Maine Session Laws (1917), 207; Michigan Session Laws (1913), 725; Mississippi Session Laws (1916), 118, 124; Montana Session Laws (1917), 250; Nebraska Session Laws (1917), 428–31; North Dakota Session Laws (1915), 294; Oregon Session Laws (1913), 489–91; South Carolina Session Laws (1917), 69; South Dakota Session Laws (1917), 488–519; Tennessee Session Laws (1913), 559–664; Texas Session Laws (1910), 33; Utah Session Laws (1913), 128–31; Virginia Session Laws (1916), 236–37; Washington Session Laws (1915), 10–11; West Virginia Session Laws (1913), 102–7. For dry support of such laws, see *American Issue*, August 1914, 6, May 15, 1915, 6, April 1913, 7, August 1913, 12, October 1913, 4, March 20, 1915, 5, 11, March 27, 1915, 1, April 3, 1915, 4, April 10, 1915, 4, May 22, 1915, 6–7, June 5, 1915, 4, July 24, 1915, 3, August 7, 1915, 3, August 21, 1915, 5, November 6, 1915, 3, November 29, 1915, 1, 7; *Union Signal*, April 30, 1914, 9, June 22, 1914, 2, September 9, 1914, 9, November 18, 1915, 2, December 1915, 2, December 23, 1915, 11, February 24, 1916, 9; *New Republic*, April 4, 1913, 1, April 25, 1913, 2, September 5, 1913, 1. The drys perfected these laws and exchanged them between states; see Picket to Webb, October 27, 1913, Weakley to Webb, April 20, 1915, Webb to Weakley, April 22, 1915, EYWP; Bader, *Kansas*, 183–84.

55. Dinwiddie to Webb, October 6, 1915, Dinwiddie to Webb, February 10, 1915, Webb to Bricket, October 15, 1913, EYWP. Fifteen states filed amici curia briefs; 242 *United States Reports* (1915) 311–32, 313–15; *Union Signal*, January 13, 1916, 9; *American Issue*, November 6, 1915, 3, May 22, 1915, 3, November 29, 1915, 1; Weakley to Webb, April 20, 1915, April 14, 1915, Webb to Weakley, April 30, 1915, Weakley to Webb, September 22, 1915, EYWP; Dinwiddie suggested that Congressmen Webb—without offending "against the proprieties"—send to Justice McReynolds a copy of Samuel Weakley's brief dealing with Webb-Kenyon and sustaining state laws before the Alabama courts, but Webb refused. Dinwiddie to Webb, May 12, 1915, and May 24, 1915, EYWP.

56. 242 *United States Reports* 320, 324–26. Justice McReynolds concurred, and Holmes and Van Devanter dissented without opinion. See Lyndsy Rogers, "Life Liberty and Liquor," *Virginia Law Review* 6 (December 1919): 156–81; Rogers, "The Webb-Kenyon Decision," *Virginia Law Review* 4 (1916–17): 558–70; Rogers, "Unlawful Possession of Intoxicating Liquors and the Webb-Kenyon Act," *Columbia Law Review* 16 (January 1916): 1–17; Rogers, "Power of the States over Com-

modities Excluded by Congress from Interstate Commerce," *Yale Law Journal* 24 (May 1915): 567–72; Clifton R. Snider, "Growth of State Power under Federal Constitution to Regulate Traffic in Intoxicating Liquors," *West Virginia Law Quarterly* 25 (November 1917): 42–55; Samuel P. Orth, "The Webb-Kenyon Law Decision," *Cornell Law Quarterly* 2 (1917): 283–98; Thomas Reed Powell, "Decisions of Supreme Court, 1914–1917," *American Political Science Review* 12 (1918): 18–22; see also Alexander M. Bickel and Benno C. Schmidt Jr., *The Judiciary and Responsible Government, 1910–1921,* Oliver Wendell Holmes Devise History of the Supreme Court (New York: Macmillan, 1987), 9:438–46.

57. USBA, *Yearbook* (New York: USBA, 1916), 312, 325; *Union Signal,* January 18, 1917, 2, January 25, 1917, 2–3; Robert Ritchie to Anti-Saloon League, January 12, 1917, E. J. Richardson to Ritchie, January 15, 1917, TPP, ser. vii; Wheeler to Webb, January 12, 1917, EYWP.

CHAPTER 8. A DRY NATION

1. Peter Odegard, *Pressure Politics: The Story of the Anti-Saloon League* (New York: Columbia University Press, 1928), 151; *American Issue,* March 1913, cover, 2, June 1913, 4, 5; *Union Signal,* March 26, 1914, 2; Ernest Cherrington, *Evolution of Prohibition in the United States* (Westerville, Ohio: American Issue Press, 1920), 321–24. Cherrington outlined the league's plans in *A New Plan of Campaign in the Interest of National Prohibition* (Westerville, Ohio: American Issue Publishing, [1913]) and *The National Prohibition Movement* (n.p., [1913]). The best accounts of the passage of the amendment and the Volstead Act are Odegard, *Pressure,* 149–80; K. Austin Kerr, *Organized for Prohibition: A New History of the Anti-Saloon League* (New Haven, Conn.: Yale University Press, 1985), 185–210, 222–26; Norman Clark, *Deliver Us from Evil: An Interpretation of American Prohibition* (New York: W. W. Norton, 1976), 118–39; Clement E. Vose, *Constitutional Change: Amendment Politics and Supreme Court Litigation since 1900* (Lexington, Ky.: Lexington Books, 1972); on the Wilson administration, see Lewis L. Gould, *Reform and Regulation: American Politics from Roosevelt to Wilson,* 2d ed. (New York: Knopf, 1986), 176–86.

2. Lewis L. Gould, *Progressives and Prohibitionists: Texas Democrats in the Wilson Era* (Austin: University of Texas Press, 1973), 94–95, 97; Erik N. Olssen, "Southern Senators and Reform: Issues in the 1920s: A Paradox Unravelled," in *The South Is Another Land,* ed. Bruce Clayton and John A. Salmond (Westport, Conn.: Greenwood Press, 1987), 50, 53.

3. *DATB,* 229–30, 441–43; *SEAP,* 1230–31, 2431; *New York Times,* June 12, 1914, 10, July 1, 1914, 10; *Cong. Rec.,* 63d Cong., 2d sess., 640, 739–40, 744; Richard N. Sheldon, "Richmond Pearson Hobson: The Military Hero as Reformer during the Progressive Era" (Ph.D. diss., University of Arizona, 1970), 195–228; "Viellard" [Hobson], "Choice in Hobsons," *Nation,* March 11, 1915, 286; Hobson to Wheeler, July 26, 1916, 1–2, box 2, RPHP.

4. *Union Signal,* May 21, 1914, 3, 4, 12, January 7, 1915, 5, *New Republic,* May 1,

1914, 4; *Cong. Rec.*, 63d Cong., 3d sess., 615–16; *American Patriot*, January 1914, 2; *SEAP*, 456, 1174; Cherrington to James Cannon, October 18, 1915, Cherrington Papers, TPP, ser. xiii.

5. *Cong. Rec.*, 63d Cong., 2d sess., 615.

6. William Anderson, "National Prohibition—What Form Should It Take?," *Outlook* 114 (December 27, 1916): 900; *SEAP*, 1174; *Union Signal*, May 21, 1914, 4, January 14, 1915, 5, December 2, 1915, 2; *New Republic*, May 1, 1914, 4.

7. *New York Times*, January 29, 1915, sec. 2, 10; *Baltimore Sun*, December 14, 1914.

8. Bailey to R. M. Johnston, December 18, 1917, 3, 4, 6, 7, JBP; *World*, quoted in *Baltimore Sun*, December 14, 1914; Trice clipping, "The Hobson Bill," enclosed in circular letter of Mercantile Protective Association of the State of Florida, May 9, 1914, box 18, RPHP..

9. House of Representatives, *Report 652*, 63d Cong., 2d sess., pt. 2, 1–7, *Report 1493*, 64th Cong., 2d sess., 1–7; *New York Times*, May 13, 1914, 16; *Cong. Rec.*, 63d Cong., 3d sess., 525.

10. *Cong. Rec.*, 63d Cong., 2d sess., 8507–8, 8931, *Cong. Rec.*, 63d Cong., 3d sess., 336, 613; *Union Signal*, January 7, 1915, 5.

11. *Cong. Rec.*, 63d Cong., 2d sess., 615, *Cong. Rec.*, 63d Cong., 3d sess., 513, 525; Stevens to Hobson, November 22, 1913, Hobson to Colleagues, May 28, 1914, box 1, RPHP; Hobson to Webb, May 28, 1914, EYWP.

12. *Cong. Rec.*, 63d Cong., 3d sess., 495, 498, 504, 510, 511, 519; see also Hobson to Colleagues, November 15, 1914, EYWP.

13. *Cong. Rec.*, 63d Cong., 3d sess., 611, App. 600; Val Peter, circular letter, December 19, 1914, box 2, Hobson to Dean, March 1, 1917, box 3, RPHP; Hobson to Webb, May 28, 1914, EYWP.

14. J. M. Gilmore to editor, *North American Review* 201 (March 1915): 463–65, 465; *Cong. Rec.*, 63d Cong., 2d sess., 745, *Cong. Rec.*, 63d Cong., 3d sess., App. 58–60, 61, 288–89; "The Folly of County Option," enclosed in Pelter to Hobson, January 15, 1916, box 2, RPHP.

15. *American Issue*, December 29, 1914, 12, 13; *Union Signal*, December 23, 1915, 3, 4; National WCTU, *Convention Minutes* 43 (1916): 128–30.

16. Elisabeth Tilton to editor, *Survey* 33 (February 13, 1915): 544, 545; *Cong. Rec.*, 63 Cong., 3d sess., App. 665–67, 612.

17. Idaho Session Laws (1915), 41–47; *American Issue*, April 3, 1915, 4, May 29, 1915, 6, June 12, 1915, 6.

18. George Gage to editor, *American Issue*, January 21, 1917, E. J. Richardson to Gage, January 27, 1917, TPP, ser. vii; *Union Signal*, February 1, 1917, 3, March 1, 1917, 3, 8, July 26, 1917, 15, August 16, 1917, 5, October 18, 1917, 15; Norman Clark, *The Dry Years: Prohibition and Social Change in Washington* (Seattle: University of Washington Press, 1965), 138–39; Jimmie Lee Franklin, *Born Sober: Prohibition in Oklahoma, 1907–1959* (Norman: University of Oklahoma Press, 1917), 65–69. For North Carolina, see Davis to Webb, January 5, 1914, Davis to Webb, October 14, 1915, Davis to Webb, February 15, 1916, February 25, 1916, "The Resolutions of the

Executive Committee of the N.C. Anti-Saloon League" (adopted January 29, 1914), enclosed in Davis to Webb, March 3, 1914, Poe to Davis, January 6, 1914, EYWP.

In Oklahoma the Catholic Church, raising the issue of sacramental use, successfully challenged a total ban on liquor; see Thomas E. Brown, "Oklahoma's 'Bone Dry' Law and the Roman Catholic Church," *Chronicles of Oklahoma* 52 (Fall 1974): 316–30. The Anti-Saloon League counted only nine bone-dry states; James H. Timberlake, *Prohibition and Progressive* (Cambridge, Mass.: Harvard University Press, 1963), 172–73, cites this total. I have found more, including some that passed laws after adoption of the Reed Amendment; see Arizona Session Laws (1917), 3–4 (referendum); Arkansas Session Laws (1917), 41; Colorado Session Laws (1919), 461–68; Florida Session Laws (1918), 1:26–28; Georgia Session Laws (1917, extra session), 7–19; Idaho Session Laws (1915), 41–47; Indiana Session Laws (1917), 15–34; Kansas Session Laws (1917), 283–88; Kentucky Session Laws (1917), 16–17; Michigan Session Laws (1917), 291; Mississippi Session Laws (1918), 210–20; Missouri Session Laws (1918), 409–416; Nebraska Session Laws (1917) 428; North Dakota Session Laws (1917), 201; Oklahoma Session Laws (1917), 350; Oregon Session Laws (1917), 46–57; South Dakota Session Laws (1917), 490, 514; Tennessee Session Laws (1917), 3, 25; Washington Session Laws (1917), 46–62; Brough quoted in *Results of Prohibition* (Washington, D.C.: World League Against Alcoholism, [1920]), 14; Laura Lindley, comp., *State-Wide Referenda in the United States on the Liquor Question* (Westerville, Ohio: American Issue Publishing, [1927]), 4, 5, 7, 21, 27.

19. 245 *United States Reports* (1917) 298–304, 304–8; *SEAP*, 765–66; *Union Signal*, December 20, 1917, 3;

20. *New Republic*, April 18, 1913, 2; *Union Signal*, April 24, 1913, 4, *American Patriot*, February 1916, 3, 16; *American Issue*, July 19, 1915, 9, May 22, 1915, 5.

21. Alabama Session Laws (1917), 9; Arkansas Session Laws (1917), 41; Colorado Session Laws (1915), 276; Delaware Session Laws (1917), 22; Florida Session Laws (1917), 323; Georgia Session Laws (1915), 105–7; Iowa Session Laws (1917), 155; Indiana Session Laws (1917), 27; Idaho Session Laws (1917), 492; Kentucky Session Laws (1918), 16; Maine Session Laws (1885), 311; Mississippi Session Laws (1916), 126; North Dakota Session Laws (1906), 276; Oregon Session Laws (1917), 963–64; South Dakota Session Laws (1916–17), 491; Virginia Session Laws (1916), 216; Washington Session Laws (1915), 4; West Virginia Session Laws (1913), 102. George M. Brown and Elisha A. Baker, *Laymen's Primer on the Oregon Dry Law* (Portland: Anti-Saloon League of Oregon, [1914]), 10; after passage of the federal law, two more states, Florida and Delaware, joined the list of states with such laws; Florida Session Laws (1917), 323, Delaware Session Laws (1917), 22. Drys also pressured newspapers into not carrying liquor ads—even in wet areas; *American Issue*, April 10, 1915, 8, May 15, 1915, 6, December 25, 1915, 10; *Union Signal*, January 6, 1916, 9. On Alabama, see *American Issue*, March 13, 1915, 3, 4, 6, April 10, 1915, 7, May 22, 1915, 3, April 3, 1915, 1, June 191, 1915, 1; Judge Samuel J. Weakley, "The Alabama Prohibition Program of 1915," in *Proceedings of Sixteenth National Convention of Anti-Saloon League of America* (Westerville, Ohio: American Issue Publishing,

[1915]), 288; James B. Sellers, *The Prohibition Movement in Alabama, 1702–1943* (Chapel Hill: University of North Carolina Press) 101–14; Virginia Van Deer Hamilton, *Hugo Black: The Alabama Years* (Baton Rouge: Louisiana State University Press, 1972), 22–68; USBA, *Yearbook* (1916), 117–18; *New York Times*, February 25, 1915, 8, March 21, 1915, sec. 3, 1, January 25, 1918, 17; Weakley to Webb, June 23, 1915, EYWP.

22. *Union Signal*, January 6, 1916, 9, February 22, 1917, 2, March 8, 1917, 3; Weakley to Aldrich, September 22, 1915, Weakley to Webb, April 20, 1915, May 10, 1915, August 21, 1915, Webb to Weakley, August 23, 1915, Middleton to Webb, November 13, 1913, Hamilton to Webb, November 23, 1914, EYWP; Weakley, "Alabama Prohibition Program," 285–89; *Alabama Citizen*, May 1908, 2, 6, 10, 15.

23. Weakley, "Alabama Prohibition Program," 288; Middleton to Webb, November 13, 1913, EYWP; *American Issue*, December 25, 1914, 10, July 24, 1915, 11, December 11, 1915, 1, September 4, 1915, 8, March 29, 1915, 1, 8, November 27, 1915, 1, October 16, 1915, 4, *American Patriot*, February 1916, 6; *Cong. Rec.*, 60th Cong., 1st sess., 479, 701, *Cong. Rec.*, 60th Cong., 2d sess., 343; Dorothy G. Fowler, *Unmailable: Congress and the Post Office* (Athens: University of Georgia Press, 1972), 102–3, 127–28; *New Republic*, January 3, 1913, 2; *Union Signal*, July 13, 1916, 2; for a typical bill, see copy of H.R. 21458, introduced February 24, 1915, in EYWP.

24. Hobson to Dinwiddie (telegram), February 17, 1917, Hobson to Baker, Gordon, and Hanly, March 5, 1917, box 3, RPHP.

25. *Union Signal*, February 22, 1917, 2, March 1, 1917, 2, 8; National WCTU, *Convention Minutes* 44 (1917): 74, 209; USBA, *Yearbook* (New York: USBA, 1917), ix; Odegard, *Pressure*, 161–62; Kerr, *Organized*, 195–98; Timberlake, *Prohibition and Progressive*, 173; William E. Johnson, *The Federal Government and the Liquor Traffic*, 2d ed. (Westerville, Ohio: American Issue Publishing, 1917), 294–97.

26. *Union Signal*, March 22, 1917, 8, July 12–19, 1917, 3, September 5, 1918, 9, October 3, 1918, 2, January 23, 1919, 2, March 22, 1919, 3; *United States v. Gudger*, 249 *United States Reports* (1919) 373; *United States v. Simpson*, 252 *United States Reports* (1920) 465; Larry Englemann, *Intemperance: The Lost War against Liquor* (New York: Macmillan Free Press, 1979), 26–27; Persons to Webb, February 24, 1917, and February 26, 1917, EYWP.

27. The best account of the role of the war in facilitating the creation of national prohibition is Christopher N. May, *In the Name of the War: Judicial Review and the War Powers since 1918* (Cambridge, Mass.: Harvard University Press, 1989), 60–86; see also Kerr, *Organized*, 185–210; Odegard, *Pressure*, 149–80; Cherrington, *Evolution*, 355–61; a good analysis of the origins, efforts, and failures of German Americans in fighting prohibition is David W. Detjen, *The Germans in Missouri, 1900–1918: Prohibition, Neutrality, and Assimilation* (Columbia: University of Missouri Press, 1985).

28. Webb to Burleson, October 9, 1909, Webb to Shuford, November 17, 1909, Webb to McMillan, December 18, 1913, Mann to Webb, August 14, 1916, Webb to Mann, August 17, 1916, Webb to Carroll, August 1, 1913, EYWP.

29. Odegard, *Pressure*, 171–74; Kerr, *Organized*, 177–84; House *Report 1493*, pt. 2, 1–7, 64th Cong., 2d sess.; House *Report 211*, pt. 3, 65th Cong., 2d sess.

30. *Cong. Rec.*, 65th Cong., 2d sess., 423; Hobson, "Brief for Proposed Changes in the Wording of the National Prohibition Amendment Prepared for the Special Committee of Nineteen" (August 20, 1915), box 5, RPHP; Hobson to Baker, Gordon, and Hanly, March 8, 1917, box 3, RPHP.

31. *Cong. Rec.*, 65th Cong., 2d sess., 424, 433; Kerr, *Organized*, 202–3; Odegard, *Pressure*, 172–74.

32. House *Report 211*, pt. 3, 65th Cong., 2d sess.; House *Report 1493*, pt. 2, 64th Cong., 2d sess.

33. *Cong. Rec.*, 65 Cong. 1st sess., 5645, 5647, 5648.

34. Ibid., 5556, App. 733–42; House *Report 1493*, pt. 3, 1, 64th Cong., 2d sess.; L. Ames Brown, "Nationwide Prohibition," *Atlantic Monthly* 115 (June 1915): 735–47; *Literary Digest* 54 (January 29, 1917): 112–13; *Independent* 89 (January 22, 1917): 138–39; William Howard Doughty to editor, *New York Times*, March 23, 1918, 4.

35. Robert Woods, "Winning the Other Half?," *Survey* 37 (December 30, 1916): 344–52; *Cong. Rec.*, 65th Cong., 2d sess., 427. Ernest Cherrington made the same argument in *The Time Has Come* (n.p., n.d.; reprinted from *American Issue*), 2.

36. *Union Signal*, May 21, 1914, 4, January 14, 1915, 5; *New Republic*, May 1, 1914, 4; William Anderson, "National Prohibition—What Form Should It Take?," *Outlook* 114 (December 27, 1916): 900; *Cong. Rec.*, 65th Cong., 1st sess., 5552, *Cong. Rec.*, 65th Cong., 2d sess., 448–50; *Union Signal*, December 2, 1915, 2. One of the first to reintroduce the antislavery absolutist analogy was Ernest Cherrington, see *Address of Mr. Ernest H. Cherrington . . . Before Congress, December 10, 1913* (n.p., n.d.), 3–4; see also *Winning Orations in the Contests of the Intercollegiate Prohibition Association*, rev. ed. (Chicago: Intercollegiate Prohibition Association, [1917]), 13, 14, 15–16, 21, 40, 109; Martha A. Hunter, *Weighed in the Balances: Or, the Trail of the Serpent* (Cincinnati, Ohio: Monfort and Co., 1916), 28–29, 17, 23, 24, 34; this work tried to make Hobson into a radical temperance advocate by putting him on the cover. In general, there was a radical resurgence in this period, and the party unsuccessfully tried to court Hobson to its cause; see Pitts to Hobson, June 30, 1916, Hobson to Pitts, July 12, 1916, box 3, RPHP.

37. *Survey* 38 (June 23, 1917): 274; John G. Woolley, *The Wounds of a Friend* (Westerville, Ohio: American Issue Publishing, n.d.), 11; Henry M. Dodd, *National Prohibition: Best Wording of the Amendment* (n.p., [1914]), 2–3; Scott to Webb, November 29, 1915, EYWP, Adamson to Hobson, December 19, 1914, box 1, RPHP.

38. *Cong. Rec.*, 65th Cong., 1st sess., 5640, 5637, 5640–41, 5537, 5555.

39. *Cong. Rec.*, 65th Cong., 2d sess., 423–25, 427; House *Report 211*, pt. 1, 3, 65th Cong., 2d sess.

40. House *Report 211*, pt. 1, 4, 65th Cong., 2d sess.; *Cong. Rec.*, 65th Cong., 2d sess., 440–42, 433–35, 447, 461, 428.

41. *Cong. Rec.*, 65th Cong., 2d sess., 423–25; Chafin to John, January 6, 1916, enclosed in Chafin to Hobson, February 23, 1916, box 2, RPHP.

42. Pollock to Hobson, September 27, 1915, box 5, RPHP; *Cong. Rec.*, 65th Cong., 2d sess., 423–25; Fabian Franklin, "Prohibition and the States," *North American Review* 207 (February 1918): 231–38, 231; *Cong. Rec.*, 65 Cong., 1st sess., 5587.

43. Odegard, *Pressure*, 174–80; Kerr, *Organized*, 207–10; *Outlook* 121 (January 19, 1918): 180; *Cong. Rec.*, 65th Cong., 2d sess., 469, 474–78. The league was also well prepared for its opponents' tactics; as early as 1914 Wayne Wheeler had already advanced arguments to defend ratification of the amendment; see Wheeler, "May Ratification by a State of an Amendment to the Federal Constitution Be Repealed?," *Case and Comment* 20 (January 1914): 548–50.

44. USBA, *Yearbook* (n.p., [1918]), 1–30, 20, 14–16, 24–25; *Ex Parte Desjeivo*, 152 *Federal Reporter* (1907) 1004; *New York Times*, January 19, 1919, 1, January 10, 1918, 7; *North American Review* 211 (May 1920): 348–54; *Independent* 101 (January 3, 1920): 24–25.

45. Wheeler to Webb, February 5, 1920, EYWP; Wayne B. Wheeler, *The Eighteenth Amendment and Its Enforcement*, Leaflet No. 3 (Westerville, Ohio: American Issue Publishing, Lincoln-Lee Department, [1920]).

46. Volstead to Wheeler, February 7, 1920, box 1, AJVP.

47. Webb to Wheeler, February 13, 1920, March 23, 1920, EYWP.

48. 253 *United States Reports* 350–411, 387; Wheeler to Webb, June 16, 1920, EYWP; *New York Times*, January 10, 1918, 7; *Outlook* 121 (February 5, 1919): 212; Wheeler, "National Prohibition," *Outlook* 117 (December 26, 1917): 673–74; Wheeler, "Is Prohibition Constitutional?," *Forum* 61 (May 1919): 563–74; 253.

49. *Literary Digest* 60 (February 1919): 11–13; *SEAP*, 1961; Cherrington, *Evolution*, 383–84; *Proceedings of the Board of Directors of the ASL of America* (Westerville, Ohio: American Issue Publishing, [1918]), 13; *Proceedings of the Board of Directors of ASL of America* (Westerville, Ohio: American Issue Publishing, [1919]), 11; Davis to Webb, December 5, 1919, EYWP. Clark, *Deliver*, 134–39, extends Joseph Gusfield, *Symbolic Crusade: Status Politics and the American Temperance Movement* (Urbana: University of Chicago Press, 1963), 119–22, on the symbolic nature of national prohibition. In Gusfield's account, the symbolic content of the act explains why it was so poorly enforced after it was adopted; Clark thinks that symbolism determined its form. For different views of the alcohol limit, see Clark, *Deliver*, 131–33; Kerr, *Organized*, 224. The disparity between the Volstead Act's opening declaration that possession was forbidden and later clauses allowing the possession in the home would seem to support the symbolic view of the law, except that this discrepancy was not the prohibitionists' idea but a result of the political process in Congress.

50. *New York Times*, January 17, 1919, 1, 4.

51. *Union Signal*, March 6, 1919, 5; Wheeler, "How War Prohibition Will Be Enforced," *Outlook* 122 (May 21, 1919): 101. On the debate on authorship, see Justin Steuart, *Dry Boss: An Uncensored Biography of Wayne B. Wheeler* (New York: Fleming H. Revell, 1928), 148–52; Charles Merz, *Dry Decade* (1930; reprint, Seattle: University of Washington Press, 1969), 47–49. Steuart claimed that Wheeler wrote it whereas Kerr, *Organized*, 223, argued for Volstead's primacy in drafting the act. But

Kerr offers no detailed proof of his claim, and Hogan disputes it; see Charles M. Hogan, "Wayne B. Wheeler: Single Issue Exponent" (Ph.D. diss., University of Cincinnati, 1986), 1–2, 189–201. The evidence is equivocal on this debate. It shows that each man had reason to claim the act: Wheeler to support his reputation as "Dry Boss" and Volstead to disprove the charge of wets (made in an article written by Theodore Tiller and published in the *Baltimore Sun* on March 22, 1920) that he was merely a tool of the temperance movement. See Wheeler to Volstead, January 17, 1920, Volstead to Editor, *Baltimore Sun*, March 27, 1920, Kent to Volstead, March 29, 1920, enclosing Tiller to editor, *Baltimore Sun*, March 29, 1920, Volstead to editor, *Baltimore Sun*, March 31, 1920, Volstead to Shea, February 10, 1934, Volstead speech to Anti-Saloon League Conference, December 8, 1921, and various newspaper clippings from 1920, boxes 3 and 5, AJVP. For a clause-by-clause examination of the first two titles of the Volstead Act showing each provision's origins in state legislation, see Archibald D. Dabney, *Liquor Prohibition* (Charlottesville, Va.: Michie Co., 1920).

52. 41 *Statutes at Large* 305–26; for a discussion of the first title of the Volstead Act, see May, *In the Name of the War*, 86–93.

53. The fruit juice exception became very troublesome when Commissioner Kramer set the allowance at two hundred gallons per year. Bronner [Brown?] to Volstead, May 18, 1921, AJVP; see also Volstead to Haynes, May 18, 1922, Haynes to Volstead, May 20, 1922, AJVP; Wheeler to Webb, June 16, 1920, EYWP.

54. 41 *Statutes at Large* 305–19, 308; Wheeler, clipping of offprint of *Current History*, May 1922, box 3, AJVP; Andrew Sinclair, *Prohibition, Era of Excess* (Boston: Little Brown, 1962), 167–69; *SEAP*, 2777–83. On the origins of nuisance provisions in state laws, see J. B. Howard, *Effective Liquor and Vice Law* (Provo, Utah: Betterment or Booze Publishing Co., [1913]).

55. Wheeler, clipping of offprint of *Current History*, AJVP.

56. *SEAP*, 1702, 1916–62; Steuart, *Dry Boss*, 145–46, H. H. Russell, "Our League—Its Future" (speech delivered in Washington D.C., December 1918), 2, folder 35, TPP, ser. xv; Allan S. Everset, *Rum across the Border: The Prohibition Era in Northern New York* (Syracuse, N.Y.: Syracuse University Press, 1978), 128; *Literary Digest* 64 (March 17, 1920): 23, 64 (January 19, 1920): 18; Wayne B. Wheeler, "The Eighteenth Amendment and Its Enforcement" (address at National Conference, Washington, D.C., September 15, 1920), AJVP; Wheeler to Webb, March 24, 1927, Webb to Wheeler, March 28, 1927, EYWP; 253 *United States Reports* 387. Wheeler wrote a law for New York that had stronger search and seizure clause, and Kansas had a similar law; see Bader, *Kansas*, 193.

57. 41 *Statutes at Large* 305, 306, 307, 308, 309. In 1920 the commissioner of internal revenue created the Prohibition Unit, and the balance of enforcement work fell to treasury agents until a reorganization on April 1, 1927; Lawrence F. Schmeckebier, *The Bureau of Prohibition: Its History, Activities, and Organization* (Washington, D.C.: Brookings Institution, 1929), 1–9; *New York Times*, January 26, 1919, 4.

58. 41 *Statutes at Large* 317–18. This provision was upheld in *United States v. Yuginovich*, 256 *United States Reports* (1921) 450, 462; but for some law enforcement

officers it was not stringent enough, and they urged use of the harsher penalties available in some state laws; see Barkman to Simonson, April 26, 1921, and enclosed Gates to Federal Prohibition Agents (Memo 9), April 14, 1921, AJVP. In 1922 in *Lipke v. Lederer*, 259 *United States Reports* (1922) 557, the tax penalties were struck down; Volstead then drafted new ones, which were also struck down in *United States v. La Franca*, 282 *United States Reports* (1931) 567; see untitled Volstead speech, typescript, undated folder, box 1, AJVP. For more on the constitutional history of this section, see Arthur W. Blakemore, *National Prohibition: The Volstead Act Annotated*, 3d ed. (Albany, N.Y.: Matthew Bender and Co., 1927), 799–814.

59. *Outlook* 123 (December 31, 1919): 564; 41 *Statutes at Large* 305–19; *SEAP*, 1516–17; H. H. Russell, "January 16, 1919," 2, Russell, "Our League—Its Future," TPP, ser. xv; Volstead to Shaw, November 13, 1922, AJVP; Steuart, *Dry Boss*, 152; Kerr, *Organized*, 223–24, 227.

60. *New York Times*, January 17, 1919, 1, 4, January 26, 1919, 4, February 22, 1919, 4; *Literary Digest* 68 (February 12, 1921) 40–44; Wheeler, *Eighteenth Amendment*, 4–5; *Nation* 110 (February 7, 1920): 166–67; Wheeler, "Law and Order," *Outlook* 124 (January 28, 1920): 146–47. Kansas, one of the driest of states, saw active league programs to insure strict enforcement; Bader, *Kansas*, 193–210; in Arkansas federal officials advised officers to "appeal for help to the Anti-Saloon League and the Woman's Christian Temperance Union, Women's clubs, Ministerial Alliance, and Church organization" willing to "take an active part in prohibition law enforcement." Barkman to Simonson, April 26, 1921, enclosed in Gates to Federal Prohibition Agents (Memo 9), April 14, 1921, AJVP.

61. *Union Signal*, March 6, 1919, 5, April 24, 1919, 2.

CONCLUSION. THE RELATIONSHIP OF THE POLITY TO REFORMS

1. This sketch of divorce reform is derived from William L. O'Neill, *Divorce in the Progressive Era* (New Haven: Yale University Press, 1967); Nelson M. Blake, *The Road to Reno: A History of the Divorce in the United States* (Westport, Conn.: Greenwood Press, 1962); Lynne Carol Halem, *Divorce Reform: Changing Legal and Social Perspectives* (New York: Free Press, 1980), 27–83; Elaine Tyler May, *Great Expectations: Marriage and Divorce in Post-Victorian America* (Chicago: University of Chicago Press, 1980); Daniel J. Boorstin, *The Americans: The Democratic Experience* (New York: Vintage Books, 1974), 64–77; Lawrence M. Friedman, "Rights of Passage: Divorce Law in Historical Perspective," *Oregon Law Review* 63 (1984): 649–69; Neal R. Fergenson, "Extraterritorial Recognition of Divorce Decrees in the Nineteenth Century," *American Journal of Legal History* 34 (1990): 119–67; Roderick Phillips, *Putting Asunder* (Cambridge: Cambridge University Press, 1988), 439–515.

2. O'Neill, *Divorce*, 235 n. 8; Friedman, "Rights of Passage," 659–60, Boorstin, *Democratic*, 67–72.

3. Woolsey quoted in Blake, *Reno*, 131–32.

4. Ibid., 141; see also O'Neill, *Divorce*, 238–40.

5. This account of juvenile justice reform is derived from the following works: David J. Rothman, *Conscience and Convenience: The Asylum and Its Alternatives in Progressive America* (Boston: Little Brown, 1980), 205–35; Steven L. Schlossman, *Love and the American Delinquent: The Theory and Practice of "Progressive" Juvenile Justice, 1825–1920* (Chicago: University of Chicago Press, 1977); Ellen Ryerson, *The Best-Laid Plans: America's Juvenile Court Experiment* (New York, Hill and Wang, 1978); Charles Larsen, *The Good Fight: The Life and Times of Ben B. Lindsey* (Chicago: Quadrangle Books, 1972); Robert G. Caldwell, "The Juvenile Court: Its Development and Some Major Problems," in *Juvenile Delinquency: A Book of Readings*, 2d ed., ed. Rose Giallombardo (New York: John Wiley and Sons, 1972), 399–423; Standford J. Fox, "Juvenile Justice Reform: An Historical Perspective," *Standford Law Review* 22 (1970): 1187–1239; and a classic of the movement, *The Child, the Clinic and the Court* (1925; reprint, New York: Johnson Reprint Corporation, 1970). The figure for the adoption of the system comes from Caldwell, "Juvenile Court," 401.

6. Evelina Belden, *Courts in the United States Hearing Children's Cases*, U.S. Children's Bureau Publication 65 (Washington, D.C.: Government Printing Office, 1920), 7–10.

7. Scholars have shown that, as institutions and practices, the various components of the juvenile justice system failed to live up to their creators' hopes. See Ryerson, *Best-Laid*, esp. 78–98; Schlossman, *Love*, 81–193; and Rothman, *Conscience*, 221–35.

8. Rothman *Conscience*, 214; for contrasting views of Lindsey, see Rothman *Conscience*, 215; Larsen, *Ben Lindsey*, 27–54.

9. For the legal setting of the juvenile courts, see Ryerson, *Best-Laid*, 57–77; Rothman, *Conscience*, 231–34.

10. The leading case in applying due process procedures to juvenile courts is *In Re Gault*, 387 *United States Reports* (1967), 1.

11. Rothman, *Conscience*, shows parallel developments in prison and psychiatric institution reform. In each case, the reformers are what I would characterize as reformationists dominated by a spirit of efficiency. And in each case the federal system, in turn, had little effect on these reformers' programs.

12. The following works explore the eugenics movement: Richard Hofstadter, *Social Darwinism in American Thought* (Boston: Beacon Press, 1955); Allan Chase, *Legacy of Malthus* (New York: Alfred Knopf, 1977); Rudolph J. Vecoli, "Sterilization: A Progressive Measure," *Wisconsin Magazine of History* 43 (Spring 1960): 190–202; Donald Pickens, *Eugenics and the Progressives* (Nashville: Vanderbilt University Press, 1968); Mark H. Haller, *Eugenics: Hereditarian Attitudes in American Thought* (New Brunswick, N.J.: Rutgers University Press, 1963); Daniel J. Kevles, *In the Name of Eugenics: Genetics and the Use of Human Heredity* (New York: Alfred A. Knopf, 1985); Nicole Hahn Rafter, ed., *White Trash: The Eugenic Family Studies, 1877–1919* (Boston: Northeastern University Press, 1988); Philip R. Reilly, *The Surgical Solution: A History of Involuntary Sterilization in the United States* (Baltimore: The Johns Hopkins University Press, 1991); Carl N. Degler, *In Search of Human*

Nature: The Decline and Revival of Darwinism in American Social Thought (New York: Oxford University Press, 1991), 42–55.

13. For the legal dimensions of the eugenics crusade, see Harry Laughlin, *Legal, Legislative and Administrative Aspects of Sterilization* (Cold Spring Harbor, N.Y.: Eugenics Records Office, 1914); Harry Laughlin, *Scope of the Committee's Work* (Cold Spring Harbor, N.Y.: Eugenics Records Office, 1914); Harry Laughlin, *The Legal Status of Eugenical Sterilization* (Chicago: Psychopathic Laboratory of the Municipal Court, 1929); Paul A. Lombardo, "Eugenical Sterilization in Virginia: Aubrey Strode and the Case of *Buck v. Bell*" (Ph.D. diss., University of Virginia, 1982); Kevles, *In Name of Eugenics*, 106.

14. For a discussion of *Buck v. Bell*, see Lombardo, "Eugenical Sterilization in Virginia"; Kevles, *In the Name of Eugenics*, 100–101.

15. Frances J. Hassencahl, *Harry H. Laughlin, "Expert Eugenics Agent" for the House Committee on Immigrant and Naturalization, 1921 to 1931* (Ann Arbor: University of Michigan Press, 1971); Laughlin to Webb, August 7, 1917, EYWP; the relationship between the two movements is covered in Bartlett C. Jones, "Prohibition and Eugenics," *Journal of the History of Medicine and Allied Sciences* 18 (1963): 158–72.

16. *SEAP*, 1585.

17. Jimmie Lewis Franklin, *Born Sober: Prohibition in Oklahoma, 1907–1959* (Norman: University of Oklahoma Press, 1971), 78; Norman Clark, *Deliver Us from Evil: An Interpretation of American Prohibition* (New York: W. W. Norton, 1976), 162–65; Wayne Wheeler, "The Success and Failure of Prohibition," *Current Opinion* 70 (January 1921): 37. Territories with insular legislatures could follow the same path. Thus, Puerto Rico, which adopted prohibition by referendum, never passed a local enforcement law; see Truman R. Clark, "Prohibition in Puerto Rico, 1917–1933" (paper presented at the International Congress on the Social History of Alcohol, May 13–15, 1993, London, Ontario, 3–8), 12. The fish and game comparison is reflective only of the states' attitudes, as most legislatures assumed that local officials in the course of their duties would go about enforcing prohibition. So general appropriations for the police, while not earmarked for prohibition enforcement, did contribute to implementation of the policy. Nevertheless, specific prohibition enforcement programs received little funding. For instance, Colorado's legislature appropriated all of $5,000 in one year to enforce prohibition; James E. Hansen II, "Moonshine and Murder: Prohibition in Denver," *Colorado Magazine* 50 (1973): 1–23, 14–15.

18. Austin Kerr, *Organized for Prohibition: A New History of the Anti-Saloon League* (New Haven, Conn.: Yale University Press, 1985), 236; Clark, *Deliver*, 167–69; Larry Engelmann, *Intemperance: The Lost War against Liquor* (New York: Macmillan Free Press, 1979) 195–96; Larry Engelmann, "Organized Thirst: The Story of Repeal in Michigan," in *Alcohol, Reform and Society: The Liquor Issue in Social Context*, ed. Jack Blocker Jr. (Westport, Conn.: Greenwood Press, 1979), 171–210, 174; *SEAP*, 1515, 1963; Laura Lindley, *State-Wide Referenda in the United States on the Liquor Question* (Westerville, Ohio: American Issue Publishing, [1929]), 6, 13, 31–32;

Report of the Special Commission on Liquor Legislation: Rhode Island (Providence, R.I.: Freeman Co., 1931), 18.

19. Charles Merz, *Dry Decade* (New York: Doubleday, Doran and Co., 1931); Larry Engelmann, *Intemperance*, 150–55, pointed out that the civil service application was not a cure-all, for it was applied mindlessly and resulted in the dismissal of "some very good agents," leading to demoralization in the service; on the history of federal enforcement, see Laurence F. Schmeckebier, *The Bureau of Prohibition: Its History, Activities, and Organization* (Washington, D.C.: Brookings Institution, 1929). Beyond the increased caseloads the federal courts also took on the extra task of regulating the federal prohibition enforcers; see Rayman L. Solomon, "Regulating the Regulators: Prohibition Enforcement in the Seventh Circuit," in *Law, Alcohol, and Order: Perspectives on National Prohibition*, ed. David E. Kyvig (Westport, Conn.: Greenwood Press, 1985), 81–96; National Commission on Law Observance and Enforcement, *Report on the Enforcement of the Prohibition Laws of the United States* (1931; reprint, Montclair, N.J.: Patterson Smith, 1968), 8–20, 43–48; David Kyvig, *Repealing National Prohibition* (Chicago: University of Chicago Press, 1979), 30; Kerr, *Organized* 211–74; Warden Moxley, "History of Reapportionment and Redistricting," in *Guide to U.S. Elections* (Washington, D.C.: Congressional Quarterly, 1975), 530–34; Clark, *Deliver*, 194; Andrew Sinclair, *Era of Excess: A Social History of the Prohibition Movement* (New York, Harper Colophon Books, 1964), 362.

20. Clark, *Deliver*, 193–94, 202–3, Kyvig, *Repealing*, 111–13, Sinclair, *Era*, 361–68.

21. A good introduction to the subject of repeal is Mark E. Lender, "The Historian and Repeal: A Survey of the Literature and Research Opportunities," in *Law*, ed. Kyvig, 177–205; the first studies of repeal—Ernest Gordon, *The Wrecking of the 18th Amendment* (Francestown, N.H.: Alcohol Information Press, 1943), and Fletcher Dobyns, *The Amazing Story of Repeal: An Expose of the Power of Propaganda* (Chicago: Willett, Clark & Co., 1940)—were dry polemics; for correctives see Sinclair, *Era*, and Clement E. Vose, *Constitutional Change: Amendment Politics and Supreme Court Litigation since 1900* (Lexington, Mass.: Lexington Books, 1972), 101–37; Kyvig's *Repealing* is the standard account.

22. Clark, *Deliver*, 165–208, especially 169–79; Sinclair, *Era*, 309–33; Bader, *Kansas*, 251–53. Paul Murphy sees the emergence in 1920s of a similar legal conception of individual rights replacing an older tradition of social morality; Paul L. Murphy, "Societal Morality and Individual Freedom," in *Law*, ed. Kyvig, 67–80. For the anti-obscenity movement (which suffered a collapse because of the same cultural change), see Paul S. Boyer, *Purity in Print: The Vice-Society Movement and Book Censorship in America* (New York: Charles Scribner's Sons, 1968).

23. Kerr, *Organized*, 211–74; Sinclair, *Era*, 350–51.

24. Kyvig, *Repealing*, 71–97, 116–36, 173–77; Clement E. Vose, "Repeal as a Political Achievement," in *Law*, ed. Kyvig, 97–122. For the working of the process in one state, see Engelmann, "Organized Thirst," 171–210.

25. Sinclair, *Era*, 242–306; Kyvig, *Repealing*, 168, 178–79; David E. Kyvig, "Ob-

jection Sustained: Prohibition Repeal and the New Deal," in *Alcohol*, ed. Blocker, 211–34; William E. Leuchtenburg, *Franklin D. Roosevelt and the New Deal* (New York: Harper Colophon Books, 1963), 46–47.

26. Not until 1937 was the federal government made fully neutral in prohibition matters. In that year the U.S. Supreme Court in *United States v. Constintine* ruled unconstitutional the revised federal tax penalty law, 296 *United States Reports* (1937) 288–99; for a brief history of the concurrent clause of the Twenty-first Amendment, see William F. Swindler, "A Dubious Constitutional Experiment," in *Law*, ed. Kyvig, 53–65, 63.

INDEX